GOLF'S BEST NEW DESTINATIONS

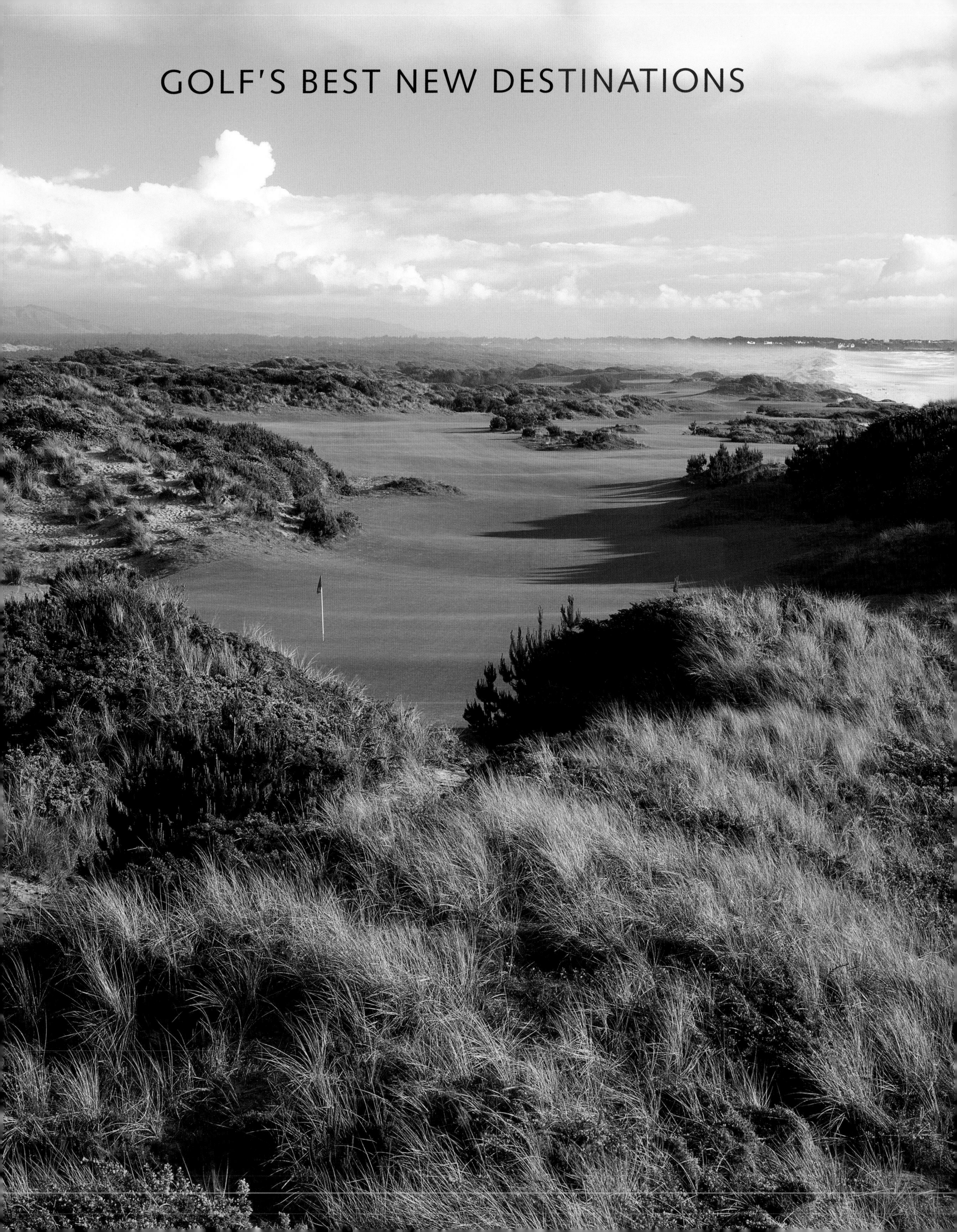

GOLF'S BEST NEW
DESTINATIONS

BRIAN MCCALLEN

ABRAMS, NEW YORK

CONTENTS

All I can say is, it seemed like a good idea at the time.

As the travel editor at *Golf Magazine* from 1987 to 2003, I had a wonderful catbird seat from which to observe the growth and development of golf at home and abroad during its most active period. My job, as I saw it, was to tell readers where to take their games on the road. During the '90s, those places were to be found mainly in the U.S., where the majority of the best projects by the top designers were being built. However, new course development in America reached its peak in 2000, when roughly 325 new layouts opened, about 80 percent of them public-access. Since the millennium, new course openings in the U.S. have declined every year.

The reasons for the slowdown are many, say the pundits. The number of golfers in the U.S. has leveled off, and their participation rates are down. Golf is expensive. Heavier workloads tend to shrink leisure time. Also, with so many new courses flooding the ranks, supply caught up with demand. In point of fact, the time was right to take stock of the recent boom at home—and also to cast my nets beyond American shores.

More than half of this book covers destinations outside the U.S. In selected regions around the globe, golf is taking off—growing steadily, or actually skyrocketing. A happy circumstance for traveling golfers, though it presented something akin to a moving target as I researched the book.

My first two books for Abrams, *Golf Resorts of the World* and *Top 100 Courses You Can Play*, were linear projects. Each was completed promptly in the span of 13 months. There was a roster of Gold and Silver Medal resorts for the first, a finite number of courses for the second.

If only the subject matter for this book were as cut and dried.

As I proceeded with my research, I found that some destinations I thought were emerging ceased to show their heads, and ones I hadn't even considered started popping up all over the place. An example: I started writing the book in earnest in July 2002 after returning from an extensive tour of Ontario. Three years later, the entire chapter required a complete update. Much like workers who paint the George Washington Bridge, once I was done, it was time to start over at the beginning.

But now I *am* done, and you are about to discover an enticing cross-section of courses and places that appeared as blips on my jerry-built radar screen.

First, a few details on how regions and courses were chosen. I used the mid-1990s debut of Tiger Woods (he turned pro in 1996 and won the Masters the following year) as a dividing line between established courses and emerging ones. In more ways than one, Tiger has ushered in golf's modern era. As for the locales chosen, I felt a given area of a state, province, or country needed to show enough promising newcomers to rate a serious golfer's attention. Great new venues, I decided, could be combined with pre-existing courses to flesh out a destination's appeal. But the burden of proof rested with the quality and worthiness of the new layouts.

I understand fully well that a golf trip is charged with anticipation and often requires significant outlays of time and money. With so much at stake, there could be no pretenders. A new or reconstituted destination had to make it through my "Would it, could it, disappoint?" Dr. Seussian wicket. Otherwise, it was DIPLOI (Destination In Pocket, Lack of Interest).

Now for the contents. Domestic golf participation rates may be stuck in neutral, but the game nationwide has flourished in selected areas of the U.S. both urban and rural. Seven different regions are represented in these pages. While new, you've probably heard of some of the places I've featured. Golf destinations, like any commodity, have gotten very good at marketing and promoting themselves. Exceedingly diverse, they share one thing in common: great golf.

Much of the geography herein goes against the grain. Emerging destinations range from the outskirts of Houston and Los Angeles, two major cities better known for urban sprawl than golf courses; to Plymouth, Massachusetts, in square miles the nation's largest municipality but still very much the place where the pilgrims stepped ashore. Orlando, home to more PGA Tour pros than any other city, continues

Terravista Golf Club, Brazil

to sprout layouts on the outskirts of its entertainment megalopolis. Las Vegas, against all odds the fastest growing metropolis in America, spawned several excellent if very high-priced courses between 1996 and 2005. Only the decreased availability of water will slow the growth of golf in Glitter City.

Two visionaries, Herb Kohler and Mike Keiser, are recognized in these pages. Kohler, the plumbing fixtures baron, joined forces with Pete Dye to create a world-class 72-hole destination where none had existed an hour's drive north of Milwaukee. Similarly, Keiser, who made his fortune in recycled greeting cards, took a huge gamble on a stretch of Oregon coast in the middle of nowhere. Now Bandon Dunes Resort, with three distinctive courses, is on every aficionado's list as *the* place to go for the most authentic golf experience in America.

I'm excited about the best and newest places to play here at home, but I'm also a realist. Half the world's golfers and golf courses are located outside America. The greatest prospects for future growth are located overseas. According to the International Association of Golf Tour Operators (IAGTO), golf tourism has grown 2.5 times faster than general "leisure" tourism since 1995, and golf visitors spend, on average, 30 percent more money at a given destination than other tourists. Overseas golf is hot because it's profitable.

Among the hottest spots are what I call the regional international destinations, our neighbors in the hemisphere: Canada, the Caribbean, and Mexico. In 2001, hockey, which is pursued with near religious fervor by Canadians, was surpassed by golf as the sport of choice. I chose to spotlight the provinces where the number and quality of new courses has been most significant, in Ontario and Prince Edward Island. But all of Canada, from British Columbia to Newfoundland, is bonkers over golf.

The Caribbean has always had the setting and the weather for golf. For years the archipelago puttered along with a few decent courses, relying on its gorgeous beaches and dreamy seascapes to do most of the heavy lifting. But now golf, thanks in part to a new salt-tolerant turfgrass called paspalum, has hit the West Indies with the strength of a hurricane. Not only have vintage resorts added to their rosters, islands that never before had a bona fide 18-hole course are getting into the game.

Mexico is perhaps the poster child for emerging destinations worldwide. Until Los Cabos, the holiday corridor at the tip of Baja California Sur, began to showcase the superlative designs of Jack Nicklaus in the mid-1990s, there was very little reason for players to trundle their clubs south of the border. Los Cabos now competes with the world's most elite tropical destinations. Modeling its success, Puerto Vallarta and the Riviera Maya have presented themselves as full-fledged golf destinations. Great beaches, lots of sunshine, refreshing margaritas—there's a lot to like about Mexico.

Europe posed a greater challenge. In my opinion, Europe's only fully-blossomed destination of recent vintage is Ireland, an enchanting place with deep roots in golf. Thanks to a booming economy and significant European Union incentives, Ireland in the past 10 years has built dozens of first-rate courses, both links and parkland, to go along with its classic venues. Add pubs and the spoken poetry of its people, and the emerald green portrait is complete.

Portugal's Algarve, like Ireland, has a fascinating mix of old and new. Once a sleepy hideaway favored by British ex-pats who arrived in the 1950s to escape the rigors of winter and who laid out courses among pine groves and almond trees above the Atlantic, the Algarve is now one of Europe's most complete golf destinations. I've also touched on Scandinavia, specifically Sweden and Finland, where golf has been embraced as a social pastime as much by women as men. The venerable spa towns of the Czech Republic west of Prague have fixed up their old courses and built new ones now that communism has gone the way of the dinosaur.

That leaves the rest of the world, a daunting task that left me truly amazed by the game's intrinsic appeal as well as its extraordinary ability to span diverse environments, from the jungled flanks of St. Lucia to the desert enclave of Dubai. The places where the British left their legacy were relatively easy to define. Three of the nations I chose to write about—South Africa, Australia, New Zealand—have a long and storied golf tradition along with some of the finest new courses imaginable. On the North Island of New Zealand, for example, a Wall Street tycoon's bold vision and deep pockets has led to the creation of a pair of courses that redefine the golf experience Down Under.

Perhaps the unlikeliest emerging destination on the international front is China, a People's Republic where communism, not chip shots, was the order of the day for much of the 20th century. But reforms in the 1980s led to a new perspective on the sport. China, right now, is poised to become a dominant golf power in the 21st century.

I may be alone in my opinion, but I believe the best golf courses have yet to be built. I predict that by the year 2050, a time when the earth's population will reach the nine billion mark according to *National Geographic*, a healthy percentage of the top 100 courses in the world will exist in countries not currently associated with golf. Whoever said all the good sites were taken by the game's Golden Age designers hasn't explored the far precincts of Asia, Africa, or South America. Gary Player, golf's roving ambassador, has described the vast subcontinent of India as the most promising nation in the golf course development industry. But its time is not now.

I salute golf-friendly governments and developers worldwide whose taste and resources make great new courses possible. But my real heroes are the designers, the gentlemen and in a few rare instances the ladies who create the fields of play we so enjoy. The best of them blend science, which you don't see, and art, which you do if you play for more than score.

The book's long gestation period had its share of fits and starts, but began happily over lunch with Margaret Kaplan, my long-time editor and friend at Abrams. It was she who suggested the formal idea for a book on "emerging golf destinations" after hearing me talk so much about the wonderful new courses that were under construction here, there, and everywhere. It was she who championed this book and guided it from conception to completion. My thanks as well to Harriet Whelchel at Abrams for her support; and to Bob McKee, who has again outdone himself in the design of the book. To former *Golf Magazine* cohort David Barrett, a tip of the hat for editing the manuscript and separating fact from fiction.

Bad breaks? Setbacks? I had my share. Two days before I left for Ireland in June 2003, I was let go by *Golf Magazine* after more than 16 years on the job. The magazine, when it was run by George Peper and Jim Frank, gave me carte blanche to cultivate a travel agenda along with wide leeway to research and write what I deemed to be newsworthy. With less opportunity to travel, I could not move forward as quickly. It didn't help that I was covering a breaking news story about up-and-coming projects halfway around the world where English was often the second (or third) language.

I'll keep my thank you list as brief as I can. To tourism board executives, public relations personnel, and directors of golf at home and abroad, I thank you for providing information on golf courses, resort hotels, and off-course amenities. "I'll send you an e-mail with an attachment" became music to my ears as I sought verification for my fanciful notions.

As mentioned, golf designers are my personal heroes. How they can look at 200 acres of wilderness and devise a routing, much less build 18 holes that cohere, is beyond me. Among my favorite practitioners: Pete and Alice Dye, Rees Jones, Tom Doak, Roger Rulewich, Jim Engh, Brian Silva, Kyle Phillips, Jim Lipe, Steve Smyers, Dana Fry, and a pair of underrated Canadians, Doug Carrick and Tom McBroom. All have spent time with me, in person or on the phone, educating me to the finer points of strategy and design, and informing me of projects I wouldn't have heard about elsewhere. A special note of thanks to Ron Fream, the Johnny Appleseed of golf design who trots the globe in his quest to build courses in the unlikeliest places, and who sends postcards to keep me informed of his progress. He is the sunniest optimist I know. Plus, my girls love the stamps on his cards.

To friends and golf pals, we now have an entire book of emerging destinations from which to cull ideas for our next trip. But mostly I'm looking forward to playing golf at local courses with Rich Kusack, John Thompson, Mark Peele, Jeffrey Anderson, Phil Johnstone, Ralph Little, and my brother, David, who has to give me more strokes every year to equalize the disparity in our abilities. To my dear friend and golf writer extraordinaire Jim Finegan, your words of encouragement meant more to me than you know.

A special note of thanks to Dr. Martin Weinberg, a cherished friend without whose generosity and technical assistance I would still be pecking away on a manual typewriter.

I'd also like to thank local pal and architect Bob Mercer, who designed an above-ground office for me so that I wouldn't have to work in the basement anymore. What a difference natural light makes.

I'd like to dedicate this book to my mom, who passed away in 2003 and who always said my letters home from camp were fun to read. It was she who instilled a thirst for knowledge and stressed the value of proper grammar. Dad, I can't believe you've been gone seven years, I still think of you every time I tee it up.

To my family, well, the race is run and the journey, at least this journey, has come to an end. To my darling daughters, Aliyah and Jordana, I never really minded when you crept into my office and fooled around with my computer, but I had to pretend I minded because I was desperately afraid of losing data. To my wife, Saddia, you've been a pillar of support and never stopped believing that I could finish the job. Now that it's done, I don't know what to say except I love you.

Brian McCallen
Stonington, Connecticut
November, 2005

Northeast

Plymouth, Massachusetts

It's known as "America's original hometown," and it's where the Pilgrims came ashore in 1620. There's even a famous rock to prove it. Today, Plymouth is where colonial history comes alive along its bustling waterfront and also among its tiny, quiet side streets. But while visitors have been busy discovering its attractions for decades, Plymouth has quietly asserted itself as one of New England's premier golf destinations since the late 1990s. It currently boasts the greatest concentration of top-quality public-access courses of any town in New England. Several more are on the drawing board.

Located an hour's drive south of Boston and five miles north of Cape Cod Canal, Plymouth is the oldest town in Massachusetts and, at nearly 134 square miles, its largest municipality. Not only are there vast tracts of land available for new course development, the land itself is ideally suited to the game. Scraped by glaciers during the last Ice Age, the terrain is generally sandy, pine-covered, and rolling. Trace the footsteps of the Pilgrims with the family in between rounds—or turn the weekend into a golf orgy of 36 holes a day on some of the best new courses in the East. Either way, Plymouth has a way of taking on all comers. Just ask the Pilgrims.

Waverly Oaks Golf Club, opened in 1998, is the course that put this historic corner of New England on the golf map when Massachusetts native Brian Silva conjured a modern classic on rolling, windswept land marked by dramatic elevation changes. Describing the site as "simply phenomenal...the best I've worked with in my 20 years of designing courses," Silva set out to extract a brawny, fast-running links from the pine-dotted sand hills, the kind of course Yankees who like to walk can relate to. Nature lent a hand. "When we shaped the second green," says Silva, "it took all of 15 minutes. On half the holes, the natural contour was that perfect." To create the other half, nearly a million cubic yards of dirt were moved, an enormous sum by local standards. Yet Silva detailed this cut-and-fill enterprise with vintage design characteristics to fashion a seamless 18.

The front nine at Waverly Oaks (ironically, there are many more pines than oaks on site) is highlighted by back-to-back par fives, both reachable by better players. The downwind 529-yard fourth dares big hitters to play down the dangerous left side where a large mound (if cleared) provides an additional 50 yards of roll. The 12th is a short par four that invites players to carry a sentinel bunker down the left side. The reward is an extra 80 yards, though the inverted saucer green, inspired by Donald Ross, is not an easy target. On the other hand, the magnificent par-four 15th has a huge punchbowl green that funnels shots to the pin. The epic par-three 17th, called "Black Hole," was designed to "play like the 16th at Cypress Point—with no Pacific Ocean but a better bail-out area," says Silva. A monstrous 30-foot-deep maw defends the banked green. From the tips at 251 yards, this is one of the most intimidating one-shotters in New England.

Bunkers were dug randomly in natural depressions and hillocks at Waverly Oaks to create an old-time look, though putting surfaces were bunkered so that duffers can roll the ball onto 17 of the 18 greens. Five sets of tees range from a benign 4,930 yards to a stern 7,114. A shingle-style hilltop clubhouse patterned after the low-rise landmark at Shinnecock Hills offers fine views of Plymouth Bay along with excellent fare in the Waverly Grille. After lunch, opt for a quick round on the club's Challenger 9, a 2,264-yard, par-33 scaled-down version of the main course. It's fun and easily walkable.

Established in 2001, the first course at **Pinehills Golf Club,** designed by Rees Jones, is the kind of layout that may have hastened the journey of the Mayflower across the Atlantic had it been around in 1620. Presented with ideal terrain—sandy soil, pine groves, and glacial footprints ranging from kame terraces and esker ridges to large enclosed depressions known as kettles—Jones crafted a versatile test that makes full use of the site's Ice Age curvature. Only four miles as

Waverly Oaks Golf Club, 17th hole

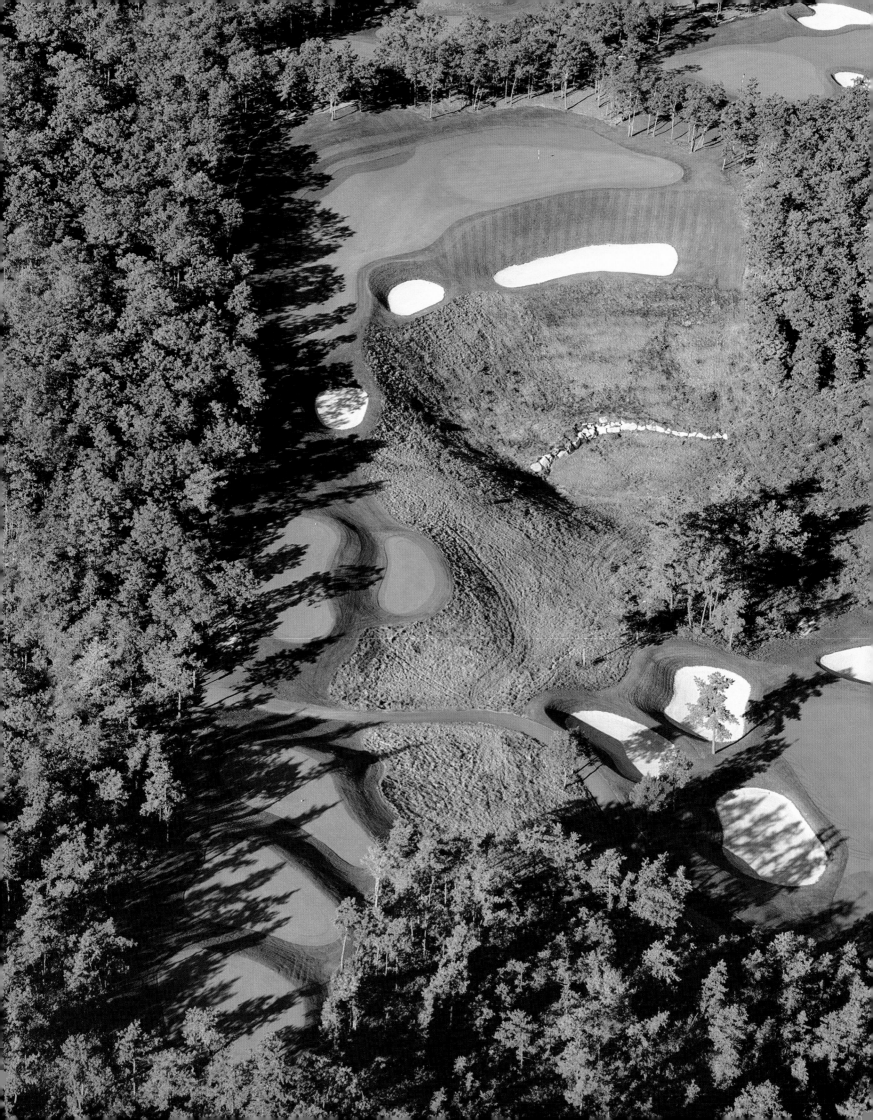

Pinehills Golf Club, Jones Course, 16th hole

the crow flies from Cape Cod Bay, the 7,175-yard layout can be breezy, which is why Jones built generous targets. However, good players are tempted at nearly every turn to gain advantage by cutting the corner of a large, sculptured bunker often recessed below the landing area. Plateau fairways routed along ridges lead to large, subtly contoured greens that spill off to close-mown hollows or well-placed bunkers.

The front nine on the **Jones Course** achieves strategic excellence, but the loftier back nine boasts a highlight reel of great holes. The 14th is a monster par three stretching to 248 yards that calls for a tee shot over a ravine to an enormous bi-level putting surface fronted by a deep, U-shaped bunker. There's a bail-out area to the left, but the chances of getting up-and-down from here are slim to none. The tee at the thrilling par-five 15th, which commands the high point of the course, teeters above a crater-like kettle overgrown with colorful scrub, the fairway rising to a pulpit green defended by deep bunkers. At 509 yards from the tips, this is one of the finest short risk-reward par fives in the state. The 16th, a boomerang-shaped par four that swings sharply to the right, dares players to fly the elongated sand pit

cut below the serpentine-like fairway. Despite a pond to the right of the putting surface, the par-three 17th appears innocuous—until you waltz onto the cloverleaf-shaped green and note the Y-shaped ridge at its center. Bucking a trend, Jones built a testing but not overbearingly difficult 18th hole, a straightforward par four that offers a chance for redemption.

By sculpting holes into glacial landforms and using the site's 60-foot elevation changes to dramatic effect, Jones established a unique identity for each hole. He also created a course that truly coheres. "It's a course you really need to think yourself around and determine what kind of shot you want to hit or are capable of hitting," he says. With numerous restorations of classic U.S. Open venues under his belt, Jones has absorbed the artistry and strategic nuances of the masters on the way to becoming one himself. His subtle, classic creation at Pinehills ranks among the very best courses on his résumé.

The Jones Course was joined in 2002 by the **Nicklaus Course,** a strong 7,243-yard test by the Golden Bear's eldest son, Jack Nicklaus II. Routed on slightly flatter land than the original course, the layout weaves around tall white pines, abandoned cranberry

bogs, and deep kettle holes. The driving corridors are ample, though the small greens are tightly guarded and demand accurate approach shots. En route to the first tee, players cross the Old Sandwich Road, a wide dirt path trafficked by the Pilgrims. It is the oldest road in America. The feature hole on the front nine is the third, a massive 243-yard par three that proceeds uphill past a gaping bunker to a skewed, tilted green divided by a prominent ridge in its center.

The back nine of the Nicklaus Course builds in interest, notably at the 14th, a brilliant short par four that doglegs to the right around a sloping ridge pockmarked with sandy potholes. Big hitters can try for the green with their drives, though the smart play is an iron off the tee to the left followed by a pinpoint approach to a severely undulating, two-tiered green. The 15th is the prettiest par three on the course, and also one of the most testing. The tee shot here is played over a broad, pine-choked kettle to a large, humped green defended in front by a multi-fingered bunker. The 18th, a long two-shotter, has a water feature on the left that pinches the fairway to a very narrow strip as players near the green. It may be the club's toughest par four.

Anchored by a handsome, 25,000-square-foot clapboard-shingle clubhouse, with outdoor dining available on its stone terrace, Pinehills offers one of the most extensive practice facilities in New England. There's a double-ended driving range, five putting greens, three chipping areas with practice bunkers, and a Dave Pelz Short Game School. In addition, the club introduced a caddie program in 2003 to give purists a chance to play the game the way it was meant to be played. All told, Pinehills is one of the finest 36-hole daily-fee facilities in New England.

Debuted in 2003, the soon-to-be 27-hole **Crosswinds Golf Club** is Plymouth's newest calling card. The golf complex is a unique hybrid: a privately-managed public golf facility built on town land. (The Town of Plymouth, recognizing it was not in the golf course construction or management business, collaborated with a local developer.) Laid out on heavily wooded land within the town's 600-acre Forges Field recreation complex adjacent to Miles Standish State Forest, this Michael Hurdzan-Dana Fry design features the biggest hills and sharpest elevation changes in the Plymouth area. Each of the nines is named for a

Crosswinds Golf Club, Jones nine, sixth hole

famous golfer. The core 18, with its Bobby Jones and Francis Ouimet nines stretching to 7,056 yards, will be joined in 2006 by the Babe Zaharias nine. Each is a stunner. The key to enjoyment is selecting the correct set of markers. The back tees, it should be noted, are for experts only.

In addition to heaving fairways that bob and weave through the woods, many of the large, gently undulating greens are set on natural plateaus or benched into the sides of hills. Reaching them in regulation is one thing; sinking a putt is another.

Among the feature holes is the dropped-in-the-woods par-three eighth on the Jones nine, where the tee shot is played over a pond to a slightly elevated green guarded by a pair of shaggy-edged, cavernous pits. Hurdzan-Fry strive for an old-style look that matches well to this rugged patch of town land. The deeply incised bunkers, many of them random, are fierce in appearance but are not overdone. Large, rough-cut boulders buttress the tee boxes. The corridors are wide, yet nearly every hole is self-contained.

Crosswinds is a perfect example of pure Yankee golf, player vs. terrain. A brisk sea breeze adds greatly to the challenge. A dramatic coastline view stretching from Plymouth Bay to the Cape Cod Canal can be glimpsed from the higher holes and seen in its entirety from the vantage point of the clubhouse.

In 2005, the Monday to Thursday visitors green fee at this well-run, well-groomed municipal facility was $47, one of the best bargains in New England.

If the sidehill, downhill, and hanging lies at the venues described above are getting you down, the **Atlantic Country Club** may get your game back on track. It's a well-groomed layout by Cornish-Silva-Mungeam circa 1995 that's fair and friendly from the white tees. Located at the south end of Plymouth off Pilgrims Highway near the entrance to Cape Cod, this is a well-mannered design, gently rolling and not overbearing. Want to experience an appetizer-sized taste of the game? Opt for a round on **Southers Marsh,** a charming 4,111-yard, par-61 track that plays over and around 100-year-old cranberry bogs as well as stands of tall white pines. With its numerous forced carries, it's not an easy test on a windy day, but it is fun.

OFF-COURSE ATTRACTIONS

Early-American history buffs can tour Plymouth Plantation, a living history museum where costumed actors recreate the lifestyle of the Pilgrims' 1627 settlement. Not only do these "colonists" speak in an arcane 17th-century dialect and still wonder aloud how they ever survived the transatlantic voyage to the New World, they milk cows and goats, tend gardens, cut firewood, and patch the walls of their modest wattle-and-daub homes. The rustic settlement is an eye-opener for those who take modern comforts for granted. In addition, Native-American interpreters on site explain how their forebears, the Wamponoag Indians, planted crops, made baskets and built canoes.

Anchored in the harbor is the Mayflower II, a full-scale reproduction of the ship that carried the 102 settlers to their new home. (It arrived from Plymouth, England in 1957 and is worth exploring.) For a unique perspective of the historic town and seaport, check in with Capt. John Boats for a narrated harbor cruise. Whale-watching cruises are also available. Exhibits at Cranberry World Visitors' Center, on the waterfront, trace the history of the tangy little berries, still an important crop, from pre-colonial days to the present. Nearby Plymouth Colony Winery produces and sells cranberry-blend wines.

After dark, join a Colonial Lantern Tour of Plymouth's plantation site, historic waterfront district, and Burial Hill. The tours are a fascinating way to learn more about America's original permanent settlement.

You can't leave town without having a gander at Plymouth Rock, which is nestled under an impressive seaside portico designed by McKim-Mead, but brace yourself—the famous rock is no bigger than a sack of potatoes. Far more impressive are the county's seven state parks and five saltwater beaches.

LODGING

Radisson Hotel Plymouth Harbor, an updated 175-room property, is centrally located opposite the busy Town Wharf. Sightseeing, restaurants, and attractions are a short walk from the hotel.

DINING

A pair of seafood restaurants on Town Wharf—Weathervane and the Lobster Hut—offer good casual dining. The chowder at both is exceptional. Wood's Seafood on Town Pier, a galley-style restaurant, also offers fresh-off-the-boat fare. Sam Diego's Mexican Eatery—"South of the Border, a Block from the Rock"—occupies the town's former fire station and offers good enchiladas, great margaritas, and an open-air patio. After the round, golfers tend to gravitate to the British Beer Company Pub, comfortably snug with a wide selection of imported beers and ales on tap. For traditional fare, head for the Colonial Restaurant in downtown Plymouth or the Hearth 'n Kettle at the John Carver Inn, staging point for Colonial Lantern Tours. Golfers can start the day with a fortifying breakfast at the All American Diner Café.

Mayflower II in Plymouth Bay

Boston

Thirty minutes west of Boston is Walden Pond, Henry David Thoreau's retreat and the place that inspired his famous essays. Somewhat incongruously, its not-too-distant neighbor is Fort Devens, a former military base and artillery range where soldiers trained for combat beginning in 1917. It's easy to find: Follow Patton (as in General) Road to Bulge (as in Battle) Road, and look for a hilly course marked by long ridges dotted with burly oaks that looks like it was built before World War I, even though the first (tee) shots were fired in 2002. Actually, authentic history was made in nearby Lexington and Concord, where the "shot heard round the world" was fired as the American Revolution began.

After the army base was decommissioned, Bay State native Brian Silva was brought in to build a golf course on a 185-acre site he describes as "wicked awesome." Many new courses claim to be multi-themed, but **Red Tail Golf Club,** named for a family of hawks that nests here, plays through a variety of environments and ecosystems. Several of the holes are routed down former oak-lined streets or reside atop army barracks foundations; others skirt abandoned gravel pits or vast sandy wastelands created when the military denuded the landscape. Traditional parkland-style holes are balanced by stark desert-style creations that would look more at home in Scottsdale than New England.

While sprinkling vintage design characteristics throughout his newfangled links, including a Redan-style par three, a giant punchbowl green, a Cape-style hole, and a few "baroque" bunkers carved into slopes, Silva, who made over 100 site visits and also drove the seeding tractor to get the look he wanted, dropped in modern defenses as well. These include random bunkering, "up" greens with "down" surrounds, and lots of options for recovery shots. Silva's "Indy 500" ramps tend to funnel the ball to the topsy-turvy greens, but Red Tail will rain bombs on the heads of unthinking players.

The par-four sixth, only 365 yards from the back tees, is typical of Red Tail, demanding accuracy and the ability to shape shots left and right in order to score. Silva's landing areas are sufficiently wide, but the designer holds nothing back on the greens. Some of the putting surfaces are as domed as a soldier's helmet; others are saucer-shaped to gather slightly errant approach shots. All the greens have slopes, ledges, and undulations, but most are defended not by bunkers—sand is a ticking bomb for most duffers— but by pronounced swales and hollows. Needless to say, the short game is fully tested at Red Tail. So is

the putting stroke: Reaching the green in regulation is only half the battle.

The closing sequence on this exciting swords-to-plowshares track is hair-raising. The Cape-style par-four 17th plays from a raised tee to a hairpin-shaped island of turf encased in tawny sand, with old ammo storage units located to the right of the green. Take dead aim or else! The sharply downhill par-five 18th can be reached in two—if you're skillful or daring enough to whack a fairway wood from a hanging lie over a waterfall-fed pond that fronts a slim, angled green.

"It's pretty incredible," muses Silva, "that this land, which is so magnificently suited to golf, was once the site of military exercises." Formerly laced with the residue of war, Red Tail has earned entry into Audubon International's Signature Sanctuary Program, golf's most demanding environmental management designation. That's not to say the hawks are about to welcome doves into their neighborhood anytime soon.

On a trio of landfills straddling the towns of Quincy and Milton eight miles south of Boston, Florida-based architect John Sanford has jumped over what he calls a "marathon of high hurdles" since 1992 to build a course the likes of which New England has never seen. Named for several abandoned granite quarries on site that yielded stone for the Bunker Hill Monument and numerous Boston skyscrapers, **Granite Links Golf Club at Quarry Hills** has been a work in progress thanks to miles of bureaucratic red tape and what Sanford describes as "a litany of constraints." But with two nines at the semi-private facility up and running as of 2004, plus a third nine slated to open in 2006, the wait may prove to be worth it.

In theory, the genesis of the 540-acre complex was brilliant, something the brain trusts at Harvard or M.I.T. in nearby Cambridge might have dreamed up. When it was learned that the state of Massachusetts was prepared to spend upwards of $200 million to dispose of the dirt dug from the city's massive Big Dig highway and tunnel construction project, wiser heads prevailed. Granite Links was more than happy to accept nearly *10 million cubic yards* of fill from the bottomless, over-budget Big Dig (that's 900,000 truckloads) to cap the landfills and create a canvas for golf, with room to spare for six athletic fields, open park space, and walking trails.

By virtue of its near-mountainous 320-foot height above sea level, not to mention its frog-to-prince metamorphosis, the domed, nearly treeless golf

Red Tail Golf Club, 18th hole

course, which skirts wetlands and prehistoric "work-shops" where Native Americans made tools 8,000 years ago, is totally unique.

First, the views. They are astonishing. On the Milton nine, where the mostly open holes are separated by steep-sided, fescue-covered hills up to 80 feet high, players enjoy unobstructed views to the north and east of the Boston skyline (notably the John Hancock Tower and Prudential Center) as well as Boston Harbor and its islets. Closer at hand is the Blue Hill Conservation area as well as church steeples in Milton that appear toy-like from the topmost holes. The Quincy nine plays around several of the old quarries, their sheer walls dropping 60 feet into limpid pools once popular as swimming holes. A handful of holes routed in between the landfills are tree-lined and exhibit a parkland appearance. They add greatly to the facility's multi-theme appeal.

Thanks to Sanford's ingenuity, the quarries are incorporated in the design and influence strategy. Fairways are bent around the rim of spent rock pits, multi-tiered greens are pushed to the brink of caverns, and a few forced carries must be made over granite cavities. Taken as a group, the short risk-reward par fours on the core 18 are outstanding. Geographically, both of the original nines start in Quincy, venture into Milton, and then return to Quincy. The Granite nine, the final piece in the Granite Links puzzle, is built entirely on the Quincy landfill. The configuration of holes on this nine is inventive and maximizes the topsy-turvy site to the fullest. The par-three eighth, which stretches to more than 250 yards and drops 60 feet to an 8,000-square-foot green, will one day rank among the Bay State's best one-shotters.

On a course where no two holes are alike and where the wind dictates strategy from day to day (and

Granite Links Golf Club at Quarry Hills, second hole

sometimes from hour to hour), players must adapt to the conditions at hand. One of Sanford's personal favorites is the first hole on the Quincy nine, a 483-yard par four that drops 70 feet to a broad fairway. It sets up as a reverse of Augusta National's famed 10th, with the landing area, parted through tall, shaggy hills and swerving to the right, rewarding a power fade with an extra 20 to 30 yards of roll. The approach shot is played to a partially hidden green sunk below fairway level.

"Building a golf course on a landfill has its own set of problems," says Sanford, whose father, Jack, grew up in Massachusetts and pitched for the San Francisco Giants. "We really had to work closely with the engineers to build a base and make it structurally sound on top of the landfills."

The first new course built inside the I-95 loop since the mid-1970s, Granite Links is a testament to municipal perseverance. Boston-area golfers didn't have to wait quite as long for the completion of this grand-scale reclamation project as Red Sox fans did for a World Series victory, but 12 years is a long haul. Their patience has been rewarded by a fantastic facility that is equal parts advanced engineering and landscape art. As much as any new course in America, Granite Links at Quarry Hills shows what a gifted architect can do with free dirt, a decent budget, and a good imagination.

Upstate New York

Against all odds, the Oneida Indian Nation's **Turning Stone Resort and Casino,** located in upstate New York some 30 miles east of Syracuse, has established itself virtually overnight as the top golf resort in the Empire State. In addition to Vegas-style gaming, live entertainment, specialty retail shops, a wide range of accommodations (there's even an RV park), and a dozen restaurants (New York deli to gourmet Asian), the resort offers three superlative courses, each by a top designer and each opened since 2000. It must seem a long time ago that the tribe was reduced to living in dilapidated housing on a 32-acre "territory" with no water or septic system.

One of the original members of the Iroquois Confederacy, the Oneidas enjoy a special role in American history, having supported the colonies in their struggle for independence from England. In their finest hour, the Oneidas carried 600 bushels of corn on their backs to George Washington's starving troops in Valley Forge in the terrible winter of 1777–78, staving off disaster. And though the federal government, through the landmark Treaty of Canandaigua (1794), gave the Oneida people special protections for their lands in return for their loyalty and courage, unscrupulous "treaties" orchestrated by New York State defrauded the tribe of their ancestral lands.

Despite the depredations of the past 200 years, the Oneida Nation survived and, through ingenuity and tenacity, eventually created a wealth of new opportunities for themselves and for the central New York region. Since the early 1990s, the 1,100-member Nation has grown into the area's largest employer,

providing jobs for more than 5,000 people. The resort's golf courses, each designed in harmony with nature, are the centerpiece of a thriving destination that ranks as one of the top five tourist attractions in the state and draws nearly five million visitors annually.

The first course to open at Turning Stone was **Shenendoah,** which debuted in 2000 and quickly established itself as the finest resort facility in central New York. Laid out by Rick Smith, the noted swing guru who works with Phil Mickelson and who typically designs one course a year, the 7,129-yard spread is a diverse layout that takes players from rolling parkland to links-style grasslands to a Lowcountry-style setting where the holes weave around wetlands. Free of housing, each hole on the course is isolated in nature, a fact not lost on Audubon International, which designated Shenendoah a Certified Signature Sanctuary shortly after it opened. Marked by broad fairways, slick greens, and deep bunkers, the course is very playable from the forward tees but shows its mettle from the tips (142 slope rating, 74.1 course rating). The layout's most memorable hole is the 18th, a 553-yard par five that plays to a wide landing area and then leapfrogs a creek and wetlands to an island-style fairway framed by bunkers. The green, tucked to the right, is defended by a very deep bunker in front. Rated the No. 2 course in New York by *Golfweek* on its America's Best State-by-State public-access course list in 2005, Shenendoah, home of the New York State PGA Championship, has also received kudos from *Golf Digest* as one of the best-conditioned courses in the nation.

The Lodge at Turning Stone

Turning Stone Resort & Casino, Kaluhyat, sixth hole

Turning Stone's second course, **Kaluhyat** (pronounced ga-LU-yut, an Oneida word meaning "the other side of the sky"), opened in 2003 to immediate acclaim. Designed by Robert Trent Jones, Jr., this well-groomed layout presents an otherworldly challenge from the back tees at 7,105 yards, playing significantly harder than Shenendoah. Dramatic elevation changes, narrow, tree-lined fairways, and a half dozen lakes that come into play at seven holes place a premium on accuracy. Shotmakers who keep the ball in play have a big advantage over risk-takers on Kaluhyat. Among the feature holes are a pair of killer par fives, 6 and 11. The sixth, stretching to 554 yards, calls for a drive that must flirt with a pond to the right. After the second shot is carried over a swath of marshland, the approach must find and hold a sloping green guarded by sand and framed by trees. The 11th, a gargantuan 621-yarder, calls for a forced carry over wetlands on the drive to a well-bunkered fairway and a second carry over soggy lowlands on the approach to a small, perched green. It's probably the toughest hole at Kaluhyat, but it's also a beauty.

stretches of open space and numerous water features, including lakes, streams, and small waterfalls. The largest pond on the course measures 13 acres and presses against three holes, including the dramatic par-five 18th, where water hugs the entire right side of the fairway.

Atunyote, with its own New England–style clubhouse and practice center, has the feel of an exclusive club in its own park-like setting, with a green-fee structure set higher than the other two courses. For high rollers accustomed to the best, Atunyote, manicured to perfection, is the venue of choice.

Pressed for time or just getting started in the game? Turning Stone has a pair of appealing nine-holers. **Sandstone Hollow,** designed by Rick Smith at the time he built Shenendoah, offers a distinctive collection of par threes framed by rock outcrops and long fescue grasses, the holes ranging in length from 110 to 230 yards. Happily, the Hollow can be played in an hour. Players can also have a go at **Pleasant Knolls,** a 3,393-yard, par-36 recreational layout set on 70 gently rolling acres dotted with water hazards. Built in 1963 and acquired by the Oneidas in 1999, Pleasant Knolls is perfect for a relaxing afternoon of fun after a morning round on one of the three main tracks.

LODGING

In 2004, the existing hotel and inn at **Turning Stone** were dwarfed by a 19-story tower featuring 266 guest rooms and 21 lavish suites geared for high rollers. Seven of these suites average a thousand square feet, and the other 14 offer views of the surrounding golf courses and New York countryside. Tower guests have access to a third-floor fitness center complete with pool, while suite guests can dine in a private, top-floor restaurant, the Top of the Tower. Also debuted in 2004 was an events center with ample space for business meetings as well as theater-style seating for 5,100.

But leisure travelers, specifically golfers, were not overlooked in favor of conference business. **The Lodge at Turning Stone,** a wood-and-stone property with 98 suites located beside the Shenendoah and Kaluhyat courses, evokes a traditional Adirondack lodge, with wooden balconies, a pitched metal roof, expansive terrace and lawn, and a scenic lake nearby. Inside, a curved wall of frosted glass illuminated from within defines the Great Room, which is dominated by a majestic stone fireplace and accented by cherry wood flooring. Connected to the lodge via a covered walkway is the Spa at Turning Stone, a 27,000-square-foot facility opened in late 2004 that features a variety of treatments as well as an indoor-outdoor grotto pool. The Lodge also boasts a spacious lounge and a 65-seat restaurant featuring classic American dishes.

The course that has transformed Turning Stone from a major casino resort with golf to a major golf destination with a casino is **Atunyote** (pronounced uh-DUNE-yote, meaning "eagle"). Unveiled in 2004, this Tom Fazio–designed layout, a burly yet flexible test stretching to 7,315 yards from the tips (it's nearly 7,000 yards from the blues), is tucked away in a secluded setting a few miles from the main property. Handed a rolling tract of land, essentially a pristine habitat for deer, fox, and a diverse array of birds, Fazio crafted a brilliant parkland course with vast

Mid-Atlantic

Atlantic City, New Jersey

With several excellent new daily-fee courses opened in the past few years coupled with a $7 billion renaissance plan, the East Coast's best-known (and often most disparaged) seaside resort is on the rebound. There was a time when Atlantic City was the reigning queen of the Jersey Shore, a time when physicians extolled the curative virtues of its ozone-rich sea air and encouraged stifled city dwellers to lounge on its sandy beach or stroll its raised wooden Boardwalk, the nation's oldest (1870). A city of firsts, Atlantic City is where saltwater taffy originated when a storm flooded a Boardwalk candy store in 1883. The nation's first picture postcards were color views of amusement piers protruding into the surf. The Miss America pageant was born here. So was the concept of a "vacation," if locals can be taken at their word. And if the street names sound familiar, it's because the popular board game of Monopoly utilizes the city's byways.

Although Atlantic City attracts upwards of 38 million visitors annually and rakes in more than $10 million daily in the casinos, it was only recently that golf became recognized as a drawing card. Many of the region's new and vintage courses, built on sandy soil dotted with pines, resemble their exalted neighbor to the west, Pine Valley. The Greater Atlantic City Golf Association, launched in 1996, packages these venues with a variety of accommodations. Says golf designer and local resident Stephen Kay, "In my opinion, there is no golf destination of the same size in the U.S. that has a better collection of golf course architecture than the Atlantic City area." Kay is admittedly biased, but he just might be right—the region's variety of courses is exceptional.

The city's ambitious redevelopment was originally intended to transform the downtrodden town into a major meeting destination. Along the way, it became hip, trendy and, according to a report in the *New York Times* in 2003, a viable alternative to the ultra-chic Hamptons. Overnight, the Beautiful People—celebrities, models, and their entourages—began to frequent the gelato shops and chic boutiques in a town formerly characterized as "tacky" by sophisticates. Other enticements: an improved airport, the Grand

Boulevard entranceway into the city, and dozens of beach bars that opened shortly after the city lifted its ban on the sale of alcoholic beverages along the shore. The runaway success of Las Vegas has not been lost on its eastern cousin—the city's newest hotels, restaurants, spas, and nightclubs aim to dazzle and please.

Because it's within easy driving distance of New York, Philadelphia, Baltimore, and Washington, D.C., their combined citizenry representing one-third of the U.S. population, Atlantic City has the virtue of convenient access. Also, the shore's mild maritime climate makes golf possible year-round. The only caveat? Green head flies and mosquitoes can be pesky in summer. Bring lots of bug spray or, better yet, plan to visit in the bug-free spring or fall months.

For years, California-based Ron Fream has trotted the globe working on far-flung projects in such spots as Korea, Bali, Nepal, Argentina, Tunisia, and even Disneyland Paris—the more exotic the better. In 2001, Fream made a detour to Ocean View, a small community 30 minutes south of Atlantic City, where the Turner family, owners of a nearby campground, asked him to have a look at their 245-acre parcel. Won over by the designer's enthusiasm, they quickly hired Fream to build **Shore Gate Golf Club** on land that was beach and dunes eons ago.

After massaging the site, one of the highest points in Cape May County, with bulldozers to displace 450,000 cubic yards of sand—this after noting sun angles and shadow patterns—Fream produced the boldest and most extroverted layout imaginable, a dynamic, visually intimidating world-beater designed to drain the plaid from a duffer's knickers. Perhaps to remind players of the site's geologic past, Fream flashed sand up the sides of tall vertical mounds at several holes to create the impression of incoming ocean waves. There are 88 formal bunkers on the course, plus seven ponds, but it's the fescue-fringed waste areas and sand-flashed mounds that scream, "Watch out!"

Despite the histrionics, the 7,227-yard course, nicely framed by maple, pine, oak, and holly, is a brilliant stage set that's quite playable from a carefully

Atlantic City County Club, 18th hole and clubhouse

A CLASSIC OPENS ITS DOORS

It's an axiom that a city built around casino gambling must have an exclusive playground for high rollers who take golf as seriously as they take their table games. In the case of **Atlantic City Country Club**, the reward for establishing a serious line of credit at a selected casino hotel (or reaching deep for a top-end green fee) is access to a truly historic venue. Thanks to a $15 million overhaul by Tom Doak in 1999 after the course was purchased by Caesars Entertainment, the formerly private club has been transformed into one of the finest layouts in the mid-Atlantic region.

The big news for visiting players is that ACCC dropped its high rollers–only policy and began to welcome daily-fee play in 2005. And while the Vegas-style rates at this once-exclusive venue may be high (at press time, $179 Monday to Thursday, $250 Friday to Sunday), the experience of turning back the pages at this historic facility is well worth it.

The legendary club, founded in 1897, is where the term "birdie" was coined in 1903, and where many great champions have teed it up, including Harry Vardon, Walter Hagen, and a strapping young Coast Guard seaman named Arnold Palmer, who was posted at Cape May in 1951 and '52. Atlantic City's storied clubhouse, its wide-planked floor scarred over the years by metal spikes, doubles as a museum of American golf. Rightfully so: the 1901 U.S. Amateur (won by Walter Travis), three U.S. Women's Opens, and the first Senior PGA Tour event, in 1980, were held there.

The original links, flat and featureless in places, was transformed by Doak into a gently rolling layout with a brilliant mix of five par threes (four of them short but deadly) interspersed among the longer holes. Seemingly innocent on the card at 6,539 yards (par 70), ACCC presents a brilliant test of golf by virtue of its stunning bayside location and varied array of challenges. To meet the gaming company's goal of creating a special retreat, Doak rerouted several front-nine holes to take old crossing roads out of play. The 10th and 11th were combined to make a strong par five that points into the prevailing wind, and the former 12th was extended by 70 yards to make it a very testing par four. But the most radical and welcome changes are found at the new 14th and 15th holes. According to Doak, "A new section of tidal marsh was dug into the original 15th (now the 14th) to create a more daunting short par four from a peninsula tee, followed by a difficult par three playing back into the southeast wind, while the earth removed from the marsh was redistributed to raise all of the coastal holes above flood levels."

These two creations, along with new definition and shaping throughout the course, have elevated the golf experience at the club to a level unimagined by early hickory-toting members. When the remedial work was completed, Doak mused that he and his crew "spent more [money] in rebuilding it than to build any of our new 18-hole designs!" Not only was every green and tee rebuilt, trees were removed to create more dramatic views of the marsh. Conversely, trees were planted along the layout's western boundary to enhance the secluded feel of the club.

With a unique blend of parkland, salt marsh, sandy wasteland, and links-style holes, ACCC is a multi-theme layout nonpareil. Manicured to perfection, this breezy spread skirts the bay and offers fine views of the city skyline across the tidal flats.

chosen set of tees (there are five). Fream's greens, most of them large, wavy, and undercut by swales, are as entertaining and unpredictable as the tee-to-green game. Among the singular holes is the ninth, a sickle-shaped behemoth of 648 yards that skirts a massive curlicued sand pit and swings around a lake en route to a huge green with fortress-like defenses. This king-sized dogleg belongs among New Jersey's grandest par fives.

Holes 13 through 15, a secluded trio, are reached via a metal bridge that spans a large swath of protected wetlands. Shore Gate's finale, a long par four into the wind with trouble galore, will not succumb to a grip-it-and-rip-it approach. "Shore Gate is a copy of no one and nothing else. The course is not minimalist, leave nature as it is. It is not stereotyped or a knockoff of others I've done," Fream wrote in a postcard from Katmandu shortly before the course opened in 2002. Kudos to a West Coast pioneer not afraid to shake up the status quo and tilt the seaboard a little closer to the sea.

Located in Swainton, 30 miles south of the Boardwalk, **Sand Barrens Golf Club** was originally intended to be a 27-hole parkland spread called Royal Oakes until co-designers Michael Hurdzan and Dana Fry discovered on site a thick layer of sand, up to hundreds of feet deep in places. Eschewing the manicured look, the architects dug deep into every designer's favorite medium, gouging holes and splicing fairways through vast sandy wastelands framed by oaks, pines, and bayberry bushes. According to Hurdzan, "The main reason for the success . . . of Sand Barrens is that the sandy soils were so perfect [they] could pass for a laboratory-selected and blended root zone for putting greens. That meant it was not only a perfect growing medium for turfgrass, it also offered perfect drainage." Added Fry, "Think of it as a public Pine Valley," though in truth this splendid creation has a look and feel all its own. The terraced greens, among the largest ever planted in the Garden State, require a sure touch—and a sense of humor. The 55,000-square-foot, boomerang-shaped double green

Shore Gate Golf Club, 13th hole

Sand Barrens Golf Club, West nine, ninth hole

that serves No. 2 North and No. 4 West, stretching nearly 400 feet from end to end, is a case in point. The dips and swales in this riotously undulating green make the haystack contours on the Himalayas putting course in St. Andrews, Scotland seem tame by comparison. This massive green is roughly nine times bigger than the average putting surface.

Landing areas at Sand Barrens are far more generous than they appear, though higher handicappers for whom sand is a chained dog waiting to strike should consider playing from the "rookie" or forward tees to assuage their fear. On the plus side, a local rule permits players to lift their ball and level their lie in the acres and acres of steep-walled waste areas draping most of the holes. A "smoothie," it's called.

Bring your trustiest sand iron to a club where even

the entryway is dotted with coarse sand bunkers. The North and West nines at Sand Barrens, opened to acclaim in 1997, were followed two years later by the debut of the equally appealing South nine. (The South's par-three ninth, played from a perched tee over a water-filled quarry to a well-protected green, is perhaps the finest one-shotter at the facility). For pure natural endowment, Sand Barrens is as good as it gets in south Jersey.

While known mainly for its casinos and beach and Boardwalk, Greater Atlantic City is also home to one of the nation's oldest wineries. Established in 1864, Renault Winery in Egg Harbor City introduced New Jersey Champagne in 1870, and today its blueberry sparkling wine remains ever popular. The

Vineyard Golf at Renault Winery, seventh hole

addition in 2002 of the 45-room Tuscany House gives the winery the look and feel of an established Mediterranean vineyard.

Opened in 2004, **Vineyard Golf at Renault Winery** is a marked departure from other courses in the region, most of which are cut through sandy pinelands. This handsome parkland spread, flanked in places by the resort's vineyards, fruit orchards, and blueberry patches, also passes by stands of tall evergreens and hardwoods planted as windbreaks long ago. Landing areas are generous, but according to designer Ed Shearon, "the design utilizes classic strategic elements, with an emphasis on diagonal hazards that offer risk/reward opportunities," a gambit popularized by Golden Age designers. Ponds, bunkers, waste areas, and spent quarries come into play, though there's plenty of room for duffers to steer clear of trouble. Better players, however, must chart a bolder route to reap a reward on a course that measures 7,213 yards from the back tees.

"You don't have to carry these angles, but your chance at par is greatly diminished if you don't," Shearon says. "I wanted a 'look hard, play easy' course that resort guests could enjoy" from the forward tees. What Shearon produced is a beautiful, flowing test of golf that marries art and utility. Imagine a wine-tasting session with a flight of 18 wines,

each related by varietal but different in character.

The balance and variety of holes at Vineyard Golf is admirable. No two are alike; only two are routed consecutively in the same direction. Located eight miles from the ocean, the open, gently rolling site invites the prevailing southwest breeze. Earthmoving was kept to a minimum. Slopes surrounding each putting surface were tied into the green complex itself to create naturalistic targets. The greens have broad sweeps, not tight contours, but most have enough shelves and saddlebacks to keep better players attentive. Fairways, built on sandy loam, drain well and are kept firm to promote the ground game.

A full-service resort, Renault Winery offers pleasant accommodations in the Tuscany House, its walls painted with colorful murals of bucolic Italian scenes and its lobby set off by greenery and a large gurgling fountain. In addition to cocktails served at a bar built from wine kegs, superb dining is available in Joseph's Restaurant and, across the street in the winery, the Gourmet Restaurant (weekends only).

Stretched across a former horse farm in Egg Harbor Township is **Twisted Dune Golf Club,** a big, treeless layout patterned after the great sand hills courses of Ireland (think Ballybunion). Its sunken fairways are framed by facsimile dunes and towering hills covered with tall native grasses that wave in the wind. Opened in 2001 and designed by Archie Struthers, a local resident and former Pine Valley caddie and assistant pro, Twisted Dune was the first course in the region to capture the look and feel of a brawling seaside links. Struthers moved more than two million cubic yards of material to simulate the stark effects of coastal erosion on the dead-flat site. Fairways are spacious—up to 90 yards in width—while the sloping greens are large. Holes 13 through 16 are routed through an old sand quarry, with water in play at the par-three 13th and short par-four 14th. The par-four 18th, at 472 yards, is one of the area's toughest finishing holes. The canyon-through-the-dunes theme is a bit repetitive, but Twisted Dunes offers a fine test of links-style golf. Only experts need apply from the tips at 7,384 yards. Walking is encouraged.

Built on a closed landfill three miles south of Twisted Dune, **McCullough's Emerald Golf Links,** a Stephen Kay–designed municipal layout, features a rare-for-south-Jersey 100-foot elevation change along with variations of holes drawn from famous British and Irish courses. Named for Egg Harbor Township Mayor James J. "Sonny" McCullough, the driving force behind the project, the nearly treeless links, dotted with grassy knobs and nearly 100 shaggy-edged bunkers, offers fine views of the Atlantic City skyline from its topmost holes.

Kay, who juggled 30 routing plans to accommodate the hundreds of methane gas extraction wells on site before finally fitting the pieces together, recreated the award-winning two-shotter that Alister Mac-Kenzie designed for *Country Life* magazine in 1914, a hole that had never been built to its original specifications. Kay described the par-four seventh, ranging from 464 to 333 yards in length, as "the largest hole we have ever designed, requiring *seven* rows of sprinkler heads across its broadest width." The mammoth hole, bulging to 160 yards at its widest point, offers three distinct options. Players can aim for the island fairway on the left; fly the huge central waste bunker, the most perilous route; or bail out safely to the right. As is true throughout the 6,535-yard, par-71 course, sound tactics are required to succeed, based on wind direction and player ability. The firm, fast links, opened in 2002, was designed to be walked.

Sea Oaks Golf Club, a Ray Hearn design opened in 2000, is yet another Egg Harbor Township entry. Carved from heavily wooded, sand-based terrain in the pine barrens, this semi-private club features rolling fairways lined with scrub pine, jack pine, and burly oaks. Cookie-cutter bunkers

frame the prime landing areas. Several of the large, undulating greens, also well-defended by sand, are multi-tiered. The stronger back nine of this 6,950-yard spread features a double green at holes 13 and 15 plus a treacherous par five, No. 16, that plummets down a roller-coaster fairway girdled by a long waste bunker and plays to a peninsula green cantilevered into a rock-rimmed pond. The club's practice facility is first-rate. Long Beach Island, the ocean, and the Atlantic City skyline can be seen from the 23,000-square-foot clubhouse.

Routed on wooded parkland dotted with 12 lakes, **Harbor Pines Golf Club,** a player-friendly layout designed by Stephen Kay in 1996, could pass for a course in the Carolinas. What you see is what you get: Fairway corridors are wide, landing areas are clearly visible, and most of the large, well-contoured greens are angled to face the golfer, allowing players to easily "read" each hole and assess the risk-reward consequences of each shot. The rough is cropped short. Also, underbrush from beneath the oaks and pines that frame the fairways has been cleared to expedite play. Flashed-face bunkers accent the holes, but most are easily avoided, as are the numerous ponds. The course owner wanted a forgiving layout the average duffer "could play and play again" without getting beat up too badly. Harbor Pines, always in good shape, fits the bill.

The **West Course** at **Blue Heron Pines Golf Club,** the region's first upscale public layout, proved to disbelievers that the high-end daily-fee concept would fly on the outskirts of Atlantic City. Opened in 1993, this is the course that paved the way for future development. Designed by Stephen Kay, it is still among the area's best. Carved from pines and hardwoods, the course is a classically-styled parkland spread marked by clever short par fours. The straightforward front nine is followed by a tougher back nine highlighted by the par-five 14th, its gaping fairway hazard inspired by "Hell's Half Acre" at Pine Valley. Sadly, the facility's **East Course,** a nearly treeless layout built in 2000 by Steve Smyers to emulate a links, a course good enough to host the U.S. Amateur Public Links Championship in 2003, is scheduled to have its plug pulled at the end of 2006, to be replaced by a housing development.

Twisted Dune Golf Club, 14th hole

FAMILY FUN

Just off the Atlantic City Expressway is the **Olde Masters Family Golf Center,** one of the largest and most complete practice facilities in the East. Set on 30 acres, the center, opened in 2001, features 86 synthetic-based hitting stations in a double-decker configuration, with 20 of the lower bays covered and heated. Four private instruction bays have computerized swing analyzers. A grass tee is available for purists. There's also a five-acre short-game practice area that features bunkers, chipping area, and practice opportunities from a variety of grasses and lies. Kids gravitate to the center's miniature golf course.

LODGING

Originally founded in 1912 as a private club, **Seaview Marriott Resort and Spa,** located in Absecon north of Atlantic City, is the region's leading full-service golf resort. Anchored by a Georgian Revival–style hotel overlooking Reeds Bay, Seaview offers 297 updated guest rooms and features fine dining in its window-walled main dining room. Seaview is home to the Faldo Golf Institute by Marriott as well as an Elizabeth Arden Red Door Spa. The resort hosts an annual LPGA event on the **Bay Course,** a Donald Ross creation routed along the shores of Reeds Bay. Its vintage features—deep sand pits, high grassy mounds, crowned or punchbowl greens—have been artfully restored. While not long at 6,247 yards (par 71), the Bay is no pushover when the wind blows. Seaview's **Pines Course,** carved from a thick forest of pines and oaks, is a rolling, narrow layout that calls for accuracy off the tee.

Borgata Hotel Casino & Spa, a dazzling 2,002-room, golden-bronze glass tower that debuted in 2003 and was Atlantic City's first new casino-hotel in 13 years, is the surest sign that the mega-hotel concept perfected by Las Vegas has moved east. The $1.1 billion property, a joint venture of Boyd Gaming Corp. and MGM Mirage, currently reigns as the city's new market leader, its marble archways, playful glass chandeliers, and other architectural flourishes drawn from Italian-themed hotels in Vegas as well as the fertile imagination of Borgata CEO Bob Boughner. The lighting in particular is very well done.

Built on a former landfill in the city's Marina District, the 43-story Borgata is linked to the Atlantic City Expressway by a $330 million tunnel opened in 2001. The trendy, monolithic property features exceedingly comfortable guest rooms, each with floor-to-ceiling windows, large bathrooms with granite countertops and marble walls and floors, and a number of stylish amenities. Borgata's 11 dining "destinations" include a branch of New York's landmark Old Homestead steakhouse and two superb Italian venues, the deluxe Specchio and the subterranean Ombra.

Headlining Borgata's live-music bars and clubs is MIXX, a "Chino-Latino" restaurant that morphs into a

Atlantic City shorefront

throbbing nightclub after 10 p.m. on weekends. The bustling hotel also has the 50,000-square-foot Spa Toccare, several specialty retail shops, 125,000 square feet of gaming space, a 1,000-seat theater called the Music Box—the works. Borgata (Italian for "little village") has raised the lodging bar in Atlantic City and forced competitors to expand or upgrade their facilites.

In addition to Seaview Marriott and Borgata, the Greater Atlantic City Golf Association packages most of the courses listed above with numerous mid-priced hotels.

DINING

You'll find everything from haute cuisine to clams on the half shell in Atlantic City. Several eateries are local institutions. White House Sub Shop in Ducktown, the city's Italian district, claims to have sold over 20 million overstuffed submarine sandwiches since 1946. Check the celebrity photos on the walls: Frank Sinatra, the Beatles, Joe DiMaggio, Tiny Tim, numerous Miss Americas. Down the street is Angelo's Fairmont Tavern, where fresh pasta and homemade sauces have been

MIXX at Borgata Hotel Casino & Spa

served up by the Mancuso family since 1935. Fresh-off-the-boat seafood? Head for Dock's Oyster House, family-owned and operated since 1897. For superb steaks and fine seafood dishes, the Knife & Fork Inn, setting for a scene in the movie *Atlantic City* starring Burt Lancaster and Susan Sarandon, has been pleasing customers since 1927.

For formal dining (jackets required at dinner), the Ram's Head Inn, located in Absecon near the Seaview Marriott Resort, is a beautiful country restaurant set on five acres that ranks among south Jersey's finest dining establishments.

OFF-COURSE ATTRACTIONS

With more than a dozen major casinos open 24 hours a day, there are no dull moments in Atlantic City. Billboards announcing top-name musical groups, entertainers, and comedians that perform at casino showrooms can be previewed on the drive into town. Shopping? There's lots of it here. A box of saltwater taffy (preferably Fralinger's) is a must. The Pier at Caesars, a new $145-million luxury retail, dining, and entertainment complex features high-end specialty shops Gucci, Hugo Boss, Louis Vuitton, Armani A/X, Burberry, and many others, in addition to nine restaurants. The Pier is connected to the Caesars casino by a skybridge.

The Walk, a $60 million, 320,000-square-foot retail and entertainment complex located in a former eight-block eyesore between the Atlantic City Convention Center and the Boardwalk, debuted in 2004 with dozens of well-known outlet stores, from Banana Republic to Timberland. There's also The Quarter, a 200,000-square-foot, old Havana-themed retail, dining, and entertainment complex opened at the Tropicana Casino & Resort in late 2004.

Ocean fishing charters are available out of Atlantic City and Cape May. The Noyes Museum near Absecon, south Jersey's only fine arts museum, has a good collection of American folk art, including vintage bird decoys. Bring binoculars to the adjacent Edwin B. Forsythe Wildlife Refuge, a 40,000-acre haven for more than 200 species of migratory birds. For a pre-gaming overview of the city, check out the sepia-tone photos and other artifacts in the Atlantic City Historical Museum.

Of course, you can always stroll Atlantic City's world-famous, seven-mile-long wooden Boardwalk for fresh air and good people-watching. Better yet, hire a "rolling chair," a Jersey version of a rickshaw.

Philadelphia

For years, the "City of Brotherly Love" was everything it was cracked up to be in the fraternity of golf—if you happened to be a member of one of its exclusive Main Line private clubs. The venues for unattached players were in most cases mere afterthoughts. However, dozens of top daily-fee courses have debuted on the outskirts of the nation's fifth-largest city since the late 1990s. Here are a handful of the finest newcomers around a town where the Liberty Bell now rings loud and clear for public golfers.

Forty minutes southwest of Philadelphia is a 175-year-old school for troubled youth with an unusual study aid on campus: a golf course. The Glen Mills School is a privately-funded educational facility for nearly a thousand court-appointed, troubled teen-age boys from around the country. The institution's superb daily-fee venue, **Glen Mills Golf Course,** opened in 2001 across a road from its Victorian-era buildings, was specifically designed to serve as an outdoor vocational classroom where students can learn landscape maintenance, golf course management, maintenance mechanics, and agronomy. According to superintendent John Vogts, "The goal is to turn out technicians who can command good pay on the market." (Green fees are funneled into a college scholarship fund for the youths, with operational funds derived from tuition and other sources.)

The layout, a rugged parkland-style design with a rough-hewn, wilderness feel, was built by Florida-based architect Bobby Weed. "Open fields, forested uplands, streams, and wetlands provided great diversity for the routing," Weed explains. "The course features rolling terrain, natural rock outcroppings, stacked rock walls, and abundant wildlife." While relatively short at 6,636 yards (par 71) from the Scratch tees, the course has plenty of teeth and cannot be overpowered. Weed built nearly 170 bunkers, many of them nasty, sod-faced pits modeled after those on the Old Course at St. Andrews, Scotland. "Most people can't go to Scotland," says Weed, "but at least the golfers in and around Philadelphia will now have the feeling of playing out of a St. Andrews–style bunker."

Shot placement and course management are all-important on this tumbling track where the slippery greens, interwoven with troughs and whalebacks, are the great equalizer. Bunkers, creeks, and trees defend the corners of the dogleg (and double-dogleg) par fives, while the five par threes, well-varied in length, play uphill, downhill, and over water. There's a pair of "driveable" par fours, at eight and 12, though the penalty for a miscue is severe. Weed advises "keeping the ego in check to achieve the optimum score."

The conditioning at Glen Mills is first-rate. According to Vogts, "Some of the students do as good a job as some of my crew, and better in certain cases."

Not far from Glen Mills in Norristown is **Jefferson-ville Golf Club,** Philadelphia's most compelling rags-to-riches golf story. Originally designed by Donald Ross in 1931, "the Jeff" had devolved into a hard-scrabble muni. Fortunately, the custodians of this town-owned course sought out local resident Ron Prichard, who has earned a well-deserved reputation as a masterful restorer of Ross courses.

The refurbished 6,450-yard layout (par 70), reopened in 2002 following a $3 million makeover, is a virtually new course that adheres closely to the Ross style. With the assistance of old photos, Prichard restored numerous bunkers that had been abandoned over time and also added 11 new ones, bringing the total to 86. After a new irrigation system was installed, all tees were leveled, reconstructed, and in some cases enlarged. The back nine was rerouted—"a rerouting of the rerouting," according to Prichard—and a large pond was dug out beside the 18th fairway. In addition, the open, rolling, lightly wooded site—Ross's ideal canvas for a golf course—was lengthened by nearly 300 yards to keep pace with modern equipment.

Jeffersonville does not belong in the pantheon of great Ross designs—it's no Pinehurst No. 2—but it presents a fair, fun test with all the master's trademarks. These include grass-faced bunkers, subtly crowned greens, and appropriate penalties for those who stray. Perhaps best of all, the green fee for walkers—$24 on weekdays, $32 on weekends in 2005—represents a genuine bargain on this much-improved classic. Somewhere Ross, a thrifty Scot, must be smiling.

In the sleepy hamlet of Williamstown, New Jersey, some 30 minutes south of Philadelphia is **Scotland Run Golf Club,** one of the brightest stars in the city's orbit. Designed in 1999 by Stephen Kay, who lists three courses in Atlantic City along with a nine-hole course built for the King of Bhutan on his résumé, the layout winds in and around an old sand and gravel quarry. The par-71 course, stretching to 6,810 yards, artfully blends woodland, quarry, and links-style holes. Expansive waste areas, 10 acres of water, and an imposing array of cliffs provide quite an eyeful during the round. Each hole has its own personality, a rare feat. Also, every tee, fairway, and

Glen Mills Golf Course, 11th hole

green area was covered with two feet of sand excavated from the old quarry, resulting in superior playing conditions year-round.

Named for a stream that defines the northern boundary of the course (the stream was named by early Scottish settlers who noted the landscape's resemblance to their homeland), Scotland Run eases players into the round but cranks up the challenge on the back nine. The green at the par-five 10th, for example, is fronted by a moat-like bunker and a sheer-sided wall of railroad ties that defends against easy assault. The par-four 16th is a classic risk-reward hole that tempts players to bite off a corner of a sprawling waste bunker to reach a prime portion of the fairway, while the fishhook-shaped 18th, a 530-yard par five, dares brave-hearted players to carry a fearsome sand pit to reach the elevated green in two. This stunning finale, with its water, sand, and curving quarry walls, sums up all that has gone before.

In *The Time Machine*, H.G. Wells takes readers on a bumpy ride into the remote future. At the **Architects Golf Club** in western New Jersey, an hour's drive from Philadelphia, designer Stephen Kay, assisted by golf historian Ron Whitten, has opened the door to the game's rich past by taking players on a fascinating tour of vintage design styles. Using the period from 1885 to 1955, Kay, who got the notion for Architects while assisting on the Donald Ross Memorial course at Boyne Highlands in Michigan in the early 1980s, fashioned a living museum piece that pays tribute to the game's legendary designers. There are no replica holes; rather, the signal features of the game's finest practitioners were reproduced on 175 acres of rolling farmland.

"We looked at three elements," Kay explains. "How the architect set up a hole strategically, the shape and style of the bunkering, and the contours of the putting surface." All the big names of the profession are represented, from C.B. Macdonald and Donald Ross (twice) to Alister MacKenzie and A.W. Tillinghast. Kay wraps up 70 years of classic design at the final two holes, which were inspired by the Canadian stylist Stanley Thompson and his protégé, Robert Trent Jones.

Five sets of tees ranging from 6,863 to 5,233 yards (par 71) make Architects a versatile test. Kay, who teaches golf design at Rutgers University, moved quite a bit of dirt to create what nature failed to provide, yet the holes appear draped on the partially wooded land tucked away in the Pocono foothills.

The course, which debuted in 2001, opens with a straightaway par five, its sod-walled pot bunkers and plateau green a dead giveaway: this is Old Tom Morris. The back nine is longer and tougher, starting with the 11th, the William Flynn hole. The elbow of the dogleg at this grand uphill par five is peppered with nearly a dozen rounded, elliptical bunkers marked by rolled-down grass faces. The small, docile green here is a tip of the hat to Shinnecock Hills, Flynn's masterpiece. The par-five 13th is a mirror image of Alister MacKenzie's famous risk-reward 13th at Augusta National, complete with a creek that cuts diagonally in front of the slippery green. It's probably the most inspired hole on the course, but not the toughest. That honor goes to any one of the two-shotters patterned after the designs of Perry Maxwell, Donald Ross, and Dick Wilson, holes 14 through 16, respectively. Each is a standout par four measuring well over 460 yards from the tips.

Kay could be accused of gimmickry, but the Architects Golf Club knits together nicely and moves seamlessly from one design style to the next. No abrupt changes, no false notes. Even if you don't give a hoot about history, the ride on this time machine is smooth and enjoyable.

When you take the Walt Whitman Bridge across the Delaware River into New Jersey, heavy industry and major transportation rear their collective noisy and unsightly head. Oil refineries dot the shore. Huge oil tankers ply the river. Across the water, jets take off or land incessantly at Philadelphia International Airport. The hum of highway traffic is constant. Not a prime spot for golf at first glance, yet on a sprawling site in West Deptford Township that was once the site of a ruinous oil spill, **RiverWinds Golf Club** has arisen, oasis-like, along the banks of the river. Laid out by newcomer Ed Shearon and expertly shaped by Pete Fazio, designer Tom's cousin, the 7,086-yard course, opened in 2002, is a nearly treeless links-style spread marked by heaving mounds, menacing bunkers, and fine views of the Philadelphia skyline. The planes and passing ships can be distracting, but most players will be too riveted by the windswept challenges to notice.

Well-defined by tall grasses, sandy waste areas, and a meandering creek, the course reaches a climax at the final five holes, which trace the shores of the Delaware. The par-three 17th, for example, plays 156 yards to an island green in the river. Steady crosswinds and a deep pot bunker in front of the green give even accomplished players pause for thought here. The breezy par-four 18th, the toughest hole on the course, drops 50 feet to a fairway pinched by wetlands and a marina basin, its undulating green protected in front and to the right by a vast waste area. Cart paths at RiverWinds are made from crushed seashells, though walking, permitted Monday to Thursday and after 2 p.m. Friday to Sunday, is the best way to go on a brilliant links revived from a "brown field."

On the Philadelphia side of the Delaware River a 45-minute drive southwest of the city, the landscape turns pastoral in Chester County. Horse farms and beautiful stone homes stretch for miles across the hills. Golf courses are the region's newest neighbors. On the outskirts of West Chester, Rees Jones crafted **Tattersall Golf Club,** an outsized roller coaster of a golf course, from a former colonial farm. The 1702 farmhouse, the original home of John Beale Bordley, a noted agriculturist, now serves as the clubhouse. The stone walls of this handsome building are several feet thick. Jones, consciously or otherwise, crafted an old-fashioned test replete with blind tee shots and tricky approaches to perched greens. Perhaps the unyielding terrain left him little choice. The putting surfaces, while not treacherous, have plenty of undulation. Says Jones, "A properly contoured and fortified green, more than any other feature, is the

Scotland Run Golf Club, 10th hole

Tattersall Golf Club, second hole

Makefield Highlands, 15th hole

place where par is preserved as a standard of excellence." No one shoots the grass off Tattersall, yet this is one of the area's most appealing courses.

Tattersall starts off with a bang at the first hole, a down-and-up par five with a forced carry over wetlands on the second shot, and a difficult third shot to a plateau green defended by a bunker-strewn slope and a grassy bank. It is a theme repeated throughout the round: Drive from a hilltop perch to a rolling ribbon of fairway that snakes down from the tee, climb back up a hill and take aim at a flag set against the sky. Stretched across three ridges on a generous 372-acre parcel, this rugged 6,826-yard layout, opened in 2000, offers generous bail-out areas to duffers. In fact, Tattersall is more forgiving than it looks, but with 150 feet of elevation change from start to finish, the terrain is downright Himalayan by Philly standards. The topsy-turvy challenge is redeemed by long views of rolling, wooded horse country from the topmost tees. Save time to experience the landmark clubhouse and its Bordley House Grille, one of the coziest dining establishments in the area.

In beautiful Bucks County some 30 miles north of Philadelphia just off I-95 is **Makefield Highlands,** a Rick Jacobson–designed course routed across the former Pleasant Valley Farm. Opened in 2004, the 7,058-yard layout occupies a gently rolling, partially wooded site featuring elevation changes of up to 100 feet and a small stream that comes into play on several holes. Landforms separate the fairways so that each hole is self-contained. Native grasses gone to seed line the periphery of each hole, while flashed-faced bunkers in the style of Alister MacKenzie provide a strategic element.

In addition to a pair of short risk-reward par fours, Makefield Highlands features a massive par five at No. 7, which measures a whopping 640 yards from the back tees. A protégé of Jack Nicklaus, Jacobson made innovative use of the property's underlying rock formations. The course, underwritten by Lower Makefield Township, preserves the farm's original stone farmhouse, silo, and rustic outbuildings. A 5,000-square-foot hilltop clubhouse offers panoramic views of the Delaware River valley.

Baltimore

Once the nation's third-largest city, Baltimore, located 35 miles from Washington, D.C. and just down the I-95 corridor from Philadelphia, is a poster child for urban renewal. "Charm City" fell on hard times in the 1950s, but the old town center and Inner Harbor were redeveloped starting in the late 1960s. The city's once-derelict waterfront is now a bustling tourist attraction marked by shops and sidewalk cafes as well as the World Trade Center and National Aquarium. Camden Yards, home of the Baltimore Orioles, is one of the most delightful retro ballparks in America.

In the corridor between Wilmington, Delaware, and a city that artfully combines urban sophistication with down-home charm, a number of superb daily-fee layouts have sprung up since the mid-1990s.

Thirty-five miles northeast of Baltimore off I-95 is Havre de Grace, home of **Bulle Rock,** hands-down the finest daily-fee course in the mid-Atlantic region. After a two-year search for a site to accommodate his dream course, Ed Abel, a successful construction entrepreneur from Pennsylvania, found a magnificent 564-acre estate high on a hill overlooking Chesapeake Bay. He then hired Pete Dye to build a public-access facility for avid players who could not gain access to an elite private club.

Havre de Grace may be a down-at-the-heels exurb, but after driving under an old stone bridge, golfers enter a vast realm of rolling hills crested with tall golden fescues that wave in the breeze. The only building in sight is the handsome white clapboard clubhouse atop its hill. In 2004, *Golf Digest* recognized only 16 five-star courses in the nation. Bulle Rock, which received special commendations for service and conditioning (the twin hallmarks of private clubs), was one of them.

According to Dye, who said he "did not undo God's work" on what he called "one of the best pieces of inland property I've ever worked with," the rolling nature of the land dictated the layout's contours, noting that very little land had to be repositioned. "Very little" is a relative term for Pete Dye. On nearly ideal terrain, the designer, who made 79 site visits, moved nearly 500,000 cubic yards of material to stamp his own inimitable brand of golf on the heaving land, its higher points offering distant glimpses of Chesapeake Bay and the Susquehanna River.

Named for the first thoroughbred horse ever brought to the American colonies from England, Dye sired a thoroughbred of his own in Bulle (pronounced Bully) Rock. Fom the tips, this is one gift horse that can't be looked in the mouth. In fact, Dye wants better players chasing pars to gallop hard (or bite the dust) from the black tees at 7,375 yards, its 76.4 course rating and 147 slope the highest in Maryland. Locals believe the layout provides a better and more interesting test than the revamped Blue Course at Congressional in Bethesda, Maryland, which hosted the 1997 U.S. Open. After all, who else but a world-class pro could reach the *uphill* 483-yard par-four fifth hole in two shots? Or master the par-five 11th, which stretches to *665 yards* from the tips, its bottlenecked fairway and sloping green guarded by 20 bunkers?

"Playing Bulle Rock from the back tees," wrote Jeff Thoreson in *Washington Golf Monthly* in 2003, "is like having a root canal while the dental assistant is dragging her fingernails across a chalkboard and the dentist has 60 watts of the Sex Pistols blowing through the office Muzak system. Oh yeah, and your wife is having an affair, your kid's college tuition bill is going up another 12 percent and that hot stock you paid $45 a share for is now selling at a buck-fifty. Bulle Rock from the back tees...is Stalin in a very bad mood."

To his credit, Dye made sure that Bulle Rock is a versatile test of golf, not just a one-trick pony for experts only. From the forward tees, less accomplished players are given free rein to have fun on an expansive layout marked by wide landing areas, open-entry greens, and a few modest forced carries over streams. More classic in appearance than many of Dye's designs, the course is an aesthetic delight, blending nicely with the old stud farm's natural features, give or take a few railroad ties and rock-rimmed ponds.

Taken as a group, Bulle Rock's par fours are among the best Dye has ever built. The ingenious ninth, 478 yards from the tips, offers players a choice of forking fairways wrapped around a pond, one broad and welcoming, the other slim and risky. However, nothing ventured, nothing gained when it comes to the best angle to the green. The 476-yard 13th, its fairway bent to the right around a grassy chasm, calls for a bold approach to a tightly defended green. The 18th, at 485 yards from the tips, has a trough of water up the entire left side of the fairway, the water wrapped like a shepherd's crook behind the deep, tapered green. This hole, which Dye claims is one of the toughest finishing holes he's ever built, can trample a scorecard in a hurry.

There is, unfortunately, a fly in the ointment. The dream that Abel and Dye both had for "golf in its purest form" faded in 2003 when Abel, who could not secure a loan to build a 225-room hotel and confer-

Opposite: Bulle Rock, 13th hole   Above: Bulle Rock, 18th hole

ence center along with a second course, was forced to sell Bulle Rock. The buyers, three Baltimore-area developers, have a long-range plan to build a gated adult community. The layout's pristine landscape may one day be blemished by houses and condos, though nothing is expected to change for the daily-fee golfer for the foreseeable future.

Another recent development is more favorable. In 2004, the McDonald's LPGA Championship signed a deal to move the event, one of four majors on the women's tour, to Bulle Rock for a period of five years. The 2005 event, won by Annika Sorenstam, was an unqualified success.

On a site in Aberdeen originally slated for industrial development located just six miles from Bulle Rock, designer Tom Doak, who in his early 20s apprenticed himself to Pete Dye, has crafted a less-is-more modern classic. Opened in 1998, **Beechtree Golf Club** is a minimalist's delight free of gimmicks and gingerbread, its fairways woven through Chesapeake woodlands and rolling farmland.

"It's always nice to work next to a great architect, to see how your own work measures up," says Doak, who understudied Dye at Long Cove Club on Hilton Head Island, South Carolina, in the early 1980s. "But I learned a long time ago that you don't try to outdo Pete Dye. You compete by building something different, but hopefully just as worthwhile. Beechtree is more of a 1920s-style course, like Five Farms [a.k.a. Baltimore Country Club, a classic Tillinghast

design], with rolling greens and lots of bunkering to vary the holes." There's also a good risk-reward scenario at nearly every turn on this straightforward layout where each hole has its own character. Beechtree lacks the muscular charge and latent drama of Bulle Rock, but it's a fine, subtle test in its own right.

Doak, a clever strategist, installed large-scale, ragged-edge bunkers as well as unmown native grasses to signpost or frame the holes on this firm, fast par-71 layout stretching to 7,023 yards. A pair of creeks and two large ponds come into play on six of the holes. These features command the attention of better players, though most driving zones and green sites offer a safe route or bail-out area to higher handicappers.

Beechtree's back nine departs the open, rolling pastures of the opening nine for more densely wooded terrain. Doak turns up the knobs on the challenge coming home, too. The stretch of holes from 12 through 15 has raised eyebrows throughout the mid-Atlantic region, especially the 14th, called Sahara, a lengthy par four with an elaborate sand pit set below an oblong green chock full of contour; and the 15th, known as Elbow, an intriguing 475-yard par four that wiggles left before veering right to a putting surface tipped at its outer edges to gather errant shots. The 18th, a spacious par five of 557 yards, features a two-tiered green that's higher in front than in back. It's a reminder that Doak still likes to throw the occasional curveball, a pitch Aberdeen native and Baltimore Orioles legend Cal Ripken can usually handle when he tees it up at Beechtree.

Above: Mountain Branch Golf Course, 11th hole   Opposite: Beechtree Golf Club, 15th hole

Moving farther north from Baltimore towards the Delaware state line is a pair of new courses that, while not quite in the same league as Bulle Rock and Beechtree, is well worth finding. **Mountain Branch,** located a mile off I-95 in Joppa, occupies rolling farmland and is the brainchild of Davis Sezna, a former Pennsylvania amateur champion who developed Hartefeld National in nearby Chester County, Pennsylvania, a club highly regarded for both its private Tom Fazio–designed course and its splendid restaurant. Mountain Branch is a homespun version of Hartefeld. Sezna, along with partners Jeff Matthai and Olin Belsinger, designed the 6,969-yard layout themselves, proving beyond a doubt that enormous budgets and massive amounts of earthmoving are not required to produce an excellent course.

The compact routing draws heavily on traditional architectural values and manages to give players a different look at every hole. The first three holes on this housing-free layout, debuted in 2000, are benign, but the course builds in interest as the round progresses, the fairways framed alternately by thick woods, rock outcrops, rolling mounds, well-placed bunkers, tall fescue grasses, or a meandering creek. The greens are quite undulating but in general are lightly guarded. The prettiest and most memorable hole at Mountain Branch is the par-five 18th, the left side of its fairway flanked by a cascading stream, with a rockbound waterfall beside the green.

Sezna, a successful restaurateur, spared no expense in the creation of a timber-pegged, post-and-beam clubhouse, its tall windows offering fine views of the course. Testament to the excellence of the fare at The Grille & Pub at Mountain Branch is the fact that many of the diners are not golfers. As long as Sezna is in charge, golfers won't find a better meal (or more exceptional crab cakes) at any other public-access track in the mid-Atlantic region.

Striking off on his own, Matthai, who assisted Sezna at Mountain Branch, also came up with a winner at **Patriots Glen** in Elkton, a stone's throw from the Delaware state line. The site for the course has a place in American history: It was here that Generals Washington, Lafayette, and Green stood in 1777 while an invasion force of 265 ships carrying 17,000 British troops landed nearby.

Despite the fact that the 6,730-yard course, opened in 2001, is the centerpiece of a residential community, the layout is buffered on one side by marshland and is crisscrossed throughout by meandering streams. Most of the holes are tree-lined and well thought out, none more so than the par-five 17th, which is shaped like a shepherd's crook and bends to the right around a lake for its entire length.

"What we wanted to do with Patriots Glen was fill a niche," said Matthai, who works for a firm that served as project engineers at Bulle Rock and Beechtree. "There have been a lot of upscale, daily-fee courses built in the area [between Baltimore and Philadelphia] with green fees in the $95 to $140 range. There are a number of existing municipal courses in the $20 to $30 range. Patriots Glen is in the $45 to $55 range. We feel that the course is a bargain for a truly fine public layout." That it is.

Frederick, Maryland

Frederick, birthplace of Francis Scott Key and today Maryland's second largest city, has been a witness to many important events in American history. Located an hour's drive west of Baltimore and Washington, D.C., it was here that Meriwether Lewis stopped before joining William Clark on their trek westward, here also that Confederate and Union troops clashed on the streets during the Civil War.

Despite its historic touchstones, Frederick was a victim of urban blight in the 1960s. Civic pride in anticipation of the national Bicentennial (1976) spurred its rebirth, and today well-preserved 18th- and 19th-century buildings, many of them occupied by eclectic shops and cafes, make up the city's 33-block historic district. In fact, Frederick's revitalized downtown area, often described as "a little Georgetown," was named one of the National Trust for Historic Preservation's "Dozen Distinctive Destinations" in 2002.

Since the early 1990s, the Frederick area of central Maryland has attracted commuters seeking more land and home for their money. At first, golf lagged behind the influx of new residents, but it has caught up quickly. Three fine new courses can be found west of Frederick; three more are located east of town. There's even a solid muni within city limits called Clustered Spires, a reference to the numerous church steeples that crowd the skyline.

Leading the charge in the rural area west of Frederick, site of Civil War battles, is **Musket Ridge Golf Club.** Located off I-70 in the blink-and-you'll-miss-it

Musket Ridge Golf Club, first hole

town of Myersville, Musket Ridge is a stellar layout by Joe Lee, the under-appreciated designer who toiled in relative obscurity for more than 50 years in the flatlands of Florida and other southern states, and who passed away in 2003 at age 81. Musket Ridge was the last of the 232 designs he produced. Lee once said, "I start with the premise that golf should be enjoyable, not a chore," and Musket Ridge, which circulates players around mountain slopes not far from where the Appalachian Trail cuts through Maryland, is living proof of his philosophy.

The golf course he produced for friend and owner Lou Brady shows that while Lee made his living in the Sun Belt, he adapted well to the heaving countryside. The 6,902-yard layout is a versatile test that places a premium on accuracy and shot-making from each set of tees. The scenery is exceptional: Fairways routed atop flattened ridges offer unobstructed views of the Blue Ridge and Catoctin mountains, both spurs of the Appalachians. Lee handled the elevation changes expertly, for the fairways drop more than they climb.

Player-friendly but no pushover (from the tips, the ratings are 140/73.0), the steep hillsides at Musket Ridge generally gather stray tee shots back to the fairway, while the large-scale bunkers are used not as penal hazards but to provide a clear direction for each hole. Open-entry greens accept low, running shots, not a bad option on a typically breezy day. Still, the course has subtle defenses and does not yield to the grip-it-and-rip-it approach. If you want to capture the high ground at Musket Ridge, you have to shoot straight.

Lee's designs were as homespun as his personality, with no underhanded trickery and all hazards in plain view. One of the prettiest and most enjoyable courses in the Old Line State, Musket Ridge is Gentleman Joe's legacy. A third nine laid out by Lee when the course was planned is expected to be built by 2006.

Down the road from Musket Ridge on the outskirts of the Victorian-lined streets of Middletown is **Maryland National Golf Club,** an excellent Arthur Hills–designed course opened in 2002. Seven years in the making, Hills made the most of his opportunity at Maryland National, a daily-fee spread that proceeded by fits and starts. Stretched across 194 acres of former farmland dotted with lakes and wetlands, the layout, carved into hillsides and ridges, has over 80 feet of elevation change. Modest on the card at 6,811 yards (par 71), Maryland National has plenty of teeth along with a sterling collection of five par threes. The course, with its demands for accurate and thoughtful play, must be caressed, not overpowered. A deft putting touch is required on the greens, which are smooth, fast, and intricately contoured.

As on most Hills courses, the look here is unadorned and pared down, a la Donald Ross. Hills borrows classic motifs to enliven the challenge, with a false-front green at the uphill par-three third, a partially hidden green recessed 15 feet below fairway level at the short par-three ninth, and a Cape-style tee shot over a long angled bunker at the par-four 11th.

"It's a very dramatic property with a lot of rolling hills, wetlands, and wonderful panoramas around the perimeter," Hills said. "The terrain was very challenging, but the golf holes fit into the landscape very well." The only dissent? The name of the course, given its homespun setting, is perhaps a bit grandiose.

Also located in Middletown is **Hollow Creek Golf Club,** a daily-fee course built to support a residential development. Designed by Rick Jacobson, the 6,610-yard, par-71 layout, debuted in 2002, occupies former farmland as well as rolling hills bisected by Hollow Creek. While much of the property lacks tree cover, it does have 100 feet of elevation change, and Jacobson worked the existing vegetation into eight holes, with the creek in play on five holes. The Catoctin Mountains frame the layout's spacious, undulating fairways to the north and east. The club's 14,000-square-foot clubhouse is one of the best in the Frederick area, its Black Truffle Bistro overlooking the 18th hole a favorite of locals and visitors alike.

Tucked away in tiny Ijamsville, south of Frederick, **Whiskey Creek Golf Club** is a stellar mountain track

that marked the design debut of Ernie Els. Joining forces with J. Michael Poellot, who has worked extensively in Asia, the two conceived a routing plan that took full advantage of the property's diverse environments and features, including springs, creeks, stone walls, broad meadows, pine forests, wetlands, rock outcrops, and the stone ruins of an old farmhouse. To their credit, Els and Poellot recognized that this choice property in lower Frederick County spoke for itself, and that extensive earth moving was unnecessary. According to Els, "Our goal was to create a golf course reminiscent of the traditional designs of the courses where I won my two U.S. Opens [Oakmont and Congressional], and I believe we have achieved that. We all knew from the start that this beautiful, rugged site would give us the opportunity to build spectacular golf holes. We tried to create shots that would be a thrill to hit—not gimmicky shots, but shots that call for skill, daring, and imagination."

The 7,001-yard layout, opened in 2000, takes its name from a nearby creek reputedly used by smugglers to float barrels of whiskey downstream during Prohibition. Arriving players drive through a mile of field and forest to reach the club, adding to the sense of privacy and seclusion.

Poellot and his design team shoehorned each hole into the landscape, creating naturalistic fairway and greenside undulations that are compatible with the significant pitch-and-roll of the site. Els was determined to make the course as playable as possible for higher handicappers, campaigning for the removal of trees on selected holes to create more generous landing areas. Most of the holes at Whiskey Creek have open approaches and run-up options, with only two forced carries in the mix, and most of the putting surfaces are gently contoured—the course itself is topsy-turvy enough.

Whiskey Creek's risk-reward par fives are unusually good. Also noteworthy are the par threes, especially the pair of toughies on the back nine, which departs the high ground for the pond-dotted lower portions of the property. The best is saved for last at Whiskey Creek. The layout's majestic par-five 18th is a genuine signature hole, the spectral ruins of a farmhouse built by German immigrants in the 1840s rising from the center of the fairway some 280 yards from the tee. The bold play is left of the ruin to a narrow strip of fairway, setting up a shot over water to the green. The safer route is to the wider section of fairway to the right of the crumbled stone walls.

A footnote: Els made a working visit with clubs in tow shortly before the course opened, hitting shots to test the holes. He hit three drives on the 547-yard 18th. The first was in the power slot to the left, and from

Maryland National Golf Club, third hole

there he rifled a 4-iron to the green on a line to the pin. He dropped another ball and hit another 4-iron on the same line and trajectory, but this one took a crazy hop when it landed. The course superintendent, standing greenside, had a good explanation. The second ball had hit the first one. As co-developer Steve Goodwin said at the time, "His [Ernie's] game is as different from mine and yours as a rocket from a rock."

Also located in Ijamsville but a world apart in ambience and challenge is the **P.B. Dye Golf Club,** a signature layout by Pete's younger son. Like his father, P.B. is his own man when it comes to golf course design. But while pere likes to push the envelope to the limit, P.B. can be excessive to the point of unfairness. Such was the case when this well-groomed course, set in the foothills of the Catoctin Mountains,

made its debut in 1999. The main bone of contention for most players, besides the sneaky blind shots and deep timber-walled bunkers, were the greens, which split the difference between the Himalayas putting course at St. Andrews and the banked turns at Indianapolis Speedway. Not only were the greens severely undulating, they were extremely fast, a deadly combination.

The owners, to their credit, heard the cries and correctly saw that some of the holes had a little too much "flair." In 2001–02, many of the layout's more penal elements were softened. A few of the greens were redesigned, i.e., were made less tumultuous and more receptive, while several of the long greenside runoffs, which previously served as exit ramps for slightly errant incoming shots, were grown with sticky rough to keep approach shots within shouting distance of

Whiskey Creek Golf Club, 18th hole

the putting surface. A few of P.B.'s cavernous bunkers were modified to facilitate recovery, and a new set of forward tees, measuring 5,391 yards, have made the course more playable for women. Having said that, meek players of either sex need not apply.

The P.B. Dye Golf Club at 7,036 yards (141 slope, 74.6 course rating) still taunts players and gives them ample reason to quit golf and take up tennis, though the fine views of Sugar Loaf Mountain are fair compensation. The course was intentionally designed to be a man-eater and will never be a pussycat, but at least in its current incarnation the incidence of six-hour rounds and boiling-mad golfers has abated.

Looking for a kinder, gentler start to your Frederick-area holiday? Head for Urbana, a mere 30 miles from Washington, D.C., and home of **Worthington Manor Golf Club,** a rolling, country club–style facility designed by Ault, Clark & Associates, a prolific Maryland-based firm that has sprinkled the mid-Atlantic region with many excellent, playable courses. Opened in 1998, Worthington Manor is a sleeper, the type of course that appears simple on the card but is sneaky-tough from the member tees. From the tips at 7,034 yards, the club carries a lofty

143 slope rating and has been a three-time U.S. Open qualifying site, most recently in 2004. It's that rare championship-caliber course that will drop its guard from the middle tees—if you exercise good course management and take the hazards, both obvious and subtle, out of play.

A lightly treed, links-style spread marked by slick, undulating greens, steep drop-offs, and numerous wetlands, Worthington Manor offers superb pace and variety. The course's acknowledged signature hole is the sixth, a beautiful par three that plays over water to a riprapped peninsula green surrounded by large bunkers. The challenge is clearly stated, but the target is generous. On a windy day from the tips at 198 yards, the hole is world-class.

Clustered Spires Golf Course, a municipal layout opened in 1991, offers the best bang for the buck in Frederick. Laid out by Ault, Clark & Associates, the 6,769-yard course, which offered a sub-$50 green fee to out-of-towners at press time, is a solid test in a lovely, rural setting that manages to offer superb conditions year-round. If you want to mingle with the locals, the Spires is the place.

LODGING & DINING

Frederick, a convenient hub for all the courses described above, offers dozens of hotels and bed & breakfast properties, with more than 2,000 guest rooms available.

For a special getaway near Maryland National and Musket Ridge, check out **Stone Manor Inn** in Middletown, an historic manor house circa 1760 set on 114 acres of formal gardens and working farmland. The New American cuisine here ranks among the finest in the Baltimore–Washington D.C. area. Room rates include continental breakfast and welcome plate from the chef.

Dining or imbibing in Frederick? Follow your nose along Market and Patrick streets, a lively quarter of town noted for its pubs and taverns. Stuck for a choice? Try the Tasting Room on Church Street, a cutting edge eatery and wine bar that occupies an old merchant's corner store. Or opt for the Brown Pelican on East Church Street, a candlelit rathskeller with a nautical motif that features superb veal and seafood dishes. Something more casual? Brewer's Alley on North Market Street, set in Frederick's former town hall and opera house, is a lively spot with better-than-average pub grub and brewed-on-premises beer.

OFF-COURSE ATTRACTIONS

In Frederick, history buffs can check out the National Museum of Civil War Medicine, featuring more than 1,500 artifacts, including a Civil War ambulance. (The museum is a starting point for a walking tour of the city's Civil War history.) Legendary battlefields on the outskirts of Frederick include Antietam National Battlefield near Sharpsburg, where Union troops repelled Robert E. Lee's invasion in 1862 in one of the Civil War's bloodiest confrontations. Seeking collectibles? The nearby town of New Market is known as the "Antiques Capital of Maryland." Got kids? Hundreds of exotic animals are on display at Catoctin Wildlife Preserve & Zoo in Thurmond, north of Frederick. Looking to take a little exercise before or after the round? The Appalachian Trail skirts the border of Frederick County. A one-hour hike will bring you to dramatic cliffs and look-outs.

South

Tennessee: The Bear Trace

Imitation being the sincerest form of flattery, the Volunteer State couldn't help but take notice of the highly successful Robert Trent Jones Golf Trail in neighboring Alabama. To bring added tourism revenue to the state and also give its residents a wonderful legacy, the government in 1993 earmarked $20 million to build a series of golf courses within existing state parks. The man entrusted with the job of designing the layouts had to be a well-known figure, someone who would bring instant credibility to the project. Only one person was considered: Jack Nicklaus, whose reputation as a designer now nearly equals his accomplishments as a player.

The name for Tennessee's fledgling golf trail, the Bear Trace, was created by combining Jack's nickname, the Golden Bear, with the Natchez Trace, a historic wilderness byway that originates in Tennessee and was trafficked by pioneers in the late 1700s. According to Jim Hardy, whose firm, Redstone Golf Management, operates the Bear Trace in a public/private partnership with the state, "Jack was once asked, 'Do you have any regrets about your career?' He said from a playing standpoint, no. But from a design standpoint, he regretted not having built more courses the average person had access to and could afford to play. Most of his work had been of the private-club, high-dollar variety. What Tennessee wanted to create provided a great opportunity for Jack."

From the forward tees, Nicklaus and his design team have crafted courses that are readily playable by the average duffer, challenging but not overbearing, well-balanced but not predictable, either. With a few exceptions, the open-entry greens are mildly contoured. Fairways are generous and corridors have been cleared of underbrush to speed play. The modest construction budget meant that Nicklaus could not indulge in massive earthmoving, a blessing given each park's natural features. Jack, of course, has yet to build a creampuff for anyone, including the state of Tennessee. From the gold pegs, each course will give the skilled player a good tussle. At press time, the Friday to Sunday green fee (with cart) ranged from $59 to $69.

The state park that encompasses each course is a peaceful world unto itself far removed from civilization's reminders. No unsightly real estate development intrudes on the golf experience. As seasoned campaigners know, the chance to commune with nature during a round of golf is exceedingly rare at new facilities these days. In addition, the courses on the Trace are walkable, an attractive option for visitors who like to hoof it.

Each course on the Bear Trace is anchored by a hand-crafted log clubhouse topped by a green tin roof that combines the feel of a rustic timber lodge with a traditional clubhouse. On a nice day, players can rehash the round on a long wooden porch set with rocking chairs. Given the state park setting, these modest down-home clubhouses are a good fit.

The Bear Trace lacks the easy access found on Alabama's Trail—only one of the courses is less than an hour's drive from a major air gateway—but this may be a blessing in disguise. To properly tour the Trace, simply tune your radio to a local country-and-western station and follow the brown state park signs posted on the major thoroughfares. To see Jack's courses, you have to see Tennessee, which is not tough duty given the state's exceptional beauty and variety of environments. Along the way, there are enough down-home diners and Southern hospitality to keep most golfers happy.

Future plans call for additional Bear Trace facilities near the major population centers of Nashville, Memphis, and Knoxville. Until then, travelers can keep the pioneer tradition alive by exploring the Trace.

Debuted in 1998, **Bear Trace at Cumberland Mountain State Park** in Crossville, located 70 miles west of Knoxville, was the first track to open on the Trace, and it stands apart as the hilliest and most rugged of the five. Extracted from a rocky site at 2,500 feet above sea level in the Appalachian highlands of east Tennessee, the course, carved from a thick forest of oak, pine, maple, and hickory on the nation's largest timbered plateau, features an elevation change of nearly 300 feet from start to finish.

Bear Trace at Cumberland Mountain, seventh hole

Like most mountain courses, this sturdy 6,900-yard track, which overlays a mantle of rock, favors precision over power.

Among the more eye-popping holes on this beautiful spread is the downhill par-four seventh, where a drive to a plateau fairway must be followed by a daunting approach over a stream to a pulpit green propped up on giant slabs of layered flagstone. It is a genuine postcard hole, a place to admire the stonemason's art, but the skewed, oblong green, fully 15 feet above the flowing water and flanked by bunkers, will command your attention from the fairway.

Departing the open pastures of the front nine, Cumberland Mountain's longer, tougher back nine is a roller-coaster ride through the woods, its elevation changes sharper and its horizons broader. The par-four 13th, 466 yards from the tips, offers several thrilling moments of hang-time on a drive launched from its skytop ledge of a tee, though the euphoria of the drive soon fades once players get a look at the target: The slim, bunkerless green is sited beyond a swath of wetlands sluiced by a tiny creek.

LODGING

Cumberland Mountain State Park offers 37 family-friendly duplex and timber lodge cabins set in the woods. These rustic but modern cabins are fully equipped for housekeeping and include all cooking and serving utensils as well as linens. The park's restaurant, offering a beautiful view of Byrd Lake, serves good Southern cuisine in ample portions.

As is true throughout the Trace, there's more to Tennessee's state parks than golf. At Cumberland Mountain, you can hike on 15 miles of trails cut through the woods; swim in the Olympic-size pool; or take a rowboat, paddleboat, or canoe onto Byrd Lake, where fishing for bass, crappie, and catfish is good. During the summer, naturalists provide guided tours, campfire programs, arts and crafts classes, and other family-oriented activities.

Hand-crafted log clubhouse at Tims Ford

The one course close to a big city is **Bear Trace at Harrison Bay** on the outskirts of Chattanooga. Unveiled in 1999, the course is routed along the shores of Chickamauga Reservoir, a body of water developed by the Tennessee Valley Authority as a "recreation demonstration area" in the 1930s. A haven for campers, boaters, and fishermen, the site was characterized as "the best natural piece of land for a golf course" by the Nicklaus design camp before ground was broken. Seven holes on this brawny 7,140-yard layout skirt the shoreline of the lake. A second-growth forest of slender pines and oaks defines the perimeter of each hole, but there is no sense of claustrophobia at Harrison Bay. In typical Nicklaus fashion, there is ample room to hit safely off the tee. The flat, open-entry greens welcome run-up shots, but Harrison Bay offers much more than a pleasant lakeside stroll. Well-placed fairway and greenside bunkers were designed to snare errant shots, and good course management is required to return a decent score.

The routing comes alive at the fourth hole, a gorgeous 184-yard par three that plays to a green perched 10 feet above the red clay shores of the lake, its right side defended by two deep bunkers. The rest of the front nine plays nip-and-tuck with the lakeshore, cozying up to peninsulas and coves where bass fisherman sit offshore in their boats, casting for lunkers.

The slightly shorter back nine at Harrison Bay seems benign at first, but the in-your-face par-three 14th throws down the gauntlet. Only a high-flying shot will carry a corner of the lake that sits between tee and green, although there is a generous bail-out area to the right of the green. The layout boasts a strong trio of holes at the finish, a pair of sturdy par fours wrapped around a subtle double-dogleg par five at 17. Slotted into a hill above the 18th green overlooking the lake is the signature log cabin clubhouse, built in the same style at each Bear Trace course. There are sure to be more than a few Chattanoogans, who have taken to this newcomer like bears to honey, observing your final strokes from the porch.

Until **Harrison Bay State Park** builds cabins along the lake, visitors seeking overnight accommodations can choose from among several major chain hotels and motels in Chattanooga. However, the city also offers a special enclave known as the Bluff View Art District. Tucked neatly atop tall stone cliffs high above the Tennessee River, the district is a creative blend of al fresco trattorias, sculpture gardens, and art galleries. There's even a bocce court and terrace clinging to the bluff.

The centerpiece of this award-winning example of sustainable urban renewal is the **Bluff View Inn,** which offers tasteful accommodations in three beautifully restored homes dating from the early 1900s. Collectively, this is the best B&B in town. The Art District is within walking distance of many of Chattanooga's top attractions, including the Tennessee Aquarium, which displays the freshwater fishes of the southern U.S. Six miles away is 2,215-foot Lookout Mountain. Its peak, which commands panoramic views of seven states, can be accessed via the world's steepest Incline Railway.

Boaters and fishermen can access the reservoir at Harrison Bay marina, which is located in one of the lake's protected harbors and offers a launch ramp. The bass fishing here is some of the best in the state. Visitors can also utilize the park's large swimming pool, shady picnic grounds, hiking trails, horseshoe pits, and other recreational amenities.

Located 90 minutes from both Nashville and Chattanooga, **Bear Trace at Tims Ford State Park** is set in the rolling hills of southern middle Tennessee down the road a piece from the famed Jack Daniel's Distillery in Lynchburg.

Stretched across a peninsula that juts into Tims Ford Lake, this elegant 6,790-yard, par-71 layout, opened in 1999, is the most pleasurable spread on the Trace. Opening holes, routed across former pastureland and cornfields, are lightly treed, links-style creations delineated by fescue-tufted ridges. Bunkers cut into these ridges have rolled-down faces, while the smooth bentgrass greens are among the finest putting surfaces on the Trace. In marked contrast to Harrison Bay, the greens are also quite undulating. The course also takes players into the park's shady wooded corners, where giant white oaks frame several tees and greens. The sparkling lake is never far away. Eight holes skirt a deep reservoir created in 1970 by the Tennessee Valley Authority to provide flood control within the Elk River Basin. As an environmental safeguard, buffer zones were doubled in size to 200 feet to protect habitat for winged creatures ranging from bald eagles to bats.

The sporty front nine at Tims Ford is followed by a sterner back nine, which kicks into gear at the 444-yard 11th hole, a U.S. Open–style par four that veers from left to right, its well-bunkered, oblong green skewed to the line of play. A battle of wits is waged at the 12th, a risk-reward par five with a phalanx of bunkers in the crook of its dogleg and more bunkers defending the second landing area.

This enchanting test reaches a climax at the par-four 18th, its back tee sited 40 feet above the lake and its sinuous fairway parted between a row of trees on the right and a huge bunker to the left. Until a newcomer comes along to displace it, this 450-yard two-shotter, its liberally contoured green flanked by bunkers, is the most attractive finishing hole on the Trace.

LODGING

Tims Ford State Park offers 20 deluxe cabins built along the wooded slopes of Tims Ford Lake. Each cabin features a gas fireplace, charcoal grills, outdoor balcony, and color TV with satellite dish. These nicely appointed cabins feature two bedrooms with two double beds in each room. Tims Ford Lake is regarded by insiders as one of the top bass fishing spots in the Southeast.

DO THE MASH

Fifteen minutes from Tims Ford State Park is Jack Daniel's Distillery, the oldest and best-known whiskey maker in America. The visitor center distills the history of its sour mash whiskey into 30 exhibits, which detail the unique manufacture of the charcoal-mellowed liquor as well as the exploits of Jasper Newton "Jack" Daniels. At age 13, young Jack was running wagonloads of hooch from Tennessee to Alabama. By 21, he was known throughout the South as a gentleman distiller whose taste for fine whiskey was matched by a love for fine haberdashery. Alas, Lynchburg, like many Tennessee towns, is dry. You can buy a distinctive square-shaped bottle of the revered Old No. 7 Brand at the gift shop, but there's no whiskey-sippin' on site.

Located an hour's drive northeast of Memphis, a mecca for blues fans and Elvis pilgrims, the **Bear Trace at Chickasaw State Park** is a 7,118-yard gem draped on some of the highest terrain in west Tennessee. A series of environmental setbacks caused delays, but once the site's wetlands issues were resolved, the westernmost course on the Trace made its debut in 2000. Heavily wooded, with an abundance of avian species in the trees, Chickasaw is for many the most beautiful layout on the Trace.

Bear Trace at Ross Creek Landing, eighth hole

Carved from a thick stand of oak, pine, hickory, and tulip poplar, the holes at Chickasaw rise and fall through the forest. Old deer stands were left in the trees to provide a rustic touch. Green sites, notched in ridges or tucked in hollows, are seamless and natural. Many of the fairways are flanked or crossed by Piney Creek and a network of spidery streams. Cat-tailed marshes pinch landing zones on the longer holes. Most are marked "Snake Habitat: Do Not Enter," with good reason. With water in play on 13 holes, deep bunkers, and sharp doglegs, Chickasaw is among the more testing of the Trace courses, though its challenges can be met, especially by cautious, accurate players who steer clear of trouble.

Chickasaw's back nine plays two to three strokes tougher than the outgoing nine. Watery graves at two short par fives, 13 and 16, more than compensate for any perceived lack of length. The finish is Nicklausian: the 17th is a 218-yard par three indented by a marshy pond to the right, while the par-four 18th is a sweeping right-to-left dogleg that proceeds uphill to a perched, well-bunkered green.

Chester County may be known as the state's redneck capital, but Chickasaw is a very sophisticated layout that deserves wider notice.

LODGING

Chickasaw State Park, which covers 14,400 acres, is complemented by 13 cabins overlooking Lake Placid. Built by WPA crews in the 1930s, these cozy, fully equipped cabins sleep four to six people. Like other parks within the Volunteer State, Chickasaw has a pleasant, informal restaurant serving Southern cuisine. Picnic tables and grills are numerous. Recreational amenities range from tennis courts and a lighted ball field to horseback riding in the summer months. The swimming beach on Lake Placid's shore is popular, as is fishing for bass, bream, crappie, and catfish.

BAR-B-QUE: THE REAL THING

Genuine pulled pork barbecue is revered in the South like no other dish. In the minds of aficionados who crave the real thing, the western Tennessee towns of Henderson, Jackson, and Lexington form the "Bermuda Triangle of Barbecue." It is here that whole hog, hickory-smoked barbecue is raised to a level beyond succulent.

Two of the best barbecue joints in the state are located a short distance from Chickasaw State Park. Five miles east of Henderson is L&L Bar-B-Que, a nondescript roadside brick building that will leave

Two hours east of Memphis and two hours south of Nashville is Clifton, a sleepy town on the Tennessee River founded by a timber baron in the late 1800s. Until the mid-1990s, Clifton's Main Street was a gravel road. But as of 2001, the town's hot new thoroughfare for golf is the **Bear Trace at Ross Creek Landing,** the fifth course on the Tennessee trail and arguably the layout that has garnered the most national attention.

The course in Clifton became a reality thanks to the generosity of the Hassell Charitable Foundation. This private fund deeded the land needed to build the course to the state as part of the state park system. Given a generous parcel and a healthy budget, Nicklaus produced the strongest test yet on the Trace, a genuine championship-caliber track of 7,131 yards capable of hosting a major competition. Ranked the best public-access course in Tennessee by *Golfweek* in 2005, this stellar creation can stand shoulder-to-shoulder with The Honors Course, a celebrated private track near Chattanooga laid out by Pete Dye.

On a rolling, wooded site flanked by the river's back channels as well as man-made ponds, Nicklaus moved more than one million cubic yards of dirt to prop up tees and greens above the 100-year flood mark. Despite the earthworks, the layout ties in naturally with its surroundings. Because special efforts were made to preserve stream corridors and specimen trees, the course looks like it's been there for decades. The shaping is so good, there's no way to tell where Jack began and nature left off. Some holes meander across lush, open meadows that invite the breeze off the river; others are framed by oak, hickory, hackberry, cedar and, in wet areas, by cypress trees. The corridors are wider and the greens larger here than on the other four courses on the Trace. This is a grand test sketched on a big canvas. "I knew the course was good," Nicklaus said at the grand opening. "But I didn't know it was this good."

The hallmark of any great course is its across-the-board playability as well as its intrinsic appeal to better golfers, notably the options it dangles in front of experts. A good example: Jack moved the back tee forward at the short par-four fourth to 292 yards to tempt big hitters to carry a hill peppered with bunkers to reach the green, though short knockers can still make birdie by playing an accurate approach. The eighth, a tremendous 556-yard par five, is a strategic marvel with an inlet of the river running the entire left side of fairway. The hole is flanked by Hassell Field Airstrip, which accepts small aircraft. (If you arrange to fly to Clifton, the golf staff will pick you up and bring you to the course.)

The epic back nine, laced with thrilling risk-reward scenarios, has "riverboat gambler" written all over it and ranks among the best nine holes Jack has ever designed. The spectacular par-four 10th plays away from the familiar log clubhouse to a rolling fairway that dead-ends at rock-lined Ross Creek. Raised well above the oxtail-brown creek is a large, peninsula-like green benched in the side of a limestone-studded hill, a lone pot bunker in front. The challenge is clearly stated: Produce a solid drive, then play a precise approach that flies the chasm and sits quickly on the rippled green.

The stakes are raised to the limit on the final holes at Ross Creek Landing, where better players stationed on the gold tees must cope with awkward angles and long carries over hazards. However, risk-averse players content to ply the middle can avoid most of the trouble from the forward tees. The 18th is a murderous 477-yard par four that plays over the corner of a pond and swings right to a green set beside the water. It may well be the toughest closer in the state.

Mark your roadmap, charter a plane, or cast your houseboat ashore in Clifton to access this magnificent course. At press time, the $54 weekday green fee (with cart) to play a Jack Nicklaus–designed course of this caliber is simply unavailable anywhere else.

LODGING

Opened in 2003 and privately-owned, the **Bear Inn B & B,** located alongside the 15th fairway of **Ross Creek Landing,** features spacious rooms decorated in a log cabin–style motif. Suites and cottages are equipped with microwave, refrigerator, and coffeemaker. Stay and play packages are available.

Georgia's Lake Country

In Georgia's red clay country 75 miles east of Atlanta is Lake Oconee (uh-KO-nee), a giant inkblot of a lake spread across more than 19,000 acres. When Georgia Power dammed a few creeks at the edge of Oconee National Forest to create the lake in 1979, much of the land acquired by industrialist and inventor Mercer Reynolds Sr. in the 1920s was flooded. But there was a silver lining. Two heirs to the land, brothers Mercer and Jamie Reynolds, had a long-range vision to create a resort and residential community, using golf as the engine of growth. And not just any golf. At press time, **Reynolds Plantation** had amassed 81 holes of golf, enticed Ritz-Carlton to build a luxurious Lodge, and in the process created one of the most appealing resort addresses in the Southeast.

There is another, more subtle reason for the success of Reynolds Plantation. About 80 miles east of the development is Augusta, as in Augusta National, home of the Masters and every golfer's idealized image of the perfect inland course. Augusta has exerted a powerful influence on golf design throughout the interior regions of the South, especially places where the land rolls and the pines grow tall. The next best thing to Augusta National? With a knowledgeable caddie on the bag and the piney woods abloom with dogwoods and azaleas, the fantasy can play out convincingly on a fine spring day at Reynolds Plantation. The experience comes with exclusivity, too, albeit on a public scale. The courses at Reynolds Plantation are open only to guests of the Ritz-Carlton, members, or those renting villas or cottages at Reynolds.

Plantation, the first course to open at Reynolds in 1987, was laid out by Bob Cupp with input from Hubert Green and Fuzzy Zoeller. Its particulars don't do it justice: a scant 6,698 yards from the tips, fewer than 20 bunkers, no holes on the lake. Yet the golf course, carved through a forest and updated by Cupp in 2005, places a premium on accurate driving and pinpoint approaches. The fairways are rolling and the greens are small. From a playability standpoint, it is the most accessible of the four courses on site.

Next came **Great Waters,** a Jack Nicklaus creation that garnered national acclaim for Reynolds Plantation and secured destination status for Greensboro (the resort's home town) shortly after it debuted in 1992. Nicklaus, who up until that time had relied upon major earthworks to create challenging, take-no-prisoners courses, decided to shelve his customary land features, such as exaggerated mounds and plateau fairways, in favor of a playable, aesthetically pleasing course. Handed a spectacular piece of land, Nicklaus turned it into an even more spectacular golf course.

Reynolds Plantation, Great Waters, 11th hole

Reynolds Plantation, Oconee, 18th hole

Half the holes at Great Waters flank the shores of Lake Oconee. Forced carries are rare: Most of the water is parallel to the line of play. The layout's pleasant front nine runs inland through a pine forest, with a man-made creek in play at four greens, while the peninsular back nine circulates players from one lake cove to the next. The final nine, in fact, may well offer the most memorable stretch of lakeside golf in the nation. And while the challenge from the tips at 7,048 yards will get a good player's attention, multiple sets of forward tees give everyone (including women) a chance to enjoy a user-friendly course that signaled a new direction for Jack as an architect.

Emboldened by the success of Great Waters, the resort's brain trust next invited Tom Fazio to have a go at a hilly tract of hardwoods and pines set back from Lake Oconee. Called the **National,** presumably in tribute to Augusta, the original 18 holes, opened in 1997, proved to have more teeth than a typical Fazio design. The corridors of what are now the Ridge and Bluff nines are generously wide, though many of the fairways are cambered, effectively shrinking their landing areas. Also, giant flashed-face bunkers intrude on the line of play and swallow errant shots, particularly around the greens, which are large, elevated, and undulating. The Bluff nine, arguably the toughest stretch of golf at the Plantation, is narrow and testing in places but offers an aesthetic gem at the fourth, a stunning 174-yard par three that skirts a bluff, with the lake below on the right.

Based on the success of the layout's core 18, Fazio returned three years later to build a third nine, called the Cove. This nine, the most picturesque and strategic on the National, doglegs through the woods on rolling terrain with nary a straight hole in the mix except for the par threes. A few of the greens have false fronts, a clever ploy, while the long, difficult par fours at eight and nine ensure that a Nassau match will not be won with indifferent shots. Bottom line? Fazio, the king of playability, has put his foot down at the National, creating a course favored by aces, not duffers.

Had they stopped there, the Reynolds family could have sat back and congratulated themselves on a job well done. Instead, they handed another choice parcel to Rees Jones, who was fresh off his U.S. Open make-overs of Bethpage Black and Torrey Pines South. Not only did Jones fashion a traditional, grand-scale test at the **Oconee,** he built a flagship track to complement its hospitality companion, the Ritz-Carlton Lodge, which debuted in 2002 shortly before the course opened.

The burly 7,393-yard layout, among the finest on Jones's distinguished résumé, comes on strong right out of the box: The first hole is a massive 579-yard par five with a pond beside the green. Succeeding holes play nip and tuck with the lake as the layout enters and departs the forest, with the lake directly in play at five holes and in view at several others. Jones carved wide corridors through the pines to create expansive fairways. Everything is in plain view; there is no caprice or chicanery. With its subtly contoured greens, the Oconee Course is a modern classic in every way, a feeling enhanced by the mandatory forecaddies or walking caddies.

Jones, a master at building drama, ramps up the challenge as the round progresses and tightens the screw on the final six holes. The par-three 15th demands a full-blooded carry over water from the tips at 192 yards, but offers a far friendlier angle for players of lesser attainment from the forward markers.

The finale on the Oconee, a gargantuan Cape-style par four of 485 yards, calls for a bold drive over an inlet of the lake followed by a solid approach to a deep green defended by sand and water. The best closing hole at Reynolds Plantation? This is it.

SHORT-GAME FIX

For players who want to hone their short game, the Dave Pelz Scoring Game School, located near the Oconee Course, offers three-day schools as well as one-day clinics. Students are grouped according to handicap and work with instructors on a four-to-one student-instructor ratio and are indoctrinated into the Pelz system of pitching, chipping, sand play, putting, and wedge play.

Spa at Ritz-Carlton Lodge, Reynolds Plantation

LODGING

Smaller and less formal than other Ritz-Carlton hotels, the rustic-luxe **Ritz-Carlton Lodge, Reynolds Plantation,** overlooking the Oconee Course, is one of the most stylish retreats in the South. The field-stone and shake-sided lodge, unveiled in 2002, makes a favorable first impression: The flagstone-floored lobby has Oriental rugs, hardwood beams stretched across its cathedral ceiling, comfortable leather couches, and a large stone fireplace. The spacious guest rooms, totaling 251, are done up in warm earth tones of amber, green, and brown. Most feature lake views from their private verandas. Indoor and outdoor pools, notably a beautiful infinity-edge pool set above the lake and its attractive man-made beach, complete the picture. The hotel's top amenity is its 26,000-square-foot spa, which features décor and treatments influenced by the Creek Indians who once inhabited the area.

Reynolds Plantation, first and foremost a residential golf community, also offers more than 200 multi-bedroom golf villas and cottages sprinkled throughout the expansive property. These nicely furnished units, designed for prospective real estate buyers, typically include a cheerful living room, a large, fully equipped kitchen, and a deck or porch with a golf course view.

DINING

Gourmet cuisine with a Southern twist is featured at Georgia's, the Ritz-Carlton's signature restaurant, where regional ingredients range from peaches and pecans to Vidalia onions, and where dinner entrees range from bourbon-glazed salmon to cornbread-stuffed quail. Also located within the Lodge is Gaby's By the Lake, a casual, open-air restaurant with savory grilled entrees and specialty iced teas. In the Oconee clubhouse adjacent to the Lodge is the Linger Longer Bar and Grill, which offers golfers a quick bite between nines as well as classic steakhouse cuisine (and hot and cold soufflés) in the evening. The Lobby Lounge is a fine place to swirl a snifter of brandy and gaze upon the lake after a meal.

OFF-COURSE ATTRACTIONS

Locals reckon there are 43 pounds of largemouth bass per acre in Lake Oconee. Guests can test the theory by hiring a guide at one of the resort's two marinas and trying their luck on a lake that boasts 374 miles of shore-line. With or without fishing rods, boating is a pleasure on the lake, especially a peaceful moonlight cruise on a pontoon boat. By day, water sports range from canoeing and kayaking to water-skiing to wakeboarding. Sporting clays and horseback riding are also available. Nature trails, ideal for hiking and jogging, give visitors a chance to see the resident wildlife, including deer, turkey, fox, otter, and waterfowl. Reynolds Plantation is also home to a resident bald eagle colony.

DAY TRIPS

Nearby Eatanton was the home of author Joel Chandler Harris, creator of the Uncle Remus Tales. Brer Rabbit himself resides at the Uncle Remus Museum. A short drive north of the resort is Madison, which was spared by General Sherman during his infamous march through the South. The town's beautifully preserved historic district offers a wealth of antebellum buildings. Madison is known for small antique shops that offer everything from heirloom jewelry to large credenzas.

Reynolds Plantation is the most significant development on Lake Oconee, but there are three other options on the lake.

The course that first drew golfers to the region was Port Armour Country Club in Greensboro, a Bob Cupp design opened in 1986. Although locals had their doubts that golf would fly in what was then a remote backwoods, the layout was soon recognized as one of state's better courses. (The club, acquired by Reynolds Plantation in 2005, was treated to a $1 million makeover by Cupp and renamed **Reynolds Landing.**) A firm 7,051-yard test marked by elevated greens, this walker-friendly design brings players to the shore of the lake at the short par-four fifth, which asks players to hit their approach to a green cantilevered into the water. Unlike the other Reynolds courses, this one accepts outside play.

The region's next course of note was the **Harbor Club,** a Tom Weiskopf–Jay Morrish creation located on the outskirts of Greensboro. Having mastered Arizona's desert, the design duo brought their subtle, strategic brand of architecture east of the Mississippi in 1991. The 6,930-yard layout is a genuine championship track with across-the-board versatility. With its intriguing challenges, including a fine pair of short risk-reward par fours, this is the course that raised the bar for excellence along Lake Oconee. Brilliantly routed to take full advantage of the lake—six holes cozy up to the water's edge, with a stream in play at four others—the designers even sought to reprise a famous hole. The eighth, a daunting 180-yard par three, was styled after the fabled 12th hole at Augusta National. The bunker placements and bean-shaped green and ominous grassy slope that drops to a watery grave in front are very similar to the original, though this inspired copy, set along a marshy inlet of the lake, lacks the terror of Augusta's 12th. Which is probably a good thing.

Cozy lobby at Ritz-Carlton Lodge, Reynolds Plantation

Cuscowilla's 14th green and Golf House Grill

The **Golf Club at Cuscowilla,** opened a year after Reynolds Plantation unveiled the core 18 at the National, cemented the area's reputation as a desirable getaway for golf insiders, a mini-mecca convenient to Atlanta but a world apart in ambience. Laid out by Bill Coore and Ben Crenshaw shortly after they completed their masterpiece at Sand Hills Golf Club in Nebraska, this low-profile, less-is-more course epitomizes the tandem's approach to design.

Currently ranked 15th on *Golfweek's* list of America's top courses built since 1960, the layout could almost be dismissed as humble based on its appearance were it not for the exceptional test of golf it presents. Designed for walkers, the 6,874-yard, par-70 layout, pared down to the barest essentials and decidedly free of frills, is a shot-maker's dream. The routing appears effortless and inevitable, but the designers took a few risks at Cuscowilla by giving golf a higher priority than scenery. Unlike most of the other courses in the neighborhood, the layout does not linger along Lake Oconee. (Only two holes border the lake.) The reason is simple. Coore found the site's open pastures and rolling, wooded terrain well-suited to golf, but most of the land endowed with golf-holes-in-the-raw waiting to be discovered was set well back from the water's edge. And so the

development's inland precincts are where the designers allowed the holes to roam.

Though understated, Cuscowilla does have impressive ragged-edge bunkers filled with red clay soil the color of crushed brick. They are as organic and eye-catching as they are well-placed. The greens, many of them of the pushed-up variety popularized in the 1920s, are very fast and liberally contoured. Players have options galore on every approach, for the ground game is welcome here. That is because Coore and Crenshaw took the time to identify and employ the site's most interesting ground contours. As in any hand-built work of art, these features are subtle. But experienced on foot with an able caddie at your side, no purist worth his straight left arm will fail to recognize Cuscowilla as a modern classic and a natural beauty that serves as a reminder of how good golf can be when the design conception is pure.

On-site accommodations range from lakefront villas to cottages and homes tucked discreetly among the pines surrounding the course. For area dining, check out the Waterside Restaurant, which commands an inlet of the lake near the 10th tee of the golf course. (It's accessible by land or water.) The theme may be casual, but the dining is first-rate, with fresh fish, good steaks, and inventive Creole fare, too.

Orlando

Thanks to the (Mickey) Mouse that roared, Orlando, the megalopolis of central Florida, is the city that won't stop growing. Home to dozens of PGA Tour pros (including Tiger Woods), Orlando, alone among Sun Belt cities, has continued to stretch its boundaries as a golf destination. It's not that it didn't have any good public-access golf until recently. Bay Hill, Grand Cypress, and Disney's 99 holes are mainstays. It's just that the city's most recent additions have amplified the choices in America's family entertainment capital. In fact, nearly *150 golf courses* can be found within an hour's drive of downtown Orlando, a figure that exceeds the number of venues available in Myrtle Beach, America's self-proclaimed golf capital.

Here's a sampling of the top newcomers built since the mid-1990s.

Deland, a sleepy little town 35 miles north of Orlando and a short drive from Daytona Beach, is known as a prime launch site for boaters who wish to explore the beautiful St. Johns River. Now, with **Victoria Hills Golf Club,** the town can boast a golf course every bit as salutary as the north-flowing river. Located within a budding golf community at Victoria Park is a splendid daily-fee course by Florida native Ron Garl that fits its setting seamlessly.

"It's always been one of our goals to have a course sit softly on the land," says Garl. "Here there's a feeling that the holes were here and the trees just grew up around them." Boasting an 80-foot elevation change, Victoria Hills, debuted in 2002, is framed by burly oaks and tall pines, with sa ndy waste areas and pris-tine lakes in play as well. This 6,989-yard layout is a walker-friendly, shot-maker's track that calls for sound course management in return for par. This is especially true on and around the large, swift greens, where creativity and skill are required to get the ball in the hole.

Garl chose his inspirations well: The fifth, a 221-yard par three, crosses a sandy preserve to a huge, oak-framed green staked out by bunkers and close-cropped swales that appear airlifted from Pinehurst No. 2. The signal feature at the downhill par-four 10th is a Pine Valley–style waste bunker that must be avoided at all costs, while renowned Cypress Point is represented at the par-four 15th, where the green

Victoria Hills Golf Club, 17th hole

Orange County National, Panther Lake, 17th hole

is partially hidden from view by severe mounds and grassy hollows. Rare for Florida, water comes into play on only three holes, yet the slope and course rating from the tips (142/73.5) are a clear indication of the resistance to scoring posed by sidehill lies, well-placed bunkers, and difficult greens.

On a former cattle ranch spliced with wetlands 10 miles north of Orlando in Seminole County, Tom Fazio was given carte blanche to conjure a playable course while leaving Mother Nature's creations intact. So pristine is the parcel of land on which the semi-private **Legacy Club at Alaqua Lakes** was built, it is one of a handful of courses worldwide to have achieved full certification in Audubon International's Signature Cooperative Sanctuary Program.

Tapping the same team of shapers that fashioned top-rated Black Diamond Ranch in Lecanto, Fazio threaded holes through a thick, old-growth forest of towering pines, moss-draped oaks, and cypress trees on surprisingly hilly terrain. (The club occupies the third highest point in the county.) The site's 158 acres of wetlands, distressed from years of cattle ranching, were restored. In addition to numerous retention ponds, broad stretches of marshland flank several of the holes. To speed play and also to maintain environmental stewardship, these delicate "habitats," marked by green-topped red stakes, are played as lateral hazards and are not to be entered, a mutually agreeable arrangement for golfers and gators alike.

In typical Fazio fashion, the Legacy Club, opened

in 1998, appears daunting at first, but the landing areas are very wide and the challenges posed are fair. The par-five 11th, the layout's tightest hole, is flanked by a conservation area up the right side where deer are common and where black bear cubs have been sighted. The side-by-side ninth and 18th holes, each indented by a common lake, return players to a handsome plantation-style clubhouse.

When the Audubon Society makes its annual bird count at the club, it usually identifies 50 species of birds and 770 individual specimens, from cormorants and herons to egrets and hawks. Bring your A-game and a pair of binoculars.

Phil Ritson, the charismatic South African swing guru who mentored David Leadbetter and many other top instructors, thinks big. Who else would have the chutzpah to borrow $137 million and obtain a 55-year lease on more than 900 acres of prime land with the idea of building four courses, a 33,000-square-foot clubhouse, a giant 42-acre circular practice range, and a 10-acre putting clock, not to mention a state-of-the-art golf institute? Ritson's vision for a definitive golf complex in Winter Garden south of Walt Disney World had to be scaled back, though two fine courses put **Orange County National** on the central Florida golf map when they opened in the late 1990s.

Routed through oak hammocks, pine forests, and wetlands on rolling land with a near-mountainous (for Florida) 65-foot elevation change, Ritson joined

Eagle Creek Golf Club, 15th hole

with design partners Dave Harman and Isao Aoki to conjure a magnificent test in **Panther Lake,** Orange County National's first course. Broad fairways and staggered tees give everyone a chance to play from the short grass, though the enormous, subtly contoured greens are well-defended by sand and water. The diversity of vegetation and variety of landscapes serve up what Ritson calls an "outstanding visual and psychological adventure," its key architectural features inspired by great courses worldwide. Several of the holes skirt lakes and creeks that give pause for thought from the back tees at 7,295 yards, though all the holes are quite manageable for middle handicappers from what Ritson calls the "member-guest tees" at 6,298 yards.

Crooked Cat, the second course to open at Orange County National, lacks the lovely natural features of Panther Lake, notably rolling hills and mature trees. Built by the same design team on more open land, this sturdy 7,277-yard layout showcases a distinct links-style flavor in its open, flowing design. Nearly treeless and therefore open to the seasonal winds that sweep central Florida, Crooked Cat's wide, terraced fairways are framed by rolling man-made berms. Redtop grass in the rough lends the course a Scottish look.

It's located a mere 15 minutes from Orlando International Airport, but the airport could just as easily be Heathrow in London, so convincing is the British links look and feel of **Eagle Creek Golf Club,** an exceptional newcomer on the city's eastern outskirts. Opened in 2004, this eclectic 7,198-yard, par-73 layout features broad fairways, boldly contoured greens, bulkheaded water hazards, and 90 bunkers. Eagle Creek aims to be the Auld Sod with better weather, and largely it succeeds. Laid out by Ron Garl and Howard Swan, the course reflects in equal measure the diverse background of its two designers. Florida-based Garl is known for creating strategically demanding yet very playable courses with ample landing areas and challenging approach areas. He is at home on a flat, sandy palette typical of the region. Swan, an Englishman, was responsible for the layout's compact greens, rectangular tees, and dramatic bunkers, many of which are revetted with stacked sod walls, a design style common on British seaside courses.

A well-balanced test, Eagle Creek hangs its hat on its quintet of par fives. Chief among them is the short 535-yard 18th, which dares go-for-broke players to reach the green in two and defines the term "risk-reward." After flying their drives over a daunting cross bunker and avoiding a large beach bunker on the right, players can take aim at a rock-walled peninsular green defended in front and to the right by water. Eagle Creek was the first course in Florida to surface its greens with Mini Verde, an ultra-dwarf Bermuda varietal that provides extremely durable and fast-rolling putting surfaces.

On the site of a former orange grove 20 miles west of Orlando near Walt Disney World, the 36-hole **ChampionsGate Golf Resort,** debuted in 2000 and part of a sprawling resort and residential complex, offers two completely different golf experiences by Greg Norman. The **International,** a prodigious 7,363-yard layout, is patterned after the elemental, treeless links of Scotland and Ireland. In addition to ragged man-made dunes flashed with sand, low choppy mounds choked with scrub and inset with bunkers enclose nearly every hole. The greens are large and swift. Strong winds often sweep the course. Unlike an authentic links, however, there's also water in play at six holes. From an incorrect set of tees, this course can be difficult and unforgiving, which is just what the Shark intended.

In sharp contrast to this rugged faux links is the **National,** a refined parkland-style course framed by woodlands, wetlands, and working orange groves. Stretching to 7,128 yards from the back tees, the housing-free National offers a pristine setting for golf. Nearly 100 bunkers and numerous waste areas frame the gently rolling fairways of this well-groomed test, its narrow greens embraced by close-mown chipping areas. The National's slightly hillier back nine comes on strong, its fairways bellied into valleys and bordered by mature oaks and pines.

Home to the 730-room Omni Orlando Resort opened in 2004, ChampionsGate is also the world headquarters of the David Leadbetter Golf Academy, a state-of-the-art learning center offering programs for all ages and skill levels.

Located due east of the Orange County Convention Center expansion and just 15 minutes west of Orlando International Airport, **Shingle Creek Golf Club** is yet another solid addition to the area golf scene. The 7,228-yard course, opened in 2003 on one of the last remaining open parcels of land in the city's tourist corridor, was designed by Dave Harman, the creative force behind the two courses at Orange County National. "The property, to be perfectly frank, wasn't Pebble Beach when we started," Harman admitted. Heavy earthmoving on the expansive 230-acre site, notably the digging of numerous lakes, led to the creation of a lush, gently rolling track framed by oaks and pines. Holes are interlaced by a series of waterways that are headwaters of the Everglades. (Water comes into play at 16 holes). The golf course, anchored by a lavish 23,000-square-foot

ChampionsGate Golf Resort, International, eighth hole

clubhouse, defines the perimeter of Rosen's Shingle Creek Resort, a massive 1,500-room property slated to open in 2006.

Another course set in the Shingle Creek basin is **Ritz-Carlton Golf Club Orlando, Grande Lakes,** a well-groomed layout with a rural front nine that proceeds through a wooded preserve dotted with lakes, wetlands, and cypress trees. By contrast, the back nine parallels a busy highway and returns players to civilization, its three finishing holes literally overshadowed by two enormous hotels, the 584-room Ritz-Carlton (the nation's largest Ritz) and the 1,000-room JW Marriott. Greg Norman's signature shaved green collars, skimpy rough, and large waste areas filled with crushed coquina sand mark the 7,122-yard layout, which opened in 2003.

If the golf course is rather generic in places, the service is anything but. As part of Ritz-Carlton's golf caddie-concierge program, an attendant accompanies each group at Grande Lakes. These ultra-polite caddies, attired in white jumpsuits, provide tips on playing the course, locate stray shots, provide yardage, read the greens, repair ball marks, clean clubs, and rake bunkers. Between shots, the caddies morph into concierges, providing a wealth of information on the services available at the two hotels and even addressing specific customer preferences. At the end of the round, an ice-cold Hoshobori towel soaked in rum and lime juice is a great reviver.

Formerly known as International Golf Club, the **Marriott Grande Pines Golf Club** reopened in 2004 after being treated to a major makeover by Steve Smyers, whose imaginative bunkering (sand features prominently in his designs) is in evidence throughout. Located a mile south of the Orange County Convention Center and a splash or two away from SeaWorld Orlando, the virtually new $6-million course, stretching to 7,012 yards, bears no resemblance to its ho-hum predecessor. Co-designed by player-consultant Nick Faldo, Grande Pines is a versatile track that can be played on the ground or through the air. Safer routes are available to conservative players on every hole, though bolder competitors can challenge the hazards to gain an advantage. Transportation to the club is available from nearby Grande Lakes, its sister facility.

Designed by former PGA Tour player Gary Koch and located two miles south of Walt Disney World Resort at the Wyndham Palms Resort & Country Club in Kissimmee, **Mystic Dunes Golf Club,** an interesting 7,012-yard test that opened in 2001, has a split personality. The front nine features British links-style holes that take advantage of the site's 50-foot elevation changes and natural sandy areas. On the Carolina lowcountry-style back nine, holes meander through oak hammocks, pine trees, and wetlands, the sunken soggy areas forcing risk-reward choices by players at all ability levels.

Koch notes that "almost every green is accessible with run-up shots, and there is mounding to help direct shots." On the other hand, many of the greens are heavily contoured, their humps and bumps resembling pods of whales en route to nearby Sea World. Far less defensible are the small pot bunkers lined with vertical planks that intrude on play and are menacing in the extreme. But then, Mystic Dunes is a course with a "Pine Valley-meets-Pinehurst-meets-Pirates-of-the-Caribbean theme," according to Ron Whitten of *Golf Digest.*

A 2,300-acre community built on a former citrus grove immediately south of Disney's town of Celebration and 15 minutes from Walt Disney World, **Reunion Resort & Club,** which strives for a "Main Street, USA" ambience, will feature three courses by 2006, each designed by a golf legend. Reunion's first course, the **Legacy,** is an Arnold Palmer–designed layout that debuted in 2003. A well-balanced test that utilizes a combination of mature trees, rockscapes, water treatments, bridges, and grass-sloped bunkers, the 6,930-yard course offers a solid test. The Legacy's more memorable holes are carved through a series of rolling hillocks.

Of far more interest is the **Independence,** Tom Watson's first design effort in Florida. Unveiled in 2004, this parkland-style layout, stretching to 7,257 yards, boasts well-placed fairway bunkers along with a 45-foot elevation change. Strategy and shot-making are required to score. The greens, several of them inspired by the huge roly-poly surfaces at Augusta National, are especially challenging. According to Watson, who only takes on a design project or two per year, "When I design a hole I attempt to make it look either harder or easier than it really is, to test a golfer's accuracy in perception and judgment." The Legacy and Independence courses, both located on the east side of I-4, share a common clubhouse.

The **Tradition,** Reunion's third venue, located on the other side of the highway, is being co-designed by Jack Nicklaus and his eldest son, Jack Nicklaus II, and is slated to debut in 2006. Each of the courses at the residential and resort development is semi-private. Three hotels are planned.

Ritz-Carlton Golf Club Orlando, Grande Lakes, 13th hole

Midwest

Sheboygan County, Wisconsin

It was when the third feasibility study stated unequivocally, as had the first two, that golf would never fly an hour's drive north of Milwaukee, that plumbing fixtures kingpin Herb Kohler knew he had to do what they said could not be done. This was in the mid-1980s, a fallow time when the game was years away from taking off. To prove to himself and to the naysayers that, done correctly, golf could work in the tidy factory town of Kohler, he tackled the idea of building a course like he did everything else, with passion and an eye to perfection.

Kohler was a twice-a-year golfer in those days, but his plan was to build a premier layout to satisfy the leisure demands of guests at **The American Club,** a former men's dormitory transformed into a beautiful hotel. The course would be built on land flanking the Sheboygan River that he had roamed as a youngster and later hunted as a young man. The first architect he consulted told him that most of the trees in the valley would need to be cut down to make way for golf. After a heated disagreement, Kohler turned him down. Kohler next hooked up with Pete Dye, like himself a hard-headed iconoclast and a Midwest native. In retrospect, it was a match made in heaven. Though the two fought like cats and dogs for years, their battles only brought them closer together. Kohler was the one with the vision, money, and land, satisfied only by the best; Dye was the design wizard who recognized among the glacier-carved hills and valleys the opportunity to build a superior course loaded with memorable shot opportunities. In 1985, ground was broken on what would become **Blackwolf Run,** named for the prominent Winnebago Indian chief from the early 1800s.

In the club's original course guide, Kohler talked about Dye's commitment to his work. "Virtually all course designers will have their staff lay out a course on paper in graphic detail before they turn a spade. Pete doesn't do this. He walks the land, and walks it again and again. He stakes the basic yardages from

Blackwolf Run, Meadow Valleys Course, 14th hole

tee to green, then moves some earth. He returns to the site once a week through completion, adjusting and readjusting. For anyone who has had the opportunity to experience the man and his work, it becomes immediately obvious that he loves the land and enjoys the people who play this game."

Alas, a torrential downpour in September of 1986—eight inches of rain fell in four hours—washed away two summers of hard work, irrigation pipe and all. Normal spirits would have been dampened. Kohler had the design team back on the job the next day. Blackwolf Run opened in 1988, a year later than planned. The golf course the pundits said would never fly in a small market with a short season was an instant hit with Wisconsin's fervent golfers as well as visitors. By the time demand for tee times began to outstrip supply at the end of the first season, Kohler told Dye, "We need another 18 holes."

With acreage for the second 18 located on either side of the original course, the only way to accomplish it was to integrate the old holes with the new, creating the **River Course** and **Meadow Valleys Course.** There was a risk in splitting the acclaimed original course, but Dye forged ahead, artfully blending the break points so that two championship courses were created in the process. The River receives more

Whistling Straits, Straits Course, 17th hole

Left: Blackwolf Run, River Course, 13th hole

accolades, but Meadow Valleys, routed on higher ground, is nearly as good, lacking only the former's dramatic river frontage. A huge boomerang-shaped double green accommodates the 18th holes of both courses. A sprawling lodgepole pine clubhouse, one of the handsomest gathering places in golf, overlooks the home green and the river.

How good are these two layouts? When I dispatched Jim Finegan, an accomplished golfer and writer to assess Blackwolf Run in 1992, he wrote of the River Course: "A look at the adjectives scattered across my scorecard is informative: exquisite, spectacular, thrilling, majestic, intimidating, delightful, magnificent. Here we have it all: dramatic elevation changes, vast and deep bunkers, water imperiling the shot on nine holes, devilishly contoured greens, plenty of trees to tangle with, surprises at every turn (a choice of *three* fairways on the short par-four ninth!), hole after hole of challenging and fair and fascinating golf." His take on the Meadow Valleys was no less stinting in its praise. His final summation: "Winged Foot would be lucky to have a 36-hole complex the likes of Blackwolf Run." The USGA was also impressed with Blackwolf Run. In 1998, it hosted the U.S. Women's Open on a composite course that reunited holes from the original layout and produced the highest scores the event has seen in recent years.

Among public-access parkland venues nationwide, only Bethpage's Black Course, site of the 2002 U.S. Open, can be placed ahead of Blackwolf Run for grandeur and challenge.

Once Kohler got the golf development bug in his bloodstream, he could not sit still. One day he told Dye that there was some acreage along Lake Michigan he wanted him to look at. The land, located nine miles northeast of the village of Kohler, was the former Haven Army Base, which operated as an anti-aircraft weapons firing range and military training camp during World War II. Seventy-foot bluffs stood above the gun-metal gray waters of Lake Michigan, though the derelict site would require the removal of underground fuel storage tanks, concrete bunkers, and an old airstrip as well as an environmental clean-up of asbestos, toxic waste, and other detritus left after years of illegal phantom dumping. Dye's palette for **Whistling Straits** would be 560 acres of spoiled land, a site the Wisconsin Electric Power Co. had held as a potential nuclear power plant location.

Dye was taking stock of the raw site that cold wintry day when Kohler threw down the gauntlet: "I want the course to look like it's in Ireland," he said,

Whistling Straits, Straits Course, 18th hole and clubhouse

dismissively. Dye had joined Kohler for many a trip via Kohler's private jet to the Emerald Isle, and both shared a love for its rugged seaside links parted through massive, heaving sand dunes. But a walkers-only, Irish-style links on a dead-flat site in Wisconsin?

After gaining permission from the Army Corps of Engineers to move the bluffs back from the water's edge to better preserve the eroded coastline, Dye set himself the task of fulfilling Kohler's dream along two miles of lakeshore, a feat accomplished with an army of bulldozers and dirt obtained from the work on the bluffs. After moving nearly *three million cubic yards* of material, a vast amount even for an old dirt devil like Dye, sand mined from local farms—more than 13,000 truckloads of it—was brought in to flash the tops of the 80-foot-high dirt hills to make them look like Ballybunion's brawny dunes. The towering hills are not only capped with sand, they're honey-combed with miles of Kohler pipe so that the sand doesn't wash into the lake during a heavy rainstorm.

The deep kettle bunkers and menacing sand pits shored up by blackened timbers look very much at home on the barren tract of land. Architecture critic Ron Whitten writes about the **Straits Course,** "There are a thousand bunkers (give or take 500) scattered about like laundry in the aftermath of a tornado. The whole course looks like a moonscape." As in Eire, scrubby broken ground and tall brown fescues divide the holes, 14 of which skirt the reconstituted bluffs above the lake. The wind is constant and can blow from any direction. When a flock of black-faced sheep was introduced to the facsimile links, the fakery of the Straits, debuted in 1998, was complete.

It is difficult to single out feature holes on a course that announces to players on every tee that a flight to Ireland may not be necessary to experience links golf in America. The par-four 10th, for example, was loosely adapted from the opening hole at Lahinch, the famed links in County Clare, only here there's a bunker in the middle of the fairway that must be avoided at all costs, and the skewed, perched green is undercut by deep bunkers.

Dye, like Robert Trent Jones before him, is aghast at the advances in modern golf equipment and the game as played by today's long-hitting pros. Dye's solution was to make the Straits appear visually intimidating from the tips, even hostile and scary in places. His goal was to provide a thrilling, one-of-a-kind test to resort players but to plant seeds of doubt in the minds of the top players. "From a visual point of view," Dye says, "I want them [Tour pros] to feel uncomfortable. These days especially, you have to push it or it won't really challenge them." That's why targets and bailouts are partially hidden from the back tees, which often are lower in elevation than the forward markers. Dye, a master illusionist, has

Fly fishing in the Sheboygan River

KOHLER WATERS SPA

Given his business, it was just a matter of time before Herb Kohler built a spa, but not before he was fully satisfied that the feel-good emporium met his exalted expectations. Occupying 16,000 square feet of space on two levels of the Carriage House, a guest-room annex of The American Club, Kohler Waters Spa is not the largest spa in America, but it is among the best, for several reasons. First and foremost, the spa is a showplace for the parent brand's premier plumbing products. The whirlpool tubs, Vichy showers, and classically-styled fixtures are of the finest quality. Peach and butter tones along with rattan furniture create a soothing atmosphere within the spa, which opened in 2000. Also, Kohler brand lotions and bathing products are infused with botanicals inspired by the village's gardens, including its signature hollyhocks. Lastly, the spa's staff of friendly, nurturing Wisconsinites cannot do enough for their charges.

At the center of the tranquil spa is a beautifully tiled pool with an eight-foot cascading wall of water. Spa-goers can sit on a bench beneath the falls to relax. Because Kohler has a long history of working wonders with water, many of the treatments and bathing experiences celebrate the therapeutic benefits of water. Treatments, notably the one-of-a-kind Renaissance Bath immersion, are greatly enhanced by the quality of the fixtures, in this case a hand-hammered copper steeping bathtub that sells for $43,000. Golfers brought low by one of Kohler's four courses can opt for the Golfer's Massage, designed to ease tension and increase flexibility. For walkers, there's the Golfer's Foot Renewal, a relaxing pedicure and foot massage that features an application of self-heating mud designed to re-energize and stimulate the feet.

LODGING

The American Club, a stately Tudor edifice that once served as a men's dormitory for Kohler Co.'s immigrant employees, is justly celebrated as the Midwest's finest resort hotel. Fifty-two suites in the club's Carriage House annex, located above the spa and debuted in 2000, are the first choice of golfers traveling with spa-goers. These are among the resort's most deluxe accommodations. The Carriage House features on-site check-in, concierge, continental breakfast, evening beverages and hors d'oeuvres, easy access to the spa, and other extras.

At the other end of the spectrum is the **Inn on Woodlake**, a moderately-priced hotel set beside a lovely spring-fed lake. The 121-room hostelry, favored by players who do not require the ultra-luxe refinement of The American Club, features comfortable rooms and beautifully appointed baths. Preferred tee times at Blackwolf Run and Whistling Straits are available to overnight guests of both Kohler resort hotels.

DINING

The resort's nine restaurants deliver everything from bratwurst to beef Wellington. The Immigrant Restaurant & Winery Bar, revamped in 2003, occupies The American Club's former laundry room, its six connected rooms decorated to honor the European heritage of the town's first arrivals. The cuisine here is eclectic gourmet. The European-style Winery Bar features a regional cheese room that, given the state's reputation as America's dairyland, is second to none. Hungry golfers usually gravitate to the Horse & Plow, a casual tavern that once served as a tap room for Kohler Co. employees. The fare is hearty. More than 80 regional beers and 12 Wisconsin beers are available on draft in a large, handsome space accented by stained glass, brass rails, and rich woods.

Pool and cascade at Kohler Waters Spa

cooked up a recipe for disaster at every single hole.

He did it not only with prodigious length—the black tees, at 7,362 yards (151 slope, 76.7 course rating) are dire beyond imagining, and the championship tees push it farther back to 7,514 yards—he did it with cunning. For instance, Dye levels the field at the 14th, "a short par four that embodies our thinking regarding longer-hitting golfers," he chuckles. "The key revolves around providing an angle to the green so that the longer the drive the more difficult the approach becomes. The short hitter has a longer distance but an easier angle to the green." The wiliest fox in the design business never stops figuring out ways to thwart long-ball artists.

The par-three 17th, one of four dramatic one-shotters that tightrope the bluffs and teeter above the lake, is a genuine tour de force, by turns harrowing and spectacular. The tee shot from the tips at 223 yards is partially blind to a long, narrow green tucked behind a volcano-like mound, the ground dropping off sharply to the left to a gnarly netherworld of coarse sand and wild fescues. The lakeshore beckons 40 feet below. The hole, called "Pinched Nerve," was amended when Alice Dye, Pete's wife, confidant, and a fine player in her own right, told him the original wasn't difficult enough. "You have to run the risk of making double-bogey," she sniffed.

While the USGA was looking into the possibility of holding a U.S. Open at the Straits Course, the PGA of America jumped in with a firm offer for the 2004 PGA Championship, which Kohler accepted. It was a tremendous coup for a new course and a feat rivaled only by Kiawah's Ocean Course, which hosted the 1991 Ryder Cup matches less than a year after opening. The USGA later selected the Straits Course to host the 2007 U.S., Senior Open, and after a successful 2004 PGA Championship the PGA announced that event would return in 2010 and 2015, to be followed by the coveted Ryder Cup in 2020.

The club's name was cooked up by Kohler himself one blustery day, and it was he who insisted on planting fescue grass in the fairways to create firm playing surfaces. The logo for Whistling Straits, a puffy-cheeked, hirsute man, his lips pursed as if to blow a mighty gale, is a dead ringer for Kohler, though the resort staff insists the image came from a piece of antique Irish furniture.

The impressive Irish-themed clubhouse at Whistling Straits once again demonstrates Kohler's ingenuity. At the time workers were building the clubhouse, Kohler suggested they reverse the stones so that the rougher, unfinished sides would face out, creating a more rustic look. Even Dye thought the notion was crazy, but the effect is convincing. However, it should be noted that very few clubhouses in Ireland can touch this one for beauty, elegance, and comfort. The restaurant in particular lays a superb table, while the upstairs bar offers a definitive selection of whiskeys and ales along with fine views from its tall windows of the vast, often white-capped lake. Alongside the clubhouse is an open, three-sided barn of a style found in Ireland, its east wall open to the elements. On a pleasant day, it's a great place to stretch your legs after the round and gaze upon the links.

DESIGNER KNOWS BEST

Since its debut, the general reaction to Whistling Straits from pros and amateurs alike has been mixed. Many of the jagged man-made hills, for example, are pitted with pockmarks from top to bottom, prompting one visiting writer to comment, "I've never before seen a golf course with a bad case of acne." Is the Straits, I asked him, a blemish on the landscape? "No," he replied. "It's probably the greatest manufactured links on the face of the earth."

Prior to the 86th PGA Championship held on the Straits in 2004, this opinion was not shared by many of the world's best players. Indeed, the forecasts for golf's fourth major were dire. Typical of the many comments by players about the course, England's Lee Westwood said, "I'd been told there are 10 difficult holes and eight impossible ones. I'm still trying to work out which the 10 difficult holes are."

But the most prescient comments came from Dye himself. "The ones playing well will get to this course," he said. "Once they go around a couple of times and get used to it, they will get locked in. If they stay out of trouble, they'll do fine." He predicted a winning total of eight to 10 under par, not the nightmarish, over-par "train wrecks" others had warned about.

The old master was right. On a course that yielded an opening-round 65 to Darren Clarke, the Straits played reasonably difficult the next two days before finally baring its teeth the final day. Close to half of the 450 rounds played at the PGA Championship resulted in scores of par or better. But with the fairways dry and firm and the winds brisk on Sunday, the field came back to the course. Justin Leonard, Chris DiMarco, and Vijay Singh tied after 72 holes at 280, eight under par. Singh, arguably the finest ball-striker in the world, won the three-hole playoff. Dye's crystal ball was crystal clear, and Herb Kohler's faith in the world's most iconoclastic designer was well-founded. Walking a tightrope, Dye had earned the respect of the game's top players without embarrassing them. In the process, his newfangled links on the shores of Lake Michigan achieved "must-play" status.

Whistling Straits, Irish Course, second hole

After the first course opened at Whistling Straits, another challenge remained for Kohler and Dye: What to do for an encore on the heels of a course that was perhaps the crowning achievement of Dye's legendary career.

By now an avid golfer with an 18 handicap who played with gusto and intent, Kohler had not only collaborated with Dye in the creation of three world-beaters, he had become his close friend and biggest fan. Dye, for his part, said, "Herb is crazy to work with. He had no knowledge of golf when he got started, and he would still fight me on so many things. I couldn't believe it, given his lack of experience and background, but he was right so much of the time."

Dye's stated goal for the **Irish Course** was to make it of equal stature to the Straits. Claiming to employ "every trick I've ever learned," Dye melded the jumbled landscape into a quirky but endearing patchwork quilt of a course, portions of which occupy broken ground behind the towering hills of the Straits. Originally conceived as a parkland test with numerous forced carries over water, the Irish Course

evolved into a counter-puncher with a multiple personality that defies better players to settle in and get comfortable. How to get comfortable on a course that sings you an Irish lullaby one moment and knocks you blind the next?

This one-of-a-kind hybrid, opened in 2000, features nine holes routed through man-made dunes flashed with sand; six parkland-style holes criss-crossed by creeks; and three holes wrapped around ponds. Wetlands pinch or cross the fairways on a few occasions. There's also a swirling breeze off the lake that makes club selection an art, not a science.

And then there's the par-three 13th, "blind man's bluff." Kohler wanted a blind par three on the order of the fabled "Dell" hole at Lahinch in Ireland. The ever-playful Dye was more than happy to comply. Only the top of the 12-foot-high pin and a tiny portion of the enormous, rippled putting surface are visible from the hole's five sets of hilltop tees, which range from 111 to 183 yards. If the tee shot is a hit and hope affair, the first putt on the sunken green, 15,000 square feet of bentgrass in turmoil enclosed by steep walls and ringed by nasty bunkers, is even more so. For many, the 13th on the Irish may be the best short par four in the Midwest.

From the tips at 7,201 yards, the Irish Course carries a 146 slope and 75.6 course rating, both slightly lower than the Straits. But the ratings from the middle tees, where most mortals play from, are comparable. Challenging, unnerving, but memorable, with long views of Lake Michigan from five holes, the walker-friendly Irish Course is a wild-eyed, red-headed cousin of the Straits.

On a farm in Sheboygan Falls where champion Holstein cattle were once raised, a farm located all of 10 minutes from the village of Kohler, Jack Nicklaus, the Golden Bear, has created an alter ego of sorts in **The Bull at Pinehurst Farms.**

Just as Pinehurst Farms had been a showcase of agriculture for more than 150 years, The Bull, melded to glacial landforms, is a supreme parkland course for the 21st century. Each hole on The Bull is named for a champion sire, from Avant Garde to Rock-N-Roll, and each offers a hefty challenge. Five sets of tees provide admirable versatility, though the rip-snorting Bull tees, at 7,332 yards, will trample all but the most skillful of matadors. The layout is seamless, classic, and fair, its well-crafted holes designed to test a player's mettle and stimulate his imagination. From any set of tees, golfers must play smart shots to score well. You may not be able to ride or tame The Bull, but you can make a truce with it.

Nicklaus and his team juggled 10 routings before arriving at a sequence of holes that takes maximum advantage of the site's specimen hardwoods, thickets of white birch, and 75 feet of elevation change. Fewer than 400,000 cubic yards of material were moved to shape the holes. "The uniqueness [of the course] is the terrain itself," Nicklaus said shortly before the course opened in 2003.

The Bull is roomy off the tee, for a reason. "People are spending $500 for a driver," Nicklaus told owner David Bachmann Jr. "I want them to be able to use it."

Expertly strategized, the course offers numerous risk-reward options occasioned by the presence of water. Ponds, wetlands, and the Onion River, a tributary of the Sheboygan, come into play on 16 holes. The 75 bunkers, each beautifully shaped and well-deployed, also give pause for thought. The greens, surfaced in Princeville bentgrass, are firm, fast and among the most imaginatively contoured Nicklaus has ever built.

The most unforgettable hole on the course is the 432-yard fifth. The scene from the tee is heart-stopping: A hairpin-shaped fairway bent sharply from right-to-left around an omigosh, 40-foot-deep ravine. The approach shot, which must fly a corner of the cliff, is frightening to behold. But carry the cavernous bunker beyond the ravine, and a hidden swale in the bail-out area to the right actually funnels the ball to the punchbowl green. The hole's "wow" factor is second to none in the Midwest.

The Bull's back nine is longer than the front, though its best hole may be the petite par-four 11th, which tempts big hitters to try for the green on their drives. In typical Nicklaus fashion, The Bull's 18th is a bear, a very rigorous par four of 485 yards that plays uphill over a lake to a silo and barn on the horizon. Wetlands and a rocky creek will swallow any shots pushed to the right.

How does The Bull compare to the River and Meadow Valleys courses at Blackwolf Run? It is more classic in appearance, with slightly better playability from its forward tees, yet just as tough from the tips. (The Bull's slope rating of 146 from the back tees is the third highest in the state, behind the River and Straits courses). Basically, the courses at both facilities are great because the land is great. Dye's holes are trickier, Nicklaus's more straightforward.

Says Bachmann, "Those [Kohler] courses are four of the best I've ever played. It's amazing what they did. If they hadn't done it, we would have been laughed out of every bank." A friendly competitor, the Bull is slightly lower in price than the Kohler layouts, yet course conditions are comparable.

The Bull at Pinehurst Farms, 16th hole

Minnesota's Far North

Talk about tundra. The northeast corner of Minnesota is about as far north as you can get in the U.S. without running into Canada (or polar bears). Among the sparkling lakes and pine forests is a land called the Iron Range, specifically the Mesabi and Vermilion iron ranges, which a century ago became legendary as rich producers of iron ore. As high-grade ore was depleted, leaving only lower-grade taconite behind, the state formed the Iron Range Resource and Rehabilitation Agency (IRRRA) in the 1940s to figure out how to turn the worn-out mining land into revenue-producing recreational facilities. One of the agency's projects was the creation in the mid-1950s of the Giants Ridge ski run in Biwabik. Later, the IRRRA, which has jurisdiction over 13,000 square miles, began considering ways to broaden the area's four-season appeal. Campers and fishermen were common, but golfers were scarce. After much deliberation, a site for a golf course was chosen at the edge of Superior National Forest not far from the cross-country ski trails at Giants Ridge used for training by the U.S. Olympic Team.

If iron ore proved to be difficult to extract for the immigrants who arrived to work the mines, the creation of the first course at **Giants Ridge,** now called the **Legend,** proved no less so. According to Texas-based designer Jeffrey Brauer, surely the least heralded in the current crop of gifted architects, the course "faced numerous challenges to satisfy environmental concerns including water quality, endangered species, wetlands, and tree preservation." When a botanical study turned up a rare marigold and an even rarer strawberry on site, Brauer and his design team, which included former PGA Tour star Lanny Wadkins, had to move holes to accommodate them, resulting in a sprawling configuration. (Golf carts are mandatory.) Brauer estimates that he juggled more than 30 different routings in an effort to accommodate all parties. "I know we did more than 26," Brauer remembers, "because we started out lettering them from A to Z and we passed Z and started numbering!"

His patience was rewarded on a rugged site strewn with car-sized boulders deposited by glaciers. The 6,930-yard course, opened in 1997, covers 275 acres

Legend at Giants Ridge, 11th hole

and is joined together by numerous bridges and nearly eight miles of cart paths, with lengthy but lovely rides between holes that double as take-a-deep-breath nature trails. And while the holes were chain-sawed from a thick forest of birch and pine and in some areas blasted from bedrock, the Legend, draped on ridges and bellied into valleys along the Laurentian Divide, appears serene, pastoral, and naturalistic. In truth, the Legend is a Bunyanesque playground, a mighty, grand-scale test that packs a big punch.

Among the feature holes is the third, a sweeping par five that doglegs to the left around an enormous footprint-shaped fairway bunker said to be left by Paul Bunyan himself, with four elongated, trench-like toes flashed with sand appending the foot. Probably the most memorable hole on the Legend is the 17th, a heroic, all-or-nothing par three stretching to 227 yards which plays from a skybox tee high above an inlet of Lake Sabin.

Touted for its excellence shortly after opening, the layout, widely considered to be Minnesota's most suc-cessful resort course, immediately developed a strong following and in fact single-handedly created a new summer tourism market in the Iron Range. Because the Biwabik area is sparsely populated, 90 percent of its customers travel 100 miles or more to tee it up here. (It's a 3½-hour drive from the Twin Cities.)

In 2003, when a second course at Giants Ridge, the **Quarry,** made its debut, interest in the region more than doubled among traveling players. According to IRRRA development director Mike Gentile, "We challenged Jeff...to build an equal or better yet differ-ent facility than the Legend, our 'Gentle Giant.' We wanted to provide a course that challenges the low handicapper, but has generous fairways and appro-priate forward tees for the high-handicapper." Did Brauer succeed? "You would never dream these two courses were designed by the same person," he said.

The land itself is responsible for many of the differences between the two venues. Though just a mile down the road from the Legend, the Quarry is defined by spent rock and sand quarries as well as broad stretches of land made barren by a century of

Legend at Giants Ridge, 17th hole

iron ore manufacture. "You might say it's the most 'unnatural' course I have ever designed," said Brauer, "because most of the land has been scarred into land of great charm and character by these previous industrial operations. We decided that instead of covering up the history of the Quarry's site, we would let the site tell its story." Deep gouges, steep embankments, and quarry spoils from mining operations mark the holes. Rusted mining implements, railroad ties, and other reminders of the site's industrial past were left in place. Each hole is named for an area mine, past and present. The burly par-four 18th, for example, is named for the Embarrass Mine, which today is a 550-foot-deep, trout-stocked lake, the deepest in the Mesabi Iron Range. It spells a watery grave for players who slice their approach shots.

Routed in parts through thick woods and in other places around lakes and wetlands, the Quarry, which welcomes walkers, offers tremendous pace and variety. It is also a course without a single chink

in its armor. Holes six through nine, the heart of the course, play over, around, and through the sand quarry, the hazards every bit as penal and dramatic as fabled Pine Valley's.

Enthusiasm for the course has been unbridled since the day it opened. According to *Golf Digest* architecture critic Ron Whitten, "What Jeff has conceived amidst deep sand pits and squeezed among high piles is as fine a set of golf holes as has been produced thus far in the 21st century. There are spots where you must get the ball airborne, but mostly it's a feed-the-ball-to-the-target layout that you could play with a hockey stick."

Very few public-access courses in the Midwest can go to the mat against this wild, wooly mammoth of a layout, which measures 7,201 yards from the tips with a course rating of 75.6 and a slope of 146. Taken together, the Legend and the Quarry at Giants Ridge offer the most diverse 36-hole golf experience imaginable, well worth a detour to the middle of nowhere.

LODGING

The **Lodge at Giants Ridge,** situated at the base of the resort's ski area near the Legend, is marked by an impressive log-built port cochere and timber-beamed lobby. It offers 92 suites (king-size bed or two queens) and an indoor swimming pool. Far better are the Villas at Giants Ridge, a group of free-standing luxury condos and cabin-style villas overlooking Wynne Lake and a private beach near the Quarry Course. Guests can swim, fish, or go boating on their doorstep. Roughing it? A nearby camping area accommodates tents, motor homes, and everything in between.

DINING

Timbers Restaurant at The Lodge offers a casual atmosphere, a spectacular view, and regional favorites, including pecan-crusted walleye and roast duckling with seasonal fruit sauce. For something completely different, drive through the Bavarian-themed town of Biwabik outside the resort into nearby Gilbert to sample authentic Jamaican food (including killer-hot jerk chicken wings) at the Whistling Bird.

OFF-COURSE ATTRACTIONS

At Giants Ridge, there's mountain biking on more than 60 kilometers of trails consisting of single track, cross-country ski trails, snowmobile trails, and abandoned logging roads. In addition, 10 miles of paved trail from Aurora to Biwabik was completed in 2003. Hiking is available in Superior National Forest (check the ranger station in Aurora for information); and to the top of Giant Ridge mountain, where the view of the surrounding lakes and forest is spectacular.

Hundreds of Minnesota's 10,000-plus lakes are found in the vicinity of the resort. These crystal clear waters abound with northern pike, bass, crappie, and walleye, the region's signature fish, which reach great size (over four feet) in these waters. There's also fishing in the pit lake beside the Quarry's 18th hole.

Hockey fans in search of a shrine need look no further than the U.S. Hockey Hall of Fame in nearby Eveleth. Minnesota's mining and immigration history is preserved at the Ironworld Discovery Center in Chisholm. Also located in Chisholm is the Classic Cars Museum, a must for car buffs.

Quarry at Giants Ridge, 13th hole

At the far end of a two-lane road cut through the wilderness some 30 miles north of Giants Ridge is **Fortune Bay Casino Resort** in Tower, the pride and joy of the Bois Forte Band of Chippewa. The casino, a north woods beacon for gamblers, has been in operation since 1986. The resort, featuring a hotel and conference center, marina, RV park, and nature trails, opened 10 years later. To enhance their economic self-sufficiency, the tribe decided to build a resort course on a rugged site near the casino overlooking Lake Vermilion, one of the prettiest lakes in North America and, with 1,200 miles of shoreline, one of the region's largest. Their architect of choice? Jeffrey Brauer, the designer of the 36-hole complex at Giants Ridge.

Calling the property "some of the prettiest land in Minnesota," with dramatic granite rock outcrops along with long views of Lake Vermilion and its inlets, Brauer set to work on **The Wilderness at For-**

tune Bay. It was Brauer who came up with the name for the course, which debuted in 2004. During one of the many field trips he made to the 250-acre site over a three-year period, Brauer said he saw "bear, deer, moose, an eagle, even a timber wolf out there. The name jumped out at me, and as it turned out, the marketing theme the resort had recently adopted was, 'We put the wild in wilderness.'"

The golf holes fit the land naturally. Because much of the rock underlying the course was immovable, Brauer designed around it. On four holes, for example, there are two distinct routes for drives or approach shots over or around the rock.

Brauer, who said he was charged with designing a popular yet challenging course, believed the natural beauty of the layout would be the major draw. Appropriately enough for a casino-based resort, he also built a course where players could take chances. "I emphasized gambling holes, while giving golfers

a good chance to, in this case, beat the designer," he chuckled.

Among the more fascinating holes on this well-groomed track is the 13th, a stunning short par four routed around the shores of Lake Vermilion that tempts big hitters to launch their drives over a corner of the lake to reach the small, well-defended green. This hole, called the Muskellunge for the voracious pike-like fish that rules the lake, is a true standout, as much an aesthetic triumph as it is a strategic gem.

The 7,207-yard layout is a heck of a place to roll the dice: Its 144 slope and 75.3 course rating from the tips makes it only marginally less difficult than the Quarry at Giants Ridge. The more demanding and perhaps more strategic Quarry course will always get the nod from purists who prefer to walk, but the carts-mandatory Wilderness spread, interwoven with classic design features, accentuates playability from the forward tees.

LODGING

Guests of **Fortune Bay Resort** are greeted by a massive free-standing stone fireplace in the lobby, with accommodations ranging from deluxe lakeview rooms and whirlpool suites to larger, extended-stay suites. In addition to ample dining and shopping opportunities, the resort offers a pool and fitness area, a game room, and day care.

For those who wish to try their luck, the resort offers two gaming floors with hundreds of popular table games (including live poker). Dinner theater, top comedians, and national recording artists round out the entertainment.

The best place for dinner at Fortune Bay is the impressive stone-and-wood clubhouse, which features a large patio for outdoor dining and a good array of entrees.

OFF-COURSE ATTRACTIONS

Boat rentals and guided fishing trips are available at Fortune Bay's full-service marina. Lake Vermilion, named one of the nation's most scenic lakes by *National Geographic,* is home to 365 islands and has been ranked the top walleye lake in the state. Pike, bass, and panfish are also taken, as is the occasional muskie.

Not far from the resort is Soudan Underground Mine State Park, which invites visitors to make a fascinating hard-hat descent a half-mile underground to see the caverns where immigrant workers extracted the world's richest iron ore in the state's first underground mine. The mine ceased operation in 1962. The temperature way down deep is 50 degrees year-round.

East of Fortune Bay in the heart of Superior National Forest is Ely, gateway to the western portion of the Boundary Waters Canoe Area Wilderness, a federally protected region of more than 1,000 lakes and streams enveloped by stony cliffs and boreal forests. Coupled with Canada's adjacent Quetico Park, this is the greatest wilderness canoeing and fishing area in the world. If you want to hear the unforgettable call of the loon, this is the place.

NORTHERN LIGHTS

Also known as the *aurora borealis* (Latin for northern dawn), these glowing streamers of light often appear in the region's black velvet sky. The throbbing lights are often colored, and move in curtains across the horizon. These displays, unique to the world's northern regions, occur when electrons from solar emissions enter the earth's atmosphere.

WILD NORTH GOLF

In addition to the headliner courses at Giants Ridge and Fortune Bay Casino Resort, a consortium known as Wild North Golf includes three nine-hole layouts for players seeking a more casual outing. **Evelyth** is a superb nine-holer nestled in a grove of pines and maples beside the St. Mary's River. **Hoyt Lakes,** another muni, has a periscope at its seventh hole that enables players to see the blind green. **Wolfridge** is a short, well-kept nine lined by tall trees and rock outcrops.

The Wilderness at Fortune Bay, 16th hole

Superior National, Canyon nine, eighth hole

SIDETRIP: SUPERIOR NATIONAL

Golfers wishing to take in the lakeside scenery along Highway 61, a thoroughfare made famous by Bob Dylan and recently designated one of "America's last great drives" by *Car & Driver,* should travel to Lutsen to tee it up at **Superior National.** Opened as an 18-holer in 1991, the club, set between the Sawtooth Mountains and Lake Superior on a vast tract of thickly wooded land, added a third nine in 1999. Laid out by Don Herfort and Joel Goldstrand, a for- mer PGA Tour player who has designed several fine courses in Minnesota, Superior National offers some of the most breathtaking golf course vistas in the nation. Above the treetops, Lake Superior stretches as far as the eye can see. Few courses anywhere blend beauty and challenge quite like this spectacular 27-hole spread. Superior National is located 90 miles from Duluth (the world's largest inland port) and is 90 minutes east of Giants Ridge.

Rockies

Summit County, Colorado

Throughout Colorado's Rocky Mountains, where the four-season appeal has increased dramatically in the past few years, the mantra often heard from locals is, "We came here to ski, but we live here because of the summers." Not only are the cool, humidity-free summers in the ski communities west of Denver ideal for golf and other outdoor pursuits, the golf ball seemingly flies forever at a mile and half above sea level.

Seventy miles west of Denver, visitors enter well-named Summit County and its stellar collection of ski resorts in the Front Range. These resorts are not only convenient to the Denver metropolis, they're ranked among the finest (and highest) slopes in the nation. Ditto its growing collection of high-altitude golf courses.

Chief among these four-season playgrounds is **Keystone Resort.** The original **Keystone Ranch Golf Course,** at 9,300 feet one of the nation's highest-altitude layouts, was well ahead of the leisure curve when it opened in 1980. For years the resort relied upon this Robert Trent Jones, Jr.–designed layout, its holes stretched across a former cattle ranch and lettuce farm framed by lodgepole pines and open meadows, to satisfy the needs of visiting players. A top-of-the-world wonder with several holes wrapped around a nine-acre lake, the Ranch is a respected hombre but a tough piece of beef for most vacationers, its narrow landing areas and numerous forced carries demanding skillful play.

Twenty years after the debut of the Ranch, Keystone's second venue, the **River Course,** made its debut on a splendid site at lower elevation where the Ute and Arapaho Indians once hunted buffalo. The design team of Michael Hurdzan and Dana Fry, known for its environmentally sensitive work, has given golfers a second reason to visit this gorgeous corner of Summit County.

Located west of Keystone Village, the River Course offers dramatic elevation changes and a longer playing season than the original. This 6,886-yard, par-71 layout is also a scenic delight, serving up views of towering peaks in the Continental Divide and the Gore Range, many of them snow-capped year-round.

Closer at hand, players traversing the front nine may occasionally see a kayaker paddle by on the Snake River, which bisects the course.

And that's just the window dressing. Given a generous parcel with no tight boundaries and very limited housing, Hurdzan-Fry were asked to create a more user-friendly counterpoint to the rigorous Ranch Course. Landing areas, many of them up to 60 yards wide, are framed by sagebrush, native grasses, and 12 different kinds of wildflowers. In addition, the large bentgrass greens are the golfing equivalent of the broad side of a barn. And while hardly a pushover from the back tees—creative shotmaking and a strategic game plan are required to score from the tips—the layout is loads of fun from the multiple sets of forward tees. (The layout can play as short as 4,762 yards.) An absence of penal hazards and only three modest carries over wetlands or water means it's possible to play the River in a reasonable amount of time without losing a dozen balls.

The front nine of the River Course is mostly flat, the fairways skirting the banks of the Snake River, though both the first and ninth holes drop 100 feet. The back nine bobs and weaves through a forest of lodgepole pines, with precipitous drops from the topmost tees. The most memorable hole on the course is the 16th, a 496-yard par four with a 200-foot vertical drop from tee to green. If you live to see your tee ball pinned against the sky for several heart-stopping seconds, you'll love this hole.

While the Ranch Course is open from the first week of June until early October, the sunnier, south-facing River Course generally adds two to three weeks to both ends of the season. The fall season, when the aspens turn gold, is spectacular, but note that Keystone's greenkeepers remove the flags in late afternoon because the resident elk have a habit of charging them!

Just down the road from Keystone in the little town of Silverthorne, designers Michael Hurdzan and Dana Fry joined forces with PGA Tour player Tom Lehman to produce a wild bronco of a golf course,

LODGING & DINING

With 1,500 lodging units located in seven villages encompassing three mountains, **Keystone Resort** has something for everyone. Townhomes and condos in West Keystone are convenient to both the Ranch and River courses, though top digs are available at **Keystone Lodge,** an upscale RockResorts property; and the historic **Ski Tip Lodge,** a former 1800s stagecoach stop since converted to a cozy bed-and-breakfast. Not only does Keystone offer free lodging for children 18 years and younger in summer, complimentary Mountain Passes provide resort guests with dozens of free activities and adventures.

Keystone's dining choices are excellent. Ski Tip Lodge dishes up what it calls the "best comfort food on the Divide," while Keystone Ranch, a beautifully restored log homestead from the 1930s that doubles as the Ranch Course clubhouse, specializes in six-course meals served with Western flair. Wild game entrees, notably elk and bison, can be paired with a superb array of wines. The Zagat Survey has recognized Keystone Ranch as the best restaurant in Colorado. Alpenglow Stube, accessible via gondola at the top of North Peak, is another of Keystone's superb dining choices. At 11,444 feet, this extraordinary room, where the cuisine is a match for the top-of-the-world views, is America's highest-altitude restaurant.

OFF-COURSE ATTRACTIONS

With dozens of miles of paved trails near the River Course as well as hundreds of miles of single-track trails and mountain roads, Keystone may well be the nation's premier mountain bike destination. From late June through early September, Keystone operates two ski lifts to transport bikers to the summits of Keystone Mountain and North Peak. The view from these ridge tops is spectacular, the downhill plunge even more so. Gentler trails are available for beginners. Keystone, which offers clinics for bikers of all abilities, is not just another place to ride a mountain bike. The resort has totally embraced the mountain bike culture and continues to maintain very steep trails for serious diehards.

Keystone also offers boating, rock climbing, fly fishing, hiking, horseback riding, horse-drawn wagon rides, scenic chairlift rides, wine tasting, and fitness classes.

Keystone Resort, River Course, 18th hole

albeit one with classic breeding. **The Raven Golf Club at Three Peaks,** a semi-private facility opened in 2000, is an entirely new design superimposed on the former Eagles Nest Golf Club. On a site with dramatic elevation changes at an altitude of up to 9,100 feet, the design team built a big course with four sets of tees ranging from 7,413 to 5,235 yards. Lehman, who loves to hit his driver, insisted on wide corridors for the fairways.

The most distinctive course feature, in addition to the astounding views of snow-capped peaks in the Gore Range, is the bunkering. The layout's massive, flashed-face bunkers, their fingers and fringes festooned with thick native vegetation, were designed to emulate those created by Dr. Alister MacKenzie in Australia's Sand Belt. Seemingly gouged from the landscape by a steam shovel run amok, these bunkers were in fact artfully crafted to "look" rough and were strategically placed to direct the line of play. The design team refers to its hurly-burly sand pits as "lighthouse bunkers," serving as beacons to guide players around the rough-and-tumble links. Just be sure to stay out of them. The layout's slick bentgrass greens are mostly open in front and invite bump-and-run shots, but a few have false fronts (another MacKenzie flourish) that reject less-than-noble efforts.

The back nine, with its more limited housing parcels, is the stronger and more scenic half of the course. Anchored by a rustic mountain lodge-style clubhouse, the well-groomed club employs an attentive, service-oriented staff, making it a country-club-for-the-day experience.

For many years, **Breckenridge Golf Club** was Jack Nicklaus's only municipal design in America. Debuted in 1985, the first nine, now called the Bear, was joined two years later by the Beaver nine. So popular was this superb mountain course set high in an alpine valley, a third nine was added in 2001. Today, the Town of Breckenridge is the only municipality in the world to own a 27-hole, Nicklaus-designed course.

A high-altitude test routed at an elevation of over 9,300 feet, the layout serves up panoramic views of the Rockies at holes that proceed from a thick forest to native grasslands. Players who secure early morning or late afternoon tee times may run across beaver, deer, elk and fox, with the occasional moose and black bear to be seen. Red tail hawks circle high overhead in the swirling mountain thermals.

The Raven Golf Club at Three Peaks, 11th hole

The Bear nine, set in a valley known to early-day gold miners as Buffalo Flats, is the most open of the three nines at Breckenridge, the holes skirting tall native grasses and pockets of wetlands. The Beaver nine, narrowest of the three, places a strong premium on accuracy. Taken together, the Bear and Beaver nines measure 7,276 yards from the Nicklaus tees, with a course rating of 73.5 and a slope of 151. From the tips, this is one of the toughest 18s in the Rockies.

While the first two nines can be considered beginner to intermediate in terms of terrain change, the new Elk nine is a black diamond trail that boasts the most dramatic elevation changes of the three as well as the most spectacular views of the Ten-Mile mountain range. Although more open than the Beaver nine, the Elk calls for accuracy. Also discretion. The short par-four sixth is a classic risk-reward hole, driveable even by medium hitters given the exalted elevation, but very dangerous for those who uncork a drive that goes long and wrong. Take a moment to savor the view on the next tee, at 9,445 feet the high point of the course and one of the prettiest spots on any course in the American West.

After the round, repair to the deck of the club's Buffalo Flats Restaurant to savor the view along with the fine refreshments. If you can plan your schedule accordingly, don't miss the club's Thursday Night BBQ, a favorite of locals.

Breckenridge Golf Club, Elk nine, seventh hole

Vail Valley, Colorado

Moving west from Summit County on I-70, the region's main thoroughfare and a marvel of engineering, travelers enter Vail, the world-famous ski resort and a gilded enclave where the current array of resort courses is now a match for the legendary slopes. Most of the region's new golf developments have arisen to the west of Vail in Edwards, Wolcott, and Eagle. Vail is of course known as a winter sports mecca, but its humidity-free summers are, for golfers, the equivalent of 300 inches of powder snow for skiers. Indeed, the weather for outdoor pursuits is ideal. Summer temperatures hover in the mid-70s and sun is abundant.

As befits one of the most affluent communities in America, the quality of life in Vail and its sister community of Beaver Creek is high. The collection of restaurants and art galleries tucked into the faux-Tyrolean buildings in pedestrian-only Vail is exceptional. Yet despite its prosperity, the purpose-built ski village and its environs are not stuffy. Posh, of course, but down to earth. Casual wear, not coat and tie, is the rule, even at the toniest dining spots.

With 54 holes of regulation golf, a 10-hole Short Course, and a fabulous European-style lodge with stellar mountain views that appear lifted from "The Sound of Music," **The Lodge & Spa at Cordillera** in Edwards is currently Colorado's premier golf resort and residential community.

The first venue to open at the Club at Cordillera was the **Mountain Course,** a burly Hale Irwin/Dick Phelps layout routed among towering firs, tall aspens, and open meadows in the shadow of the majestic New York Mountains. Debuted in 1994, it was renovated a few years later to enhance playability, i.e., landing

The Club at Cordillera, Summit, 16th hole

OFF-COURSE ATTRACTIONS

Needless to say, there are no couch potatoes in Vail. Here's the short list: Whitewater river rafting, jeep tours, scenic chairlift and gondola rides on Vail and Beaver Creek mountains, swimming, kayaking, sailboarding, hiking, mountain biking, tennis, hot-air ballooning, art gallery walks, horseback riding, sporting clays, cattle drives, and rock climbing. Excellent fly-fishing is available on Gore Creek as well as the Eagle and Colorado rivers.

For ultimate excitement, adventurers can try a guided thrill-sledding tour. (It's the fastest way down Vail Mountain.) The sleds have a hand-activated hydraulic brake system and ride on four independently suspended wheels. Also available is the gravity cart, a recumbent four-wheel, gravity-powered go-cart that races down the mountainside.

DINING

With as many restaurants to choose from as hiking trails, Vail's dining options are unsurpassed in the Rockies. A few favorites: The Wildflower in The Lodge at Vail serves excellent meals (including a gourmet breakfast) on an open-air patio set beside a gorgeous flower garden. Terra Bistro, located in the Vail Mountain Lodge & Spa, features innovative cuisine in an upbeat atmosphere. For 20-plus years, Sweet Basil has been pleasing patrons with Asian-influenced dishes as well as superb service. The Swiss Chalet at Sonnenalp features six different types of fondue, raclette, and other traditional alpine dishes. For great steaks, try Chap's Grill & Chophouse in the Vail Cascade Resort & Spa. The Left Bank and La Tour present award-winning French cuisine. There's even fresh seafood available at Billy's Island Grill and Montauk Seafood Grill.

At nearby Beaver Creek Resort, the top dining spot is the Grouse Mountain Grill, where the distinctive Rocky Mountain menu features superb side dishes and hearty portions along with a definitive wine list (a Vail-area specialty). The views of the valley from the restaurant's outdoor dining deck are lovely.

MUSIC, ART & CULTURE

Culture-wise, Vail has the clout of a major city with the added bonus of a spectacular mountain setting. *PRIMA*, the Vail Valley's cultural calendar, brings together three major arts festivals: Bravo! Vail Valley Music Festival, presenting chamber music, orchestra, and jazz concerts in beautiful mountain venues at Vail and Beaver Creek; the Beaver Creek Theatre Festival, founded in 2001 and already acclaimed for its diverse offerings of both classic and fringe performances; and the Vail International Dance Festival, featuring world-class dance artists in seasoned classics, contemporary masterpieces, and world premiers. Also noteworthy are the Vail Jazz Festival; the Hot Summer Nights concert series held at Gerald Ford Ampitheater in Vail (performances are free); and the Beaver Creek Film Festival.

Rock climbing in the Colorado Rockies

Whitewater river rafting near Vail

SHOPPING

Shopping in Vail has cemented the town's status as a premier destination. Native American handmade turquoise, coral, and silver pieces, such as Concha belts, earrings, necklaces, and bracelets, along with story wheels, are available at Squash Blossom. In addition to jewelry stores owned by artists such as Tom Hughes and Jim Cotter, other superb jewelry stores include Karats (known for one-of-a-kind commissioned pieces), Currents, A Place on Earth, and Gotthelf's, which offers a fine collection of American and Italian glass. The Golden Bear boasts the "signature of Vail" trademark, a golden bear set in rings and bracelets or worn on necklaces and earrings.

Gorsuch, one of Vail's oldest and best-known establishments, carries clothing for men, women, and children from top European lines along with high-end furnishings and linens. Pepi's Sports is the place for ultra-luxe skiwear. Need shoes for hiking, biking, and running, plus cowboy boots, clogs, and summer specials on ski boots? Check out Colorado Footwear, Vail Sports, Vail Boot & Shoe, Christy Sports, or Kenny's Double Diamond.

The Club at Cordillera, Summit, 13th hole

areas were widened so that players other than the arrow-straight Irwin could find the fairways. The Mountain is still a mountain that cannot be moved from the tips at 7,716 yards (the slope is 145, one of the highest in the area), this despite the extra yardage gained at 8,250 feet.

Cordillera's second course is a different kettle of fish. The **Valley Course** is a stellar Tom Fazio design routed in the shadows of the majestic Sawatch Range at an elevation 2,100 feet lower than the Mountain Course. Opened in 1997, this 7,413-yard layout is the perfect place for players who like to let out the shaft on their tee shots. Routed on south-facing slopes, Cordillera's Valley Course enjoys an extended season, with play available from April to November. Fazio's trademark playability is firmly in place, but cross hazards, notably creeks and chasms, must be negotiated. Indifferent approach shots tend to disappear in fescue-covered mounds or roll into deep, well-placed bunkers.

Routed through the high desert, its bowl-like fairways framed by piñon pine, sagebrush, and ancient junipers, the Valley Course is a poster child for the beauty of the Colorado Rockies. Fazio, a master at creating contours that blend with existing landforms, sculpted holes that minimize the vertigo-inducing effect of the mountain sideslopes. Even skiers who've never given golf a second thought have dropped by the clubhouse to take in the floor-to-ceiling view of this fabulous spread.

Want to go a little higher than the Mountain or the Valley? The course for you is the **Summit,** a Jack Nicklaus-designed behemoth unveiled in 2001. Crowning the pinnacle of the exclusive mountaintop retreat, this is the course that vaulted Cordillera to the top of the heap in the Colorado Rockies.

Marked by dizzying drops from tee to fairway, the aptly-named Summit, at just under 9,200 feet above sea level, is one of the highest 18-hole layouts in the nation. At nearly 7,600 yards from the tips (Nicklaus quipped that "All I need is 15 minutes and a weed whacker" to stretch the course to 8,000 yards), it's also one of the longest, but at this altitude, the added length is necessary to keep big hitters on their toes.

On what he called "one of the most dramatic sites I've ever seen," the Golden Bear scaled the heights to fashion a multi-theme track that begins in a forest of aspen and spruce, opens onto an alpine meadow, skirts a few wetlands, and weaves around rock outcrops. A round of golf here is nothing less than a turfgrass sleigh ride through the mountains. Earth-moving was kept to a minimum—Jack sought to blend his mammoth layout into the craggy terrain. Not only are the fairways lightly shaped, the slick bentgrass greens are among the most subtly contoured Nicklaus has ever built.

The Summit's back nine, with its sharper drops and steeper climbs, comes on strong. The 12th, a broad, downhill par four ranging from 375 to 504 yards, calls for a drive over a diagonal rock outcrop that doubles as a cross hazard. The only water on the course is found to the left of the 12th green, but keep an eye on the rocky bluffs beyond the putting surface: Two active bear dens have been identified among the cliffs. The par-three 16th gives players an unobstructed view of the three million acres in the

White River National Forest adjoining the course, while the par-four 18th, a bruiser at 474 yards from the tips, offers panoramic views from the high point of the layout.

From late May through early October, the sage-brush-covered hills at this Everestian spread are alive with the sound of golfers gasping for superlatives.

In addition to the three main tracks, Cordillera also offers the **Short Course,** a 10-hole par-three course designed by short-game guru Dave Pelz. The modestly scaled layout is designed to boost a begin-ner's confidence but also challenge experts to sharpen their pitching, chipping, and putting skills.

A 21st-century version of luxe life in the Rockies? **Red Sky Golf Club,** centerpiece of a $100-million golf community in Wolcott 25 minutes west of Vail, defines it.

While it's a private membership club, Red Sky's 36 holes are also open to guests of properties owned and managed by Vail Resorts. The club's enlightened policy dictates that members and guests alternate

Yoga at Cordillera

LODGE & SPA

Cordillera's centerpiece is a slate-roofed Lodge inspired by luxurious chalets in the Pyrenees. The 56-room manor-style hotel is staffed by internationals schooled in the fundamentals of European-style service. Spacious, high-ceilinged rooms, many with wood-burning fireplaces, have balconies or patios facing the majestic Sawatch Mountains. In addition to the beautifully-appointed Lodge, the resort also makes available for rent three-, four-, and five-bedroom homes in a variety of architectural styles and locations.

The resort's European-style Spa, designed to nurture body, mind, and spirit, features wellness programs, body treatments, massage, facials, and nail treatments. Among the signature treatments is the invigorating Wildflower Scrub, which uses mineral-rich sea salts to exfoliate the skin and stimulate circulation.

DINING

Cordillera boasts four distinctive restaurants, each with a different menu, décor, and high-country setting.

Restaurant Picasso, Cordillera's signature dining room, features light interpretations of gourmet European fare in a room highlighted by original Picasso lithographs. The wine list is extensive. Chaparral is a casual steakhouse, while the Timber Hearth Grille in the Mountain Course clubhouse features American cuisine with Western flair. And then there's Grouse-on-the-Green, an authentic pub (its interior was designed and built in Ireland) that functions as both eatery and clubhouse for the Short Course. Shepherd's pie, fish 'n chips, and other traditional entrees pair well with the pub's fine selection of microbrew beers.

play daily between the two layouts, designed by Tom Fazio and Greg Norman. This flip-flop system is the ultimate win-win for an unattached player at a club where the invitation-only memberships start at $175,000, and home sites—just the dirt!—average $750,000. Members and guests are each served by their own clubhouses.

The two courses, completely different in personality, are divided by a massive ridge that serves as a wildlife corridor for deer and elk. Unveiled in 2002, the **Fazio Course** at this 780-acre development unfolds at more than 7,000 feet above sea level on a former sheep ranch, with holes routed through sage-covered hills and thick groves of aspen. A 7,113-yard tour de force that switchbacks its way up a steep mountainside, the Fazio Course, carpeted with lush bluegrass fairways, was built wide to accommodate all styles of play. Elevated tees serve up stellar views of Castle Peak to the west and Vail's fabled Back Bowls to the east.

After a front nine that ambles through a high-desert setting, the back nine delves deeper into the Rockies. The 12th hole, like the third, is a short par four that tempts big hitters to go for the green, but the direct route at both is perilous. As on all Fazio designs, the accent is on playability, although players expecting a carefree round should check the club's address: Bellyache Ridge Road. (The large, speedy greens have been known to tie an unsteady putter's stomach into knots.) However, the major challenge here is concentrating on the task at hand, so breathtaking is the scenery—and the 600-foot elevation change from start to finish.

Loads of dynamite were required to make way for the course. "The rock blasting here was unbelievable," says director of golf Jeff Hanson. "We knew these were the Rocky Mountains, but we didn't think they were *that* rocky." To the development team's credit, more than 23,000 sage plants and another 2,200 juniper and serviceberry bushes were salvaged during course construction and later replanted as part of an extensive revegetation program.

Red Sky's Fazio Course was joined in 2003 by the **Norman Course**, the Shark's first design in the Rockies. Stretching to 7,580 yards from the tips, the Norman Course, situated high above the Fazio layout and separated from it by a ridge, is set in a deep, bowl-like valley. Holes criss-cross back and forth through aspens, junipers, and twisted knots of scrub oak. Craggy red-rock outcrops, deep gulches, a fast-flowing river, and wildflower meadows frame the fairways. In other words, it is a true wilderness expe-

Red Sky Golf Club, Fazio Course, finishing holes and clubhouse

rience—with plenty of teeth. The Fazio Course can be negotiated from the forward tees by golfers who play the percentages and master (or at least avoid three-putting) the large, slippery greens. The longer, narrower Norman Course presents a much firmer test for the simple reason that Norman, like Jack Nicklaus early in his design career, tends to build courses that meet his own scintillating standards of play. There is, to be sure, adequate room to drive the ball, with several inviting downhill tee shots in the mix, but the greens, defined by shaved bentgrass collars, are well-bunkered and medium-to-small in size. They're also tilted, crowned, or multi-tiered. These slender targets are tough to hit and even tougher to putt.

That said, players who choose the correct set of tees for their ability level will encounter a firm but fair test, one with minimal rough off the fairways. Only Norman or a visiting Tour player would choose to tackle the tips, especially on the ninth hole, a beastly

par four that measures *559 yards*. Then again, players will understand that Red Sky's motto—"Elbow room for the soul"—is no idle boast from the topmost tees of the spectacular Norman Course.

There was indeed a golf building boom in the Vail Valley around the time of the millennium, but most of the new venues were built at upscale resorts and exclusive clubs. In fact, until Arnold Palmer rode in on his white horse to open **Eagle Ranch Golf Course** in 2001, there hadn't been a new 18-hole daily-fee course built in the Vail area since 1975. Eagle Ranch has fulfilled its mandate to give locals and visitors alike a great new place to tee it up at reasonable rates.

Located 30 miles west of Vail, Eagle is one of the prettiest and best-preserved small mountain towns in America. On a former cattle ranch on the outskirts of town, Palmer, along with design associates Vicki Martz and Eric Larsen, fashioned a roomy test of golf with five sets of tees per hole. Set at an altitude of 6,600 feet above sea level (1,600 feet lower than Vail), the course gives experts all they can handle from the tips at 7,530 yards, yet from the forward tees even the Happy Gilmores of the world can have a blast without getting flattened. Landing areas are *wide*—Palmer loves to hit his driver, and wants you to enjoy taking a rip with yours, too. Also, the subtly contoured greens are sizable, averaging well over 7,000 square feet. A fun course that accommodates all styles of play, Eagle Ranch encourages creative "bump-and-run" shots around the greens.

Backdropped by craggy spires in the Sawatch Range, the layout's gently rolling fairways, stretched across the floor of Brush Creek Valley, are staked out by large-scale bunkers, many of them dotted with grassy islands. Water is a dominant theme at Eagle Ranch and comes into play at half the holes. Streams cascade through rock outcrops and feed many of the ponds on the course. According to Martz, "Mr. Palmer loves the sound of moving water." So will golfers if they can avoid it.

Unlike higher-altitude courses in the area marked by sharper elevation changes, Eagle Ranch can be walked without fear of bumping into a bighorn sheep or expiring due to lack of oxygen. The region enjoys a salubrious banana-belt climate—Eagle's golf season is two months longer than it is in Vail itself, with play extending to early November.

LODGING

Red Sky Golf Club is open to guests of lodging properties owned and managed by Vail Resorts, the club's developer. These include many of the top lodging entities in the valley: the **Lodge at Vail,** the **Inn at Beaver Creek, Vail Marriott Mountain Resort & Spa,** the **Pines Lodge,** plus condos and private homes in the Vail/Beaver Creek Resort Properties portfolio. Also included is the valley's most prominent newcomer, the **Ritz-Carlton Bachelor Gulch,** a 237-room property inspired by grand old National Park lodges at Grand Teton, Yosemite, and Yellowstone. Opened in 2002, the hotel, nestled at the base of Beaver Creek Mountain, is accented by rough-hewn logs, tons of indigenous stone, and 100 fireplaces, one of them an impressive three-story fieldstone chimney that rises from the lobby's polished barn-wood floor. "Parkitecture" is the name that's been coined for this rustic-chic style. The Ritz-Carlton, located 15 minutes from Red Sky, offers complimentary transportation to the club. At press time, golf packages at this deluxe property were a relative bargain: In 2005, it was possible to stay-and-play there for $280 per night.

Red Sky Golf Club, Fazio Course, 14th hole

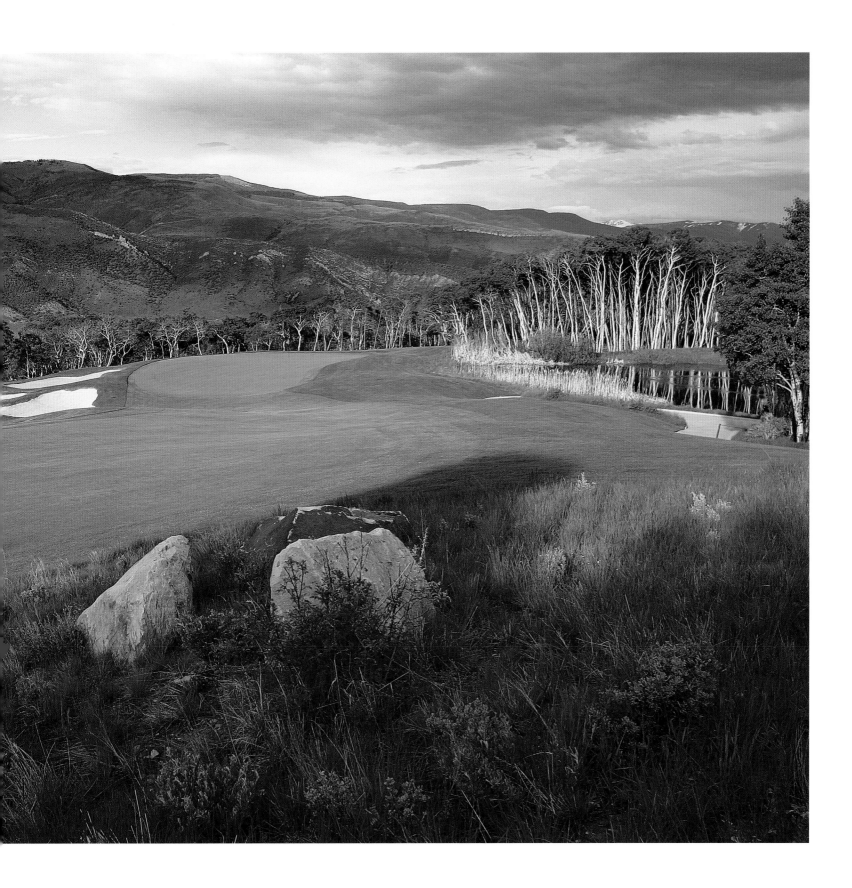

Southwest

Las Vegas

Like most success stories, it happened overnight. What began as a scrubby plot of Nevada desert with a modest hotel-casino in the mid-1940s is now a turbo-charged gaming and entertainment mecca that continues to grow by leaps and bounds. The destination, of course, is Las Vegas, a frenzied city of dreams known as much for its quickie weddings (and divorces) as its endless rows of one-armed bandits.

In the pale Mojave Desert on the outskirts of an unashamedly glitzy city that gets more sun and less rain than just about any other place in the nation, a number of stellar daily-fee courses have sprung up in the past few years. WARNING: If you're squeamish about shelling out lots of money for a green fee, if anything well into three figures makes you tremble when you reach for your wallet, skip Vegas. The sub-$100 fee here is rare. The top tracks—*ka-ching!*—start at $250. What you generally get for your money is a well-groomed spread by a name designer, one with firm, fast greens and emerald fairways woven through raw desert or mountain foothills (or a housing complex).

When the round is done, there's enough to do at night to make all other Sun Belt destinations despair. Vegas is hot and stays hot by constantly reinventing itself. Nearly 40 million people visited Las Vegas in 2005 to catch the excitement and discover for themselves if this ultimate symbol of hubris and money is everything it's cracked up to be. Verdict: the "wow" factor is so big in Vegas right now, only the most jaded travelers leave unimpressed. Even for those who don't gamble, Vegas boasts the greatest assemblage of hotels, restaurants, spas, and nightclubs on earth, many of them crowded along a four-mile-long, neon-lit boulevard called the Strip. Bring a taste for (or a willingness to appreciate) the phantasmagorical, and Glitter City, which celebrated its centennial in 2005, will not disappoint.

Drawbacks? The mercury routinely hits 115 in the summer months. (Spring and fall are the best times to go.) And water, or rather the lack of it, generated by aquifers and the Colorado River Basin, may limit the number of new courses that can be built in the years ahead.

HENDERSON

Many of the top public-access facilities in the vicinity of Vegas have arisen 40 minutes southeast of The Strip in Henderson, itself one of the fastest-growing small cities in America. Located along the main route to Hoover Dam and Lake Mead, Henderson, with a population of more than 210,000 (its growth rate since 1990 is over 170%), is a progressive municipality where the median age is 35.9 years and where the pace of life is slower and quieter than in Vegas itself. If you like your weather dry and bright, this is the place—annual rainfall is four inches, relative humidity is 29 percent, sunny days number 320-plus.

From this arid desert at 2,000 feet above sea level has arisen **Lake Las Vegas Resort,** a $4.5 billion destination built around the state's largest privately-owned lake, a placid body of water with 10 miles of shoreline. This upscale Mediterranean-themed development—Italy is no stranger to Vegas—offers two superb resort courses with a third on the way.

Like most of Jack Nicklaus's recent design work, **Reflection Bay Golf Club,** debuted in 1998, is playable by mere mortals, not just by the Golden Bear in his prime. Five holes on this oasis-like spread in the desert play directly along 1 1/2 miles of Lake Las Vegas, with five additional holes highlighted by major water features.

The tone at Reflection Bay, currently ranked 36th on *Golf Magazine's* list of the "Top 100 You Can Play," is set from the start. A complete sensory experience, players follow a cascading stream laced with waterfalls that eventually spills into a pond on their way from the range to the first tee. Opening holes are routed around canyons on sloping terrain skirted by arroyos and backdropped by stark peaks. Symmetrical in design, the early holes on each nine rise in elevation along the deep-cut canyons, reverse at midpoint, and play dramatically downhill thereafter. The finishing sequence on each nine reaches a memorable climax beside the man-made lake. Along the way, players are treated to a pair of strategic gems at the par-four second and 13th holes, each with a central bunker to direct players left or right. And then there's the improbable 40-foot-high waterfall beside the green at the fifth. After parking the golf cart in a shady oasis, players reach the putting surface by crossing a stream on large, flat stepping stones.

Like all fine courses, Reflection Bay builds in interest as the round progresses. The boomerang-shaped par-five 18th, with water in play up the entire right side of the hole and nests of bunkers and beaches working in and out along the shoreline, is a grand finale to one of Nicklaus's most versatile layouts. In fact, with the possible exception of his Hawaii designs, Reflection Bay is Jack's finest resort course in the U.S. This memorable, well-groomed test, stretching 7,261 yards, is anchored by an elegant 32,000-square-foot waterside clubhouse.

Nicklaus and Tom Weiskopf, who are as competitive with each other in the design field as they were as PGA Tour players, have each created venues at multiple-course facilities, notably in Palm Springs and Mexico. On the heels of Reflection Bay, Weiskopf was handed an extremely rugged parcel near the entrance to Lake Las Vegas, a barren, craggy site that appears lifted from an ochre-and-tan planet. Not even cactus grows in these desolate badlands. The designer, who has crafted some of the finest courses on his résumé in the Southwest, turned out a gravity-defying layout called **The Falls Golf Club,** which opened to acclaim in 2002.

The first six holes on this surreal 7,243-yard *wun-derkind* are splayed among rocky arroyos on descending land, the broad, rolling fairways trimmed with sagebrush and staked out by large, sculpted bunkers. There's a hint of things to come at the seventh, a narrow, uphill par five dropped into a rocky defile and crossed by an arroyo at the green, but there's nothing to prepare players for the back nine of The Falls, which is named for a cascade that tumbles from a stony cliff high above the course.

The layout reaches its zenith at holes 12 through 14, a trio that appears airbrushed on the rocks. The golf holes may seem improbable, but the herd of bighorn sheep that grazes here is real. The 12th, a jaw-dropping par five routed up and over the side of a mountain, calls for a blind tee shot to a rising fairway, a semi-blind second over a saddle, and then a downhill approach to a green that appears to hang in the air, with a dizzying view of the Vegas skyline far below. Take aim at the Stratosphere Tower on the Strip, the tallest building west of the Mississippi.

The par-four 13th, beautiful and stark, is a genuine original. The hole plunges from a skybox tee to a narrow, well-bunkered fairway laid into a canyon, a peek-a-boo green tucked to the right behind a perforated fist of rock. It's not long at 388 yards, but only an accurate drive and a leap-of-faith pitch will do. The 14th is a "driveable" par four that drops nearly 200 feet to an artfully bunkered fairway, although a nice straight tee shot leaves only a wedge—and a chance for one's heart rate to return to normal.

Reflection Bay Golf Club, ninth hole

The Falls, the yang to Reflection Bay's yin, is not a golf course in the traditional sense. It's a geology field book and rock climber's guide with fairways and greens mixed in.

As good as The Falls and Reflection Bay are, they could be equaled or perhaps even surpassed by **Rainbow Canyon,** a Tom Fazio–designed layout currently under development at Lake Las Vegas. The course, with four to five holes routed beside the water, will offer a combination of lake, mountain, and desert settings. A 2008 debut is anticipated.

Etched into the rolling foothills of the Black Mountain Range on the outskirts of Henderson is **Rio Secco Golf Club,** a target-style test carved into steeply pitched terrain spread out among canyons, plateaus, and a river bottom. Designed by Rees Jones in 1997, this imaginatively routed layout, framed by an upscale housing development, leapfrogs from one interesting land feature to the next. In fact, there are three distinct themes at Rio Secco. Six holes are stretched across high plateaus, with fine long views of Vegas; six holes occupy a dried-up riverbed and a broad desert wash; and six holes are laid into V-shaped canyons. So carefully was the course draped onto the terrain, only one hole at Rio Secco was dynamited to alter the landscape for golf.

Among the feature holes on this brawny 7,332-yard layout is the par-four seventh, its fairway encased in a box canyon and its green set below a sheer 40-foot wall of rock. But the best holes at Rio Secco are its heroic one-shotters, notably the 180-yard 12th, which calls for an all-or-nothing, trans-canyon tee shot to a pedestal green. Befitting a championship-caliber spread, course conditions are fast and firm. Home to the Butch Harmon School of Golf, Rio Secco is where Tiger Woods, Harmon's former star pupil, honed his swing in his early days on Tour. Owned by Harrah's Entertainment, Rio Secco is available to guests of the Rio Suite Hotel & Casino.

Another fine Henderson complex can be found at **The Revere Golf Club,** its pair of Billy Casper/Greg Nash courses set within a housing community. **Lexington,** the original layout, is paved through steep canyons, although nearly every drive is played downhill, a confidence-builder. **Concord,** debuted in 2002, is softer and more forgiving, with wider fairways and more accessible greens. There are, however, significant elevation changes, with the par-five 18th plunging 150 feet from tee to green. The courses, among the

best-conditioned in Vegas, are named for the first two stops on Paul Revere's historic midnight ride.

DragonRidge Golf Club, a semi-private facility set in the foothills of the McCullough Mountains in Henderson, was laid out on topsy-turvy terrain by Jay Morrish and David Druzisky in 2000 and offers panoramic views of the Vegas skyline and the valley below from its topmost holes. Large directional bunkers and blackened lava rock outcrops characterize the layout, its holes placed into canyons and intersected by arroyos. The 441-yard seventh, which bends to the right around a lake and waterfall and plays uphill to a well-defended green, is one of the best par fours in Vegas.

Another area option is **Wildhorse Golf Club.** According to *VegasGolfer Magazine,* "Wildhorse has changed its name almost as many times as Liberace changed his shoes." Known as Paradise Valley Country Club when it opened in 1959 and former host to a PGA Tour event, the 7,053-yard course, centerpiece of the Green Valley community, was reworked in 2000 by Bob Cupp and Hubert Green. The layout's watery finish is one of the strongest in Vegas. There's also a Nike Golf Learning Center on site.

Among the region's newer venues is **Boulder Creek Golf Club,** a 27-hole municipal facility built for $22 million and opened in 2003 in Boulder City near Henderson. The club's first two nines, Desert Hawk and Coyote Run, are laid into raw desert as well as oasis-like settings accented by palm trees, lakes, beach bunkers, and waterfalls. A newer third nine, Eldorado Valley, is a big hitter's paradise with plenty of elbow room and gorgeous mountain views, though creeks come into play at several holes. The golf throughout is straightforward: no blind shots, no hidden hazards. At press time, weekday green fee rates starting at $75 were a relative bargain by Vegas standards. Walkers can subtract $15 from the fee.

For a pleasant country-club-style experience, head to **Tuscany Golf Club,** a Ted Robinson design set within a golf course community north of Lake Mead. This player-friendly course, unveiled in 2003, has water features at four holes along with fine views of the surrounding mountains and distant Vegas skyline. The club's green fee structure is well below the area norm.

LAS VEGAS
Given the city's explosive growth in the past decade, course construction has kept pace with the surging real estate market. New fields of play have popped up to serve locals and visitors alike, especially to the north and west. Downtown, the Strip is a place of unbridled change, with new hotels, casinos, restau-

The Falls Golf Club, 13th hole

Left: Rio Secco Golf Club, seventh hole

Top: Rio Secco Golf Club, ninth hole

Above: The Revere Golf Club, Concord, 18th hole

WHERE TO STAY/HENDERSON

The 496-room, Moroccan-themed **Hyatt Regency Lake Las Vegas Resort,** terraced into a hillside on 21 acres opposite Reflection Bay Golf Club, made its debut in 1999. Guest rooms have views of the lake, mountains, and palm-lined fairways. The primary location for the filming of *America's Sweethearts,* starring Julia Roberts, Catherine Zeta-Jones, Billy Crystal, and John Cusack, the Hyatt Regency features a full-service spa and fitness center as well as innovative Pacific Rim cuisine (and excellent sushi) in its signature restaurant, Japengo. In addition to two swimming pools with palm-shaded terraces and a waterslide, the hotel's European-style Casino Baraka offers slot, video, and table games.

One-fifth of the rooms and suites at the 349-room **Ritz-Carlton, Lake Las Vegas,** unveiled in 2003, occupy a replica of the Pontevecchio Bridge in Florence, its arches spanning the lake's inner harbor and linking different quarters of MonteLago Village, a stage set evocative of Tuscany, Portofino, and tiny hillside hamlets in northern Italy's lake district. Specialty shops, waterside restaurants, and outdoor cafes ring the shores of the lake. A 40,000-square-foot casino, accessible by a grand staircase from the village plaza, is attached to the hotel. Adjacent to the Ritz-Carlton is a deluxe 30,000-square-foot spa. Dining is available both poolside and within the resort, which ranks among the most architecturally daring in the Ritz-Carlton chain.

OFF-COURSE ATTRACTIONS/HENDERSON

At Lake Las Vegas Resort, take a bike ride or long walk around the lake, or rent a kayak, paddleboat, canoe, sailboat, or an electric boat for a spin around the water. Catch-and-release fishing for largemouth bass is also available. Self-guided hikes to the area's unique desert rock formations, notably the Rainbow Gardens Geological Preserve a mile from the resort, are popular.

A 30-minute drive east of Henderson is the Boulder City Historic District as well as Hoover Dam, an engineering marvel that captured the nation's attention when it was built to block the Colorado River in 1936. Tours of the 727-foot-high, 660-foot-thick dam and power plant are available daily. Behind the wall of cement is Lake Mead, at 247 square miles the largest man-made lake in the western hemisphere. One of the Southwest's largest recreation areas, it offers water skiing, jet skiing, and other water sports. Sightseeing boat tours are also available. Black Canyon raft trips, which visit caves, hot springs, and sandy coves, are as impressive as the dam itself.

Valley of Fire, Nevada's oldest state park, derives its name from brilliant red sandstone formations created by shifting sand dunes. Mysterious drawings scratched on the sandstone by Anasazi Indians centuries ago can be viewed. Hummer tours of the park can be arranged.

Hyatt Regency Lake Las Vegas Resort

DragonRidge Golf Club, seventh hole

rants, shopping arcades, and entertainment spectacles emerging on almost a daily basis to keep Vegas fresh.

Some 20 miles northwest of the Strip is **Las Vegas Paiute Golf Resort,** a housing-free, 54-hole complex developed by the Paiute Indians on a reservation given to the tribe by Congress in 1983. Massive 11,918-foot Mt. Charleston and smaller peaks and spires in the Sheep Range backdrop the resort's three Pete Dye courses.

The resort's first layout, **Nu-Wav Kaiv (Snow Mountain),** debuted in 1995, could pass for a course in Palm Springs. Fairways are broad, green approaches are open, and the white tees at 6,035 yards take most of the rattler habitats and watery graves out of play for duffers. Fairways are framed by shaggy-trunked Joshua trees, creosote bush, and

other vegetation that can survive on the scant four inches of rain per year the region receives.

Tav-Ai Kaiv (Sun Mountain), opened in 1997, is a compact layout with more pronounced mounding beside its fairways and greens. Players also must contend with more bunkers and waste areas on this 7,112-yard desert links, though very few golfers tee it up from the tips. Bogey shooters can have a good time from the regular tees at 6,074 yards. Built on a rock pile, Tav-Ai Kaiv, like its predecessor, boasts very swift greens.

The resort's top venue and shot-for-shot one of the best in Nevada is the **Wolf,** which opened to raves (and howls) in 2001. The design of the course was a family affair, with Pete Dye assisted by sons Perry and P.B. as well as his niece, Cynthia Dye McGarry. The look—raw, vast, and wild—is totally different from the other two courses. Cone-shaped mounds and ridges strewn with rocks delineate the Wolf's undulating fairways, which are broad but strategically bunkered. All is not bleak, however: Beautiful red and orange mission poppies blanket a landscape dotted with yuccas and Joshua trees, with the stark Spring Mountains a strong presence in the distance. The layout's tabletop greens, while sizable, are artfully defended by pot bunkers, grassy hollows, and steep drop-offs. From the regular tees, the enticing par fives average well under 500 yards, but the Wolf may have the sharpest teeth in town from the technology-proof tournament tees at 7,604 yards (149 slope, 76.3 course rating).

For serious players who choose to wrestle the Wolf from the waybacks, the finish will provide all the answers to your questions. There's the obligatory island-style par three at the 15th, only here the green is triple-tiered and trimmed with rocks, not railroad ties. At 182 yards, it's also quite a bit longer than the original at the TPC at Sawgrass. The concluding trio—three murderous par fours of 427, 486, and 496 yards, each calling for a long, straight drive and an unerring approach to a well-defended target—is merciless. Playing the Wolf is like being stalked by one, unless you exercise more prudence than valor in choosing a set of tees (there are five).

The Wolf commands a premium above the other two courses, but this stunning desert links is a premier test of golf. The tribe has plans to build a fourth course by Dye as well as a resort hotel and other amenities at their $500-million complex.

An excellent newcomer west of the Strip is **Bear's Best** in Summerlin, a compilation of Jack Nicklaus's signature holes drawn from desert and mountain environments in the southwestern U.S. and Mexico. It must be a wonderful thing to get to a point in your career when you can borrow from yourself to produce something of value. The holes are not merely inspired by Nicklaus's favorite designs, they are exact duplicates that capture the look, feel, and challenge of the originals. Selections for the design of each hole were based on how well the topography matched the original location. Much care and thought went into this process, which is why this greatest-hits collection from the game's greatest player is a winner.

Opened in 2001, this 7,194-yard stunner, set at 3,200 feet above sea level, is a big, brawny course pushed up against the base of the Red Rock Mountain range. Broad sandy washes snake across several of the fairways. As is true throughout the valley, the greens are extremely quick. Many of the putting surfaces are elevated and set on a diagonal to the line of play, making them tough to hit. There's a generous bail-out on every hole, but shot-makers need to take a few risks in return for par. Driving zones are wide, but the uphill second shots are very demanding on the longer holes.

Among the more striking recreations at Bear's Best is the par-three fourth, which was inspired by a one-shotter at Old Works in Montana and, like the original, has glistening black slag in its bunkers. A pair of par fours lifted from Eldorado and Palmilla in Baja California Sur, Mexico, Nos. 5 and 6, are excellent, even without the Sea of Cortez at their feet. And while an ocean could not be imported, Bear's Best goes the extra mile where possible. There are tall saguaros to match the cacti at six Arizona holes. There are pines on the eighth in tribute to the 14th at Castle Pines in Colorado, and palms alongside a pair of holes that replicate holes drawn from PGA West in the California desert. The magnificent 463-yard 18th, patterned after the 18th hole on the Resort Course at PGA West, may be better than the original.

Steve Wynn, the visionary behind the Mirage, Bellagio and other major casino hotels, helped to spur a building boom in Vegas in the late 1990s. Wynn was chairman of Mirage Resorts, Inc. until the company was sold to MGM Grand for $6.4 billion in 2000. The sale included Shadow Creek. Not one to sit still, Wynn embarked on a new $2.7 billion project: **Wynn Las Vegas.**

Located on the site of the former Desert Inn, which he bought for $270 million and soon demolished,

Las Vegas Paiute Golf Resort, Wolf, 15th hole

Bear's Best, fifth hole

Wynn's 2,716-room mega-resort, opened in 2005, is an ultra-luxe property located directly on the Strip. Contained within a gleaming, crescent-shaped tower, the hotel's rooms and suites feature floor-to-ceiling windows, plush European linens, and high-speed wireless Internet access.

Entertainment? Wynn and Franco Dragone, the creative mastermind behind Cirque du Soleil's productions, have created a show (lots of female synchronized swimmers in red stiletto heels) for the hotel's 2,100-seat theater called "Le Reve" (French for "The Dream"). The art gallery features works by Picasso, Monet, Van Gogh, and Matisse. The resort also offers nine fine dining restaurants and six casual food outlets, including a Daniel Boulud Brasserie. The property's ample shopping arcade has upwards of 30 high-end retail shops. In the market for shiny new Italian wheels after a good night at the tables in the 110,000-square-foot casino? Wynn Las Vegas offers a full-service Ferrari Maserati dealership.

When the time came to blow up the Desert Inn's golf course and create a parkland track for the 21st century amid the bustle and neon of downtown Vegas, Wynn called Tom Fazio to rekindle a design partnership forged in the 1980s at Shadow Creek. Their creation is pure Vegas. For starters, the first tee is all of 50 feet from the pro shop on the hotel's ground floor, which means this verdant spread dou-

bles as a backyard for the resort. There is a deliberate sense of containment here: The 7,042-yard, par-70 layout is marked by dished-out landing areas walled in by high, rolling berms landscaped with flowers and trees. These berms sequester players from the city's feverish pulse and also corral stray shots. Most of the holes are routed on a north-south bias to accentuate the play of light and shadow on the undulating fairways and sculpted bunkers.

While there is plenty of challenge from the tips, the course is player-friendly from the forward tees. No struggling or searching for stray shots in the rough. The layout's five par threes, three of which have water in play, rival "Le Reve" for theatricality. Wynn, a master showman, ensured that the course builds to a dramatic finale. The 17th, at 498 yards from the tips, may be the toughest two-shotter in town, but it's the oasis-like 18th that lingers in the memory. This stunning 448-yard par four leads to a large, sloping green with water left, sand right, and a 37-foot-high, horseshoe-shaped waterfall behind the putting surface. Stagecraft at its finest.

The golf course is open to resort guests only. The green fee is a regal $500. Each group is assigned a forecaddie. For high rollers who want to gaze upon green grass when they arise, 36 of the resort's one- and two-bedroom suites are sequestered in villas spaced along the 18th fairway.

BATTLE OF THE HIGH END: CASCATA VS. SHADOW CREEK

OK, you're a Player. Not single-digit. *Multi-digit.* You will establish a serious line of credit and/or have oodles of ready cash to be wagered. But you're also a golfer. You want to tee it up at a very special place, a place where the "experience" is more, much more, than the sum of 18 holes. You have two options. By the way, while others will pay, you will be comped, of course.

Get cozy at a Caesars Entertainment casino hotel, namely Caesars Palace, Bally's, Paris, or Flamingo, and your venue of choice is **Cascata,** an enclave unto itself on the outskirts of Boulder City south of Henderson. Built for a reported $60 million, Cascata, Italian for "waterfall," exudes privilege. A Rees Jones design sculpted from the side of a mountain and creased by ancient stream beds now revived with water, the 7,137-yard course, opened in 2000, was landscaped with thousands of flowering plants and date palms to soften the stark terrain. Each hole occupies its own corridor, separated from the others by tall ridges. Where necessary, green sites were dynamited from rock cliffs. For speed and quality, the putting surfaces are comparable to any fine private club you care to name. Man-made water features—streams tumbling down stony hills, rushing greenside waterfalls—are abundant. Cascata is both a premier test of golf and an aesthetic triumph. On a clear day, the panoramic views from the topmost holes across El Dorado Valley to purple-tinged mountains in the far distance are breathtaking.

The golf course is just the beginning at Cascata. A river rushes through the center of the facility's ultra-swank, Tuscan-themed clubhouse. All requests—a beer, a cigar, you name it—are fulfilled graciously. Cascata, in sum, defines the ultra-luxe golf experience. The club revamped its invitation-only policy in 2004, welcoming guests of any of the aforementioned Caesars Entertainment hotels—at a price. Green fees are $350 on weekdays, $500 on weekends. Cart is included.

Looking for something as high-end as Cascata but a little more "traditional"? Your club of choice is **Shadow Creek,** which dates to 1989—positively vintage by Vegas standards. Currently ranked ninth on *Golfweek's* list of America's Top 100 Modern Golf Courses (post-1959), this Holy Grail for high rollers in North Las Vegas, a once ultra-exclusive enclave built by Tom Fazio and casino mogul Steve Wynn for an estimated $46 million, offers a limited number of tee times from Monday through Thursday to guests of MGM Mirage hotels. These include the Bellagio, MGM Grand, Mirage, New York-New York, and Treasure Island. The $500 fee includes cart, caddie, and limousine service to and from the club.

As a golf course, Shadow Creek is the realized dream of a visionary kingpin who was not afraid to spend lots of money to create something where nothing had existed. From a desiccated site, Wynn and Fazio built their own temperate zone, complete with lush vegetation and exotic birdlife. There are specimen trees, gurgling streams, and verdant, rolling fairways. Conditions are flawless. An engineering feat extraordinaire—the oasis-like setting arises from a dead-flat parcel of raw desert—Shadow Creek is, quite simply, one of the greatest manufactured courses on earth. To create features where none existed, Fazio and his design team dug deep into the desert floor and bulldozed three million cubic yards of earth into rolling mounds and ridges. The stands of transplanted pine and cottonwood trees are so thick, it appears the fairways were actually carved from a forest!

Shadow Creek, in sum, is the greatest feat of legerdemain imaginable. No Vegas illusionist can top it.

A river runs through Cascata's clubhouse

Cascata, seventh hole

Located in North Las Vegas, **Aliante Golf Club,** opened in 2003, was designed by Gary Panks, an Arizona-based architect who works almost exclusively in the desert. Numerous water features, spacious landing areas, and the strategic use of mature trees highlight the design of this 7,022-yard course. But true to his roots, Panks made the signature element at Aliante a meandering arroyo that comes into play at 14 holes and gives players the sensation of feeling slightly elevated. Experts are challenged by interesting fairway contours and clever hole angles, while higher handicappers can expect an enjoyable outing—if they can steer clear of the ever-present arroyo.

If you want to play where the pros play, head for the **TPC at the Canyons,** which is one of two courses that hosts the PGA Tour's Las Vegas event (the other, the TPC at Summerlin, is private). Situated nine miles northwest of the Strip, this beguiling layout has slim landing pods that look like green band-aids placed into the desert. Designed by Bobby Weed and Ray Floyd, the course, debuted in 1996, is set within a housing development but has fine views of the Vegas valley and nearby Red Rock Canyon. To speed play and keep egos intact, the raw desert and winding canyons that pinch the fairways are played as lateral hazards. The bentgrass greens, embraced by sculpted hollows and swales, are liberally contoured and very speedy. With little fanfare, the J W Marriott prop-

erty at the far end of the course, originally built as a Regent, quietly retains its stature as one of the finest hotels in Vegas. Its European-style spa is exceptional.

More choices on the northern outskirts of town? There's **SilverStone Golf Club,** a Bob Cupp design that offers three distinct nines, its Desert-Mountain tandem a solid 18-holer highlighted by the Mountain's par-five third, at 653 yards Nevada's longest hole. Or **The Badlands,** a severe 27-hole target-style layout woven through dry washes that has little margin for error and takes no prisoners. ("Like an E-ticket ride at Disneyland," designer Johnny Miller calls it.)

For a more sedate outing, head 20 minutes west of the Strip to **Siena Golf Club,** a well-groomed, country club-style spread in Summerlin marked by six lakes and nearly 100 bunkers. Its oasis-like neighbor is the Arnold Palmer-designed **Arroyo Course** at **Red Rock Country Club.** Opened in 2003, the Arroyo, routed through a series of desert canyons, relies on dramatic water hazards for its challenge. The course will remain open to outside play until its membership rolls are filled.

The only course of note east of the Strip is **Royal Links Golf Club,** a fast-running, links-style track sprinkled with holes lifted from British Open venues old and new. Designer Perry Dye, Pete's elder son, moved 1.4 million cubic yards of dirt and installed over 120 stacked sod wall bunkers to create the Auld

Shadow Creek, eighth hole

Sod look at the base of Sunrise Mountain. The course and its faux-castle clubhouse, opened in 1999, are totally ersatz conceptions in this barren landscape, but it's Vegas, so somehow it works.

Located on the Strip itself within a chip shot of the action is **Bali Hai Golf Club.** This South Seas–themed design, landscaped in jasmine, honeysuckle, and thousands of date palms, is a good strategic test, its front nine staked out by flashed-face bunkers, black lava outcrops, and water hazards, its back nine routed through a U-shaped drainage basin. Bali Hai, however, is no pristine South Pacific hideaway. The golf course is located directly in the flight path of McCarran International Airport. The distractions are too great given the extravagant green fee, which at press time topped out at $295. Within the clubhouse is Cili, a superb Balinese-themed restaurant run by Wolfgang Puck.

If you don't have time for a full round, check out the **Callaway Golf Center** near the airport, which offers an expansive grass driving range and a par-three nine-holer lit for night play. There's also **The Greens of Las Vegas,** a 24-hour putting complex that features putting surfaces inspired by Augusta National, St. Andrews, and other famous venues. The facility is located near the airport, just in case you need to drain a long one before heading home.

ONE TO WATCH

In 2004, **PGA Village at Coyote Springs** was announced as part of a planned 43,000-acre development spanning Clark and Lincoln counties north of Las Vegas. The standard-bearer for the project, which carries the imprimatur of the PGA of America, is Jack Nicklaus, who will craft a collection of courses to be marketed as "The Bear Trail." The first layout is expected to open in 2006. The center will serve as a western complement to the PGA Village in Port St. Lucie, Florida. The new destination will also be home to a PGA Learning Center and PGA Historical Center.

The PGA Village is the first part of the vast Coyote Springs project to open. Ultimately, the development could include several town centers, a range of housing options, additional golf courses, hotels, parks, and more. Because the parent company, Coyote Springs Investment, owns the site's water rights, green fee rates are expected to be lower than at comparable facilities in the area. (As much as $50 per round pays for water at a typical Las Vegas golf course).

Wynn Las Vegas, fourth hole

The Strip in Las Vegas at night

WHERE TO STAY/LAS VEGAS

With nine of the 10 largest hotels in the world to its name, many of them extravagant versions of European cultural landmarks, finding a place to stay in Vegas is not a problem. Only in Las Vegas can a 3,000-room hotel qualify as a medium-sized establishment! (**The MGM Grand,** with 5,005 rooms, is topped in size only by Thailand's Ambassador City Jomtien, which claims to have 5,100 rooms).

Two properties are generally rated among the best hotels in Vegas: **Bellagio,** a grand Italianate hotel fronted by a faux Lake Como and known for its dazzling fountains; and **The Venetian,** its hand-painted frescoes, replica of St. Mark's tower, and recreation of the Grand Canal (complete with singing gondoliers) a tip of the hat to Venice. But arguably the hippest, most exciting, and least self-conscious hotel on the Strip is **Mandalay Bay,** a 3,200-room property with a gleaming metallic bronze exterior. Guest rooms are large and beautifully appointed with fine furnishings and marble bathrooms. The hotel's 16 restaurants are diverse and appealing, from Border Grill (authentic Mexican) to Trattoria del Lupo, Wolfgang Puck's version of a Milanese café. The 30,000-square-foot Spa Mandalay is one of the largest in town. There's also an 11-acre tropical lagoon with a wave pool capable of creating six-foot surf; and Shark Reef, a two-million-gallon walk-through aquarium. Finally, the hotel's adults-only Moorea Beach Club blends South Beach with Vegas—"European bathing is permitted."

A sister property, called simply **THEhotel,** debuted in 2004 with 1,117 luxurious one-bedroom suites contained in a 43-story tower and designed for upscale business travelers. Something more tranquil? The **Four Seasons Hotel Las Vegas,** an understated yet exceedingly comfortable 424-room sanctuary occupying the 35th to 39th floors of the Mandalay Bay tower, is the hostelry of choice for those seeking a quiet, cosseted retreat in Glitter City. (It's the only hotel on the Strip without a casino.)

FUTURE GROWTH

Nothing stops Vegas from expanding and reinventing itself at a breakneck pace. In 2004, **MGM-Mirage** disclosed plans for a $4 billion "CityCenter" on a 66-acre site on the Strip between the Bellagio and the Monte Carlo. Plans in the first phase call for a 4,000-room hotel-casino; three 400-room boutique hotels operated by upscale hospitality brands not currently represented in Las Vegas; and 550,000 square feet of retail, dining, and entertainment venues, plus 1,650 hotel, condo, and residential units. Construction of the first phase is expected to begin in 2006, with an anticipated opening in 2010.

OFF-COURSE ATTRACTIONS/BEYOND THE STRIP

Yes, there is a world beyond the gaming tables. Twenty miles west of the Strip is the Red Rock Canyon National Conservation Area, where sedate tourists can pay a small admission fee to travel the one-way, 13-mile scenic drive from dawn to dusk. It is a beautiful drive, but hikers are the true beneficiaries here: Numerous trails wind below sheer sandstone cliffs and twisting ravines.

For true respite from the hustle of Vegas, travel 35 miles northwest of the city to Spring Mountain Recreation Area, which is commonly known as Mount Charleston, at 11,918 feet the tallest peak in southern Nevada. There is skiing in the winter. During the warmer months, hiking is available on trails designated by the U.S. Forest Service. Though it's five hours by car from Vegas, Grand Canyon National Park, one of the world's great natural wonders, can be readily accessed by helicopter or small plane. A number of companies in Vegas offer daily flightseeing tours.

DINING

All-you-can-eat buffets are a thing of the past in Las Vegas. Celebrity chefs have taken the city by storm in the past few years. No city, not even New York, can match Vegas for upscale eateries because no city can afford to shell out what Vegas does to attract top culinary talent.

To wit: Wolfgang Puck, the superstar chef credited with spearheading the Vegas gourmet revolution in the early 1990s with the opening of Spago in the Forum Shops at Caesars Palace, now has four acclaimed eateries on the Strip. Food Network star Emeril Lagasse runs Delmonico Steak House at the Venetian as well as Emeril's New Orleans Fish House at MGM Grand. Jean-Georges Vongerichten heads Prime at the Bellagio. Alain Ducasse oversees Mix at THEhotel, Mandalay Bay. Tom Colicchio of Craft in New York has Craftsteak at the MGM Grand. Nobu Matsuhisa has made a splash with his eponymous eatery at the Hard Rock Hotel. Thomas Keller, the visionary behind the French Laundry in Napa Valley, opened Bouchon in the Venezia tower at The Venetian in 2004. Daniel Boulud, one of New York's top restaurateurs, debuted a signature dining room at Wynn Las Vegas in 2005. Guy Savoy, who runs a Michelin three-star restaurant in Paris, will open Restaurant Guy Savoy at Caesars Palace in 2006.

In addition to its entrenched culture of celebrity chefs, Vegas also boasts outposts of famous restaurants from around the nation: Commander's Palace from New Orleans, Joe's Stone Crab from Miami Beach, Aqua from San Francisco, New York's Carnegie Deli. The list goes on and on. If you're a foodie, you'll be more than satisfied in the nation's new culinary hotspot.

WINING

One of the city's best-kept secrets is its remarkable concentration of master sommeliers—and, of course, the wines they serve. There are slightly more than 100 master sommeliers worldwide. At press time, the United States was home to 56 of them. Incredibly, a quarter of these U.S.-based master sommeliers are living and working in Las Vegas. For serious oenophiles, Vegas combines the best of old-world charm with modern technology to offer unparalleled wine-tasting experiences in the top restaurants and bars.

ENTERTAINMENT

Las Vegas can rightly call itself the world's entertainment capital. Anyone who's anyone—from Madonna to the Rolling Stones, not to mention a small army of Elvis impersonators—performs here.

On the heels of Mystere and O, a third Cirque du Soleil show, the adult-themed Zumanity, opened at New York-New York in 2003. The troupe's latest extravaganza is KA, a $165-million production that opened at the MGM Grand in 2004. The show explores the nature of duality through the saga of a twin boy and girl who, separated at birth, embark on a dangerous journey to fulfill their linked destinies. The cast, dressed in Asian-themed costumes, tell their story through acrobatic performances, martial arts, puppetry, multimedia, and pyrotechnics. Like all of Cique du Soleil's shows, it is original, inspired, and compelling.

Reserve early to see your favorite acts—top stars perform twice nightly in showrooms of major hotels, but headliners sell out quickly.

A word of advice: Plan a few leisurely days back home to recover from a trip to Las Vegas. This never-never land never sleeps and expects that you won't, either.

Houston

A sprawling metropolis girdled by interstates at the fringe of the East Texas piney woods, Houston is an oil town run by New Age wildcatters with a strike-it-rich mentality. Stetsons and cowboy boots are in evidence, yet the city is closer in style and spirit to New Orleans than El Paso. Think bayous, not buttes. Crawfish, not rattlers.

The city today encompasses a land area of 617 square miles, half the size of Rhode Island. An energy capital, medical hub, and business center, Houston is America's fourth-largest city. Golf-wise, Houston is a smorgasbord. With the possible exception of Chicago, Space City offers the finest and most diverse array of public-access facilities of any major city in the nation. Golfers can drive in any direction from downtown and find not dead-flat oil fields—the common misconception of the area—but an attractive array of layouts set on rolling, wooded land. Since 1998, the exurbs of the Big H have sprouted dozens of top daily-fee courses, to the point where supply currently outstrips demand, a nice scenario for players seeking good value and plenty of options.

Houston's most venerable municipal facility is **Memorial Park Golf Course,** but it's been reborn since receiving a $5 million facelift in the mid-1990s. Designed by John Bredemus in 1936, and the site of the Houston Open from 1951 to 1963, Memorial Park had devolved into a dusty, worn-out muni before it was renovated by Baxter Spann, with input from Houstonians Jay Riviere and Dave Marr. This oasis of urban golf west of downtown, set within one of the city's prettiest parks, now features a Spanish Mission-style clubhouse and a golf museum created from the original clubhouse. With glass-and-steel towers rising high above the fairways, Memorial Park is one of the nation's finest urban munis. If you want to rub elbows with the locals, this is the place.

At **The Woodlands Resort & Conference Center** north of the city, golfers can tee it up on a pair of fine courses. In 2003, the resort reworked its formerly private Pines Course into a stellar new daily-fee spread called **Panther Trail.** With eight revamped holes and six new ones sculpted from rolling land framed by hardwoods and ponds, the layout offers an enjoyable

Meadowbrook Farms Golf Club, sixth hole

test to duffers and aces alike. There's also the **Oaks Course,** a solid test redesigned by Jay Morrish in 1999. Large, undulating greens, huge greenside bunkers, and broad fairways framed by tall oaks mark the 7,044-yard layout.

Not far from The Woodlands is the 54-hole **Cypresswood Golf Club.** The club's **Creek** and **Cypress** courses, both woven through a thick pine forest, are pleasant and straightforward, but the star attraction is the **Tradition Course,** a Keith Foster–designed layout debuted in 1998 and named to *Golf Magazine's* "Top 10 You Can Play" list of the best new courses from that year. Carved from tall pines and live oaks on rolling land marked by sand flats and deep ravines, the Tradition is an old-fashioned shot-maker's course designed to rekindle the charm of the game's past. The pair of gaping sand pits at the par-three 11th hole, for example, were inspired by the famed Spectacles bunkers at Carnoustie in Scotland. Clever risk-reward scenarios will delight experts and novices alike—if they can avoid the meandering brooks, rock-rimmed ponds, and deep oblong bunkers. Many of the greens are raised above fairway level and skewed to the line of play. The Tradition at Cypresswood is perennially ranked the No. 1 public course in the area by the *Houston Sports News.* At press time, the $55 green fee for walkers represented one of the best bangs for the buck in America.

West of the city is **BlackHorse Golf Club,** a 36-hole complex spread across rolling, wooded ranchland. Horses were once raised here, but Harris County, the club's locale, looks like the kind of place where buffalo roamed. The **North Course,** debuted in 2000, is intersected by a creek and dotted with thick-waisted oaks. A brawny track marked by wide corridors and large greens, the North is a big-time test from the tips at 7,301 yards, even for PGA Tour pro and course co-designer Peter Jacobsen. The facility's **South Course,** opened in 2001, is a little shorter at 7,171 yards and quite a bit tighter, with trees pinching the fairways and water in play on 14 holes. The club's finest holes are found on the South's back nine, a few of which are routed around the rim of a spent sand quarry that has long since filled with water and is now a cavern of reedy wetlands. After the round, drop by Jake's Grill, one of the best 19th holes in town.

Also situated west of Houston is **Meadowbrook Farms Golf Club,** a well-groomed course that offers exceptional diversity on seemingly redundant terrain that does not inspire at first glance. After consulting with the Lady Bird Johnson Wildflower Center in Austin, Greg Norman and his design crew chose to revitalize the fast-disappearing Texas Gulf Coast

Cypresswood Golf Club, Tradition Course, 11th hole

prairie, planting Little Blue Stem and other tall native grasses along with wildflowers to attract birds and also create a nice frame for the holes. The look is simple, pure, traditional; the holes fit the gently rolling land hand-in-glove. The plateau greens at Meadowbrook Farms, many of them embraced by close-mown humps and hollows, are very slick. Stacked-sod bunkers and a tree-lined bayou add to the challenge of a well-strategized course. This subtle, beautifully manicured test, opened in 1999, is one of the finest designs on Norman's résumé and one of the most respected venues in town.

The Gulf plain flattens east of the city, but a superior golf experience awaits at **Redstone Golf Club** in Humble. While the club's original layout has turned private, the **Tournament Course,** opened in 2005, was specifically designed to host the Shell Houston Open. The mandate to Rees Jones was simple: Design a course that tests the world's best players without overwhelming bogey shooters. Handed a heavily wooded site flanked by a bayou, Jones turned out a versatile spread built for today's risk-reward style of play. The gently contoured greens, among the speediest in the region, are defended by rough-hewn bunkers that look transported from the 1920s. The pacing of the holes—a driveable par four, a pair of (theoretically) unreachable par fives—is excellent. According to player-consultant David Toms, "There's a lot of variety so that not one type of player has an advantage, which is what we need on Tour now."

For those who enjoy replica tracks, Houston offers two good copycats. **Tour 18,** opened in 1992 east of George Bush Intercontinental Airport in the flatlands of Humble, was the first public-access facility in the nation to borrow hole designs from famous clubs. The club's homage to Amen Corner, inspired by holes 11, 12, and 13 at Augusta National, coupled with holes drawn from Inverness, Colonial, and Oakmont, provide an enjoyable, déjà vu–style test.

In 2000, the developers of Tour 18 produced **Augusta Pines,** its front nine inspired by the storied back nine at Augusta National, a string of holes imprinted on the national consciousness by the Masters. The layout's incoming nine borrows from Pinehurst No. 2, Oakland Hills, and other classics, though the holes are "inspirations," not cookie-cutter copies. Site of a Champions Tour event, Augusta Pines, characterized by small, undulating greens and plenty of water, offers a solid test on heaving land framed by tall pines. The only thing lacking is Magnolia Lane, the famed tree-lined entrance to Augusta National. This semi-private club is slated to go fully private in the future.

Outer space may be the "Final Frontier," but for dyed-in-the-wool golfers, links-style golf is the last stop on the shuttle. A few miles south of the NASA-Johnson Space Center is **Magnolia Creek Golf Links,** a 27-hole complex that simulates an authentic links. The rolling, tumbling fairways on this nearly treeless site are pinched by manmade hillocks and "dunes" cloaked in tall native grasses. Situated a scant 20 miles from the Gulf of Mexico, the facility's Ireland, Scotland, and England nines are invariably swept by steady winds. Conditions are firm and fast, and bump-and-run shots into the open-entry greens are encouraged. Designer Tom Clark, who moved 1.5 million cubic yards of dirt to create the course, did himself proud here. Magnolia Creek may lack centuries of tradition, but it saves visitors the trouble of making an overseas trip to the U.K.—or booking a flight to the moon.

Tour 18, sixth hole, a simulation of Augusta National's 12th hole

LODGING

At the edge of Memorial Park near the Galleria is **The Houstonian Hotel, Club and Spa,** a leafy 18-acre enclave that functions as an oasis of serenity in the middle of the city. Floor-to-ceiling windows in the revamped guest rooms offer wooded views. Nestled among the city's skyscrapers is the **Sam Houston Hotel,** a venerable 10-story brick edifice that reopened as a 100-room boutique hotel in 2002 after a major makeover. Guest rooms, equipped with high-speed Internet lines and marble bathrooms, are done up in shades of brown and taupe. Traveling on business? The **Hilton Americas-Houston,** a 1,200-room contemporary hotel debuted in 2003, adjoins the George R. Brown Convention Center.

For a pleasant full-service resort experience, there's **The Woodlands Resort & Conference Center** 18 miles northwest of the airport. Built in the mid-1970s, this Frank Lloyd Wright–inspired resort has steadily expanded and improved itself. It offers 490 rooms and suites, two fine courses, five restaurants and lounges, a spa and fitness center, 21 tennis courts, 120 miles of jogging and biking trails, and a new water park.

DINING

Local institutions mix with eclectic newcomers in a culinary melting pot where Texas Creole and Asian Cajun got their start. Ever-popular Café Annie has elevated Southwestern cuisine to a gourmet level. Local ingredients (crawfish tails, venison sausage) are spun into delectable entrees. Hugo's veers sharply from basic Tex-Mex to the haute cuisine of Mexico City. Where else to get duck *mole,* achiote-rubbed grouper grilled in a banana leaf, or masa pancakes topped with shredded rabbit? Artista, located within the new Hobby Center for the Performing Arts, invites diners to select a range of sauces for their entrees. It's trendy mix-and-match cuisine.

Among Houston's many steakhouses, there are chain outposts of Morton's of Chicago, Fleming's and Ruth's Chris, but for local flair and fine beef with wines to match, check out Pappas Bros., a cigar-friendly haunt favored by oil tycoons.

Among the city's beloved mainstays is Goode Company Barbecue, a cafeteria-style smokehouse that slow-cooks some of the best brisket in Texas. Save room for the pecan pie. For spicy gumbo and oven-roasted oysters, head for Goode Company Texas Seafood.

NASA-Johnson Space Center

OFF-COURSE ATTRACTIONS

Explore the evolution of manned space flight at Space Center Houston, the official visitors center for the NASA-Johnson Space Center. See retired spacecraft, touch moon rocks, sample astronaut food, view an IMAX film. Reliant Stadium, home of the NFL's Houston Texans, is also home to the Houston Livestock Show and Rodeo, the world's largest rodeo. The event usually is held in March. Minute Maid Park, home of the Houston Astros baseball team, is a retro-traditional ballpark with natural turf, a retractable roof, and a fine view of the city skyline. There's also the Downtown Aquarium, its exotic sea life contained in 500,000 gallons of aquariums. Located within Hermann Park is the Houston Museum of Natural Science, its main attraction a live butterfly center.

On the arts side, Houston's 17-block downtown Theater District is home to the Houston Grand Opera and Houston Ballet at the Wortham Center, the Houston Symphony at Jones Hall, and the Alley Theater. Among the highlights of the city's museum district is the Museum of Fine Arts, which houses an amazingly diverse collection in a series of wings and galleries, a few of them designed by Mies van der Rohe.

Shopping? It's a competitive sport in Houston. The never-ending chase for the perfect whatever can be pursued at The Galleria, an enormous mall that houses hundreds of upscale retailers.

West

Bandon, Oregon

For those steeped in the traditions of the game, those who appreciate the time-honored custom of strolling a links with a caddie on the bag, there may be no finer destination in America than **Bandon Dunes Golf Resort.** Sited along the southern Oregon coast 100 miles north of the California state line, the resort has become a cult destination since its first course opened in 1999. Conceived by an against-the-grain thinker, this low-key retreat was intended for purists who relish a non-commercial atmosphere as well as the chance to play three stellar courses: the original Bandon Dunes links; the newer Pacific Dunes course; and Bandon Trails, the latest gem. All three venues are walkers-only—no golf carts! Most aficionados rank each member of this trio among the top 50 courses in the U.S.

Alone among the nation's premier getaways, Bandon Dunes is all about the golf. There are no frills. In fact, there is nothing to distract players from the prospect of tackling three heroic links stretched across headlands 100 feet above a deserted beach washed by the mighty Pacific. A place unto itself, Bandon Dunes offers welcome respite from the workaday world. Observed *Travel + Leisure Golf* in 2004, "Unless one managed to get on Cypress (Point) and Pebble (Beach), Pacific Dunes and Bandon Dunes constitute, without question, the best pair of courses a human being can play on the same day anywhere in the hemisphere." And that was before Bandon Trails opened in 2005.

Let's start with the original venue. In early 1998, I received in the mail a picture postcard of a golf course routed on bluffs high above by the sea. The postmark read "Bandon, OR." I called the number on the card and asked if the photo had been airbrushed or doctored in any way. No, came the reply. There really is a course taking shape on the southern Oregon coast, said the voice, a course that will redefine the golf experience in the Northwest. And so I made plans to visit later that year, driving 250 miles south from Portland to find out if the postcard hole was for real. (Air connections, I later learned, are available into North Bend 35 minutes from Bandon.) My curiosity was amply rewarded.

Chicago-based Mike Keiser, an avid golfer who made his fortune in recycled greeting cards, entrusted the design of the resort's first course, now known simply as **Bandon Dunes,** to an unknown 29-year-old Scot, David McLay Kidd. At the time, the budding architect was listed as lead designer for Gleneagles Golf Developments, a Scottish firm. While Kidd had only a few solo design credits on his résumé (and none in the U.S.), what he did have is an intimate knowledge of exactly what comprises an authentic links. That knowledge, along with his brogue, landed him the most enviable commission imaginable.

The land, probably the finest made available for a golf course in America since Alister MacKenzie (another Scot) was shown the site for the Cypress Point Club on the Monterey Peninsula, is a sea of tumbling dunes anchored by prickly gorse and other seaside vegetation. Some of these wind-tossed dunes are 40 feet high. Interspersed among them are knob-like hummocks, wind-twisted pines, and scalloped craters created by wind action and erosion. Far below is a tawny beach strewn with driftwood. Migrating gray whales spout offshore from fall to spring. Bald eagles, osprey, and other birds of prey sail overhead. Looking south from the cliffside holes is the sleepy fishing village of Bandon, its sea stacks and monoliths rising like chess pieces from the roiling sea. Punctuating a broad sweep of coast 15 miles north is the Cape Arago Lighthouse. Fortuitously, the breeze on the links is generally steady but not overwhelming. And while the Oregon coast is notoriously foggy, the sun usually shines at Bandon Dunes.

The course itself is a big, brawny track stretching to 7,212 yards (five sets of tees give everyone a chance), its broad fairways staked out by stacked-sod bunkers. The sand-based turf is firm, which means low, running approach shots will scamper onto the open-entry greens. Seven holes skirt the edge of a bluff overlooking the beach; all 18 have a view of the Pacific. The long years of environmental permitting endured by Keiser must now seem well worth it, for this is the course that grabbed the golf world by the lapels and brought the resort immediate acclaim.

Bandon Dunes, fourth hole

Handed a three-quarter-mile stretch of headlands, Kidd, working without benefit of a routing plan "or even a single drawing," set about finding the course in the field, identifying holes as he went along. Moving very little material, Kidd accentuated existing features and softened a few of the site's bigger rolls to shoehorn the holes into the terrain. "Basic Scottish cultural practices" were employed during the construction phase. No soil amendments, for example, were made to the enormous, mildly contoured greens, which were built atop clean beach sand. The layout's chief merits are its naturalness and individuality: No two holes are alike, and no hole conspicuously resembles any from a famous links abroad. Why? "I designed this course in the *Bandon Dunes* style," Kidd remarked incongruously. His only regret? "It's very likely I'll never again see a site this good for the rest of my career."

More's the pity. But then, the young man made the most of his opportunity. "I imagined the routing having the structure of a symphony," Kidd wrote before the course opened. "A strong start, a sense of anticipation, small crescendos, and an incredible finishing sequence along the Pacific. The course had to provide not only a challenge to every skill level, but a sense of adventure and an exploration of this great landscape." The postcard was for real, all right. Bandon Dunes was overnight the greatest resort course in the Northwest—until Pacific Dunes opened two years later.

For longer than his peers care to remember, Tom Doak, the *enfant terrible* of the design business, has been an outspoken critic of all that he has surveyed in the world of golf course architecture. But the opening of **Pacific Dunes** in 2001 gave him the goods to back

up his bare-knuckled opinions. On what he called "one of the 20 best pieces of property anybody has ever worked on," namely a stunning expanse of sandy ridges and dunes on a windswept headlands high above the Pacific a mile north of the original Bandon Dunes course, Doak and his able band of shapers coaxed an epic links from the rippling duneland. In fact, Pacific Dunes compares favorably to the finest courses ever evolved by nature and refined by man. Yes, it's that good.

If Bandon Dunes approximates Scotland, Pacific Dunes is all about Ireland. It delivers "the kind of golf that people play in their most ecstatic dreams," as Bernard Darwin once remarked of Royal County Down, the Ulster links that Pacific Dunes most closely resembles.

Drawing upon his encyclopedic knowledge of great courses worldwide, the then 40-year-old dirt artist allowed the U-shaped valleys spread among the broom-covered dunes to dictate the routing. Alister MacKenzie, the legendary designer and Doak's biggest influence, once wrote: "On a seaside course...little construction work is necessary; the most important thing is to make the fullest possible use of existing features." This Doak has done, harnessing undulations large and small while "imitating the beauties of nature so closely as to make his work indistinguishable from nature itself," as MacKenzie advised.

"Most of it was laying there for us to find," Doak says, though a few holes required modest earthworks. "We made it hard for you to pick out which ones are natural and which ones we built." Doak's take on the opportunity of a lifetime: "Even a lot of the great architects, like Ross and Tillinghast, never had a site this dramatic. If you're lucky enough to get a job like this, you feel the weight of the world to not mess it up."

Honoring the land gave Doak the freedom to build a 6,633-yard, par-71 anomaly with non-returning nines, back-to-back par threes (at 10 and 11), and only two par fours on the back nine. One of them, the magnificent 444-yard 13th, rolls along the bluffs, the ocean below on the left and a huge broken dune rising to 60 feet along the right. From the fairway, the rising green looks as if it's about to be engulfed by an enormous cresting wave of sand. It is the most dramatic hole at Pacific Dunes and one of the finest two-shotters in the world.

This walkers-only links may appear short on the scorecard, but the lumpy fairways, perched greens, fringed "blow-out" bunkers, and brisk coastal breezes provide ample defense. Brilliantly routed,

Bandon Dunes, 16th hole

the naturalistic layout, free of connective tissue and "filler" holes, pitches and tosses through pockets in the dunes, the riotous fairways leading to cleverly-defended greens that call for precise approach shots. The journey from dunes to open plain to cliff's edge and back again is as memorable as any in the sport. There is a sense of purity and solitude while abroad on the links. For the duration of the round, a golfer hears only calling seabirds, distant boat whistles, and the dull thud of waves hitting the beach.

A match play–style course intended to inspire amateurs, Pacific Dunes is a throwback, an adventurous track that rewards creative play, specifically low, punched shots that cheat the wind. Clever chips and crisp pitches are also a necessity. Each hole, unique to itself, presents an appealing problem to solve. Tactics, not brawn, are required to score. Built for a scant $2.5 million, this splendid newcomer manages to be what many new courses aren't: fun to play. Judging by its primeval appearance, its lack of cart paths and housing, Pacific Dunes could pass for a links circa 1900.

Covered on foot on a cloudless day with a light zephyr sweeping the links and a local caddie by your side (likely a moonlighting lumberjack or fisherman), Pacific Dunes offers an experience comparable to any in Ireland or Scotland. Because the wind constantly changes direction and velocity, players rarely encounter the same course from day to day at "Pac Dunes," as the locals call it.

It didn't take long for the resort's collective excellence to catch the eye of the USGA: The Curtis Cup, a prestigious biennial match between a U.S. women's team and one from Great Britain and Ireland, will be held at Pacific Dunes in 2006, while the U.S. Mid-Amateur will be held on Bandon Dunes and its newer sibling in 2007.

The resort's latest addition, unveiled in 2005, is **Bandon Trails,** a Bill Coore–Ben Crenshaw creation that begins in broad-shouldered dunes, cuts inland across verdant meadows, crosses into thick woodlands, and finishes in meadows and dunes. While no portion of the course is stretched along the cliffs, nearly half the holes on this walkers-only, 6,839-yard layout (par 71) offers ocean views. Every golfer will know where they are: The crashing surf can be heard from all 18.

A genuine multi-theme track, Bandon Trails straddles a huge sand ridge beyond the 18th hole of the original course and can be likened to Spyglass Hill on the Monterey Peninsula, but it is in fact more varied and expansive than Spyglass. Sharp elevation changes set it apart from the Kidd- and

Pacific Dunes, 13th hole

Pacific Dunes, 11th hole

Doak-designed venues. In addition, the brows of the gaping bunkers at Bandon Trails have been planted in kinnickinnick, a native ground cover also known as bearberry. Its furry look is distinctive.

Said Coore, "We have tried to tread softly on this spectacular landscape, laying out a golf course that required very little alteration to the site while providing golf as diverse as the landscape itself. As its name implies, Bandon Trails will take you on a journey, a nature walk if you will, through windswept dunes, meadows of vegetation framed by indigenous shrubbery, and through woodlands of towering fir and spruce trees." The journey, he added, could range from tumultuous to serene depending on a player's game and the weather.

Among the feature holes on the Trails, which is evocative of Pine Valley in places, is the petite par-three fifth, which plays to a rollicking green fully 50 yards deep. The layout pitches and tosses through hummocky terrain set back from the sea, reaching a climax at the 14th, a short par four that offers a spectacular view of the course from its perched tee. From the high or low side of its split-level fairway, the approach shot at 14 is played uphill to a domed green that falls away on three sides. It is Crenshaw's favorite hole on the course.

With its swirling winds, rolling duneland, and thick ground cover off the fairways, Bandon Trails is often cited as the toughest test of golf at a one-of-a-kind resort whose cup now runneth over. (Amazingly, Mike Keiser has plans to build up to three more courses on his 2,400-acre golf paradise in Bandon.)

Above: The Lodge at Bandon Dunes   Right: Bandon Trails, second hole

LODGING

Because management at **Bandon Dunes** has distilled
the essence of the game's appeal, there is no frippery
to detract from the nirvana-like setting. The 21-room
Lodge and multi-unit Lily Pond Cottages, while spar-
tan in a Euro-Zen kind of way, nevertheless have an
appropriate sense of place. Furnishings are simple, but
the mattresses are firm. Lily Pond rooms, contained
in cottages spaced around a natural lily pond, feature
a spacious sitting area, two queen beds, fireplace,
private bathroom, and balcony or patio. In addition to
19 single rooms, the Lodge offers two four-bedroom
suites. Most rooms have views across Bandon Dunes.
The Chrome Lake suites are slightly plusher, while
the new Grove Cottages were specifically designed
to accommodate a foursome in no small amount of
comfort. The resort staff, by the way, is friendly and
competent, but they don't wear white gloves. Spa?
There's a large stainless steel hot tub in the lower level
Lodge that's ideal for reviving oneself after battling
the elements on the links. Deep-tissue massages are
also available.

DINING

The Gallery Restaurant, located just off the lobby
in the Lodge, dishes out simple but savory fare in
generous portions. The most popular entree at lunch
is Grandma Thayer's Meatloaf Sandwich, a home-
style staple served with pan gravy and haystack onion
strings. Dinner brings starters like crispy oysters,
flash-fried calamari, and steamed Little Neck clams,
with main courses ranging from Muscovy duck with
Bandon cranberry sauce to a delicious Thai seafood
"Cioppino." Oregon wines, white and red alike,
pair well with everything on the menu. Tables are
set near windows overlooking the Bandon Dunes
course and the sea. Next door to the Gallery is the
Tufted Puffin Lounge.

McKee's Pub, the resort's Scottish-style eatery,
serves traditional pub fare along with regional
microbrews and classic single-malt whiskies. The
wood-burning fireplace is welcome on a cool day.
Downstairs in the Lodge is the Bunker Bar, its walls
hung with photos of the world's most famous bunkers.
With its pool tables, dart boards, and wide selection
of microbrews and whiskies, it's a perfect 19th hole.

Trail's End Clubhouse, opened in 2005, offers
casual dining along with a fine view of the 18th
green at Bandon Trails. The open-pit fireplace outside
the clubhouse has become a popular post-round
gathering spot.

OFF-COURSE ATTRACTIONS

Tear yourself away from the links and spend an afternoon touring charming Bandon-by-the-Sea, a working
ocean port. Stroll the renovated Old Town, poke your
head in a few of the art galleries, antique stores, and
gift shops. Well worth a visit is the Bandon Cheese
Factory (try the smoked cheddar or spicy Jalapeno
Jack); and Cranberry Sweets (handmade fruit candies
made with local berries). Drive slowly along the Beach
Loop Drive, which winds along the coast near many
of the craggy sea stacks offshore, including Face
Rock, Table Rock, and Elephant Rock. Native legend
maintains that Face Rock was formed from the face of
an Indian maiden who was frozen into stone by an evil
spirit, who also cast her animals into the sea to create
Cat and Kittens Rock. Watch for tufted puffins, an
endangered species that nests among the rocks along
the shore. (The resort's logo was inspired by this bird).

Los Angeles

Here's an L.A. Confidential: Simi Valley and Moorpark, a pair of towns in Ventura County about an hour's drive north of the city, have debuted several courses since the late 1990s that rank among the finest new daily-fee tracks in the state. Far from the smog-choked concrete freeways and high above the coastal fog belt, these courses, cut through canyons and creased by arroyos in dramatic mountain foothills, offer a glimmer of hope to L.A. denizens and visitors starved for a place to play.

Tinseltown's biggest blockbuster of the new century turned out to be grander in scale than any silver screen could ever hope to capture. On 1,640 acres in Simi Valley 45 minutes north of Hollywood, Pete Dye deferred to what he called a "higher authority" in designing **Lost Canyons** on a spectacular site walled in by soaring peaks in the Santa Susana Mountains. Dye, the indefatigable dirt devil, underplayed his hand on a portion of Big Sky Ranch where *Little House on the Prairie, Bonanza, M*A*S*H*, and hundreds of other serials were shot.

"The Man upstairs is responsible for this one," Dye said of the ethereal **Sky Course** at the 36-hole facility. "All I had to do was wiggle the bunkers and make it as plain and playable as possible. There was no need to try to trick anything up. The ambience and challenge were already here."

Dye rarely goes out of his way to assist the average golfer, but he relented a little in the nearly treeless canyons, building a course that generally funnels errant tee shots to the twisting fairways. The greens, several of which crown hilltops and resemble lolling tongues or blistered potato chips, are something else again. At 5,605 yards, the Sky's white tees are G-rated for generous, but the black tees, at 7,250 yards, are an X-rated horror show that only player consultant Fred Couples and his Tour pals ever see.

The front nine of the Sky Course is marked by back-to-back par fives and a superior Cape-style par four at the ninth, while the back nine skirts ridgelines and barrancas below the deeply incised flanks of White Face Mountain, its dun-colored slopes dotted with sage and chaparral. The feature holes are 17, a stellar par three that looks 30 miles beyond the hanging, hourglass-shaped green to the crest of Angeles National Forest; and 18, a sharply downhill par four paved through a steep box canyon and framed by elongated sand pits. It may be the most fun finishing hole Dye has ever built.

Lost Canyons, Sky Course, 18th hole

So enthusiastic was the reception for the Sky Course when it opened in 2000, there were serious doubts the sequel would be as good as the original. But at Lost Canyons, the **Shadow Course** turned out to be every bit the equal of the Sky Course. Where the Sky, on higher ground, is a guns-blazing western, the Shadow, unveiled in 2001, is film noir, its setting more intimate, its blind shots inscrutable. The non-returning nines, stretched across a canyon floor below the mountains, feature rolling fairways pinched by barrancas and trench-like bunkers. Dye's greens, as always, are amusing and nearly indecipherable. The fifth, an uphill par four, corrals players into a box canyon, yet hanging greens at other holes invite the eye to travel to distant vistas.

The parcel for Shadow was slightly bigger than Sky, and less grading was done, but the newcomer is a little tighter and less forgiving to loose shots. Like most of Dye's work, the routing is shrewd, the flow of holes unforced. For pure challenge and drama, the final eight holes are as good as it gets, notably the pair of short par fours at 13 and 14 that detour into mountain foothills and call for careful shot placement.

After initial outcries of unfairness at a few holes where the punishment did not fit the crime, Dye returned to shine a little light on the Shadow to enhance playability. Still, the ratings are 75.0/149 from the tips at 7,005 yards. Asked by management when his work was done if the course was walkable, Dye replied, "No one rides in the U.S. Open, do they?"

As a place to suspend reality far removed from the concrete sprawl of Los Angeles, Lost Canyons is an Oscar-winning double feature. Which is why Hollywood stars, rock musicians, and professional athletes can often be seen milling around L.A.'s finest public-access club.

Built on a former sheep ranch in Moorpark a short drive west of Lost Canyons, **Rustic Canyon** became an instant cult classic among fans of minimalist design when it debuted in 2002. The inaugural $30 fee for walkers not only qualified it as the best deal

Lost Canyons, Shadow Course, 17th hole

Rustic Canyon, 16th hole

in the greater Los Angeles area, but as one of the best bangs for the buck in the nation. Even at the top rate at press time of $53, Rustic Canyon, a throwback to the kind of naturalistic courses built at the time Hollywood was making black-and-white movies, delivers.

Laid out by Gil Hanse along with design associate Jim Wagner and golf writer Geoff Shackelford, an expert on the work of George C. Thomas, the 6,935-yard layout is a traditional links-style design that emphasizes the ground game over the aerial game. Very little earth, a mere 17,000 cubic yards, was moved to create the broad fairways, approach areas, and retro-style green complexes that are Rustic Canyon's signature element. These large, imaginatively contoured surfaces, some built to grade, some domed, and a special few built on subtle plateaus, are embraced by huge close-cropped chipping aprons defended in places by shaggy-edged bunkers. According to Hanse, the tightly-mown, free-form areas encircling the greens "give the average player more opportunity to score because he can putt, chip, or play bump-and-run shots from off the green. It also creates indecision for the better players."

As on any memorable course, the holes at Rustic Canyon build in interest as the round progresses. The incoming holes ascend to higher ground and wind through steep-walled canyons, their fairways crisscrossed by rock-strewn barrancas. The desert motif is strong: sagebrush and cactus in the rough, stunted oaks and white sage in the washes. These holes, notably the brace of long, compelling par fours at 11, 14, 16, and 18 are alone worth the very reasonable price of admission on this low-profile gem that could pass for a course built in the pre-bulldozer era.

Rustic Canyon's newest neighbor is **Moorpark Country Club,** a co-design by PGA Tour veteran Peter Jacobsen and swing guru Jim Hardy that was named to *Golf Magazine's* "Top 10 You Can Play" list for courses opening in 2003. Stretched across coastal foothills, this semi-private club, which added a third nine in 2004, is ravishing. Unlike Rustic Canyon, the holes here are not of the minimalist variety and certainly were not "identified" in the natural landscape. Nestled high in Ventura County's citrus and avocado country, this extremely rugged course is marked by sharp elevation changes and long ridges that drop off into deep canyons and washes, wet or dry depending on the season. Of the 27 holes, only two, the seventh and 12th, were built at natural grade. All the others were carved and shaped: Two tons of rock chipped away to reveal a few ounces of golf. The second fairway, for example, was lowered some 50 feet in order to make it accommodating enough for daily-fee play.

According to Jacobsen, "We've worked on several excellent designs where we were obliged to create drama and strategy from pretty tame terrain. At Moorpark, however, the exercise was just the oppo-

Moorpark Country Club, Creekside nine, fourth hole

site: take a spectacular piece of property and make it playable. I think we met that challenge. The fairways are wide and the elevation makes several holes appear more intimidating than they actually play—and that dynamic is fun for public golfers." There is no shortage of drama and visual splendor, but what sets Moorpark apart are its strategic nuances and risk-reward options.

Golfers are treated to several different looks during the course of a round. The first nine, called Ridgeline, winds along a ridge before plunging into rocky canyons for three holes. The second nine, Creekside, plays through a parched valley crossed by arroyos that come into play on four holes. The newest nine, Canyon Crest, commands the high point of the site and may offer the most spectacular golf at Moorpark.

Predating both Rustic Canyon and Moorpark in nearby Simi Valley is **Tierra Rejada,** a target-style Bob Cupp design built on precipitous terrain in the

foothills of the Santa Susana Mountains. Opened in 1999, this 7,015-yard layout features an improbably hilly front nine, its greens sited atop crested hills. In anyone else's hands, this up, up, and away layout might be downright unplayable, but Cupp, a gifted artist who studied painting in college before seeking a career as a golf professional, somehow crafted a fair test that yields to artful play.

The shorter back nine occupies flatter terrain. Ironically, the incoming holes, while they lack the steep climbs and vertiginous drops of the front, are nearly as difficult. Sharp doglegs, narrow landing areas, and well-bunkered greens warrant against easy scoring. The most memorable hole among these is the tiny 17th, a 105-yard par three inspired perhaps by the famed seventh at Pebble Beach.

Tucked against Angeles National Forest in Santa Clarita some 25 miles east of the Moorpark/Simi Valley stronghold of courses is **Robinson Ranch,** a 36-hole complex built on 400 acres of former ranchland. The facility, owned and managed by its pere-fils design team, Ted Robinson Sr. and Jr., has two courses, Mountain and Valley. Both layouts opened in 2000, yet each is quite different from the other.

The **Valley Course,** set in a low-lying area on the east side of the clubhouse where alfalfa was once grown for horse feed, ranges from relatively flat to gently rolling, its fairways staked out in places by burly oaks. The medium-size greens are unusually fast and true. This pristine, housing-free layout ambles along pleasantly on the front nine and is equally placid for three holes on the back nine, but the finish, notably holes 13-18, comes on strong. So strong, in fact, that the final stretch on the Valley Course has come to be known as Death Row. Or Death Valley.

In a region chockablock with tough tracks and killer holes, the par-four 17th could be the toughest hombre of them all. Both the drive and approach must favor the right side of a curling dogleg cut through trees, with a dry wash fronting the green. The 18th, a risk-reward par five, offers a stunning 40-foot waterfall to the right of the green. (Dramatic waterscapes features are a signature element in Robinson designs.)

The **Mountain Course,** built on higher ground, is shorter than the Valley (6,508 yards, par 71) and relies on heaving fairways and semi-blind shots for its challenge. The corridors here are quite tight in places, though the grandeur of the Santa Clarita Valley and its dun-colored, haystack-shaped hills can be admired from the topmost tees. The Robinsons moved 1.6 million cubic yards of dirt to create a 300-foot elevation change on this shot-maker's course. Trimmed in sage and chaparral, the Mountain is a sporty counterpoint to the championship-caliber Valley.

Nestled at the base of Angeles National Forest in L.A.'s northern city limits near Burbank, **Angeles National Golf Club,** a desert-style track that debuted in 2004, appears airlifted from California's Mojave Desert. Routed across a rock-strewn flood basin dotted with thorny scrub and cottonwood trees, the housing-free club was 17 years (and four name changes) in the making. Lead designer Steve Nicklaus, Jack's son, built a cleverly-bunkered track with a subtle, classic touch, albeit one with plenty of muscle from the tips at 7,141 yards. The scenery is special: Soaring mountain peaks rise behind several greens, a la Palm Springs.

Among the feature holes on this well-conceived, much-anticipated course is the third, a long Redan-style par three where players can feed their tee shots from the right to the back left section of the green, avoiding a menacing arroyo directly in front. The 406-yard 17th doglegs sharply to the right and brings the Tujunga wash into play, while the par four closer climbs 40 feet to one of the most heavily contoured greens on the course, with water in play up the entire left side of the hole.

Robinson Ranch, Mountain Course, fourth hole

Ojai Valley Inn & Spa

LOST AND FOUND AT OJAI

Less than an hour's drive northwest of Simi Valley on the road to Santa Barbara is **Ojai Valley Inn & Spa,** a vintage hideaway once favored by Hollywood's elite. Dubbed "Shangri-La" by locals, a reference to Frank Capra's 1937 film, *Lost Horizons,* which was shot in Ojai, the revamped resort is tucked away in a secluded valley walled in by rugged 7,000-foot peaks in the Topa Topa mountains. Legendary architect George C. Thomas designed many fine private clubs in southern California in the 1920s, notably Riviera, Bel-Air, and Los Angeles Country Club, but he left only one public-access spread, the short but charming par-70 layout at Ojai.

Following an update to the course by Jay Morrish in 1988, the resort in 1999 reinstated two "lost" holes by Thomas that were abandoned during World War II around the time the U.S. Army took over Ojai as a training camp. These holes included a par three with a semi-punchbowl green flanked by a deep ravine (now the seventh), a hole that was hailed as one of the world's finest one-shotters when the course debuted in 1923. (Built to resemble the third hole at Pine Valley, it was said to be Thomas's all-time favorite par three.) At 203 yards, with a sharp drop on the left and OB to the right of a concave green fronted by a minefield of bunkers, it's still a grand conception and just as great today. So is the revived eighth, a brilliant par four bordered down the right side by an overgrown barranca, its large, slick green bisected by a trough and ringed by bunkers. Imagination and touch, not brute strength, are required to score on this petite but challenging spread tucked in a valley surrounded by mountains.

THE APPRENTICE MOVES WEST

Trump National Golf Club, Los Angeles, located in Rancho Palos Verdes and formerly known as Ocean Trails, has recovered from a difficult start now that Donald Trump has poured his own special brand of magic over the ill-fated facility. Built by Pete Dye on a stunning but compact parcel on bluffs overlooking the Pacific, the layout's 18th hole fractured and plunged into the sea in 1999 six weeks prior to its grand opening. The landslide, caused by heavy rains and a leaky sewage pipe, bankrupted brothers Bob and Ken Zuckerman, who had sunk tens of millions of dollars into the daily-fee course. To fix the problem—the 18th fairway actually became detached from the mainland, creating a deep, wide gash—the cliff had to be reconstructed from sea level up at an astonishing price of $61 million, much of it paid by an insurance company. In 2002, Trump bought the course out of bankruptcy for a mere $27 million.

Because of its narrow corridors and cramped design, Ocean Trails received lukewarm reviews from discerning visitors at the time it operated as a 15-hole course. (Holes nine and 12 were closed and used to backstop dirt while the 18th was under reconstruction.) But

Trump, who unabashedly claims the property is "probably the best piece of land in the U.S." (it boasts two miles of ocean frontage), bankrolled more than $200 million in improvements and enhancements. He also is credited with a redesign, which widened fairways, eliminated blind shots, created three new holes, and stretched the yardage to 7,322. The course hosted an LPGA event in September of 2005 on a special permit before it opened to the public. "The Donald," a fan of eye-catching water features, has used native Palos Verde stone to create two huge waterfalls on site, including a double-decker cataract behind the first green.

The only public facility in Trump's stable, this L.A. outpost, anchored by an opulent Spanish Mission–style clubhouse, is priced in the neighborhood of Pebble Beach, with green fees in the $250 range. "Everything I'm doing there is to compete with Pebble Beach," Trump said of the first and only oceanfront golf course in Los Angeles County. At press time, Trump had proposed to build a 225-room hotel on the site of his immodestly titled facility.

Trump National Golf Club, Los Angeles, 13th hole

San Diego North

From coastal communities and inland valleys to mountains and deserts, San Diego North is a unique destination established in 2001 to represent 19 distinct townships. The communities that visitors gravitate to are found along the coast, for this is the origination point of the mythic southern California lifestyle, the carefree world of surfing and cars and fun, fun, fun the Beach Boys sang about in the 1960s. Here the average daily temperature year-round is 70 degrees and the gentle ocean breeze is scented with eucalyptus. The combination of gorgeous scenery, al fresco dining, excellent shopping, and world-class accommodations prompt visitors to return again and again to places like La Jolla (Spanish for "the jewel"). a picture-postcard village nestled along seven miles of gently curving coastline.

San Diego North has always offered good golf, but the choices have gotten better since the South Course at Torrey Pines, the nation's finest seaside muni, was treated to a major makeover. After the course landed the 2008 U.S. Open—a tremendous coup for a city-owned facility—traveling golfers began to size up the region as a prime destination given its salubrious climate and superlative venues. Just note that there are precious few bargains in God's country: Green fees in this neck of the woods run well into three figures.

The United States Golf Association was lauded for taking the U.S. Open, its marquee event, to the renovated Black Course at Bethpage State Park in New York in 2002, but a case could be made that the decision to bring the national championship to a genuine public course wasn't just timely—it was long overdue.

Golf in America has evolved from an elitist pastime to a popular sport enjoyed by a cross-section of players drawn from a broad spectrum of economic and cultural backgrounds. And yet, before Bethpage, U.S. Open venues had been confined to private clubs and a pair of pricey resorts, Pebble Beach and Pinehurst No. 2. Public golfers everywhere, specifically those in southern California, rejoiced the day the **South Course** at **Torrey Pines,** a municipal facility in San Diego revamped by Rees Jones in 2001, beat out Riviera, a private club in Los Angeles, for the honor of hosting the 2008 U.S. Open.

Rees Jones was justifiably celebrated for his handiwork at Bethpage Black in preparation for the 2002 U.S. Open, but his fixer-upper of A.W. Tillinghast's masterful design at the Long Island state park pales by comparison to the work he did at Torrey Pines north of La Jolla. The "Open Doctor," as he's known, performed a nip-and-tuck facelift at Bethpage, formalizing bunkers and restoring lost features. At Torrey Pines South, he created a Frankenstein for the 21st century, superimposing a brawny 7,607-yard course (with a charming personality, no less) on a previously dull, lifeless layout that endured nearly 100,000 rounds yearly.

Following a lackluster makeover in the mid-1970s, the 1957 William F. Bell–designed layout "was not a Billy Bell, Jr. golf course anymore," according to Jones. Hired by the Century Club, a local business group, to work his magic on the worn-out muni, Jones came to regard the course, routed on gently rolling headlands tilted to the Pacific, as a blank slate. He pushed back tees, enlarged and recontoured every putting surface, and moved a few green sites up to 50 yards to create new angles of attack and also bring the barrancas and coastal canyons into play. Small, oyster-shaped sand traps were replaced by more than 60 sweeping bunkers that frame the resodded fairways and new greens. The lush, thick rough, previously skimpy, is now a genuine hazard, swallowing errant shots. The cypress, eucalyptus, and rare Torrey pines on site, which lend the clifftop holes a parkland look, were saved or transplanted.

"We were fortunate to have enough room to push the features to the edge of the natural areas and also improve the views," Jones reported when the $3.3 million overhaul was completed in 2001. At full stretch, Torrey Pines South is a paradigm of the modern championship course, with no weak holes and a handful that might scare the bejesus out of

Torrey Pines, South Course, 18th hole

The Grand Golf Club, 12th hole

the world's best players on a breezy day. The layout's postcard hole is the long, downhill par-three third, its new green pushed to the brink of a ravine and back-dropped by the sea, though every hole has a view of serrated cliffs, La Jolla Cove, or the deep blue Pacific.

Beauty aside, the South bares its teeth on the par fours, three of which—4, 12, and 15—can be set up to exceed 500 yards from the tips. The quartet of par fives, formerly a birdie-fest for experts, now have enough length and hazards to give the top guns pause for thought, especially on a windy day. To help protect the course against the onslaught of new technology, Jones placed several of the new putting surfaces on a diagonal, with terraces in back that ask pros to play "hit and release" shots to greens that will be as hard and fast as polished marble by the time the U.S. Open arrives in 2008.

For drama, challenge, and any other set of criteria a golfer cares to cite, this flawless headlands layout now has few if any rivals in southern California. As a test of golf, it can be mentioned in the same breath with Pebble Beach. (Like Pebble, the course is very manageable for mid-handicappers from the forward tees.) Jones's makeover of the South is perhaps his best re-do ever, no small feat given the fact that he has prepped several courses for the national championship. Overnight, Torrey Pines South has become the most sought-after tee time in southern California.

The **North Course** at Torrey Pines, a 6,874-yard layout also built by William F. Bell, while not a U.S. Open–caliber venue, has prettier views than the flag-ship track. From the middle tees, it offers a charming, scenic test and, at the par-three sixth and 12th holes, two of the most scenic one-shotters in the West.

Formerly known as The Meadows Del Mar, this Tom Fazio design was renamed **The Grand Golf Club** and treated to a $1 million redesign in 2005. Under Fazio's direction, the 16th hole, previously a par four, was lengthened by 110 yards and transformed into a risk-reward par five. The change brings par for the course to 72 and pushes the design to 7,054 yards from the tips.

Marked by sharp elevation changes, the layout is intricately routed over a heaving site creased by barrancas. Tumbling fairways and wavy greens are framed by coastal sage, thick native scrub, and California pepper trees. The layout traverses meadows high and low, with many of the fairways bellied into steep, narrow valleys. A few of the greens are of the hanging variety, and invite a player to allow his gaze to wander far beyond the target.

The club, located near the tony enclave of Rancho Santa Fe, is expected to debut a new 50,000-sqaure-foot clubhouse in 2006. In addition, a 24-acre parcel within the club's grounds will encompass The Grand Del Mar, a 261-room resort hotel.

Located in the foothills of Poway east of Rancho Santa Fe, semi-private **Maderas Golf Club** has become an area favorite since its debut in 1999. A collaborative design by Robert Muir Graves and

The Lodge at Torrey Pines

LODGING & DINING

Located beside the 18th hole of the South Course is **The Lodge at Torrey Pines,** a 175-room hostelry that embodies the region's early 1900s Arts and Crafts–style architecture, its wing-like rooflines, shingle- and sandstone-bluff exteriors, and subdued color palette designed to blend the building into the coastal landscape. Spacious guest rooms, most with balconies and many with fireplaces, have granite-topped bars, leather chaise lounges, and Stickley-replica furniture.

In addition to a 9,500-square-foot spa where marine and botanical-based products are used, the Lodge offers fine dining in A.R. Valentien, an elegant, timbered room overlooking the golf course. (Following a round of golf, sample the superb fish tacos served in The Grill, a more casual dining spot.) Perhaps best of all for visiting players, the Lodge, surely the only AAA Five Diamond hostelry on the doorstep of a world-class muni, is granted tee times for five foursomes daily on the South Course at Torrey Pines.

Only time for one meal in lovely La Jolla? Make a beeline for George's at the Cove on Prospect Street, the storybook town's main drag. Skip the downstairs dining room in favor of the more casual upstairs restaurant, George's Ocean Terrace, a lively, open-air room where the light, southern California cuisine is delectable and the wonderful view is of a craggy section of coast with the limitless Pacific flooding the horizon. The Lodge offers complimentary transportation to La Jolla (in a Mercedes, no less).

NATURE SPOT

Adjacent to the Lodge is Torrey Pines State Reserve, a 2,000-acre botanical and geological wonderland. Here are found hiking trails, sandstone formations, and beautiful beaches (including the nation's largest nude beach). The Reserve is one of only two places where the rare Torrey pine tree grows naturally. (The other is Santa Rosa Island off the northern California coast.) Trails within the park trace a spidery path along bluffs up to 300 feet above the sea, with panoramic views of La Jolla to the south and Del Mar to the north. Overlooks along the Guy Fleming Trail are prime spots for whale- and dolphin-watching.

Johnny Miller, this brawny 7,115-yard layout is tucked among secluded canyons and ravines. Vintage oaks and sycamores along with massive rock outcrops frame the fairways, with meandering creeks, lakes, and waterfalls spicing the challenge. Forty acres of wildflowers provide some visual balm for 10 months of the year on this tough track, which rises and falls 200 feet during the round. A 2004 survey of local pro shops to determine the best greens in the San Diego area prompted an "off-the-chart" response. Indeed, the putting surfaces at Maderas are consistently smooth, fast, and true.

Tucked away in Carlsbad 30 miles north of San Diego, **Four Seasons Resort Aviara** is a spectacular Spanish Colonial–themed resort set on a plateau overlooking the Batiquitos Lagoon, a restored waterway and wildlife preserve that's home to 130 species of shorebirds. Due to environmental constraints, the resort's Arnold Palmer–Ed Seay golf course was 10 years in the making. It was worth the wait. Lakes, streams, and waterfalls frame several holes on the beautifully landscaped, 7,007-yard course, which made its debut in 1991.

The course unfolds in a magnificent garden dotted with lovely water hazards. Sculpted through three valleys, there's more than just eye candy at Aviara: Sloping terrain, undulating greens, and ocean breezes warrant against easy pars. Ready for a swing fix? Aviara Golf Academy, headed by revered instructor Kip Puterbaugh, is one of the nation's best. The luxurious five-story hotel, set atop a hill, has 329 richly–appointed rooms and suites, each with a large marble bathroom and a balcony or landscaped terrace.

One of the nation's first major health retreats, **La Costa Resort & Spa,** cradled in a valley in Carlsbad's Costa Brava hills, has had its share of ups and downs since its inception in 1965. The 36-hole golf complex, laid out on the valley floor by Dick Wilson and Joe Lee, offers traditional, parkland-style golf that has stood the test of time, serving as the long-time host of the Tournament of Champions and then the WGC-Accenture Match Play Championship. This vintage feel-good getaway completed a $140 million renovation in 2004, its centerpiece a new spa with 28,000 square feet of Feng Shui–inspired indoor space.

SIDETRIP: BARONA CREEK
The winding drive up Wildcat Canyon Road 30 miles east of San Diego is a tip-off: You've left civilization behind and entered the Wild West. Haystack-shaped hills covered in sage and dotted with pale boulders eventually give way to a desert plateau ringed by peaks at 1,500 feet above sea level. It is here, a world away from the beachfront in San Diego, that the Barona Band of Mission Indians has built a $225-million hotel and ranch-themed casino on its reservation. The golf course is a major component in the master plan, and it is terrific.

Laid out by Gary Roger Baird and Todd Eckenrode in 2001, the 7,088-yard **Barona Creek Golf Club** blends seamlessly into its setting, which is what the tribe wanted. More than 170 mature native oaks were transplanted from other parts of the reservation and placed around the course, including one in the middle of the fairway of the par-five first hole. Nearly 100 sharp-edged, multi-fingered bunkers were cut into the open, rolling landscape. Rock outcrops frame several greens. Also, the designers built a series of lakes and ponds fed by spidery streams that were strategically routed to heighten the challenge.

A firm, fast track that encourages bump-and-run shots, Barona has very slick greens, pronounced by Notah Begay III as faster than most of those he has seen on the PGA Tour. Each tee marker is etched with a unique cattle branding mark, a few dating to 1932, a time when each Barona family was provided one wagon, five cows, and two horses. With one of the premier courses in the San Diego area offered at a fair price (at press time, the green fee was $75), the tribe has come a long way since then.

Barona Creek Golf Club, second hole

Canada

If there's an international destination that's been taken for granted or treated lightly by the typical American campaigner, it's Canada, our unassuming neighbor to the north. Let's skip the silly jokes about the "frozen north," eh? Let's get right to the stats. The participation rate—roughly 20 percent of the Canadian population plays golf—is one of the highest in the world. (Perhaps that is why Canadians on

Journey Behind the Falls, Niagara Falls

average live nearly three years longer than Americans.) The land of the maple leaf counts more than 2,000 courses stretching from British Columbia to the Maritimes. Eighty percent of these courses are within 100 miles of the U.S. border; most are public-access. And then there's the value factor. At press time, $1 U.S. equaled $1.25 Canadian, which makes everything north of the border—accommodations, meals, green fees, etc.—a good deal.

But golf in Canada isn't just cheap. It's very good and in some cases exceptional, for the simple reason that Canada's landscapes are so varied and compelling. This is especially true in Ontario, which offers a superb variety of new layouts from Niagara Falls to the metropolis of Toronto to the Muskoka region, and on Prince Edward Island, where the lobster suppers, an island tradition, are just as memorable as the tiny province's spectacular new seaside courses.

Stanley Thompson, a Scottish-born Canadian who was one of the first architects to apply principles of art to his strategic designs, not only left behind an incredible set of memorials from coast to coast, he inspired two generations of architects to find new ways, as he did, of extracting fabulous holes from rugged terrain. The new crop of designers—Tom McBroom, Doug Carrick, Graham Cooke, and others—are sparking a second wave of interest in Canada with their stellar layouts.

Lastly, the ancient Scottish game has more of a European feel in the world's second-largest country. Golf is a walking game in Canada, and the pace is generally brisk. Hockey players, it turns out, walk nearly as fast as they skate.

Niagara Falls

How mighty are the world-famous Niagara Falls? You'd have to empty one million bathtubs per second to approach their torrential force. On the Canadian side of this thundering cataract, a mere three miles upstream from the perpetual veil of mist rising from the Horseshoe (Canadian) Falls, is a 700-acre golf complex built by the Niagara Parks Commission (NPC) adjacent to a War of 1812 battleground. The Battle of Chippawa pitted American regulars against British troops in the last major invasion of Canada on July 5, 1814. The skirmish essentially ended in a draw, but Americans have returned in droves to do battle on the facility's pair of exceptional courses.

Debuted in 2002, **Legends on the Niagara** features the work of two of Canada's top designers, Doug Carrick and Tom McBroom. Friendly competitors, the two Ontario-based architects collaborated on the overall golf plan for the Legends but flipped a coin to divide the property. Carrick landed the north parcel, a relatively flat stretch of lightly wooded farmland that nevertheless gives players marching down the 13th fairway a view of the Niagara River shortly before it surges over its limestone ledge.

What nature failed to provide, Carrick built at the **Battlefield,** a sturdy test with four sets of tees placed from 5,500 to 7,309 yards. He created movement in the fairways, scooped out swales around the greens, and installed more than 110 flashed-face bunkers to signpost the holes. These bunkers are in your face at every turn, notably off the tee. Straight hitters can avoid them simply by aiming around them, but to the wayward these penal pits spell terror.

The closing holes on each nine, pressed along the opposite shores of a 20-acre lake, play to greens set below a 35,000-square-foot stone-and-cedar clubhouse patterned after a 19th-century fort. The par-five 18th, a strategic tour de force, bends from left to right around the water, with beach bunkers eating into both fairway and green. In addition, gauntlets of cross bunkers defend the landing areas for the drive and lay-up. If you've managed to escape the musket balls thus far, this may be the hole that does you in. Go for the green in two? You might have better luck going over the Falls in a barrel.

Ussher's Creek, McBroom's creation, is an entirely different golf course. Heads or tails, Mc-

Legends on the Niagara clubhouse

Legends on the Niagara, Ussher's Creek, third hole

Broom came away the winner, for he landed the superior parcel. Traditional in appearance—rectangular tees, grass-faced bunkers—this more wooded course backs into river lowlands, with rehabilitated Ussher's Creek, a tributary of the Niagara River, flanking or crossing more than half the holes. McBroom relies upon plateau greens, subtle doglegs, cleverly placed bunkers, and the meandering, slow-moving creek to keep players honest.

The back nine of this attractive, well-wrought design, which ranges from 5,421 to 7,180 yards, is a little longer and tougher than the front. One of the prettiest holes is the par-four 11th, which beckons

with a wide, gently rising fairway that bends slightly to the left around a lone hardwood. The creek makes a final appearance at the long par-four 18th, which has the widest fairway but perhaps the shallowest green on the course. The green, naturally, is perched above Ussher's Creek.

In addition to the two 18s, both of which were ranked in the top 20 of Canada's Top 100 Public Courses by Toronto's *Globe and Mail* in 2005, there's **Chippawa,** a walkable nine-holer co-designed by Carrick and McBroom. It's ideal for families, beginners, and seasoned campaigners who want to work on their short shots—or settle a bet. From the blue tees,

NEW CASINO ON THE BLOCK

On a 23-acre site on Murray Hill overlooking the Horseshoe Falls on the Canadian side of the border and the American Falls on the U.S. side, the massive **Niagara Falls Casino Resort,** a $900 million project completed in 2004, boasts a giant 200,000-square-foot casino complex and a 374-room hotel affiliated with Hyatt. Other venues within the property include a 750-seat buffet restaurant and the Galleria, which offers nearly 50 retail shops and food outlets. The project, part of a larger vision to transform Niagara Falls into a year-round tourist destination, is expected to boost area tourism to 20 million visitors by 2010 and has prompted numerous area hotels to upgrade and expand their facilities.

SEEING THE FALLS

Don't be skeptical. Niagara Falls—both the American Falls and the Horseshoe (Canadian) Falls—are among the most beautiful and impressive cataracts in the world. Only Victoria Falls in Zimbabwe is larger. There's a reason nearly 14 million tourists (70 percent of them from the U.S.) visit annually to be dumbstruck by the power and beauty of the Falls.

Seeking adventure? The self-guided Journey Behind the Falls permits visitors to descend 125 feet by elevator and walk through a short tunnel to two outdoor observation decks and two portals located directly behind the Horseshoe Falls. Located opposite the American Falls is the Maid of the Mist, which has been carrying visitors to the base of the Falls since 1846. Disposable raincoats are provided with admission. The Niagara Spanish Aero Car, suspended below the Canadian Falls, allows thrill-seekers to view the river as it crashes through the narrowest channel in the gorge. Nature guides describe the geology and natural wonder of the Falls during the Great Gorge Adventure, which brings visitors to a whitewater boardwalk on the river's edge. The Horseshoe Falls are illuminated by colored spotlights at night year-round.

Nature lovers can visit the Niagara Parks Butterfly Conservatory, which is located on the grounds of the magnificent Botanical Gardens and features the world's largest glass-enclosed butterfly habitat. At the Mosaiculture Garden, unveiled in 2002, nature imitates art: Here hundreds of thousands of living plants have been sculpted into larger-than-life creatures, including moose, bear, and birds. Close by is the Floral Clock, its 20,000 small plants artfully used to create one of the largest working clocks of its kind (40 feet in diameter) in the world. Skyhunters is an interactive live show with live flying demonstrations by falcons, hawks, owls, and a bald eagle. Something more active? Bike, hike, stroll, or rollerblade the Niagara River Recreation Trail, which traces the path of the Niagara River from Fort Erie to Niagara-on-the-Lake.

Maid of the Mist, Niagara Falls

Whirlpool Golf Course, second hole

the course measures 2,202 yards (par 30), with three par fours and six par threes. Chippawa's "Little Legends" configuration, designed to put the holes within reach of children, offers three each of par threes, fours, and fives. It measures 1,972 yards.

The practice facility at the Legends, perhaps the finest of its kind in Canada, boasts a 45-acre, 360-degree "firing range" with facsimile fairways and bunkered targets; a huge moated practice putting green inset with sod-walled bunkers; and a teaching academy headed by Canadian Hall-of-Famer Cathy Sherk.

Golf packages with major chain hotels in Niagara Falls, including the **Renaissance Fallsview, Sheraton Fallsview,** and **Hilton Niagara Falls** are available.

A burgeoning golf destination, the Niagara region has more than 40 courses, with more on the drawing board. Niagara, in fact, is gunning to become the Pinehurst of Canada. With its relatively mild climate and close proximity to the U.S., it just might

succeed. Here's a sampling of excellent new courses and a pair of venerable old-timers within a short distance of the Falls.

On a rolling, wooded site beside the Niagara River, Rees Jones has crafted the first of two courses at **Grand Niagara Resort,** a facility that will further boost the region's appeal as a golf destination. Called the **River Course,** the 7,425-yard layout skirts the Welland River and offers a glimpse of the mist produced by the Falls. Jones said he borrowed liberally from several Golden Age designers, including Alister MacKenzie, Seth Raynor, and Charles Banks, to produce a scenic, neo-classic test marked by perched greens and bold, sweeping bunkers. The short par fours in particular are well-executed. Jones's layout, debuted in 2005, will be followed by the **Vineyard Course,** a links-style creation by Greg Norman with two holes laid out along the river.

Also opened in 2005 was **Thundering Waters Golf Club,** a John Daly–designed layout a mere two blocks from the Fallsview Resort District. Promoted as "the closest greens to the falls," the 7,208-yard layout, designed in collaboration with Canadian architect Bo Danoff, is a parkland track with links-style accents. Fourteen holes wind through a mature forest of maple, oak, and hickory. The remainder are more open, their broad fairways parted through fescue-covered hills. Thundering Waters features numerous do-or-die scenarios, most of which only a golfer of Daly's caliber should attempt from the tips.

Royal Niagara, a 27-hole semi-private club that opened in 2001, has three distinct nines spread across a beautiful stretch of rolling land. The first nine is nestled below a long, wooded ridge known as the Niagara Escarpment, the second is landmarked by a giant Iron Bridge circa 1860, and the third skirts the Old Welland Canal and a series of ponds. Fairways are gently moguled, while the multi-tiered greens on this Ted Baker–designed layout are smooth and fast. Most of the holes are framed by oval-shaped bunkers, grassy swales, and fields of tall fescues, with creeks cutting across several fairways.

Hunters Pointe is a modern links-style design with five sets of tees ranging from 5,332 to 6,884 yards. This semi-private club, laid out by Graham Cooke, occupies open, treeless land beside the "new" Welland Canal. Debuted in 2000, the course strives for the look of a British Open links right down to the yellow checkerboard flags. Holes are framed by tall fescues, heaving mounds, and large bunkers filled with gleaming white sand. The 14th hole, high point of the course, gives players a distant view of Niagara Falls.

Whirlpool Golf Course is, like Legends on the Niagara, part of the Niagara Parks Golf Trail. Adjacent to the Niagara Gorge a few miles downstream from the falls, Whirlpool is a Stanley Thompson design opened in 1951 that underwent numerous changes in the 1990s. The overall impression at Whirlpool is one of pleasant holiday golf, but it is a strong, strategic test with plenty of bite from the tips, especially on a breezy day. Careless approach shots will leave players with devilish chips to sloping greens, while the multi-lobed bunkers are in all the right places. To a seasoned player who chooses to walk, Whirlpool will seem as soothing and familiar as an old melody. The renovation included new tees, redone bunkers, and a refurbished clubhouse. But not all changes were for the better. The par-four second was converted into a jazzy "signature hole" with the addition of a greenside pond that is out of character with the rest of the course.

History buffs will want to check out **Niagara-on-the-Lake,** a petite nine-holer on the shores of Lake Ontario, which opened in 1875 and bills itself as "North America's Oldest Golf Course."

NIAGARA-ON-THE-LAKE

The Loyalist feeling is strong in this beautifully preserved town, which in every aspect resembles a quaint little corner of England. An early capital of Canada and annually voted one of its prettiest towns, historic Niagara-on-the-Lake, located 20 minutes downstream from the falls at the point where the Niagara River empties into Lake Ontario, has the welcome mat out for visitors, with nearly 4,000 bed-and-breakfast homes and century-old cottages available. Horse-drawn carriages ply the tree-lined streets of a storybook village full of green parks, lush gardens, and magnificent Victorian-era homes. Its main boulevard, Queen Street, is lined with art galleries, sidewalk cafes, chocolatiers, wine merchants, craft shops selling period furniture, and the likes of Greaves Jams and Marmalades, which has been producing small-batch jams on the premises for four generations.

WINERIES OF ONTARIO

Somewhat incredibly, there are more than 40 wineries on the Niagara Peninsula. The climate in the region is similar to that of several of the world's finest wine-producing regions—Burgundy, the Loire Valley, Oregon, and New Zealand. In addition, the moderating effect of two Great Lakes (Erie and Ontario) ensures a cool spring and an extended autumn season ideal for growing grapes (and pleasing golfers). The soils—from the fertile lands surrounding Niagara-on-the-Lake to the imbedded limestone at the base of the Niagara Escarpment—are well-suited to vineyards.

All the major grape varietals are grown here, but the Niagara region has becomes famous for its Ice Wines, which are harvested in winter and pressed from frozen grapes. The grapes, having achieved full ripeness in October, are left untouched on the vines until the first cold snap, freezing the grapes solid. Ice Wine is characterized by intense natural sweetness, a highly aromatic bouquet of tropical fruits, and a depth of flavors that can hold its own with any dessert wine. At roughly $50 for a half bottle, Ice Wine is not inexpensive, but it is exceptional. One of the top Ice Wine producers is Inniskillin in Niagara-on-the-Lake. Tours and tastings are available.

Toronto

The metropolitan area of Canada's largest and most cosmopolitan city boasts more than 200 golf courses, many of them within an hour's drive of downtown. With the possible exception of Chicago, more top-notch public-access courses can be found in the rolling, wooded hills on the outskirts of Toronto than any other major North American city. There are a few venerable mainstays, including long-time Canadian Open host site Glen Abbey, but the newer tracks, a bevy of them designed in various styles by area resident Doug Carrick, are the ones to play.

The original course at **Angus Glen,** a stellar facility in Markham, is a firm test designed by Carrick in 1994 on roller-coaster terrain marked by sharp elevation changes, wetlands, and a very brawny collection of par fours. The layout, now called the **South Course,** hosted the 2002 Canadian Open. From the tips at 7,400 yards, its 143 slope and 76.0 course rating give a fair indication of its resistance to scoring. The facility's **North Course,** a collaboration between Carrick and Jay Morrish that opened in 2001, is a grand links-style track marked by broad fairways and dramatic sod-walled bunkers, its larger greens

embraced by flowing swales and grassy hollows. A strategic tour de force—the stacked-sod bunkers used to signpost the course are the most distinctive in the province—the North Course will itself welcome the Canadian Open in 2007.

Osprey Valley has a genuine surfeit of riches set in the rolling hills of Caledon, an hour's drive northwest of Toronto. Having built the popular **Heathlands Links** in 1993, a compact, links-style design walled in by a sea of heaving fescue-covered mounds, with deep pot bunkers framing the open-entry greens, Carrick returned in 2001 to build two additional venues, fancifully named **Hoot** and **Toot.** Hoot, dropped into a rolling expanse of sandy wastelands dotted with spruce and pine, was inspired by Pine Valley, the legendary course carved from similar terrain in southern New Jersey. Carrick gouged huge pits from the land and filled them with 10,000 tons of local sand, creating a raw, untamed links favored by shot-makers. Toot, by contrast, is a handsome parkland spread marked by numerous elevated tees that fits its rolling, glacier-carved landscape hand-in-glove. On a typically breezy day, Toot could pass for a course in the Scottish Highlands. Hoot and Toot

Angus Glen, North Course, 14th hole

have combined to elevate housing-free Osprey Valley to must-play status in the greater Toronto area.

Tucked away in tiny Kleinburg, **Copper Creek** is a multi-themed course by Carrick that finally opened in 2002 after being tied up for 10 years in the permitting process. The course has 11 good holes on upper tableland, three very good holes stretched across a meadow, and four exceptional holes routed 80 feet below the topmost holes and fortress-like clubhouse in a valley skirted by the east branch of the Humber River. Carrick moved plenty of dirt to provide interest on the farmland series of holes, but left well enough alone in the valley, where a series of interconnected ponds and clusters of old white pines delight the eye.

Eagle's Nest is yet another Carrick design, just down the road from Copper Creek but entirely different in concept and appearance. Working on portions of an old sand and gravel extraction pit, Carrick transformed the barren landscape into a compelling links-style track, the site's sand scars amplified to resemble eroded dunes. Marked by huge plateau greens, fescue-covered hills, and sandy wastelands dotted with grass islands, this strategic gem's sod-walled bunkers are a tip of the hat to the Auld Sod.

The course, a mere 45 minutes from downtown Toronto, opened to acclaim in 2004.

Wooden Sticks, a Ron Garl design that debuted in 1999 in Uxbridge, is a replica course that recreates several of the world's most famous holes. Admirably, it is not hokey. There are three holes imported from the Old Course at St. Andrews, notably the infamous Road Hole, and a prodigious par five inspired by the fearsome sixth hole at Carnoustie. The key holes at Augusta National's Amen Corner, 12 and 13, are replicated here, as is the island green at the TPC at Sawgrass Stadium Course. Four holes were lifted from Pine Valley, but six of the holes are Garl originals, and they are among the best on the course.

Want to get in one last round before heading home? **Royal Woodbine** is a venue very near the flight path of arriving and departing jetliners, a 6,446-yard, par-71 layout a mere runway-length from curbside check-in at Toronto Pearson Airport. Designed by Michael Hurdzan in 1992, the course is wedged between the wetlands of Mimico Creek and the looming facades of airport hotels. Compact and glove-tight, Royal Woodbine has enough water and sand in play to keep good players honest.

Osprey Valley, Toot, third hole

Copper Creek, 10th hole

Copper Creek, eighth hole   Opposite: Eagle's Nest third hole

Muskoka

Two hours north of Toronto is one of the continent's most venerable summer retreats. This is the "cottage country" of Muskoka, loosely translated from the Algonquin Native language as "the land of red earth." But maybe the Indians were looking on the bright side, for Muskoka isn't known for its soil. It is said that the last person who was disappointed by Muskoka was surely a farmer.

Peeking through the region's thin layer of topsoil is the Canadian Shield, the main continental block of the earth's crust underlying North America. Composed of Precambrian rocks, the Shield is a craton, the geological center from which the continent first evolved. Stretching from Labrador to Alberta and from the Arctic Ocean to the southern U.S., the Canadian Shield is the largest craton in the world.

During successive ice ages, thick glaciers scoured the region, creating 1,600 island-dotted lakes. In time, forests of fir and spruce, birch and maple sprang up.

Muskoka, a place unto itself, is where southern Ontario ends and a new geography begins. Canada's first wilderness resort was built in Muskoka in 1870, and it was to this region that residents of sooty industrial cities—notably Pittsburgh—would escape for the summer. As Muskoka's reputation as a summer getaway grew, so did the size and grandeur of its resort hotels. In its heyday, High Society—the Mellon banking family, the Rockefellers—dined to the accompaniment of live chamber music and waltzed to full orchestras in the grand pavilions of the finer establishments.

Flash fires and fickle holiday habits ended the region's golden era, but lately Hollywood stars and Canadian hockey legends have rediscovered Muskoka, building lakefront cottages every bit as grand as those of yesteryear. Best of all for traveling players, Muskoka has blossomed as a golf destination, its rockbound stage one of the most visually arresting in the game.

Taboo Resort, seventh hole

Deerhurst Highlands, 10th hole

For years, the Canadian Shield was the bane of golf course developers in Muskoka. Then architect Tom McBroom decided to insert himself between a rock and a hard place. "In golf architecture," McBroom says, "bedrock has generally been treated like a bad family secret—best covered up and forgotten." Except for stone boundary walls (common in Scotland), rock historically has not had a place in golf.

McBroom believes that "rock can provide great beauty, character, and strategic nuance in golf design, especially where it is an indigenous, dominant element," as it is throughout the Muskoka region. The key to using the Shield as a design motif, he says, is to keep it out of play for all but the poorest offline shots—no one likes to see a golf ball dance crazily on rock. But in capable hands, the Shield, selectively power-washed and used to create harmony between the course and its surroundings, can be a compelling design element. Which is why some of the best new courses in North America, namely the brace of venues on the **Muskoka Golf Trail** established in 2003, have been hewn from its granite underpinnings.

Ninety minutes north of Toronto is Gravenhurst, the self-proclaimed "Gateway to Muskoka." On the south shore of Lake Muskoka is one of the region's vintage properties, **Taboo Resort,** f.k.a. Muskoka Sands Resort. Founded in 1927, the original hotel, called the Muskoka Beach Inn, was destroyed by fire in 1959, but a new hotel was built closer to the lakeshore. New ownership later brought a wave of changes, all

for the better. In addition to expanded lodging, the decision was made to build a world-class golf course at the 1,200-acre resort. Played from an incorrect set of tees, this stunning newcomer, opened in 2002, is nothing but trouble. Designer Ron Garl, a scratch golfer with a flair for showmanship, built a championship track stretching to 7,174 yards (par 71)—the 75.2 course rating and 146 slope are the region's highest—but multiple sets of forward tees give everyone a fighting chance.

After Garl spent the better part of two years devising a routing plan that "would lie softly on the land," more than 350,000 cubic yards of sand was used to plat the rugged site. Carved from a thick forest of black and white spruce, jack pine, balsam and poplar, Taboo also showcases generous portions of the Canadian Shield. "The rock formations were the biggest challenge in routing the course," Garl says, "and are integrated through the entire layout to add character and challenge." He had little choice. No amount of TNT could have rearranged the rock.

Taboo's back nine, with sharper elevation changes and bigger trees than the front, presents one of Muskoka's toughest stretches of golf as it barrels through the wilderness. The stunning par-five 18th, 558 yards at full stretch, is a case in point: an elevated tee set on a rocky perch, a fine view of Lake Muskoka on the horizon, massive granite outcrops on both sides of the zigzag fairway, pot bunkers and grassy hollows bracketing the diagonal green. It brings a brilliant course to a rousing climax.

Tucked away on the shores of Peninsula Lake outside Huntsville is **Deerhurst Resort,** a full-service resort with a 19th-century pedigree and home to the course that put Muskoka on the golf map: **Deerhurst Highlands.** Carved from a forested granite ridge above glacially-formed Peninsula Lake, the Highlands, laid out in 1990 by veteran designer Bob Cupp and Tom McBroom, marked a significant departure from the tamer venues in the region. In the past, architects limited by budgets and technology—and possibly imagination—avoided Muskoka's rugged, dramatic terrain. Deerhurst Highlands was the first course in the area to embrace hills, cliffs, woods, creeks, and wetlands. The result is a wilderness tour de force that, from the gold markers at 7,011 yards, remains one of the most exacting courses in Canada. Commented Lorne Rubenstein of the Toronto *Globe and Mail* shortly after the course opened, "The Canadian Open could be held here. Any PGA Tour event could be held here. The course is that good." Because of its relative remoteness, no major events have been contested at Deerhurst Highlands, but that hasn't stopped grail seekers from putting their games to the test on this fire-breather.

The first tee at the Highlands, with Peninsula Lake pinned to the horizon, is an eye-opener. Tee shots at this mid-length par four plummet 100 feet to a generous landing area flanked by deep woods, although flat lies are hard to come by in the sloping fairway. The green is small, well-defended, and anything but flat. Early in his career, McBroom championed liberally contoured greens replete with multiple decks and shelves intended to drive even the best of putters close to the edge. The greens on the Highlands are of this variety—14 of them have *at least* two levels.

The most spectacular hole on the Highlands, the one that most fully embraces the Canadian Shield, is the massive par-four 10th, where a 40-foot-high curtain of rock hems in the right side of the tumbling fairway. The hole swings to the right past the rock and leads to a large, undulating green staked out by saucer-like bunkers to the left and right. This is one of the great two-shotters in the province.

The Highlands thunders on thereafter, with water in play at the final five holes. However, average players who minimize their mistakes from the white tees at 6,012 yards (the blues are 6,506 yards) can find their way round in relative safety. The trick is not to try for too much.

If the Highlands presents too stiff a challenge, opt for **Deerhurst Lakeside,** a near-perfect venue for holidaymakers. Originally designed by C.E. "Robbie" Robinson in 1966, this 4,712-yard, par-65 charmer, reconfigured by McBroom, is a scenic delight.

DAY TRIP/GRAVENHURST

In the early 1900s, steamships plied the waters of Muskoka's numerous lakes, ferrying passengers from one resort destination to another. Gravenhurst is the home port of the R.M.S. *Segwun,* the oldest operating steamship in North America. Built in the 1880s, it was retired in the late 1950s, but restored in 1981 by the Muskoka Steamship and Historical Society. From June through October, visitors can embark on scenic voyages through Muskoka waterways on the *Segwun.*

The restored Gravenhurst Opera House, a century-old landmark, features more than 200 shows throughout the year and comes to life in the summer months. Catch the StrawHat professional summer theatre festival or any of the comedies or dramas staged in this grand 350-seat theatre, its stage, according to local legend, haunted by a ghost.

OFF-COURSE ATTRACTIONS

At Muskoka Heritage Place in Huntsville, the Portage Flyer Steam Train (rides available) and Pioneer Village combine to portray life in the region in the early 1900s. The working village includes farm animals, a general store, sawmill, blacksmith shop, nature trails, wagon rides, a telegraph station, plus two museums. It's ideal for a family outing.

Thirty minutes from Deerhurst is Algonquin Provincial Park, one of eastern Canada's finest wildlife sanctuaries and recreation areas. Created in 1893, this vast 2,910-square-mile park protects the headwaters of five major rivers and offers world-class canoeing over hundreds of miles of calm lakes and rushing rivers. Two major hiking trails also crisscross the park.

Located on one of the highest points in Muskoka a short drive east of Huntsville is Echo Valley Observatory, a three-story domed facility perfectly situated for "deep sky viewing." Because there is very little light pollution in the region, stargazers on a dark, moonless night can clearly see the moons of Saturn, the cloud belts of Jupiter, and other solar system highlights. The observatory's 40-centimeter telescope is capable of revealing celestial objects 10,000 times fainter than the faintest objects visible to the naked eye. In addition, the treetop observation deck permits unobstructed binocular viewing of the entire night sky for constellation and planet identification. Nightlife in Muskoka? Echo Valley is it.

A MUST-HAVE

Ontario's north woods breed unusually voracious mosquitoes that must be repelled at all costs. Generic stay-away ointments won't get the job done. Available in most Muskoka golf shops is Ben's 100 Insect Repellent Spray, a very strong cutter made in New Hampshire that may smell noxious, but will keep away the biting bugs.

Lake Joseph Club, eighth hole

Some 30 miles southwest of Huntsville in the little town of Port Carling is the **Lake Joseph Club,** another McBroom creation that notched his reputation a little higher when it opened in 1997. This facility gave McBroom another chance to make his mark in Muskoka, and he delivered a player's course worth getting to know. In fact, "Lake Joe" needs to be played more than once to unravel its mysteries, for it is a visually intimidating layout that spells doom for wayward hitters. Better players would be well-advised to bag the driver at several holes in favor of the club they hit straightest, for "Muskoka rough"— loose rock, thorny brambles, soggy wetlands—hems in the fairways.

Routed on land that pitches and tosses through dense woods and past the Shield's granite outcrops, this well-conditioned layout is a brute from the tips at 6,985 yards. Forward tees gives players with double-digit handicaps a fighting chance, but the premium here is on shot placement. Also the ability to forget the status of the game for a moment and drink in the woodsy beauty from the many elevated tees.

The par-three eighth, only 158 yards from the gold tees, is a genuine postcard hole and perhaps the prettiest one-shotter in Muskoka. Players mount an elevated tee and gaze 40 feet below to a long, well-bunkered green prefaced by rock and backdropped by a wooded granite cliff. What a place to hit a crisp short iron!

Lake Joe's back nine is longer and firmer than the front, with wetlands and a few ponds pinching the fairways or guarding the greens. McBroom shuffles the deck constantly, never allowing the look to repeat or the challenge to stale. The putting surfaces have plenty of speed and contour but are not nearly as Himalayan as the greens at Deerhurst Highlands.

Novices and families seeking a more carefree outing can have a go at Lake Joe's charming nine-hole Academy Course.

With Deerhurst Highlands and Lake Joseph under his belt, Tom McBroom was ready to make his biggest architectural statement to date and serve on a granite platter the quintessential Muskoka golf experience: **Rocky Crest Golf Club.** Located in tiny MacTier at the north end of Lake Joseph, Rocky Crest, says McBroom, "was inspired by my lifelong love affair with Muskoka and by lessons learned during a decade of designing courses in the region." To say McBroom expanded upon his notion of incorporating the Canadian Shield as a key strategic element in the design of the course is an understatement. Players might consider carrying a pick-axe as a 15th club, so pervasive is the rock. Opened to acclaim in 2000, Rocky Crest is that rarest of venues, a course where you feel invigorated by the challenge and awestruck by the setting.

Opposite: Rocky Crest Golf Club, 16th hole   Above: Grandview Golf Club, Mark O'Meara Course, 18th hole

Spread across more than 300 acres, this links-in-the-wilderness, framed by old-growth hemlock, white pine and birch, roams across gently rolling terrain dotted with wetlands. Each hole occupies its own wooded compartment, yet greens and tees on this walker-friendly layout are proximate, a tribute to the soundness of the routing. McBroom hauled in more than 500,000 metric tons of sand (that's 26,000 truckloads) to provide a growing medium where none had existed. He also used high-pressure hoses to peel back dirt and expose granite outcrops to further articulate his "golf on the rocks" theme.

"We exposed more rock not only in the foreground at Rocky Crest, but also in strategic areas, to define a turn in a dogleg and to frame greens," McBroom explains. "The trick was to make sure the rock didn't come into play. We wanted to celebrate our natural Canadian features and...show off the spectacular beauty of the rock." This celebration helps explain why there are only 35 bunkers at Rocky Crest. Several greens have no bunkers at all—McBroom felt none were needed either for strategic challenge or visual enhancement. Mostly, the holes tread lightly on the craggy landscape. No tricks, no gimmicks.

The ability to work the ball in both directions is the key to scoring from the gold tees at 6,943 yards (par 71), although four sets of forward tees (from 6,755 to 5,251 yards) offer the promise of an exhilarating round. Especially to those who choose to walk. The theme for the day looms into view on the tee of the par-five first hole: A large shelf of gray rock protrudes from the outside corner of the dogleg, with smaller outcrops popping up left of the green near a pair of bunkers.

While the front nine is relatively sporty—only 3,309 yards from the golds—the longer back nine, a sturdy 3,634 yards from the tips, will rock your world from any set of tees. The tremendous par-five 18th sums up all that has gone before. The tee shot is played over wetlands to the left of a rock-studded hill, the rising fairway hiding a view of the green. Upon cresting the hill, players are treated to a delightful sight: a well-proportioned green set below a mammoth rock ledge and behind it the outdoor terrace of a clubhouse perfectly matched to the course. Built from giant pine logs harvested in nearby Bracebridge, this 8,000-square-foot edifice is a fanciful version of a wilderness lodge adapted for golf.

McBroom is under contract to design a second course at Rocky Crest, but after building the top public-access course in Ontario, he has a tough act to follow—his own.

155

The Muskoka region would seem an unlikely place for PGA Tour veteran Mark O'Meara to make his architectural debut, but **Grandview Golf Club** in Huntsville, opened in 2001, is where the likeable pal of Tiger Woods chose to launch his design career. Judging by the results achieved on the **Mark O'Meara Course** (an additional layout by Curtis Strange and Nancy Lopez is planned at Grandview), O'Meara, winner of the Masters and British Open in 1998, can look forward to a brilliant second act in the golf design business.

Working on a spectacular site marked by steep hills, tall trees, and plenty of rock, O'Meara fashioned a rugged but also refined American-style design with wide fairways, big bunkers, and large, slick greens. Where McBroom's designs tiptoe lightly around the landscape, O'Meara has created a "statement" course intended to separate the men from the boys. It gets down to business quickly. The first hole, a par four, plays from an elevated tee and calls for a long carry over a sunken, weedy pond to a plateau fairway that swings to the right past a scalloped bunker. From the white tees, the carry is well over 170 yards, a prodigious pop for most duffers on their first swing of the day. The par-five second hole is even more daunting: The fairway, while broad, plays up a very steep hill that is an exercise in discouragement for higher handicappers.

The course presents itself as a roller-coaster ride through a boreal forest, around rock outcrops that resemble whalebacks, and past wetlands posted by Ducks Unlimited Canada. The holes are uniformly dramatic, demanding, and well-strategized for the top-flight player, less so for the duffer. The layout is fair in the sense that good shots find their reward, but probably requires a second go-round at minimum to unravel a few of its idiosyncrasies. Those who don't bring their "A" game to the Mark O'Meara Course might wish to confine themselves to Grandview's nine-hole Academy Course.

Grandview's magnificent clubhouse, overlooking the first tee and 18th green, is a regal 30,000-square-foot, stone-and-timber edifice that has elicited "clubhouse envy" among the region's other golf facilities. Commanding a hilltop, it's as much of an architectural statement as the golf course.

The name may be more explicit than artful, but **The Rock,** debuted in 2003, is a rolling, compact course marked by narrow corridors and more than 75 flashed-face bunkers. Much of the underbrush beside the fairways on this Nick Faldo–designed layout, located at Minett Landing on Lake Rosseau, has been cleared and sprinkled with wood chips to facilitate recoveries. However, the course twists and turns tightly through the woods, calling for carefully placed shots. Dramatic granite outcrops—the Shield in all its glory—come into play at more than half the holes.

The relative lack of distance—The Rock measures 6,545 yards against a par of 70—is more than com-

The Rock, fourth hole

pensated for by small, liberally contoured greens and the chipping areas that embrace them. Several holes are flanked by vast waste bunkers, but two holes, 11 and 16, are bunkerless, relying on terrain contours and sheer rock for their challenge. Says designer Brit Stenson, who collaborated with Faldo on the layout, "I've worked with rock before but never quite the same combination of rock, wetlands, and elevation you find in Muskoka. There's really no place like this anywhere in the world."

The Rock will be part of the 1,400-acre Red Leaves Resort on Lake Rosseau, with a JW Mariott hotel and interval ownership property expected to open by 2007–08.

The time was the Roaring '20s, which Canada enjoyed with just as much pomp and revelry as the United States. American industrialist Charles Orlando Shaw built the grandest and most expensive hostelry in Muskoka on Bigwin Island outside Huntsville, with accommodations for 500 guests. The enormous 12-sided dance pavilion of his party palace was cantilevered over Lake of Bays. During the heyday of the big bands, Duke Ellington, Count Basie, and Guy Lombardo performed here. The great Canadian designer Stanley Thompson was brought in to build a golf course, but his creation was abandoned when the resort sank into ruin in the late 1960s. Nearly 30 years later, a group of local investors called in Doug Carrick to superimpose a new course on the old site.

Carrick utilized some of Thompson's original corridors and green sites on the rolling, wooded land, but **Bigwin Island Golf Club,** unveiled in 2001, is entirely his own creation. In an age when far too many courses are designed to seek out a golfer's weaknesses and exploit them, Bigwin was designed for pleasure. It offers plenty of challenge from the back tees (there are four sets ranging from 7,166 to 5,346 yards), but the course is never overbearing.

The mood is set upon arrival. After a five-minute ferry ride from Norway Point across Lake of Bays, players arrive at a "golf dock" where bags are unloaded. Peaceful and inviting, Bigwin Island is all of one piece, the whole greater than the sum of its parts. The tree-lined fairways are unusually wide—no hunting for stray balls in thick rough here. Large, flashed-face bunkers filled with tawny silica sand as well as subtly contoured hilltop greens offer resistance to scoring, but Bigwin is all about enjoying the game and perhaps catching sight of the albino deer that roam the course. Mount the back tee at the par-four sixth for one of the prettiest views in Canadian golf: Spread out below this exalted perch 150 feet above the fairway is a panorama of beautiful Lake of Bays and its forested islands.

The time to play Bigwin Island, which is priced well above other Muskoka area courses (roughly $120 to $170 U.S. at press time), is now. Once the membership is filled, there's a good chance this enchanting club will become private.

Bigwin Island Golf Club, sixth hole

Deerhurst Resort on Peninsula Lake

MUSKOKA LODGING & DINING

Muskoka Golf Trail packages are available through Ultimate Golf Vacations. The Trail promotes two- and five-night programs utilizing four different resorts, though golfers can create their own packages by choosing any number of nights and rounds of golf. Properties can be mixed-and-matched. Rates are reduced from early September through October 31.

Taboo Resort offers a wide variety of new and renovated lodge rooms, one- and two-bedroom suites, and multi-bedroom cottage chalets. Suites and condos feature balconies and fireplaces; many condos have saunas and whirlpools. The resort claims to have more guest rooms and suites overlooking water than any other Muskoka resort. In 2003, Taboo opened its SweetGrass Spa. The resort's top dining spot is the Wildfire Grille, where eclectic Asian-fused creations using local ingredients are featured.

Deerhurst Resort, built in 1896 as a wilderness retreat for wealthy American industrialists, was the region's first summer destination property. Significantly expanded over the years, the 800-acre resort offers a wide array of bayside rooms and multi-bedroom villas. There's also a solarium-enclosed swimming pool near Peninsula Lake, an Aveda Concept Spa, and a long list of recreational activities, from squash to sailing. Among the dining options at Deerhurst is Eclipse, which occupies a window-walled room with open-beam ceiling and offers an eclectic menu (local game, fish, and produce, notably wild mushrooms). After dinner, be sure to catch the resort's latest musical stage show (country star Shania Twain's career was launched here).

Rocky Crest Golf Resort, reopened in 1999 after a major facelift, features an all-suite property with 65 one-bedroom, two-bedroom, and multi-level units, many of them overlooking Lake Joseph. Family-friendly, the 350-acre resort has a beach, an outdoor pool, kayaking, hiking, and a children's program. There's also a fitness center and an AMBA Health and Beauty Spa. The Lake Joseph Dining Room offers a superb menu complemented by an extensive wine cellar. More casual fare is available at the open-air Bayside Patio. The resort is 10 minutes from the golf club.

Delta Grandview Resort, set on 850 acres overlooking Fairy Lake, is a vintage property that dates to 1911. Completely renovated in 2002, Grandview welcomes families but is more oriented to business groups. Accommodations range from standard rooms to luxury suites. The resort's Owl's Nest Lounge has been transformed into a lobby bar with a magnificent stone fireplace. The clubhouse dining room is the summer venue for Grandview's well-known Sunday brunch.

Prince Edward Island

The Micmac Indians called the island *Abegweit*, meaning "cradled on the waves," and indeed everything on this slim crescent of land in the Gulf of St. Lawrence revolves around the sea. Well, nearly everything. Prince Edward Island's rich red soil yields high-grade potatoes and excellent berries, but its most interesting crop of late has been golf courses. More than 25 golf courses can be found from one end of the 140-mile-long island to the other, several of them built since the mid-1990s. A few are modest nine-holers, but the majority are full-sized 18s by top Canadian designers that take full advantage of the gently rolling terrain and lovely sea views. Thanks to the warming influence of the Gulf Stream, golf is played six months a year on PEI.

Until fairly recently, the only way to reach PEI was by ferry across the Northumberland Strait from New Brunswick or Nova Scotia. But the opening of the nine-mile-long Confederation Bridge in 1997, the island's only link to mainland Canada, literally paved the way to this amiable little province. Tourism, in fact, has increased by 60 percent to upwards of 1.2 million visitors per year since the bridge opened, yet PEI retains its unhurried pace and rural sensibility.

Even avid golfers should tear themselves away from the links long enough to see Charlottetown, PEI's charming capital city. The city's original settlement, located near the harbor, is a historic district of beautiful tree-lined streets, wood-framed homes—and pubs that feature traditional Celtic music.

Despite its northern latitude, PEI has some of the warmest salt water north of the Carolinas, with mid-summer temperatures reaching 70 degrees. The island's red-sand beaches, while popular, are rarely thronged. There is also the bounty of the sea itself: some of the sweetest lobsters in North America are drawn from PEI's waters. Malpeque Bay oysters are highly prized, as are plump native scallops and farm-raised mussels.

PEI itself has had a hand in its success as a golf destination. Several of the top courses are owned and operated by the provincial government. As is true throughout Canada, green fee rates are well below the norm and offer superior value given the quality of the layouts. Perhaps best of all, the pace on PEI is leisurely. The island delivers something that is in very short supply in a world that runs at gigabyte speed—tranquility.

The Links at Crowbush Cove, 11th hole

Developed by the provincial government, **The Links at Crowbush Cove,** opened in 1993, is the course that established PEI as a world-class golf destination and paved the way for future development. Laid out by Toronto-based Tom McBroom, the 6,903-yard design sprawls across a magnificent site on the island's north shore 30 minutes from Charlottetown. Taking its cue from Scottish and Irish links courses, about half the holes overlook the ocean (actually the Gulf of St. Lawrence) and skirt rolling sand dunes, which McBroom mimics with his landforms. Parkland-style holes were carved from thick stands of native spruce, with salty marshes and wetlands favored by waterfowl also in play.

With a slope of 148 from the tips, Crowbush, on a windy day, is not for the meek. Clusters of deep pot bunkers defend the inside corners of the doglegs, while cavernous bunkers are cut below the liberally contoured greens. Heavy underbrush and tall fescue grasses swallow shots that depart the fairway. The fairways are generous, and the forward tees give the average player a fair chance, but Crowbush was built to challenge the best.

Although the collection of holes at Crowbush is well-paced and varied, the eureka moment comes at the spectacular par-five 11th, its back tee perched on a high dune. From this elevated vantage point, players can scan for miles along the sandy coast looking east and west, the languid gulf issuing a cool, delightful breeze. Golf-wise, it is one of the prettiest spots in the Maritimes. With water cutting across the fairway near the green, it's also quite challenging, though the petite par-three 17th, a scant 113 yards from the tips, is more devilish. "Distress awaits any errant tee shot as dramatic slopes surround the green," reads the scorecard. Enough said.

At the eastern end of the island within **Brudenell River Resort** is the big, brawny **Dundarave Golf Course,** at 7,284 yards one of the longest, strongest courses in Atlantic Canada. Designed by Americans Michael Hurdzan and Dana Fry in 1999, the course, its name taken from the home estate of the region's first Scottish settlers, is a wild, natural beauty, a grand-scale test marked by the widest fairways and largest greens in the province. Holes are set beside the Brudenell River, a tidal inlet, or wind through a dense forest of pines. Each fairway is isolated from the others by trees, hills, or wetlands, which makes a round here as peaceful as life itself on PEI. Dundarave's most striking feature is its collection of

Brudenell River Resort, Dundarave Golf Course, eighth hole

Mill River Golf Course, seventh hole

deep, penal bunkers. All 190 of them are filled with red-tinted sand. (High iron content gives PEI soils their reddish hue.)

With its non-returning nines, Dundarave roams far from the clubhouse across surprisingly hilly terrain. According to the designers, four distinct types of golf are found here—links, heathland, coastal, and inland. Most visitors favor the holes that run along the river, notably the par-four eighth. From an elevated tee, you can see the green beckoning from the far end of a peninsula on this right-to-left dogleg. However, the drive must carry a narrow inlet of the river to find a hairpin-shaped fairway staked out by several saucer-like bunkers. Too long, you're in the trees. Too short, you're wet. One of Dundarave's prettiest interior holes is the par-three 17th: Spread before the elevated tee is an abbreviated fairway, a shelf-like green, and, in the far distance, the bunker-strewn 18th fairway and clubhouse.

Predating Dundarave by 30 years is the resort's **Brudenell River Golf Course,** a solid C.E. "Robbie" Robinson design that consists of six par fives, six par fours, and six par threes. At 6,591 yards, this well-groomed course, while no pushover, provides a nice counterpoint to the lovely but tough piece of Scottish beef that is Dundarave. Recent upgrades by Graham Cooke have fine-tuned the facility's original venue. Players of lesser attainment can have a go at the resort's Academy 9 Golf Course, an enjoyable nine-hole, par-30 course by Hurdzan-Fry overlooking the river. The scaled-down course is the centerpiece of the Canadian Golf Academy, one of the nation's top teaching facilities.

At the western end of PEI some 90 minutes from Charlottetown is the **Mill River Golf Course,** another vintage Robbie Robinson design touched up in the mid-'90s by Graham Cooke. A long-time favorite of locals and visitors alike, the layout's higher ground offers fine vistas of an ocean inlet off Cascumpec Bay. Mill River has become infamous over the years for its par-four seventh hole. From an elevated tee tucked in a wooded slot, players look to a narrow fairway split down the middle by a chain of small ponds. Neptune's necklace, it could be called. The drive must be placed to the right of the creek and its pools to set up an approach to an elevated green. A tee shot pulled to the left may leave your second shot blocked by trees, while a straight ball ends up in the drink. Controversial? Yes. Forgettable? No. Mill River will give you all you could want from the tips at 6,827 yards, though forward tees give higher handicappers a fighting chance—except at the seventh.

In 2000, Charlottetown welcomed a new course just 10 minutes from the city's center. Located across the Hillsborough River in Stratford, **Fox Meadow Golf & Country Club,** routed on old farmland by Robert Heaslip, offers a good mix of open and wooded holes in a pleasant, rural setting. Adapting a "less is more" design philosophy, Heaslip transformed the rolling, wooded hills into an enjoyable test stretching to 6,836 yards. Several of the holes appear dropped into the forest, with drives played through narrow chutes; other holes wander across more open, windswept land. Crowned greens and swirling winds preserve the integrity of par.

Among the more memorable holes at Fox Meadow is the par-three seventh, its green encircled by water. The course, which offers occasional views of Charlottetown Harbour, finishes in style at the 18th, a testing, tree-lined par five that plays uphill to a sizable green defended by three huge bunkers.

New Glasgow, a tidy little community 30 minutes west of Charlottetown known for its lobster suppers, welcomed in 2001 the first 18 of a planned 27 holes at **Glasgow Hills Resort & Golf Club.** Located a short drive inland from Cavendish, home to some of PEI's best beaches, the layout was sculpted from rolling hills by Calgary-based Les Furber, a former project director for Robert Trent Jones and one of western Canada's leading designers.

Furber, with a flair for the dramatic, has crafted a 6,915-yard course that takes full advantage of the site's stunning views of the River Clyde and the Gulf of St. Lawrence. Ledged greens dissected by ridges and deep recessed bunkers mark this rugged course, which appears exiled from the Scottish Highlands and does not resemble any other course on the island. Blind shots and sidehill lies can prove disconcerting on a breezy day, but this bold, strategic test is a brilliant conception that begs to be played more than once.

After years of tuning up some of the more established courses on PEI, Graham Cooke, a seven-time Canadian Mid-Amateur champion, got a chance to create a course of his own at **The Eagles Glenn Golf Resort** in Cavendish. Opened in 2002, the 6,855-yard layout, spread across 300 acres, is an elegant, refined parkland course, its beautifully sculpted landforms blending nicely with the rolling, wooded hills.

With a slope of 143 from the tips, there is plenty of resistance to scoring for golfers who play to Cooke's high standards, but the designer does not abandon higher handicappers at the Glenn. In fact, most of the serious trouble only comes into play for better golfers

Glasgow Hills Resort & Golf Club, 13th hole

striving for an advantage. Those content to avoid
risks will do just fine on this nicely-groomed course
framed by Kentucky bluegrass roughs and tall fescues. All of one piece, Eagles Glenn relies on canted
lies, deep troughs, grassed gullies, split fairways, and
well-placed bunkers for its challenge. Many of the
greens are raised and tiered and well-defended by
water or sand, but only a few are heavily contoured.

On the heels of his triumph at Eagles Glenn, Cooke
returned to build a second course in the Cavendish
area, **Andersons Creek Golf Club,** which overlooks
New London Bay and its marram-covered dunes.
Opened in 2003, this beautiful newcomer, crisscrossed by meandering Andersons Creek, is perhaps
even more picturesque than its predecessor. Multiple
tee decks give everyone a fighting chance on this
delightful spread, while the five tee markers, in a
departure from the normal color-coding, are named

for famous hiking trails in the area, from Harvest
(6,651 yards) to Stanley (4,912 yards). The par-four
15th has *eight* tee decks so that golfers of all ability
levels can select one that gives them a fair chance of
carrying the creek with their drives.

The best of the island's long-established courses is
Green Gables Golf Course, a vintage 1939 design
by the legendary Stanley Thompson located within
Prince Edward Island National Park in Cavendish.
The layout, a cornerstone of PEI golf, takes its name
from a farmhouse made famous in the *Anne of Green
Gables* series of books.

Extensively modified in the early 1980s—for
example, the ninth green was relocated farther away
from the Green Gables House, a target for errant
shots—the course nevertheless retains a number
of Thompson trademarks among its original holes.
Classic and traditional in appearance, the 6,459-

A bird's eye view of Green Gables Golf Course

yard layout brings trees, salt marshes, and cat-tailed ponds into play, its elevated tees offering stirring views of the Gulf of St. Lawrence and the park's rolling dunes. About half the greens retain Thompson's racy contours, though old-timers still get misty-eyed when describing the lost fairways that once wandered through the windswept dunes near the shore. On the bright side, a plan to renovate and preserve Thompson's work at Green Gables was under review at press time. Moreover, Green Gables is the centerpiece of Cavendish Beach Golf, a destination within a destination that groups the landmark course with the area's three newcomers (Glasgow Hills, Eagles Glenn, and Andersons Creek), along with Forest Hills and Red Sands, a pair of sporty nine-holers.

Established as a nine-hole course in 1893, historic **Belvedere Golf Club,** a semi-private club located a few minutes from Charlottetown, is today an 18-hole parkland design that tests finesse more than strength. Upgraded by the ubiquitous Graham Cooke, who built new tees, greens, and bunkers, Belvedere is the home course of LPGA star Lorie Kane.

NINE-HOLERS

Usually, nine-hole courses are architectural afterthoughts turned out by novices. Not on PEI, which boasts no fewer than eight good to excellent nine-holers. Among the ones worth checking out for a late-afternoon quickie: **Rollo Bay Greens,** which rolls to the shore of the sea at the eastern end of the island; **Eagles View,** a sturdy 3,360-yard course in tiny Murray River, its holes routed around MacLure's Pond, PEI's largest body of fresh water; and **Belfast Highland Greens,** a par-37 design (with four par fives) revamped by Graham Cooke that serves up fine views of Orwell Bay from its clifftop location east of Charlottetown.

LODGING

The provincially-owned golf facilities on PEI, Crowbush Cove, Brudenell River, and Mill River, each has an on-site property operated by Rodd Hotels & Resorts. While the hotel company is value-oriented, **Rodd Crowbush Golf & Beach Resort,** located beside the Links and opened in 2001, is one of Atlantic Canada's more deluxe resorts. The main hotel offers 25 rooms and 24 suites with living room and Jacuzzi tubs. There are also 32 one- and two-bedroom cottages at the resort. **Rodd Brudenell River,** debuted in 1992 and later expanded when Dundarave Golf Course opened, is a larger property with hotel rooms, suites, cabins, and two-bedroom cottages available. **Rodd Mill River,** a more budget-minded property, has 90 rooms and a variety of suites with views of either the golf course or Mill River Provincial Park. Golf packages that mix and match the courses at each site as well as additional venues on PEI are available.

For a singular experience, book into **Dalvay-by-the-Sea,** a grand wainscoted mansion built in 1895 by a wealthy American industrialist as a summer home 20 minutes north of Charlottetown. Now a resort hotel and a National Historic Site of Canada, Dalvay, overlooking an expansive lawn set with Adirondack

chairs and located across the street from a glorious beach, offers 26 guest rooms and eight contemporary cottages. The hotel lays a fine table, has mountain bikes for rent, and is convenient to seven of PEI's top courses, including Crowbush.

Another eclectic option is **The Inn at Spry Point,** located north of Brudenell River Resort on the island's east coast. Set at the tip of a 110-acre peninsula with nearly 9,000 feet of shorefront, the Inn offers 15 bright, summery guest rooms, 11 with private balcony, four with garden terrace. Walking trails along the shore lead to Sally's Beach, a secluded sandy strand. The candlelit dining room, overlooking the Northumberland Strait, has a table d'hote menu utilizing fresh seafood and organically-grown vegetables and herbs shared by the resort's sister property, The Inn at Bay Fortune. A secluded retreat, The Inn at Spry Point offers a golf package featuring play at Crowbush, Brudenell River, or Dundarave.

For accommodations in Charlottetown, the **Inns on Great George** consist of 11 historic townhouses on a shady street in the town's historic district. The 47 rooms include 24 in the main building, each in a different style but with a light 19th-century touch (fireplaces, clawfoot tubs). There are also suites with contemporary furnishings in the newer Stable House.

Confederation Bridge links Prince Edward Island to mainland Canada

DINING

Dating back to the late 1950s, Lobster Suppers are a cherished tradition on PEI. Originally held as parish fund-raisers, the suppers have grown into large-scale commercial enterprises, though many are still held (at moderate prices) in church basements. Meals typically include a good-sized steamed lobster plus all-you-can-eat mussels, seafood chowder, salad (potato, garden and/or coleslaw), and dessert. Save room for dessert: PEI is known for its blueberry pie, though New Glasgow Lobster Suppers, a large family restaurant that's been serving lobster dinners since 1958, is famous for its lemon meringue pie.

SCENIC DRIVES

There are three scenic drives on the million-acre garden that is PEI. Each traces a portion of the coastline, all are clearly marked, and each takes in most of the island's attractions.

Blue Heron Drive, which forms a 110-mile loop that begins and ends in Charlottetown, circles the island's center county of Queens and swings near the north shore's national park beaches and red sandstone capes. The popular town of Cavendish is the drive's northern terminus. Highlights include the Green Gables House and New London Bay, which is known for its population of great blue herons.

North Cape Coastal Drive, formerly known as Lady Slipper Drive, explores the westernmost third of PEI, where the villages are small and the way of life traditional. This is Acadian country, home of the island's original French settlers. This route leads from Summerside to the fishing centers of Tignish and Alberton, where tons of tuna, cod, and lobster are taken in the Gulf of St. Lawrence; and Malpeque Bay, which produces famously succulent oysters. This is also the region where pie is made from seaweed.

Kings Byway follows the coastline of Kings County for 233 miles at the quiet east end of the island. Geese and ducks can be observed in their natural habitat at Moore's Migratory Bird Sanctuary, while fishermen can cast for rainbow trout in the Sturgeon River. At the northeast tip of PEI is North Lake, the "tuna capital of the world," where catches of 1,000-pound bluefin tuna are common.

Want to leave the car behind? PEI's Confederation Trail is part of the Trans-Canada Trail, which is built on historic rail lines. Spanning more than 215 miles, the trail wanders through woods and farm fields, crosses rivers, and also skirts the waterside. The Confederation Trail is graded with fine gravel for easy walking and cycling.

Charlottetown historic district

Mexico

Mexico is hot. Not just the weather, which is reliably sunny, but the golf scene. The old joke about Mexico is that people would head south of the border with a T-shirt and a $100 bill and not change either one in a week. That has changed with the infusion of world-class golf in several key regions. More than 700,000 U.S. and Canadian golfers teed it up in Mexico in 2005. The average expenditure per golfer was roughly $1,600, three times more than the average tourist expenditure. From Los Cabos to Cancun, billions of dollars have been committed to new golf resort and real estate developments. Clearly, the old Scottish game has become Mexico's most valuable promotional tool for upmarket tourism.

Las Ventanas al Paraiso, Los Cabos

Jack Nicklaus, the Golden Amigo, should take a bow. Thanks to a carte-blanche arrangement with the government, Nicklaus has single-handedly catapulted Mexico into the golf vacation stratosphere with his prolific output since the early 1990s. At press time, Nicklaus Design had 12 courses open for play throughout Mexico, six under construction, seven in the design phase, and no fewer than 11 prospects for future development! (His goal, according to insiders, is a total of 50 facilities south of the border.)

Mexico's best-known golf destinations—Los Cabos and Puerto Vallarta—will soon be joined by the Riviera Maya south of Cancun. Each of these areas may one day be matched by other regions with the money, land, and vision to realize the incredible touristic value of top-shelf golf. Add a favorable exchange rate and convenient flights from the U.S. to the nation's major gateways, and Mexico emerges as one of the finest and fastest-growing golf destinations in the world. Olé!

Los Cabos

Mexico's premier model for high-end golf is found at the southern tip of Baja California Sur in Los Cabos ("The Capes"), the designated name for a 20-mile coastal corridor bookended by San Jose del Cabo (a quaint colonial town) and Cabo San Lucas (Margaritaville with marlin fishing). The region, boasting a handful of world-class venues with more on the way, registered nearly 200,000 rounds in 2005, or roughly 20 percent of all the resort golf played in Mexico.

Washed by the Pacific Ocean to the west and the Sea of Cortez on the east, the rugged Baja Peninsula is a stunning tropical desert, its mountains reaching to 6,000 feet and its deserts covered with hundreds of varieties of cactus. The Los Cabos scenery? Picture the view from the Monterey Peninsula's 17-Mile Drive as it winds its way along the sea in Northern California. Same weathered rocks, same pounding surf, same bracing sea air. Subtract the fog, add desert vegetation and diving pelicans—and perfect weather. The average annual temperature here is 75 degrees. Located 15 miles below the Tropic of Cancer, Los

Cabos boasts 350 sunny days a year, low humidity, and a cooling sea breeze. The weather for golf, or any outdoor activity, is perfect from November through May.

As a destination, Los Cabos has enough first-rate layouts and more than enough deluxe hotel rooms to attract visitors who typically might go to Hawaii, Scottsdale, or Palm Springs on holiday. Only a two-hour flight from Los Angeles, improved airlift from other major U.S. gateways has given travelers easier access to Mexico's trendiest destination. This sun-drenched paradise at land's end is expected to welcome two million tourists a year by 2007–08. Despite the influx, the corridor is still blessed with great open spaces.

Once a rustic, sleepy hideaway favored by retired pirates and fishermen in search of trophy marlin, Los Cabos, in a brief span from 1992 to 2001, reinvented itself as an elite golf getaway in a totally unique environment. Single-handedly, it has served as Mexico's stepping stone into the 21st century of golf.

Palmilla Golf Club, Mountain nine, fifth hole

Palmilla Golf Club, home to 27 holes of Jack Nicklaus–designed golf and now part of a resort complex known as **One&Only Palmilla,** is the landmark facility that set the stage for growth in Los Cabos. In a box-shaped canyon backdropped by stark brown peaks in the Sierra de la Laguna range, Nicklaus created a core 18 in 1992 (the Mountain and Arroyo nines) on terrain that would have given Butch Cassidy and the Sundance Kid pause for thought. Palmilla, a target-style tour de force, was the first course in the hemisphere to combine ocean, mountain, and desert scenery. (Imagine Tucson with the Sea of Cortez at its feet.) This powerful combination sparked the interest of globetrotting golfers in search of the Next Place.

Nicklaus routed holes around boulder-strewn arroyos, long waste bunkers, and several irrigation ponds, with five sets of tees providing admirable versatility. Several holes call for do-or-die forced carries over No Man's Land, but Palmilla overall exhibits the kind of playability for which Nicklaus has come to be known.

After years of manufacturing extremely difficult courses that only he could play, Jack came of age as a designer in the early 1990s. Palmilla is a perfect example. The design is user-friendly, with wide, decked fairways and generous bail-out areas for players of lesser attainment. Better players, too, are presented with more shot options and risk-reward holes than were available in Nicklaus's previous work. Strategy is as important at Palmilla as the ability to appreciate a setting that appears lifted from *Treasure of the Sierra Madre.* There is, of course, plenty of resistance to scoring from the back tees. Nicklaus has yet to bake a patty cake for anyone.

Palmilla's Arroyo and Mountain nines cannot be considered apart from their environment. Giant cardon cacti, a cousin of the saguaro and many of them centuries old, stand sentinel beside tees and greens. Angular *torote* ("elephant") trees shade the cart paths. The variety of cacti—barrel, cholla, galloping, organ pipe—is staggering. Ocotillo, *palo verde,* and ironwood trees occupy the rough. Created with a great deal of sensitivity to the environment, the holes appear airlifted into the desert.

Above: One&Only Palmilla spa   Opposite: Palmilla Golf Club, Ocean nine, third hole

Cabo del Sol, Desert Course, fourth hole

While the Arroyo nine plays around and across canyon-like washes up to 100 feet deep, its topmost holes serve up fine ocean views. Palmilla's signature hole is the fifth on the Mountain nine, one of the most thrilling par fours on Nicklaus's résumé. From a hilltop platform, the tee shot is a forced carry over the deep Arroyo Seco to a long, sinuous fairway that resembles a green island floating in a blue sky. The approach shot is equally demanding. Situated well below fairway level and benched above a dry river bed is a very slick green protected by a pair of deep sand pits.

Palmilla's Ocean nine, added in 1999, features a 600-foot elevation change from the first tee to the sixth green, carrying players from the mountains to the sea. While it doesn't have as many ball-swallowing arroyos as the core 18, the greens on the new nine are more undulating. Overall, the routing of the Ocean nine, revised to accommodate a housing development, is a bit cramped and disjointed. Certainly Nicklaus did not have carte blanche to roam the land in search of the best hole sites as he did on the Arroyo and Mountain nines.

While Palmilla was instantly the best resort course in Mexico the day it opened, Nicklaus's design work at nearby **Cabo del Sol,** with seven holes on the Sea of Cortez, is the course that placed Los Cabos squarely on the international golf map. Debuted in 1994 and now called the **Ocean Course** at Cabo del Sol—a second layout by Tom Weiskopf has since opened at the 1,800-acre resort and residential playground—this thrilling test of golf, currently ranked 73rd on *Golf Magazine's* list of the Top 100 Courses in the World, is a seaside masterpiece worth crossing a continent to play.

The opening of the course was a 30-year dream come true for Nicklaus. Jack first visited Cabo San Lucas in 1964 to go deep-sea fishing and get away from the competitive pressures of the PGA Tour. At that time the town was a sleepy little village. On his flights in and out, Jack looked out the window and imagined what a beautiful golf course might one day be built at land's end. Now he can look down with pride at the course that completely changed the area's travel dynamic.

Intent on producing the "Pebble Beach of the

LODGING & DINING

Built in 1956 by the son of a former president of Mexico and operated as a club for serious deep-sea fishing enthusiasts, including Bing Crosby, John Wayne, Ernest Hemingway, Desi Arnez, and Dwight D. Eisenhower, the original Hotel Palmilla was an elite hideaway perched on a rocky point that juts into the azure-blue waters of the Sea of Cortez. In 2002, leisure baron Sol Kerzner acquired a 50 percent interest in the property. Kerzner International committed $80 million to renovate and expand the resort and also signed a long-term management contract. The resort, contained within a 900-acre enclave, reopened in 2004 as part of the hotel company's One&Only collection, a portfolio of ultra-luxe properties that includes the Ocean Club in the Bahamas. Though the resort has been significantly upgraded, Palmilla's old Mexico ambience and charm have been preserved.

As part of the renovation, the **One&Only Palmilla** was expanded from 115 to 172 rooms. Accommodations, a tasteful blend of hand-crafted furniture, terra cotta or river stone floors, tiled sinks, and wrought-iron fixtures, are contained in single-story and three-story hacienda-style buildings that encircle the grounds along the peninsula's edge. Rooms and suites each have a spacious patio or balcony facing the sea as well as 24-hour butler service. Personal comforts? Guests have a choice of sheets (Egyptian cotton, pressed linen, or cotton sateen); and bathrobe (terry or cotton).

A prime amenity is the resort's beach, one of the very few along the Los Cabos shore that is swimmable. Excursions for fishing, scuba-diving, snorkeling, or desert eco-tours can be arranged. The One&Only Spa offers therapies in private treatment villas. Each is a discreet sanctuary with an open-air garden daybed, rain shower for two, and air-conditioned massage pavilion. The spa also has a fitness center and yoga garden.

The resort's top dining spot is C, a signature restaurant by acclaimed chef Charlie Trotter. A blue-glass fantasy set near the tip of the peninsula, C reinterprets traditional Mexican seafood dishes. The alfresco balcony of C Bar, overlooking the beach, is the ideal place to enjoy a pre- or post-dinner cocktail. Also available is Agua, a more casual indoor-outdoor restaurant serving "Mexiterranean" cuisine.

Relaxing in a hammock at One&Only Palmilla

Baja" on what he described as "the most magnificent piece of golf course property I've ever seen," Nicklaus charted grand-scale holes across gently sloping land creased by shallow arroyos and backdropped by rugged mountains. A combination of giant cardon cacti, granite rock outcrops, and deep sinuous bunkers frame most of the greens. Like Pebble, the figure-eight routing is seamless, the look natural, unforced. Very little earth (a mere 200,000 cubic yards) was moved to create this fabulous test, which at full stretch (7,103 yards) is all the golf course anyone could want. This is especially true when the sea breeze stirs, which it usually does early and late in the day.

There are a handful of death-or-glory shots to be played across Bahia de las Ballenas (Bay of the Whale), its waters the color of Aqua-Velva, though staggered tees put most of the danger out of harm's way for the duffer. Playability is the byword at Cabo del Sol. According to Jim Lipe, Nicklaus's senior design associate, "If a golf course isn't playable by all types of golfers, some of the sheen comes off it, no matter how spectacular the setting."

As at Pebble Beach, the seaside holes at Cabo del Sol have an eloquence all their own, though the inland holes, all with sweeping views of the sea, are the strategic glue that holds the design together. Each is ingeniously routed, and each provides a counterpoint to the giddy high of teeing it up beside the turquoise-blue sea. For example, holes six and seven, each a jaw-dropping par three placed beside the sea, are astounding, but the 458-yard par-four fifth, which drops from a perched tee and marks the layout's transition from high desert to ocean coastline, dares better players to cut the corner of a sandy waste area on the right without drifting through the fairway into the base of steep hillside on the left. Strategically, it's the best hole on the front nine.

The incoming nine on the Ocean Course is chockablock with great holes. The short par-four 11th has a split fairway divided by a massive bowl of sand; the par-five 12th calls for a bold drive over a hellish half-acre of scrub and an accurate approach to a perched green undercut by bunkers; the all-or-nothing par-three 13th, the only one-shotter on the course that does not touch the sea, plays downhill over a soapbush-filled arroyo to a cleverly bunkered green encased in cactus. And so on, each hole as good if not better than the one before it.

However, it is the finishing holes on the Ocean Course that have placed this exalted design at the

Cabo del Sol, Ocean Course, 18th hole

pinnacle of Latin American golf. The 17th, ranging in length from 178 to 102 yards, is as thrilling as any par three in the world. Golfers play from an elevated tee built atop a decomposed granite cliff and fly their shots over a sandy cove where turtles lay their eggs on moonlit nights. The pulpit green is nestled among sea-blackened rocks and, while not very large, is not nearly as small as it appears from the tee.

The final hole on the Ocean Course, a mirror image of the 18th at Pebble Beach, is a classic, ocean-hugging par four that traces the curve of the shore, only here the water is on the right, making it a slicer's nightmare. The muffled roar of the surf hitting the rocks below the cliffs serenades golfers from tee to green and tends to dispel any misfortunes that may have been experienced earlier in the round. Whale sightings are a nice bonus. Like the 18th at Pebble, this majestic hole provides an appropriate climax to the round.

Said Nicklaus of the closing tandem, "I firmly believe that these are the two best finishing holes of any course in the world."

Perhaps resort management has taken the great man's words to heart, for the price tag here is as breathtaking as the scenery. At press time, the tariff to play the Ocean Course in peak season was a regal $295. There are compensations, however. Fish tacos, a delectable local specialty, are served to players gratis under a shady *palapa* midway through the round.

To his credit, Nicklaus has returned often to tweak his pet project. Reopened in late 2004 after a complete agronomic upgrade, the layout, its subtly contoured greens resurfaced with a fine-bladed bermudagrass, is today the finest course in Mexico and among the very best Nicklaus has produced.

In 2001, Cabo del Sol's **Desert Course,** a Tom Weiskopf design routed in mountain foothills high above

Cabo Real Golf Club, seventh hole

the Ocean Course, made its debut to immediate acclaim. And while the 7,097-yard layout lacks a hole on the ocean, all 18 holes serve up a panoramic view of the Sea of Cortez. Shoehorning holes into rugged desert terrain crisscrossed by canyon-like arroyos, the broad fairways and large greens staked out by rock outcrops and gnarled, peeling *torote* trees, Weiskopf produced a masterful design, his first in Mexico. Semi-blind drives, visually intimidating approach shots, and excellent variety have kept players coming back for more. There's a reason. According to Weiskopf, "Even though you may be a little uncomfortable over the shot, there's nearly always a lot more room than you think." Five sets of tees enable the course to play comfortably for all skill levels. Each tee is an island of green in the decomposed granite, the sandy rock raked as carefully as a Zen garden.

Rarely is a golf architect invited to improve his work on an already highly-regarded course. But Weiskopf, spurred by a revised land plan, was asked to make significant changes to a few of the holes. Major revisions on five of the layout's less compelling holes, namely wholesale changes at holes 1, 2, 3, 14 and 15, have established this superb layout as second only to the Ocean Course as the top resort venue in Los Cabos. The course reopened in late 2005 following a $2-million makeover.

The only drawback? The course name. As Jaime Diaz wrote in *Golf World* in 2004, "'The Desert Course' is a buzzkill...While it does not have holes on the water, you can see the Sea of Cortez on every hole." His suggestion? "Because there are all manner of deep gullies to carry on the Weiskopf track, and to give it a little Latin feel, I modestly propose 'the Barranca Course.'" I second that emotion.

Both the Desert and Ocean courses at Cabo del Sol are served by a spectacular Mexican Colonial–style clubhouse accented by open-air verandas, landscaped terraces, a spacious golf shop, and indoor/outdoor dining facilities. Sweeping ocean and fairway views are available throughout the handsome 40,000-square-foot facility, its cantera stone fountain in the courtyard entrance creating a wonderful first impression.

LODGING
Two hotels are currently attached to **Cabo del Sol,** with a Ritz-Carlton in the planning stages. They are **Fiesta Americana Grand,** a deluxe 288-room beachfront property located near the fifth hole of the Ocean Course that debuted in 1999; and **Sheraton Hacienda del Mar,** a comfortable, earth-toned, low-rise property with 171 rooms that is patterned after a colonial Mexican village.

ONE TO WATCH

A third venue at Cabo del Sol, currently unnamed, is slated to be built on a spectacular site nearly 500 feet above the sea, with dramatic views of the Baja shoreline all the way to Los Arcos. Scheduled to open in 2009, the layout will take full advantage of the sharp elevation changes and also maximize real estate values on steeply pitched terrain overlooking the sea. At press time, Nicklaus headed a short list of possible designers for the new project.

The combination of Palmilla and Cabo de Sol would be reason enough to visit Los Cabos, but there's more. In the mid-1990s, Eduardo Sanchez-Navarro, heir to the Corona beer fortune, developed **Cabo Real,** a large-scale, 2,800-acre resort and residential project with three miles of beachfront as its centerpiece. Now that its Jack Nicklaus–designed flagship course, Eldorado, has turned private, the main golf attraction for visitors is the Robert Trent Jones, Jr.–designed **Cabo Real Golf Club.** This Jekyll-and-Hyde design has steeply pitched holes chiseled into the mountains as well as flatter holes routed along the seashore.

Jones, Jr. showed his versatility here, reconfiguring nine pre-existing holes at the property and melding them to nine new holes. The front nine of this sturdy 6,988-yard layout is routed on the north side of the highway. Rolling fairways climb to undulating greens backed into mountain foothills bristling with thorny vegetation. The high point is the sixth tee, which rises 460 feet above sea level. The course then stair-steps down to the sea.

Cabo Real's back nine, completely refashioned by Jones, boasts a memorable three-hole stretch a chip shot from the beach. The green at the par-four 14th, the entire par-three 15th, and the tee at the uphill 16th are all propped up on seaside bluffs. In the winter months, golfers can spot gray, blue, and sperm whales breeching, spouting, and cavorting with their calves. Recreated sand dunes at the 14th and 15th greens lend a links-like appearance to this outstanding trio, though the layout's most challenging holes rise and fall among the hills high above the sea.

Like Nicklaus at his Los Cabos courses, Jones hasn't let the inherent drama of the setting upstage the shot values of the holes. His is a more flowing style, though Cabo Real can play plenty tough from the championship tees. The key word here is balance: The uphill holes generally play downwind, the downhill holes play into the wind, and the green contours and fairway mounding mimic those of the surrounding mountains.

Beachfront table at Las Ventanas al Paraiso

BATTLE OF HIGH-END LODGING

There are two exceptional properties that compete with One&Only Palmilla for the upper end of the market in Los Cabos.

The resort hotel that gave the region its first blush of high-class sheen when it opened in 1997 is **Las Ventanas al Paraiso** (Windows to Paradise), a Rosewood property located on the beach near Cabo Real's 15th hole. This exclusive retreat, one of the most sumptuous in the Americas, features 61 Mexican-tiled suites with wood-burning adobe fireplaces, latilla-shaded terraces, hand-carved cedar doors, and other fine appointments, including computerized telescopes for stargazing or whale watching. The public spaces, linked by winding walkways graced by hand-laid pebble borders, are flowing and romantic. The Baja-Mediterranean cuisine (and fruit-flavored margaritas) featured at the Sea Grill, set a few paces from the sandy beach, is sublime. Las Ventanas also was the first area property to provide specially mixed iPods (from the Beatles to Beethoven) to its guests. Now every upscale hotel in Los Cabos has them.

Fronting Punta Ballena (Whale Point) a mile or two from Cabo del Sol is **Esperanza,** which is just as deluxe as Las Ventanas but offers a contrast in style. Debuted in 2002 and operated by Auberge Resorts, Esperanza offers 56 suites, none smaller than 950 square feet, spread across a sprawling, terraced property perched on bluffs above the rocky shore. The two- and three-bedroom beachfront suites, each with a huge terrace, whirlpool spa, and butler, are the summit of luxury. The site's drama is incomparable: two sparkling coves on the Sea of Cortez beckon far below the cliff-top. With a friendly staff attired in native dress, Esperanza comes across as a welcoming, high-end Mexican ranch by the sea. Under an enormous *palapa* high above the beach is El Restaurante, which occupies three stone terraces and showcases ingredients from local organic farmers as well as area fishermen.

Entrance to Las Ventanas al Paraiso

Sitting area at Esperanza

A COURSE APART

The only golf course in Los Cabos with a view of El
Arco, the distinctive sea arch at land's end that has
become the region's symbol, is the **Raven Golf Club,**
formerly known as Cabo San Lucas Country Club. A
semi-private course laid out in 1994 by the late Roy
Dye, Pete's brother, and completed by Roy's son Matt
after his death, this gently rolling, 7,220-yard design
compares favorably to courses in the Arizona desert,
its well-groomed fairways girdled by long waste
bunkers. While it lacks the rugged terrain and ocean
frontage of the region's A-list courses, the Raven is a
fine test in its own right. Laid out in a dry wash so wide
it appears as a sandy gash from outer space, the fairways here are framed by cardon cacti and the feathery
crowns of the *palo blanco* tree. Numerous ponds bring
water into play at more than half the holes.

ONES TO WATCH

While Eldorado Golf Club was taken off the shelf
for visiting resort players in 2005, the Cabo Real
Group has a new course, **Club Campestre,** a public-
access venue with a real estate component located on
the outskirts of San Jose del Cabo. Laid out by the
Nicklaus Design company, with Gary Nicklaus, one of
Jack's sons, listed as designer, this moderately-priced
facility, which hopes to attract local play, is expected
to open in 2006.

At the corridor's east end outside San Jose del
Cabo, the quieter and more traditional of the two
towns in Los Cabos, Eduardo Sanchez-Navarro,
the mover and shaker behind Cabo Real, has put his
considerable resources behind **Puerto Los Cabos,**
a mixed-use resort community that will feature a
state-of-the-art marina with its own town plaza,
village-style hotels, beach clubs, an ecological park,
a museum—and two golf courses, one each by Greg
Norman and Jack Nicklaus. Set in rolling foothills
that tumble down to the Sea of Cortez, the courses
will be championship-caliber. (Norman's layout,
stretching to 7,465 yards, will be the region's longest
and will eventually turn private.) The marina, which

can accommodate up to 535 boats, is slated to open in
2006. The golf courses will follow in 2006–07.

A third project on the east end is being developed
by **Mayan Palace,** which has planned a full-service
timeshare and hotel property with two golf courses.
In addition, the hotel company has greatly improved
the golf facilities at the modest nine-hole Club de
Golf San Jose del Cabo built in the late 1980s by
FONATUR, the government's tourism development
arm. The family-friendly 3,141-yard, par-35 layout,
anchored by an interesting Spanish Arabic–style
clubhouse, is now known as **Mayan Palace Golf Los
Cabos.**

Moving farther west is **Cabo Pacifica,** a 1,200-
acre mega-development in the foothills of the
mountains near Pueblo Bonito Sunset Beach Resort,
a handsome blue-trimmed, white adobe hotel near El
Arco. In addition to hotel sites, villas, and residences,
two courses are planned, one by Greg Norman, who
is beginning to work as steadily in Mexico as Jack
Nicklaus; and the second by Arnold Palmer.

FUTURE HOTSPOT

A 2 ½-hour drive north of Los Cabos on the east
coast of Baja California Sur is La Paz (City of Peace),
which overlooks a lovely bay and is sheltered from the
sea's open waters by a long sandbar. While Los Cabos
is now a jet-set destination, La Paz, the capital of
Baja Sur, is a provincial settlement with 16th-century
roots. Like Los Cabos, it was just a matter of time
before golf caught up with this tranquil desert town
by the sea. Work has begun on three major projects,
with several more in the planning stages.

In 2004, Arthur Hills broke ground on his first
design project in Mexico, called **Paraiso del Mar**
(Paradise by the Sea). The course, part of a residen-
tial/resort development, is routed through sandy
dunes and cactus. The minimalist, links-style layout
showcases views of the Sea of Cortez as well as the
Cape of La Paz. A late 2006 opening is forecast.

Forty-five minutes southeast of La Paz is a budding
4,300-acre development on the Sea of Cortez called
Bahia de los Suenos (Bay of Dreams). Master-
planned for two golf courses, including one by rising
star Tom Doak scheduled to open in 2008, Bahia de
los Suenos will feature a luxury boutique hotel plus
a low-density, second-home real estate community.
This development has the potential to do for La Paz
what Cabo del Sol did for Los Cabos in the 1990s.

OFF-COURSE ATTRACTIONS

While golf has quickly established itself as the region's hottest new sport, Los Cabos will always be known as a world-class fishing destination. A mixture of nutrient-rich currents from Central America, the Pacific Ocean, and the Sea of Cortez collide offshore, creating one of the richest game-fishing grounds in the world. Marlin, sailfish, tuna, dorado, wahoo, and roosterfish are among the prize catches taken a mere 10 miles offshore. A 50-pound fish is considered small in these fertile waters. The best season for large marlin is November through January. Thrill-seekers can rent kayaks, paddle silently into the midst of schooling tuna and dorado, and go one-on-one with a powerful fish. In lieu of the deep-sea adventure, enthusiasts can hire a 22-foot ponga boat to fish the area's inshore waters.

Surfing, sailing, snorkeling, water-skiing, and windsurfing can be enjoyed year-round in Los Cabos, which also boasts the best scuba diving on Mexico's west coast. Playa Palmilla, Santa Maria Bay, Chileno Bay, Playa Medano, and Playa de Amor are ideal places to swim and snorkel. Another attraction for divers is the world's only sand falls located 90 feet below Pelican Rock at El Arco. These unique underwater accretions of sand were discovered by Jacques Cousteau.

The whale watching season is January through April. Boat tours are available for those who want a closer look at these great mammals.

Glass bottom boat excursions to El Arco ("The Arch," also called Finisterra, or Land's End) are available in Cabo San Lucas. At the exact spot where the Pacific Ocean meets the Sea of Cortez, sea lions bask in the sun, and large colonies of sea birds cling to the bleached flanks of the enormous rocks.

Shopping? A colorful and diverse selection of handmade artisanry is available in San Jose del Cabo. Open-air bazaars are found in several locations, including the marina in Cabo San Lucas.

Nightlife? A few bars and nightclubs in San Jose del Cabo offer live music and dancing, but genuine party pandemonium is the rule in Cabo San Lucas. Squid Roe is a three-story quonset hut on the main drag where tequila shooters and table dancing are popular. At the Giggling Marlin, patrons can sample the signature drink, Skip and Go Naked, and be hoisted up like a trophy fish. Wave, located next to the Hard Rock Café, is a throbbing disco. Crazy fun also reigns at Cabo Wabo, a dance club opened by '80s rock star Sammy Hagar.

DINING SIDETRIPS

For the most part, the dining options in rowdy Cabo San Lucas are nondescript or commercial or both. A notable exception is Nick-San, a Japanese restaurant owned by a Mexican fisherman who sends out two boats at the crack of dawn each morning. The raw tuna and yellowtail prepared by his expert sushi chefs are incomparable, but many of the best dishes are lightly seared for under a minute and served with a delicate sauce.

In San Jose del Cabo, a genuine colonial-era city, top tables are found at Tequila Restaurant, a lovely courtyard café that turns out excellent cuisine in a very romantic setting. Casa Natalia, a small, trendy hotel in San Jose, lays a fine table at Mi Cocina, an elegant, European-style restaurant that nevertheless specializes in fine Mexican fare. Try some of the wines produced in Baja California Norte, especially the whites. For good casual fare on the outskirts of town, check out Zippers, its tables set a yard or two from Costa Azul Beach. A local's hangout, this is the place for juicy burgers, beer-battered fried shrimp, and a cold beer.

An hour's drive north of Cabo San Lucas past deserted Pacific beaches and steep cactus-studded hills is Todos Santos (All Saints), a former Jesuit mission and now a sleepy artist's colony that is home to the Hotel California, inspiration for the famous song by the Eagles. Here also is Café Santa Fe, an Italian restaurant located off the town's main plaza. With its gurgling fountains and shady patios, the café appears lifted from Tuscany or Umbria. The homemade pastas and seafood dishes are as exceptional as the setting.

Puerto Vallarta

Located on the Pacific coast an hour's flight west of Mexico City, Puerto Vallarta first came to light in 1963, when director John Huston arrived with a cast and crew (including Elizabeth Taylor and Richard Burton) to film Tennesee Williams's *The Night of the Iguana* in what was then a sleepy colonial seaside village. Liz and Rich's torrid off-screen affair during the making of the movie made international headlines, gaining instant fame and, in short order, destination status for Puerto Vallarta.

While it boasts 16,000 hotel rooms and welcomes more than three million visitors annually, it took a while for first-rate golf to arrive in Puerto Vallarta. Finally, at the turn of the millennium, ClubCorp, the American golf development firm, hired Jack Nicklaus and Tom Weiskopf to build a pair of courses on an upcountry site 15 minutes from the hotel zone and marina. A year after the Nicklaus Course at **Vista Vallarta Golf Club** opened, it hosted the 2002 WGC-World Cup.

Unlike many new developments in Mexico, the golf corridors, not the maximization of real estate value, were the first priority at Vista Vallarta. Two small hotels and a limited number of condos and private homes are planned on the 700-acre site, but the fairways will not be choked by haphazard housing. For golfers, this is the 36-hole treasure of the Sierra Madre.

Vista Vallarta Golf Club, Nicklaus Course, 13th hole

The **Nicklaus Course,** routed across heaving land nearly 500 feet above sea level, pushes up against the foothills of the mountains, its topmost holes serving up fine views of Puerto Vallarta and the broad sweep of Banderas Bay, one of the largest and deepest natural bays in the world. Giant ficus trees, tall palms, and sloping hillsides frame the holes, with a spidery network of arroyos and creeks in play throughout. A jagged crestline of wild, jungled mountain ridges rises from the eastern perimeter of the layout.

The 7,073-yard layout gave World Cup contestants plenty to ponder, especially on the greens, which have more corrugations than a deep-fried taco. Perhaps Jack, like Pete Dye and others before him, has come to view the putting surface as the last line of defense in the equipment technology wars.

The holes themselves are varied and well-strategized from each set of tees (there are four). Even the longer holes call for careful positioning, not brute strength. For example, central bunkers were deployed to force players to choose a left or right path off the tee at several par fours. Nicklaus chose to work with the natural undulations of the former ranchland, which means the holes have more individuality and character than he himself could have created. Traditional, straightforward holes are offset by quirky, one-of-a-kind gems where Jack left well enough alone.

Pool at Paradise Village Resort

On the lower west end of the complex, Weiskopf was handed a rugged, densely vegetated parcel marked by deep ravines and swift creeks. "The site is one of the most dramatic inland properties I've seen anywhere in the world," Weiskopf commented before ground was broken. The **Weiskopf Course,** also unveiled in 2001, stands in marked contrast to the Nicklaus Course. The holes here were dropped into a lush jungle of swaying palms and towering *papalio* trees, the rolling fairways routed on ridges above deep-cut arroyos and verdant greenery. What it lacks in expansive views, it more than compensates with pace and beauty.

The brawnier back nine on the 6,993-yard Weiskopf Course opens with the longest par five at the facility, a 624-yard marathon, but its standout hole, the spectacular 15th, is simply one of the finest one-shotters in Mexico. This hole plays anywhere from 124 to 190 yards and calls for a trans-arroyo tee shot to a deep, bi-level green set above a tawny, exposed bluff and staked out by bunkers large and small. There is no fairway—an all-or-nothing shot must be played.

Golf packages are available through a number of area hotels, including the **Marriott CasaMagna Resort,** a 404-room oceanfront property that offers golfers a buffet breakfast and roundtrip transfers to Vista Vallarta. Puerto Vallarta, by the way, is on the same latitude as Hawaii and enjoys perfect weather from November through May.

Nuevo Vallarta, a burgeoning resort area located north of the city, welcomed **El Tigre Golf Course** in 2002. This Robert von Hagge–Rick Baril creation was laid out beside **Paradise Village Resort,** a 649-room property that offers a fine beach, a wide range of restaurants, and a European-style spa. A well-groomed test stretching to a sturdy 7,239 yards, El Tigre, a relatively flat, windswept course, has 42 acres of lakes on site as well as a meandering creek and dozens of well-placed bunkers. The final three holes at El Tigre, named for a caged Bengal tiger behind the 17th tee, are among the toughest in Mexico. The 18th, in particular, is a bruiser—621 yards from the tips, into the teeth of the prevailing wind, water up the entire left side. The layout is anchored

Puerto Vallarta beachfront

by an attractive 45,000-square-foot clubhouse, but the most impressive edifice on site is the enormous Mayan-style arch that marks the entrance to the course.

Ten minutes from Paradise Village is the region's oldest course, **Los Flamingos Golf Club,** which dates to 1975. New management has breathed new life into the course by way of a $3 million renovation program and the recovery of old championship tees that had been lost to the jungle, though one aspect of the facility remains unchanged: its incredible cast of migratory and resident birds.

Also located in Nuevo Vallarta is the **Mayan Palace,** a colorful yet refined 529-room hotel that overlooks the ocean. Routed around the hotel and along the banks of the Ameca River that flows into the sea is the resort's golf course. Previously a humdrum layout, the course was redesigned in 2001 by Jim Lipe, one of Jack Nicklaus's senior designers. This is unapologetically an enjoyable resort spread, with open, lightly bunkered fairways staked out by palms and other tropical trees.

DAY TRIP/PUERTO VALLARTA

Hugged by lush, wild mountains on one side and 25-mile-long Banderas Bay on the other, Puerto Vallarta, a quaint, romantic town known for its cobblestone streets and Spanish Mission-style colonial buildings, is perfect for a stroll.

Following the *malecon*, a waterfront promenade, stop by City Hall for a look at Manuel Lepe's whimsical mural of the city. Rest along the way on white wrought-iron benches, or duck into a café overlooking the sea for a cool drink. Later, ascend any of the hills for a panoramic view of the bay as well as the crowned steeple of the Church of Guadalupe, the city's most distinctive landmark. Cuale Island, on the river of the same name that divides Puerto Vallarta, is a good place to shop for items ranging from Taxco silver to Oaxaca pottery. Also on the five-acre island is a small botanical garden and an archaeological museum that displays Indian artifacts from the nearby states of Colima and Nayarit. Puerto Vallarta is also known for the excellence and variety of its restaurants. Café des Artistes and Café Maximilian are two of the best.

Moving an hour's drive north of Puerto Vallarta is the **Four Seasons Resort Punta Mita,** the first Four Seasons Hotels and Resorts property in Latin America. Not taking any chances, the Canadian hospitality company commandeered nearly 1,500 acres on a slim peninsula set between the blue Pacific and the foothills of the Sierra Madre. Opened in 1999, the resort quickly became one of Mexico's most idyllic hideaways.

Situated at the northern end of Banderas Bay, the setting is exquisite. Scalloped strands of pulverized coral stretch away from the property's low bluffs, the ocean's flat horizon broken in places by piles of sea-blackened rocks offshore. Ancient wooden doors in the main building lead to an open-sided, thatched *palapa* that rises to 60 feet at its apex. Peeking through the palm fronds outside is a free-form, infinity-edge pool set well above the turquoise-blue sea. To the south loom distant peaks in the Sierra Madre. Add a cool sea breeze that keeps temperatures in the mid-70s in winter and the mid-80s in summer, and the resort approaches perfection.

For golfers, it gets better. Two miles from the 140-room hotel is the kind of world-class site that only the greatest player in the game's history gets a chance to assess before ground is broken. Routed in all directions across a narrow neck of land, with portions of five holes on (or in one case in) the Pacific and an additional three holes skirting Banderas Bay, Punta Mita is a dazzling Jack Nicklaus layout, its ebb and flow inspired perhaps by Pebble Beach and other great seaside designs. However, the beautifully groomed course already is in danger of being eclipsed by its 19th hole. No, not the post-round watering hole, though it shares the same name: Tail of the Whale.

During course construction, Nicklaus and his design team noticed a squib of volcanic rock in the shape of a catcher's mitt a little less than 200 yards from shore. The island's rear rock walls seemed to deflect salt spray kicked up by incoming waves. Which meant grass might survive out there. What if...Without further ado, the decision was made to create hole 3-B, an optional par three, its target possibly the only natural island green in the world, and certainly the only one in an ocean. The meek of heart can have a go at hole 3-A, an excellent land-bound one-shotter. But go-for-broke gamblers prepared to

Hole 3-B, an optional par three at Four Seasons Resort Punta Mita

brave the onshore breeze can attempt to carry the ball at least 180 yards in the air to a generous-sized green that beckons incongruously from the sea. It's a thrilling, do-or-die shot that most guests try no matter what. Sure-footed players can stroll the hand-laid stone walkway to the green at low tide to putt out. At high tide, players travel to the island in a six-wheeled amphibian vehicle driven by a staff member. The only problem with hole 3-B is coming back to earth to play the rest of the course.

Landscaped with 1,800 palms and framed throughout by dune-like mounds and vast waste bunkers, Punta Mita, with five sets of tees ranging from 7,014 to 5,037 yards, is one of the most cleverly plotted resort spreads Nicklaus has ever built. On most courses, par fours provide the sinew and challenge. Punta Mita has many fine par fours, notably the spectacular seaside 18th, but it's the lengthy par threes that provide the muscle. Conversely, four of the layout's par fives are risk-reward teasers that average 501 yards from the gold markers at 6,641 yards. Also, forward tees put the longer holes well within reach of free-swinging holidaymakers. Many guests not only match their handicaps at Punta Mita, they shoot career low rounds. (When queried, most are mum on whether or not they included the Tail of the Whale in their tally).

The club's practice facility, featuring a large tee with 40 stations, a tub-shaped hitting area, six target greens, and a stunning mountain backdrop, is one of Mexico's finest. So is the golf shop. In addition to a fine array of luxurious sportswear, there's also a jewelry store with beautiful trinkets for sale.

ONES TO WATCH

New layouts by Jack Nicklaus and Greg Norman are earmarked for **Punta Mita,** which is being expanded beyond the Four Seasons property into an exclusive, low-density resort community. Rosewood will open the 70-suite **La Solana,** one of four boutique hotels planned for the development, in 2007. With a design inspired by the ranch houses and country estates of old Mexico, La Solana will feature individual suites with private plunge pools and terraces along with an oceanside spa and beach club.

The next hotel will be a **St. Regis** resort to be built on the site of Punta Mita's original fishing village in a traditional, low-lying style. The Punta Mita community will also include private homes and shared-ownership villas nestled into a hillside overlooking the sea. The Nicklaus-designed course is expected to open in 2007 and the Norman-designed course in 2008.

LODGING & DINING

The simple, elegant guest rooms at **Four Seasons Resort Punta Mita,** each beautifully furnished with original art, are housed in low-rise, tile-roofed *casitas* terraced up the side of a hill overlooking the sea. Accommodations, including 114 rooms and 26 suites, feature oversized bathrooms as well as a private terrace or balcony overlooking the beach and sea. The resort's public spaces are uncluttered and inviting. Native wood and fossilized stone were used to accent open-air spaces oriented to the sea. Shapes are rounded; there no sharp edges at Punta Mita.

The resort's top dining spot is Aramara, which features exceptional "Chino Latino" cuisine, a brilliant fusion of Latin American and Asian flavors. The char-grilled jumbo prawns in a mango chili glaze over sauteed vegetables and couscous are spectacular. More casual fare is available at the Ketsi poolside restaurant, where a bathing suit and T-shirt is acceptable attire.

The Apuane Spa at Punta Mita, like most spas at the world's top new luxury properties, is magnificent. A chamomile body scrub followed by a tequila-spiked sage oil massage is highly recommended.

In addition to water sports at the resort's beach (everything from kayaks and sailboats to wind-gliders to windsurfers are available), some of Mexico's finest surfing beaches are located north and south of the resort. The resort can also arrange snorkeling or scuba diving excursions to the Marietas Islands Wildlife Preserve due west from Punta Mita, where the underwater visibility and marine life are excellent. Seasonal whale watching cruises are available from December to March. Deep-sea fishing, hot air balloon rides, horseback riding, all-terrain vehicle tours, and nature hikes round out the list of activities.

Cancun/Riviera Maya

Cancun is a household name among Mexican destinations, especially for those seeking sun and fun on the Yucatan Peninsula. After all, Quintana Roo, the state in which Cancun is located, is the only place in Mexico that touches the Caribbean Sea. But with 18 new courses planned for the Cancun area, soon there will be enough critical mass to transform the region, renowned for its ancient Mayan ruins and world-class water sports, into a premier golf destination.

The turnaround would be nothing short of miraculous, but then, it wouldn't be the first time. Cancun was a sleepy fishing village in the 1960s. Enter FONATUR, the government agency charged with creating new resort destinations, which chose Cancun as its first experiment. Endowed with natural attributes, notably a stunning expanse of white sand lapped by a turquoise-blue sea, sun-drenched Cancun was an immediate success, blossoming into a major vacation hub in the 1970s. Today, its 14-mile-long

hotel zone boasts more than 100 hotels lined cheek-by-jowl along the beach. An unabashedly mass-market destination, Cancun attracts upwards of three million visitors a year.

To golfers, the Cancun area offers a couple of vintage courses and a growing list of newer ones in and around the main tourism corridor. However, some of the most arresting new developments are located farther south along the Riviera Maya, a nearly 90-mile stretch that begins south of Cancun and extends to the impressive Sian Ka'an Biosphere Reserve, a UNESCO World Heritage Site. Golf-wise, it will soon be the Next Place to tee it up south of the border.

Hurricane Wilma, which pummeled Cancun and the Riviera Maya in fall 2005, damaged several works-in-progress, but at press time most developments had regained their footing and revised their construction schedules.

Golf Club at Moon Palace, Lakes nine, fifth hole

The region took a major step forward in 2003 with the debut of the **Golf Club at Moon Palace,** a Jack Nicklaus signature course. Created to harmonize with the site's lush vegetation, the 7,165-yard design is flanked by dense jungle, natural wetlands, and strategically placed waste bunkers, many of them dotted with small grassy islands. Host of the Mexican Open in 2004–05, Moon Palace is a world-class layout that is nevertheless playable from the forward tees thanks to its wide fairways.

While the site's elevation change amounts to no more than a subtle ripple, each hole is encased in its own jungle corridor, creating a feeling of containment. Among the signature holes, and there are several, is the sixth, a "driveable" par four of 337 yards that doglegs almost 90 degrees to the right over sand and water to a large green that slopes away from the fairway. Moon Palace finishes in style at the grand par-four 18th, a 445-yarder that calls for a carry over wetlands from the tee. A large fairway bunker down the right side forces players chasing par to hew close to the water on the left for a better angle into a large, skewed green that tilts abruptly from back to front.

As fine as the course is, it's not all about the golf at Moon Palace. A round of golf here is also a nature safari. Crocodiles sun themselves on the sandy banks of the lagoons. Iguanas and aardvarks occasionally appear at the place where the rough vanishes into the jungle. Deer and fox can often be seen early and late in the day.

Based on the immediate success of the core 18, Nicklaus returned to build the **Dunes,** a desert-themed nine holes designed to complement the verdant, tropical theme of the original layout. The new nine opened in 2005. A fourth nine is also planned.

All-inclusive golf packages are available at Moon Palace, a giant 2,031-room property, most with ocean views and all with double Jacuzzis and private balconies. The sprawling resort is located 10 minutes from the airport and 40 minutes from downtown Cancun. Golf packages are also available to guests of Moon Palace's sister properties, including **Sun Palace, Aventura Spa Palace,** and **Xpu-Ha Palace.**

While Nicklaus's new course set a new standard for the area, the all-inclusive Palace Resorts also offers the **Golf Club at Playacar,** a 7,202-yard layout by Robert von Hagge that opened in 1994 on the southern outskirts of Playa del Carmen an hour's drive from Cancun. With a slope rating of 148 from the tips, this broad-shouldered course, carved from a dense jungle rooted on a limestone plateau, offers one of the stiffest tests of golf in Mexico. To his credit, von Hagge managed to build the course without

Golf Club at Playacar, 18th hole

disturbing more than 200 Mayan ruins on site. He also incorporated in the design a number of cenotes, or sinkholes, used by the ancient Mayans to collect rainwater.

There is ample evidence of von Hagge's "vertical expression"—steep mounds inset with bunkers rise from the perimeter of the targets and provide a foundation for the bunkers. The mounds provide some containment, but the slim fairways and tiny greens leave little margin for error. In fact, Playacar is the ultimate macho course, an airtight test of golf skills, chutzpah, and ego. Novices need not apply. The fearsome 468-yard seventh (formerly the 16th) is not only long, it plays uphill into a prevailing headwind. The narrow green is fiendishly guarded in front by deep bunkers. The hardest par four south of the border? *Si, mi amigo.*

Guests of the aforementioned hotels plus numerous other Palace Resorts in the area have access to this archaeological site and searing test of golf rolled into one.

The region's first course, built in 1976, was Pok-ta-Pok (stroke by stroke), a Robert Trent Jones, Jr. design located in Cancun's hotel zone. Recently renamed **Club de Golf Cancun,** the layout, nestled between the Nichupte Lagoon and the Caribbean Sea, was treated to a $500,000 overhaul and a much-needed irrigation system in 2005. A series of ancient Mayan ruins can be seen from the tees and fairways of this pleasant 6,602-yard layout. With its fine views of the shore and sea, it offers an enjoyable experience to golfers of all abilities.

El Camaleon Golf Course at Mayakoba

ONES TO WATCH

Seven miles north of Cancun on a small, secluded peninsula nestled between the Caribbean Sea and the Chacmochuc Lagoon is a budding 930-acre development known as the **Playa Mujeres Resort.** Promoted as a $1.5 billion project, Playa Mujeres, endowed with four miles of white sand beach, will eventually feature four luxury hotels (including a Ritz-Carlton), a high-end retail shopping component, horse stables, a 50-slip marina, and 50-plus exclusive waterfront homes with plans for 1,000 more interior home sites. In addition, a 1,200-year-old Mayan temple discovered on the property will be studied, restored, and opened to guests for tours. Two eco-sensitive golf courses by Greg Norman are in the works: Both are expected to open by 2007–08.

Located on the west side of Cancun seven miles south of the airport will be the **TPC of Cancun,** centerpiece of a 2,000-acre residential golf community to be known as La Roca Country Club. The TPC of Cancun golf course, designed by Tom Fazio and Nick Price, is expected to open in 2007. The PGA Tour, which governs the network of Tournament Players Clubs, is providing technical assistance. At full build-out, La Roca will include over 2,800 residential units and an additional course to be designed by Fazio and Price.

Another promising newcomer on the horizon is **Puerto Cancun,** a Tom Weiskopf–designed course slated to be built between Cancun's hotel strip and the downtown area. The layout, scheduled to open in 2007–08, will feature ocean and tropical forest views, with numerous water hazards in play.

Finally, there's **Costa Cancun,** which is earmarked for two Jack Nicklaus–designed courses. At press time, a 2007–08 opening was forecast for the first 18 holes.

Moving south to the Riviera Maya we find the **Iberostar Paraiso Maya,** an upscale all-inclusive property with 432 junior suites. Opened in 2004, the hotel's towering entrance is a replica of the pyramid-shaped temple at Chichen Itza. It joins three other pre-existing Iberostar hotels on site. In spring 2005, a P.B. Dye–designed golf course opened at the complex. While the site was solid rock, the water table was low enough for Dye to dig down 15 feet. "And if I can go down 15 feet, I can go up 15 feet," he chuckles, referring to his conspicuous mounds and bold shaping. The course is covered from tee to green in paspalum, the salt-tolerant turfgrass that is driving golf growth along the Riviera Maya just as surely as it has in the Caribbean. Iberostar guests receive preferred tee times, but the course is open to the public.

Forty miles south of the mass-market destination of Cancun, a Madrid-based development group has been grooming an eco-sensitive project called **Mayakoba** (Mayan for "city on the water") since the mid-1990s. The stated goal was to create an anti-Cancun, a place

the ancient Mayans themselves might enjoy. Instead of crowding the beach with high-rise hotels, the design team placed the resort's low-rise properties well inland from a dune ridge and a mile-long strand of sandy white beach. In addition, the site's thick mangrove swamps were left intact. Mangroves serve to purify organic materials and prevent runoff from clogging reefs, in this case a pristine coral reef that extends to Belize and is rated the second largest in the world.

While it appears natural, Mayakoba's extensive system of lagoons and canals was man-made. Crystal-clear water from subterranean aquifers flows through the site's porous limestone to fill these waterways. The 1,600-acre complex, with a Greg Norman–designed golf course and five luxury hotels in its first phase, is closed to vehicular traffic. Guests get around on foot, on bicycles, in golf carts, or in canopied electric boats called *lanchas* (they look like floating tiki huts).

El Camaleon Golf Course, one of Norman's admirable "least-disturbance" designs, has sinuous fairways shoehorned into the jungle, the holes tracing the curve of the meandering waterways. The 7,067-yard layout, surfaced in salt-tolerant paspalum grass, transitions from dense forest to mangrove swamp to holes flanked by the limestone-edged canals. Cenotes, the underground caverns or sinkholes that occur naturally in the limestone bedrock of the Riviera Maya, also come into play. Many of the tee shots are hit-or-miss affairs—El Camaleon transitions very quickly from short grass to impenetrable jungle. Also, water comes into play at nearly every turn. Two of the holes beckon from rippled seaside dunes, but for the most part, the golf experience, like the hotel experience, is set well back from the ocean. A tasteful clubhouse with a three-tiered copper roof and an Argentinian steakhouse on its second floor overlooks the 18th green. In 2007, El Camaleon will host the Mayakoba Classic, the first official event on the PGA Tour to be held in Mexico.

The first of Mayakoba's five luxury hotels, each connected to the sea by its beach club, is the low-rise **Fairmont Mayakoba,** its 401 rooms and suites set beside the jungle-fringed waterways. Like the golf course, its scheduled opening was delayed until mid-2006 following damages sustained by Hurricane Wilma. Rooms and suites, done up in a sun-bleached palette of gold, soft reds and oranges, call to mind an elegant Mexican beach house. In addition to the golf course, which it manages, the Fairmont offers five restaurants (including Las Brisas, an oceanfront dining room) and a 20,000-square-foot spa with treetop treatment areas. **Laguna Kai,** a 120-room Rosewood Resort, will debut in late 2006, to be followed by properties managed by Banyan Tree, Viceroy, and La Casa Que Canta. Mayakoba is 15 minutes from the town of Playa del Carmen.

Seaside dining at Mayakoba

DAY TRIP/COZUMEL

In ancient times, Mayan women traveled to the island of Cozumel to worship the goddess of fertility. Next came Jacques Cousteau in 1961, who proclaimed the waters around the island among the finest for diving on the planet. Today, this rocky, 24-mile-long island in the Caribbean Sea remains a laid-back jungle oasis outlined by *palapa*-dotted beaches. It enjoys tremendous popularity as a spring break capital, but mostly Cozumel is known for its superb snorkeling and scuba diving. Indeed, its gin-clear waters, rare black coral, and abundant marine life attract divers from around the world.

But the sleepy island's sports focus changed slightly in 2001, when **Cozumel Country Club,** the island's first (and only) course made its debut. Chiseled from coral rock, the 6,734-yard layout is hemmed in by red mangroves, expansive wetlands, inland lagoons, and even shallow coral canyons. Turned out by the Nicklaus Design Group, this challenging spread was built with cruise ship passengers in mind, though it's no carefree lark. Forced carries over water hazards and marshy areas are called for, but the nature show is fair compensation for a few lost balls. Crocodiles patrol the lagoons, iguanas sun themselves on shore, and exotic birds, including more than a dozen members of the heron and egret families, roost in the trees.

Lodging is available at several nearby resort hotels, including two that offer unlimited golf (guests pay cart fees only) as part of their all-inclusive program: **Playa Azul Golf & Beach Hotel;** and **Paradisus Cozumel.** Ferries run on the hour to Cozumel from Playa del Carmen.

Beach at Playa del Carmen

DAY TRIP/PLAYA DEL CARMEN

The St. Tropez of the Riviera Maya? Perhaps that's a little too fancy-sounding for the former fishing village of Playa del Carman with a lovely beach and a wonderful sense of place. It doesn't take long to fall in love with this sultry seaside enclave, a fun little town built on the broad slope of a hill that is equally popular with Europeans and Americans. The best place to commence a tour of Playa del Carmen is Quinta Avenida (Fifth Avenue), a pedestrian thoroughfare lined with colorful boutiques, artisan galleries, small B & B's, trendy little hotels, and bustling open-air cafés. This is a town that attracts the young and young-at-heart. Filling the streets are couples holding hands who visit to enjoy the palpable sense of fun the town exudes. If ever there was a place to loll away an afternoon sipping a margarita in the shade, Playa del Carmen is it. Looking for a beach of your own? A short walk north brings you to empty stretches of sand.

OFF-COURSE ATTRACTIONS

An hour's drive from Cancun and only minutes from Playa del Carmen is Xcaret, a one-of-a-kind eco-archaeoiogical attraction that combines nature, history, and activities. Xcaret translates as "inlet," and the limestone rock of this park is honeycombed with cenotes and subterranean rivers. You can learn how sea turtles are raised for release back into the wild, interact with dolphins, wander through a wild bird aviary filled with dozens of exotic species, and be surrounded by butterflies within the world's largest butterfly pavilion. There's also a lovely botanical garden and an evening cultural show at Xcaret.

Established in the 1980s, Xel-Ha (pronounced she'l-ha), Mayan for "where the waters are born," is a gorgeous 22-acre nature park and one of the Yucatan's largest eco-attractions. Serene and natural despite its many recent expansions, Xel-Ha, like Xcaret, is built around an inlet of the sea, in this cas a centuries-old trading port used by the Mayans. A large lagoon teeming with tropical fish is fed by a river that flows from a jungle. Xel-Ha is a perfect place to snorkel in a protected sanctuary where coral reefs and rock formations create an ideal habitat for marine life.

The region's third major attraction is Tulum, located 40 miles south of Playa del Carmen. One of Mexico's more fascinating archaeological sites, Tulum, a walled city dotted with 60 masonry-and-stucco structures, is highlighted by El Castillo, an imposing fortress that commands a limestone bluff overlooking the sea. Also of interest are the rare Mayan paintings found within the Temple of the Frescoes. The edifices at Tulum date to the late Post-Classic period (between 1200 and 1500 A.D.). They are relatively small compared to other Mayan cities, but the setting is magnificent. So are the diving opportunities in Hidden Worlds Cenotes Park in Tulum, which offers guided dives as well as snorkeling into cenotes. The water is so clear in these underground caves, it's practically invisible.

Caribbean

After a long fallow period that ran from the mid-1970s through the early 1990s, a time of slumber when few layouts of enduring merit were built in the Caribbean, this multi-cultural collection of tropical islands, scattered from the tip of Florida to the north coast of South America, began to surge forward shortly before the millennium. Most exciting of all have been the 18-hole layouts that have

Ritz-Carlton Golf & Spa Resort, Rose Hall, Jamaica

opened or will open on virgin islands that previously had no full-scale golf.

In addition to far-sighted developers and island governments who recognize the value of golf as a tourism tool, a newly developed salt-tolerant turfgrass, paspalum, has begun to drive golf growth in the tropics. Overall, course conditioning in the islands, an iffy proposition in the past, is now much improved. Of course, the beauty quotient of Caribbean venues has always outweighed their cosmetic flaws, but now avid golfers can have it both ways. In addition, new or upgraded hotels, cutting-edge cuisine, and improved levels of service have transformed the vacation experience throughout the islands.

The settings for the game in the Caribbean are among the most rapturous and diverse in the world. Some courses scale the jungled flanks of dormant volcanoes; others are as flat and firm as a Scottish seaside links, but in place of the thorny gorse and chilly wind are swaying palms and warm, sultry air. Parkland-style layouts carved from thick tropical vegetation, headlands courses perched on bluffs a la Pebble Beach, desert-style tracks dotted with cactus and scrub—the Caribbean has a little bit of everything.

Bahamas

A sprawling archipelago of over 700 coral islands and 2,500 cays scattered across a giant arc from the east coast of Florida to the tip of Cuba, the Bahamas, favored by pirates 300 years ago and renowned for its gin-clear waters and pristine beaches, has had its ups and downs as a place for golf. The Bahamas emerged as a full-fledged destination by the early 1970s, but then went into the doldrums. Since the late 1990s, however, America's closest offshore vacation spot has committed itself to golf as a prime tourism draw and is ready to take its rightful place as a top golf getaway. Its prime selling points are its beaches: Search far and wide, you won't find prettier white and pink sand beaches than those in the islands of the Bahamas.

Grand Bahama Island (GBI), which shed its "Freeport" moniker several years ago as part of a re-branding initiative, is a mere 55 miles off the coast of south Florida and a short flight from either Miami or Fort Lauderdale. GBI showcases the vintage work of Dick Wilson, whose U.S. credits included Bay Hill and Doral's Blue Course, but even his creations had grown stale over the years. The "new" golf on GBI includes the renovation of a few of Wilson's timeless designs.

Our Lucaya Beach & Golf Resort, stretched along 7 ½ acres of white sand beach on the south shore of GBI a few miles from the duty-free shopping mecca of Freeport, is a new development but counts a

An aerial view of the Lucayan Course

previously existing Wilson course (formerly private) among its 36 holes along with a new Robert Trent Jones, Jr. design built from scratch on the site of a defunct course. Our Lucaya, unveiled in 2000 and hailed as the resort that spearheaded the rebirth of GBI, is the inspired creation of a Hong Kong–based shipping company and multi-national conglomerate that has spent nearly $450 million to build an upbeat resort with 1,350 guest rooms and suites, 14 restaurants and lounges, the Senses Spa and Fitness Center, and the Isle of Capri Casino. There's also a long list of off-campus diversions, including dolphin encounters in the open Atlantic.

The **Reef Course,** Jones's links-style design, presents an open, windswept test with water in play at 13 holes. Many of the greens, inspired perhaps by the work of his father, are raised above fairway level and bracketed by large cloverleaf bunkers. The first new layout to be built in the Bahamas in over 30 years when it opened in 2000, the 6,930-yard course stands in marked contrast to GBI's other venues, most of which are hemmed in by thick vegetation. The Reef can play tame on a calm day, but

tradewinds routinely sweep the links during winter and spring, creating a rigorous examination where only sound course management and solid ball-striking will enable players to skirt the water hazards, bunkers, and clumps of love grass.

The resort also offers the **Lucayan Course,** a 1962 Wilson design ranked among his best. A rolling, parkland-style layout carved from tall pines and thickets of palmetto, this well-groomed 6,824-yard course favors precision over power. Elevated greens guarded by steep-faced bunkers demand accurate approach shots, especially on the lengthy par threes. The signature par-four 18th hole, its hairpin fairway bent to the left around a lake that guards its two-tiered green, is notable for the weirdly-shaped concrete sculptures that rise from a landscaped island in the center of the lake. (They once spit fire and water in the go-go '60s!) But even this silly bit of stagecraft cannot detract from the integrity of an updated layout.

For those seeking improvement, there's also a Jim McLean Golf School at the Lucayan. One- and three-day packages are available, as are private lessons.

LODGING & DINING

In 2002, Starwood Hotels & Resorts assumed management of the accommodations at **Our Lucaya Beach & Golf Resort**. The 749 guest rooms in the Lighthouse Point and Breakers Cay portions of the resort were reflagged the **Westin at Our Lucaya,** while the 514-room, family-style Reef Village entity, overlooking the Sugar Mill Pool with its 60-foot stone tower and spiral water slide, is now the **Sheraton at Our Lucaya.** Twenty-five luxurious Lanai Suites that open onto the beach and feature steward service are also available. In addition, the Camp Lucaya kids club, located at the Sheraton, offers activities designed to entertain, teach, and challenge children.

The resort's 14 themed restaurants are uniformly excellent, with kid-friendly Barracudas (a 1950s-style diner) and Willy Broadleaf (eclectic buffet-style dining) drawing most of the attention. Noteworthy for its Pacific Rim fusion cuisine is China Beach.

SHOPPING

Across the street from the resort is Port Lucaya Marketplace, a 10-acre complex with more than 80 shops encircling Count Basie Square, a popular venue for live music. Fine imported goods—china, crystal, fine jewelry, fragrances—are sold at duty-free prices. In the straw markets, native artwork and colorful handicrafts are available along with the usual swimwear, sandals, and T-shirts.

OFF-COURSE ATTRACTIONS

GBI is one of the top eco-tourism islands in the Bahamas. Nature lovers should make a beeline to the Bahamas National Trust Rand Nature Centre, a 100-acre preserve and flamingo sanctuary near Freeport that is home to 130 native plants, including 20 species of wild orchids. It's also the island's birding center. Farther afield is Lucayan National Park, its 40 shoreline acres laced with trails and walkways cut through wild tamarind, gumbo limbo trees, and mangrove swamps set above a secluded beach. A descending spiral staircase leads to a portion of the park's vast system of underground limestone caverns. Kayak nature tours on secluded inland creeks are also available.

Located in Port Lucaya is UNEXSO, the Underwater Explorers Society, where novices can learn to scuba dive in three hours. Experienced divers can frolic with bottlenose dolphins in the open ocean or observe sharks being hand-fed at Shark Junction. Or opt for the Dolphin Experience, an interactive and educational program featuring trained dolphins.

Want to spend a day on a perfect beach? The broad expanse of white powdery sand at Taino Beach east of Freeport and Lucaya is perfect for water sport enthusiasts as well as families. The island is also a premier deep-sea fishing destination, with marlin, sailfish, and yellowfin tuna available.

Beachfront at the Westin at Our Lucaya

Manor house lobby at Our Lucaya Beach & Golf Resort

Waterslide at Atlantis

LODGING & DINING

Rare among island resorts, Royal Oasis promotes value. Its all-inclusive, air-and-land golf packages (with charter departures from selected East Coast and Midwest gateways) feature updated accommodations at the 392-room **Crowne Plaza Resort Grand Bahama Island Tower.** The entire resort boasts a total of 965 rooms and suites. There's also a wide choice of restaurants and lounges, including Coconuts Bar & Grill, a popular sports bar.

The resort boasts one of the largest American-style casinos in the Caribbean and claims the island's only "Sports Book." There's also a European-style spa, but its zero-entry beach pool with waterslides and waterfalls make it family-friendly, too.

WHERE'S THE WARMTH?

A caveat: The weather on GBI can be quite cool and breezy in the dead of winter. Spring and fall are the best times to visit for ideal golf weather. On the plus side, an abundant fresh water source—GBI sits atop a huge aquifer—ensures that the courses at Our Lucaya and Royal Oasis are among the best-conditioned in the Bahamas.

SHOOTING THE MOON: THE MEGA-RESORT

GBI's profile may not be high at the moment, but it will be in the future if the world's largest resort—a multi-billion-dollar, lunar-themed complex off the island's north coast—gets built. Proposed by a Canadian company and set for completion by 2010, the resort, called **Moon Bahamas,** would sit on five man-made islands. After $4.5 billion in construction costs, the complex, covering 10 square miles, would feature the world's largest casino and largest resort wine cellar; its biggest mega-yacht marina; and its largest and tallest hotel, with 12,000 suites stacked in a 100-story tower. The over-the-top resort would also feature four golf courses, 50 restaurants, 10 cruise ship terminals, a massive convention center, and 22,000 condos, all encircled by the world's largest artificial coral reef.

Fifteen minutes from Grand Bahama International Airport is the **Royal Oasis Golf Resort & Casino,** which reopened in 2002 after a $42 million facelift. Visiting players can tackle two fine courses here. Formerly known as the Bahamas Princess (and later Bahamia), the 1,500-acre complex is built around a 36-hole facility that was treated to a $6 million refurbishment shortly after the millennium. Jim Fazio, Tom's older brother, was brought in to completely redesign the **Ruby Course,** a Joe Lee creation that had grown claustrophobic over time. Fazio changed hole configurations, widened corridors, installed new tees, enlarged bunkers, and built larger, more undulating greens. Stretching to nearly 7,000 yards, the Ruby is a big, roomy, and virtually new track.

Fazio also restored the resort's **Emerald Course,** a Wilson design circa 1965. A subtle, flowing test woven through palmettos, pines, and thickets of lush vegetation, the Emerald has no intrusive housing and no parallel holes. On a breezy day from the tips at 6,679 yards, even accomplished players will have their hands full on this well-conditioned track. Fazio, who wisely kept the sequence of holes intact, reshaped bunkers, re-contoured greens, and also pushed back a few tees on this classic resort spread.

On **New Providence Island,** which goes by the name of Nassau, the nation's capital, all eyes are on Paradise Island, a thin sliver of land accessible via causeway from the north shore of the main island. Here visionary South African leisure tycoon Sol Kerzner has spent $800 million to turn a once-ailing property owned by Merv Griffin into **Atlantis,** one of the most exciting themed destination resorts in the world. This sprawling oceanfront resort features 2,349 rooms in three large towers, the largest casino in the islands, and a 14-acre water park boasting the world's largest open-air aquarium. There's also a re-creation of the Lost City of Atlantis called The Dig, an elaborate maze of rooms and corridors that takes visitors through the faux ruins of an 11,000-year-old lost continent, with more than 50,000 sea animals (most of them Bahamian) on view. Starting in 2007, golf will join the Atlantis mix with a new 18-hole course on nearby Athol Island, part of a project that also will add 1,200 more rooms.

A short drive from Atlantis but a world apart in atmosphere and ambience is another Kerzner property, the **One&Only Ocean Club,** a posh enclave once owned by Huntington Hartford II, heir to the A & P fortune. (Hartford wisely changed the name of the island from Hog to Paradise in the early 1960s.) Kerzner has transformed the property into one of the most elegant getaways in the hemisphere.

Superimposed on the former Paradise Island Golf Club, a Dick Wilson layout on the eastern tip of the island that had become a hodgepodge of design styles over the years, is the **Ocean Club Golf Course,** a brilliant 7,159-yard layout by Tom Weiskopf. Flanked on three sides by the sea, this spectacular, well-balanced course features an ocean view from every tee plus seven holes that touch the sea. Wind, which can quarter at any direction, dictates play not only from day to day, but hour to hour on this lightly treed spread. Weiskopf took out 7,000 trees, mostly casuarina pines, to enhance the ocean views, but he also planted

LODGING

The tranquil, low-key **One&Only Ocean Club**, beautifully landscaped and set on a lovely two-mile stretch of beach, offers 105 opulent guest rooms in its Crescent and Hartford Wings, with Bahamian-style beachfront suites and garden cottages available. In addition, three luxurious villas were debuted in 2004. Nice touches include round-the-clock butler service as well as champagne and strawberries served every afternoon.

After the round, guests can relax and unwind at the One&Only Spa, where treatments are available in eight Balinese-style villas with open-air terraces; and the resort's freshwater pool, which sits cloistered below terraced gardens patterned after those at Versailles. Crowning the top of a hill are the arches of a 14th-century Augustinian cloister, which Hartford bought from William Randolph Hearst and had reassembled on site.

The Ocean Club's signature dining outlet is Dune, a beachfront eatery with a spare, British Colonial theme, operated by renowned international chef Jean-Georges Vongerichten. The eclectic French-Asian cuisine benefits from the use of local herbs taken from an organic garden outside the kitchen door.

The most luxurious golf spot in the Bahamas, the Ocean Club does not come cheap—at press time, winter room rates started at $750 per night. The golf course is accessible to guests of both Atlantis and the Ocean Club, but with a high-season green fee of $245, there are very few emigrés from the Lost City on the links.

Terraced gardens at One&Only Ocean Club

500 palms to lend a tropical feel. An excellent strategic test, with wide corridors and well-placed hazards, the course can be managed from the forward tees by average players who don't try for too much glory. The fairways are covered in salt-tolerant paspalum grass.

The prettiest hole on the course is the par-three 12th, which plays from an elevated platform near the clubhouse. The shot, usually hit into a crosswind, is carried over water to a very large green staked out by bunkers and backdropped by swaying palms. The sapphire-blue sea floods the horizon behind the green.

A haven for celebrities—Michael Jordan owns a home at the resort and Cindy Crawford was married there—even the Ocean Club's pro is a star. He's Ernie Els who, like Kerzner, hails from South Africa.

ONE TO WATCH

Ever since Sol Kerzner took the Bahamas by storm with the creation of Atlantis, the notion of creating mega-resorts has proved irresistible to developers. In 2005, Baha Mar Development Company Ltd. purchased the 700-room Radisson Cable Beach Resort, its golf course, and two additional properties. While the company immediately spent $15 million to upgrade the three hotels, the renovations are a prelude to a $1.6 billion joint venture with Harrah's and Starwood in a 1,000-acre oceanfront project along Nassau's Cable Beach. The **Baha Mar** development, scheduled to be completed by 2010, will feature a water park, a 100,000-square-foot casino by Caesars, celebrity-chef restaurants, luxurious spas, a wide range of retail outlets, entertainment venues for live performances, and 2,700 guest rooms. Hotels will include Caesars, St. Regis, W, Westin, and Sheraton. Baha Mar also signed Jack Nicklaus to design a course on property accessible via a specially designed waterway.

Great Exuma, largest of the 365 mostly uninhabited islands and cays sprinkled across the Exuma archipelago, is an unsullied island of only 3,400 residents known mainly to fishermen, scuba divers, and sailors. For years there were rumors of a resort and golf course to be built on one of the island's prettiest bays. Now it is a reality.

Unveiled in 2004, the **Four Seasons Resort Great Exuma at Emerald Bay,** a 470-acre resort and residential community, is the first major hotel to open in the Exumas. Its key ingredient, and the island's first golf course, is the **Four Seasons Golf Club,** a Greg Norman design plotted through mangrove swamps and coral rock outcrops. The highlight of the 7,001-yard course is the stretch of holes from 11 through 16, which trace the perimeter of Emerald

Four Seasons Golf Club, 15th hole

Bay's rocky peninsula, bringing players face-to-face with the turquoise-blue sea as it lashes the encrusted shore. Truly spectacular, they tend to overshadow the layout's well-crafted interior holes, where the shots values are better.

Thoughtful, accurate play is required to score at Emerald Bay. Norman, in fact, has an expectation that a golfer, even a refugee from the Snow Belt, can hit the ball reasonably straight. Landing areas are

tight and targets are small, though most of the grade-level greens are open in front.

The finest hole at Emerald Bay is the 12th, a majestic par four that sweeps from right to left along the shore, the fairway rising to a long, narrow green at land's end, the sea pounding in from the left, an elaborate waste bunker dotted with scrubby islands on the right. A yanked approach will dance crazily on the ironshore before tumbling into the boiling sea.

Bring your mid-season guile, your punch shots, your wind-cheaters—or elect to go snorkeling in the bay's crystal-clear waters.

The entire course is a verdant shade of emerald green thanks to the paspalum used to carpet the tees, fairways, and greens. It's the only grass varietal that could thrive on a rocky, windswept site moistened by sea spray.

LODGING

The $400-million, 183-room **Four Seasons Resort Great Exuma at Emerald Bay**, its pastel-colored, low-rise units clustered around an exquisite crescent-shaped bay and sandy beach, is the first luxury property to be built in the Out Islands of the Bahamas. Guest accommodations—140 oversize rooms and 43 suites—are Bahamian Colonial in style. Each room has a teak-furnished balcony or terrace with an ocean view.

Landscaped in bougainvillea and hibiscus, the resort features a 32,406-square-foot spa and fitness club. Salts extracted from local salt beds along with indigenous herbs, flowers, and oils are used in the treatments and homeopathic therapies. A secluded Tranquil Garden is the venue for the resort's wellness program, which includes yoga and meditation.

The protected deep-water marina, with slips for 100 ocean-going vessels, offers yachtsmen the only first-class stopover between Freeport and the Virgin Islands. Full-day and half-day sails as well as sunset cruises can be arranged on *Emerald Lady,* the resort's custom-built, $1-million catamaran. Sea kayaking, a popular family activity, is available at newly designated Moriah Cay National Park. Some of the world's most renowned sport fishing can be found in Great Exuma, its vast flats providing a perfect habitat for bonefish, a.k.a. the "silver ghost."

The resort staff are very friendly, and happy to be home. Many Exumans left the island years ago to work in Nassau and other busy tourist areas in the Bahamas, but the opening of the Four Seasons has given them a chance to return to their beautiful rock in the sea.

DAY TRIP

Beyond Emerald Bay is Exuma Cays National Land and Sea Park, a 176-square-mile preserve founded in 1959 and the first of its kind in the world. Home to brilliant coral reefs and exotic marine life (including graceful manta rays and the rare Bahamian iguana), the park welcomes visitors, above water or below, to a sanctuary unspoiled by fishing or hunting. Many of the coral stands reach nearly to the surface, enabling snorkelers to partake of underwater beauty usually reserved for scuba divers.

BAHAMAS CUISINE

Bahamian cuisine derives its individuality from the seafood, produce, and spices of the Caribbean, accented by the polyglot cultures of the people. Conch meat—a national delicacy said to be an aphrodisiac—is one of the most popular dishes. A shellfish similar in texture to scallops, the white meat of the conch shell is served in chowders, sandwiches, and fritters. A delicious salad, generally found at small roadside kiosks, is made by combining conch, tomatoes, onion, celery, sweet and hot pepper, lime juice, and sour orange. A traditional dish (and staple fare for Sunday dinner) is Peas and Rice, a medley of pigeon peas, bacon, onion, celery, thyme leaves, hot pepper, and rice. From the sea come kingfish, wahoo, dolphinfish, and grouper. Caribbean herbs and spices—curry, ginger, allspice, marjoram, thyme, and saffron—add tantalizing flavor. Regional fruits—guava, mango, papaya, tamarind, pineapple, plantain—are incorporated in recipes. The local beer is Kalik, a fine, pale lager.

Guest room terrace at Four Seasons Resort Great Exuma

Barbados

The easternmost island in the Caribbean, Barbados, traditionally favored by British travelers, has been increasingly patronized of late by Americans and has become a major player in the West Indies golf scene virtually overnight. In fact, this "Cornwall of the Tropics" has a handful of top-shelf courses available, with several more on the drawing board.

Following three years of rebuilding, **Sandy Lane,** a glamorous jet-set resort on the west coast of Barbados, reopened in 2001 after a $450 million overhaul by its new Irish owners. The hotel was demolished and rebuilt from the ground up, with no expense spared. Architectural flourishes from the old Sandy Lane, which opened in 1961 and for years was the favored Caribbean hideaway for royalty, celebrities, and heads of state (Queen Elizabeth, Frank Sinatra, Jacqueline Kennedy, and Mick Jagger, to name a few), were incorporated into the new design.

The exclusive 112-room resort is set in an old mahogany grove overlooking a broad crescent of coral sand and a turquoise-blue bay. The hotel itself was redone in the same neo-Palladian style as the original, complete with oceanside dance floor and white coral stone rotunda. In addition to 24-hour butler

Sandy Lane, Green Monkey course, 16th hole

Pool and spa at Sandy Lane

service and a 47,000-square-foot spa, the new Sandy Lane, which unlike its predecessor welcomes children at all times of year, offers seven bars and restaurants, including fine dining in L'Acajou, an 80-seat seafront restaurant created by London architect and designer David Collins. The cuisine, built around island seafood, is French with Asian accents.

As sumptuous as the creature comforts are—the beachside service includes sunglass cleaning, Evian misting, and refreshing sorbets—golfers will find the resort's trio of courses every bit their equal. Sandy Lane's sporty 18-hole course circa 1961 has been transformed into the **Old Nine,** a charming, walkable, tree-lined nine-holer that winds its way through the old estate's mahogany trees. It is delightful, but the big buzz is all about Tom Fazio's new creations, his first major designs outside the U.S.

Sandy Lane's **Country Club** course, unveiled in 2001, is a 7,060-yard layout carved into a broad slope high above the Caribbean Sea. A true resort-style spread, it offers wide fairways, but these fairways are angled and swept by tradewinds. Deep ravines and gullies gobble off-line shots, while five lakes, well-placed bunkers, and liberally contoured greens serve to keep players honest. The course, which features a fine view of the sea from nearly every hole, offers what many resort courses promise but few deliver: an enjoyable but not overbearing test of golf. In 2006, the Country Club course will host the WGC-World Cup of Golf.

Routed on higher ground nearly 300 feet above sea level is Sandy Lane's **Green Monkey** course, which made its much-anticipated debut in 2005 following a lengthy construction process that involved much

earth-moving—and just as much legerdemain. Portions of the 7,389-yard, championship-caliber course occupy a former coral stone quarry, with 100-foot-high walls rising around several fairways and greens. Spectacular from start to finish, the Green Monkey, an engineering extravaganza marked by abrupt elevation changes, is destined to become the greatest course ever built in and around a rock quarry. Nearly half the holes are stretched across the rim or floor of the old stone pit, but Fazio created quarry-like settings for other holes to "transition" golfers from one environment to the next without a hitch. It's his most inspired (and expensive) creation since Shadow Creek in Las Vegas.

Tiered like a fantastic wedding cake, its feature holes slotted at different heights within the sun-bleached limestone walls of the quarry, the Green Monkey's netherworld setting is *sui generis.* On many Fazio designs, the holes are aesthetically pleasing but sometimes lack a strategic element or a muscular quality. Not here. Fazio has grafted a gorilla-like backbone onto the Green Monkey. Rocky gorges, huge abysses, and mammoth bunkers come into play. So do sparkling little ponds. There is a daring risk-reward element on the longer holes, and the penalty for a failed effort or a bad gamble is often severe. Fazio's trademark playability is on display for holidaymakers, but from the tips, the Green Monkey is a major-league test that ranks among the most difficult courses the designer has ever crafted.

Perhaps the most memorable hole on the course is the novel par-three 16th, which plunges 60 feet to a lake in the heart of the quarry, the target a semi-island green backdropped by sheer rock walls. Beside the green is a massive bunker with an artfully-etched grass island in the shape of a green monkey in its center.

Both the Green Monkey and Country Club courses, by the way, are shared with Bajan green monkeys that live in the gullies found on both courses. These playful creatures occasionally gambol across the fairways early and late in the day.

The Old Nine and Country Club courses are open to daily-fee play, but the Green Monkey is available only to resort guests (at roughly $300 per round) and property owners. (A limited number of one- to three-acre lots are spaced around the quarry rim.) All three venues are served by a palatial 50,000-square-foot clubhouse that overlooks the golf courses and the sea, its shaded veranda an ideal place to savor the round over a cool Banks beer, a Bajan brew.

The tariff at Sandy Lane is imperial—in 2006, the least expensive room in high season started at $1,100 per night—but this completely new resort, far less

Royal Westmoreland, sixth hole

stuffy than its hail-the-Empire predecessor, is at or near the top of the finest golf vacation experiences available anywhere in the world. Which is probably why Tiger Woods chose to get married at Sandy Lane in 2004.

For high drama and visual splendor, **Royal Westmoreland,** a semi-private club tucked within a 500-acre resort community a few miles north of Sandy Lane, set a new standard for Barbados when it opened in 1995. Designer Robert Trent Jones, Jr., who claims he "spent $14 million and spent it well" on the project, conjured a beguiling layout on a former sugarcane plantation and limestone quarry nearly 300 feet above sea level, melding golf architecture with landscape art. This is the course that paved the way for the island's future golf developments.

The 6,870-yard layout's front nine is a multi-theme affair marked by decorative grasses, artful bunkering, and holes set into coral rock canyons. Feathery ornamental grasses bordering the fairways emulate the rippled movement of the sea when the tradewinds blow, which is often. Bunkers, most of them modified cloverleafs, mimic the shape and color of the puffy white clouds that dot the sky, providing another aesthetic reference. The game, by the way, is won or lost on the greens, which are very slick and difficult to read.

Royal Westmoreland's endearing front nine is followed by a ferocious back nine that turns the tables on players seduced by the winsome beauty of the opening holes. Coral bedrock on this upcountry section was dynamited to make way for holes framed or bisected by deep ravines choked with vegetation. Many of the bunkers are of the "saving" variety, designed by Jones to spare players a fate worse than sand. (Dense growth off the fairway is easier to attack with a machete than a five iron.)

A proposed third nine at Royal Westmoreland will occupy a grassy savannah below the current 18. Two- to seven-bedroom villas, fully staffed, are available on site. Guests have beach access at the nearby Fairmont Royal Pavilion hotel. Similarly, hotel guests can gain access to the golf course.

A nicely landscaped villa at Royal Westmoreland

On the southern tip of Barbados 10 minutes from the airport is **Barbados Golf Club,** which reopened in 2000 after a $7.2 million overhaul. The original Barbados Golf and Country Club, built in 1977, had gone belly up and lay vacant for more than 20 years. The government, which owned the land, enlisted a private firm to resurrect the layout and create a public facility. Ron Kirby, a former Gary Player design associate, was brought in to fashion a new course on the old site. The current spread, a gently rolling, 6,805-yard layout with subtle humps and hollows in the fairways, benefits from mature trees strategically planted along the fairways at the time the club was built. In addition to well-defined corridors, the golf course, sculpted to simulate a links, has a pair of lakes that come into play at five holes as well as a series of coral waste bunkers carved through four holes. Barbados Golf Club offers preferred tee times to the guests of several area hotels, including **Colony Club, Tamarind Cove,** and **Turtle Beach Resort.**

SIDETRIP

At the Mount Gay Rum Visitors Centre in St. Michael, located five minutes outside Bridgetown, visitors can learn the colorful history behind the world's oldest rum. (The famed distillery celebrated its 300th anniversary in 2003.) The spirit is made from molasses produced from Barbados cane sugar. The molasses is mixed with water in huge oak vats, distilled batch-by-batch in copper stills, and aged in charred white oak barrels from Kentucky formerly used to mature bourbon. These barrels impart a distinct smoky flavor and a hint of vanilla to the amber-colored Eclipse rum, Mount Gay's signature label. Visitors can linger for cocktails and tasty cuisine, notably flying fish, a Bajan specialty, in the airy veranda restaurant.

Dominican Republic

The second-largest country in the Caribbean, the Dominican Republic occupies the eastern two-thirds of the island of Hispaniola, which it shares with Haiti. Led by its premier resort, Casa de Campo, the Dominican Republic is currently the hottest spot for golf in the islands, and also its best value. The formula? Ambitious developers + inexpensive labor = great new projects. Add friendly Dominicans, beautiful beaches, fine cigars, lots of sunshine, excellent airports convenient to the major resort areas, and the oldest city in the Americas (Santo Domingo), and the Dominican Republic emerges not merely as a superb island for golf, but as a sizable country with unlimited potential.

Twist Pete Dye's arm, and he'll probably admit that his favorite course among the many he's designed is **Teeth of the Dog** at **Casa de Campo,** ("House in the Country"), the vast 7,000-acre playground on the island's southeast coast that has evolved, thanks to a $125 million expansion and improvement since the late 1990s, into the Caribbean's most complete resort. It's also among the most convenient, located 10 minutes from La Romana International Airport, a gateway served by major carriers with direct flights from the U.S.

Named for the jagged coral rocks that buttress its seaside tees, Teeth of the Dog was hand-built by Dye and 300 Dominicans in 1970. Seven of the holes skirt or cross the Caribbean Sea; the remainder are routed through fields of sugar cane and stands of almond and teak trees. From the white tees, it is the most enjoyable resort course in the Caribbean, yet "the Dog," currently ranked 41st in the world by *Golf Magazine,* can growl on a windy day. And that was true before Dye, who turned 80 in 2005, pried open the jaws of his prize creation the same year to have a look at its choppers. At first, a minor makeover was contemplated, but the indefatigable designer, who maintains a thatched roof home at the resort and shows no signs of slowing down, ended up creating a new smile for his masterpiece.

Casa de Campo, Teeth of the Dog, 16th hole

After the greens on this seminal tropical links were resurfaced in salt-tolerant paspalum grass, Dye, who realized the dimensions of the course were a bit short by today's standards, began pushing back tees, digging new bunkers, and altering hole angles. With significant alterations at nearly every hole, Dye, originally inspired by the links of Scotland, turned his seaside gem into a tartan beast. At the par-five third, for example, he added 50 yards to bring the right-hand fairway bunkers into play. By taking out the restrooms behind the fourth tee, he added nearly 100 yards to a formerly petite par four that now dog-legs sharply to the right.

Dye also redid the brilliant stretch of holes at 15, 16, and 17, each of which hugs the coast and plays into the prevailing wind. The par-four 17th, a demanding Cape-style hole that calls for a bold carry over an inlet of the sea, now stretches to over 475 yards, its back tee sited on a corner of the 16th green. The hole plays to an enlarged green that Pete somehow made look smaller.

In sum, Dye ended up turning his pet spaniel into a pit bull, at least from the new black tees at 7,470 yards. From the regular markers, Teeth of the Dog remains one of the most delightful resort courses in the hemisphere.

How does the revamped Teeth of the Dog compare to Casa de Campo's new **Dye Fore,** the architect's upcountry tour de force that stairsteps down bluffs high above the Chavon River? From the back tees, Teeth is nearly as challenging and, with its daunting forced carries over the sea, more uproarious. But Dye Fore, intended to redefine golf in the tropics and withstand the onslaught of equipment technology (at least for a few years), is as striking as anything the architect has ever done.

Opened in 2003 after five years of planning and construction, Dye Fore is a massive creation marked by sharp elevation changes and stunning views of the Caribbean Sea, interior mountains, and Altos de Chavon, the resort's cliff-hanging replica of a 16th-century Mediterranean village. It was a monumental engineering feat, requiring serious earthworks—entire valleys and ravines were filled to make golf possible on the deeply incised tableland. Multiple sets of tees allow the course to play from 5,445 to an ungodly 7,770 yards, although most holidaymakers will have all they can handle from the white tees at 6,420 yards, given the visual intimidation, optical illusions, and sheer scale of the facility.

The fourth and fifth holes are possibly the best back-to-back par fours in the Caribbean. The fourth is a downhill, downwind par four that sweeps from right to left and measures more than 500 yards from the gold tees. The fairway snakes along the top of a promontory as it descends, the mouth of the river and the sea beyond flooding the horizon. The green, like many on the course, is a rippled, infinity-edge wafer that makes distance assessment difficult. The entire left side of the fairway drops off steeply to jungled growth from which there is no recovery. The fifth is another downhill par four that bends to the left along the bluffs, only here the overall distance is shorter and the angle of the dogleg is sharper.

Dye Fore's incoming nine, which initially reverses direction and heads north toward a range of sawtooth peaks in the far distance, is jaw-dropping. The 12th is the first of two world-class par threes, a king-sized one-shotter that calls for a bold stroke over a deep, angled ravine, its amber rock face dotted with agave plants. Far below to the right of the green are the lush banks and flood plain of the Chavon, the very place where the helicopter scenes in the film *Apocalypse Now* were shot. The 15th is comparable in terms of terror, only here the hole heads south into the prevailing tradewinds, with the lazy coils of the brown river far below on the left.

As a grand-scale test, Dye Fore has few rivals in the tropics or anywhere else for that matter. It offers ample room to drive the ball, but there are serious consequences for wayward approach shots. Dye's artful chicanery is in evidence, too. In the words of Gilles Gagnon, the resort's long-time director of golf, "Pete has the ability to make the easy holes look hard, and vice-versa."

Dye's epic new course will, in time, be joined by another venue that he and his wife, Alice, are conjuring on bluffs near the current 18. By the end of the decade, Dye Fore will be split in half to accommodate the new loops. Until then, the current layout, stretched regally along the river bluffs, has enough drama and spectacle to entertain all comers. Coupled with Teeth of the Dog, Dye Fore is the perfect bookend to Dye's now-legendary design career.

Visiting players looking for something a little less taxing also have access to **The Links,** an upcountry design by Dye that climbs into rolling hills above the resort's polo fields, its fairways lined by tall guinea grass and thick stands of trees. Small greens and numerous lagoons keep players honest. Women can have a ball on this well-groomed course from the red tees at 4,437 yards (par 71). These markers were placed with care by Pete's wife Alice, a fine amateur player.

Casa de Campo, Dye Fore, 18th hole

Entrance to Casa de Campo

LODGING

Befitting a property of this size, **Casa de Campo** has a wide variety of accommodations. The resort offers 300 updated hotel rooms and suites; two- to four-bedroom villa homes; as well as deluxe EXCEL Club villas. These beautifully appointed, multi-bedroom villas, staffed with a maid and butler, feature a private garden and a pool or whirlpool, made-to-order breakfast each morning, and many other extras, including a shiny red golf cart to get around the property. All-inclusive golf packages are available in each category of accommodation.

In 2004, Casa de Campo's villa inventory expanded to include Exclusive Villas, which enter the ultra-luxe category. These individually priced, fully staffed private homes are beautifully appointed and command prime locations—several are located oceanside. Expecting a crowd? One of the homes in the Exclusive Villas programs has eight bedrooms and sleeps 20.

DINING

With its numerous restaurants, bars, and lounges, **Casa de Campo** has something for everyone, although at present there is no temple serving haute cuisine for foodies. Among the long-time favorites is Lago Grill, an open-air, thatched-roof restaurant overlooking Teeth of the Dog and the sea. It offers a fresh juice bar and made-to-order omelettes in the morning. El Pescador, located at one end of Casa's private Minitas Beach, is a breezy al fresco café serving good salads and grilled seafood for lunch. For superb Italian fare, La Piazetta, at Altos de Chavon, features a large antipasto bar and excellent pasta dishes. In addition, the restaurant's humidor holds a wide assortment of fine cigars. Besides a new 19th Hole Bar at Dye Fore, the resort has debuted a new Pot Bunker Sports Bar in the main complex.

OFF-COURSE ATTRACTIONS

In addition to Pete Dye's three courses, the resort is a mecca for outdoor sports enthusiasts. There's a tennis center with 13 Har-Tru tennis courts, 10 lighted for night play; an extensive shooting facility with over 200 sporting clay stations and a 150-foot tower with multiple launch levels; a large equestrian center (guided trail rides, English or Western saddle); world-class polo from November through May; all manner of water sports; fishing (river and ocean); the list goes on. There are also supervised programs for children (4 to 12) as well as teenagers at this family-friendly property. A $30 million marina and yacht club with waterside cafes and trendy shopping outlets, opened in 2002 near the mouth of the Chavon River, resembles a piazza in the Italian Riviera. Visitors are often treated to impromptu *merengue* lessons at night.

VILLAGE IN THE SKY

Altos de Chavon, a replica of a 16th-century Mediterranean village that crowns a bluff high above the Chavon River, is a one-of-a-kind stage set and architectural marvel. Under the direction of Italian cinematographer Roberto Copa, the rustic village, distressed to look centuries old, was hand-built of stone, wood, and iron by local artisans in the mid-1970s. Rough cobblestone streets (wear comfortable shoes), shady pathways, cool fountains, a tiny church, and the Regional Museum of Archaeology are found here, as are balustrades cantilevered over the cliffs that offer dizzying views of the river, sea, and mountains. In addition to craft shops, art galleries, and boutiques, there's also a 5,000-seat open-air ampitheater where concerts are held. (Native son Enrique Iglesias, Julio's son, is a frequent performer.)

RARE GEMS

Amber, a fossilized resin that oozed from prehistoric pine trees and trickled down mountain slopes some 50 million years ago, is found only in the Dominican Republic, Russia, and Germany. Among other outlets, amber jewelry is available at L'Atelier in Altos de Chavon. Many of the amber pieces, ranging in size from teardrop to egg-sized, collected flora as well as small creatures and insects before they hardened. These flotsam are preserved within the semi-transluscent tree sap. "Stories in stone," the locals call them.

Also available at L'Atelier is larimar, a stone that is unique to the Dominican Republic. Noted for its hardness, larimar derives its distinctive pale blue color from the unusual presence of copper in the stone. Resembling turquoise, it is made into rings, bracelets, and necklaces.

DAY TRIP

Cigar lovers can travel five minutes from Casa de Campo to La Romana's Industrial Free Zone, where tours can be arranged to Tabacalera de Garcia, Ltd., the world's largest premium cigar factory. Here the lengthy, elaborate, and delicate process of creating a hand-rolled cigar is detailed, from the fermentation of the tobacco leaf to the actual rolling of the cigar. The factory produces more than 30 million cigars per year for the likes of Montecristo, H. Upmann, Dunhill, and others. A must for cigar aficionados.

TURFGRASS OF THE FUTURE

Around the time Pete Dye was planning his third course at Casa de Campo, now known as **Dye Fore,** he was told that his use of fresh water would be monitored by the water company. He was also informed that a dammed lake, located near the site of the new course, would be available to him. The hitch: the damn lake was filled with sea water! Necessity being the mother of invention, Dye went in search of a grass that tolerates salt water. He found a research professor at the University of Georgia, Dr. Ronny Duncan, who had been studying a grass called paspalum since 1993 under a grant from the USGA.

Paspalum, which requires a fraction of the amount of pesticides, insecticides, and fertilizer required by normal grasses, not only tolerates sea water but thrives on it with proper salt management. (It also can be irrigated with brackish or recycled water.) Stiff-leafed and waxy, a golf ball perches nicely on it. Divots fill in quickly. The grass responds well to lower mowing heights, and the speed of ball roll is comparable to that of hybrid Bermudas.

A drought-tolerant, disease-resistant hybrid, paspalum has application anywhere that calls for a durable grass (roadsides, sports fields, business landscape areas, etc.). The Sea Isle One and Sea Isle 2000 strains, each a genetically pure cultivar, were released in 1999. Each has already changed the face of golf not only in the Caribbean, but at courses worldwide where fresh water is in short supply.

Guavaberry Golf & Country Club, 15th hole

Among the new golf facilities cropping up east of Santo Domingo, the nation's colonial capital, is **Guavaberry Golf & Country Club,** a dramatic 7,156-yard, Gary Player–designed course opened in 2002 in Juan Dolio. Contrasting several large waste bunkers built around the coral rock formations, Player and lead designer Warren Henderson created a lush garden-like setting that makes artful use of the indigenous vegetation. For example, more than 700 rare corozo palms, which grow only on the island's coastal plains and are remarkable for the rows of needle-like spines that protrude from their trunks, were transplanted alongside the fairways. Giant saman and oreja trees, their thick branches spread wide, frame several greens. The mascot species, guavaberry, which produces a spicy, bittersweet liqueur prized by Dominicans as an aphrodisiac, is also present.

The signature hole is the 13th, a self-contained par three carved into an old limestone quarry. Dividing the two greens—yes, there are alternate targets—is a 15-foot-high waterfall that cascades over a yellowed rock wall into a pond in the bottom of the quarry. The left green is closer but more perilous; the right green is farther away but larger. Pin placement and the prevailing wind dictate strategy.

Guavaberry's 18th hole is a tremendous par four that ranks among the most challenging finishing holes in the islands from the tips at 466 yards. Visible from the tee is a large field of exposed rock to the right of the rising fairway, the remnant of a coral shelf pushed off the ocean floor some 200,000 years ago. Workers cleared the rock of vegetation and carefully removed debris to heighten the visual drama of this unyielding hazard.

In addition to a superb practice facility that includes three warm-up holes, Guavaberry is anchored by a cupola-topped, Spanish Mission–themed clubhouse.

Guavaberry is affiliated with the nearby **Costa Caribe Coral by Hilton,** an upbeat, all-inclusive, 534-room resort hotel and casino set along Juan Dolio Beach. Snorkeling, tennis, a full-service spa, a disco, five bars, and three restaurants are available, including a seaside beach barbecue at lunch. The resort is 20 minutes from Las Americas International Airport and 45 minutes from Santo Domingo.

A mile from Guavaberry is a sister property, **Los Marlins Golf Resort,** which features a sporty Charles Ankrom–designed course opened in 1995. The 6,398-yard layout, which has a nice blend of water, sand, and mounds, is well watered and nicely groomed. Not a championship track by any means, but a fun test of golf. The course, located within Metro Country Club, is attached to an **Embassy Suites Hotel** that debuted in 2003, its spacious two-room suites offering private balconies as well as golf course or garden views. Children under 18 years of age stay free at the hotel (a Hilton affiliate) when accompanied by an adult in the suite. Preferred tee times at Guavaberry are available to guests at Embassy Suites.

DAY TRIP/SANTO DOMINGO

Santo Domingo, the first city built by Europeans in the New World (1496), has much evidence of Spanish civilization in the 12-block Zona Colonial on the east bank of the Rio Ozama. Among the significant architectural sights in this UNESCO World Heritage Site is Alcazar de Colon, a Renaissance-style limestone castle built in 1517 that was used as a residence by Christopher Columbus's son, Diego Colon. Now a museum, its 22 rooms are furnished in period style. Casa del Cordon, dating to 1503 and the hemisphere's oldest surviving stone house, is where the city's women reputedly lined up to hand over their jewelry to Sir Francis Drake, the notorious English corsair who was later paid a ransom to dissuade him from destroying the city. Also found along the cobbled streets of the Zona Colonial are churches, cathedrals, and monasteries dating to the early 16th century. After touring the historic sites, cool your heels in one of the many tree-shaded cafes bordering Parque Colon, its centerpiece a huge statue of Christopher Columbus, who set foot on the island in 1492 (according to legend, he's buried in the capital).

P.B. Dye, the younger son of the famed designer, fashioned a seaside course of his own on the easternmost tip of the Dominican Republic in 2000 at 43, the same age his father was when he built Teeth of the Dog at Casa de Campo.

Seeking to make the most of a marvelous site at the 15,000-acre **Punta Cana Resort and Club,** P.B. also sought to redeem himself from previous design efforts, many of them over-the-top creations that were judged to be visually stunning but virtually unplayable. P.B., who's fluent in Spanish and has been visiting the island since he was a child, was determined to climb out of the proverbial sandbox and put his talent to good use at his home away from home. Which for him meant less is more.

The 7,152-yard **La Cana** course sits opposite a long sandy beach dotted with tall coconut palms fronting the Mona Passage, the body of water that separates the Dominican Republic from Puerto Rico. This is the dry side of the island, but there's a cooling sea breeze at most times of year. Dye was presented with

Punta Cana Resort and Club, La Cana course, seventh hole

Jack Nicklaus on site at Cap Cana

a valuable parcel that gave him room enough to route four holes directly along the sea, with the other 14 offering glimpses of the ocean. There was one problem, however: The entire site was a shelf of coral rock.

"Basically, we had to manufacture everything, including the soil," says P.B. of a process similar to his dad's regimen at Casa de Campo in the late 1960s. After two million cubic meters of caliche (limestone pulverized for road-bed gravel) was spread across the dead-flat site to create contour and movement, Dye capped the rock with sand and carpeted the fairways with paspalum.

Dye goes for the jugular at the quirky seventh hole, a short par four that bends sharply to the left and leads to a tiny atoll-like green awash in sand and fronted by a hellish netherworld of deep swales, gnarly mounds, and 21 pot bunkers. Dye calls this area "hecklebirnie," or golfer's purgatory, according to Scottish legend. A few too many whacks here, and you'll be bleating for mercy, especially if your ball keeps skipping across the domed "hood-of-a-car" green into sand.

The back nine comes on strong and finishes in style. The grand par-five 18th, a gentle dogleg to the left, is clearly patterned after the famous 18th at Pebble Beach, only here the shoreline is sandier, the water bluer, and the journey from tee to green longer and more perilous. P.B. may lack his father's creative flair and uncanny knack of permeating each hole with strategic nuance, but Punta Cana offers a solid test.

Punta Cana's thatched-roof clubhouse, decorated by famed Dominican couturier Oscar de la Renta, overlooks the 18th green and the sea. Beautifully appointed with marble floors, it is the resort's most attractive structure.

Punta Cana's second course, **Corales,** designed by Tom Fazio, will open in late 2006, skirting the resort's north shore within an enclave of luxurious vacation homes. These beachfront residences belong to the likes of de la Renta, Julio Iglesias, and Mikhail Baryshnikov.

Spread across 39,000 acres a mere six miles from Punta Cana's airport is **Cap Cana,** an ambitious oceanfront development with three Jack Nicklaus courses planned. The first layout, **Punta Espada** ("Tip of the Sword"), which Nicklaus assessed as one of the top 10 sites he had ever seen for a golf course, is a majestic spread slated to open in mid-2006 that lays out along the serrated coast. Eight holes are carved into a flat coral shelf washed by the pale blue sea; the remainder are tucked below a curving limestone bluff. Nearly every hole has a view of the ocean. The effect is of a desert course by the sea, with the brittle caliche taking the place of decomposed granite.

This stunning tropical links, unabashedly Jack's answer to Pete Dye's Teeth of the Dog course at Casa de Campo, is Nicklaus's first full-fledged design in the Caribbean. From start to finish, the 7,382-yard course is a firm but fair test that will accommodate bogey shooters from the forward tees but will send big hitters who spray the ball directly to the snorkeling center.

The layout gets off to a rousing start at the first hole, a mid-length par four that plays downhill from the limestone bluff to an angled fairway guarded to the left by a long waste bunker. Hooked drives should be abandoned unless you like reptiles: A six-foot iguana is known to inhabit a cave near the sandy wasteland.

Punta Espada's back nine, marked by five seaside holes, is *muy grande.* The layout's signature hole was

LODGING

Punta Cana Resort offers a variety of guest rooms distributed in oceanfront and tree-shaded villas. Top accommodations are found at Tortuga Bay, a deluxe beachfront villa complex created by Oscar de la Renta and opened in late 2005. All-inclusive golf packages are available.

In addition to three miles of white sandy beach, resort amenities include a full-service marina, tennis, horseback riding, a nature preserve, fishing, snorkeling, sailing, windsurfing, and scuba diving. In 2002, the Punta Cana Dive Center joined with the Dominican Navy to sink *Patricia,* a 200-foot cargo ship, near an offshore reef. The sunken ship has created a new habitat for marine life and protects the beach from sea surges.

Punta Cana offers unparalleled access. Contained within the resort is the world's first and only privately-owned international airport, its handsome open-air terminal a hub for nonstop and direct flights from major gateways in the U.S. and Europe.

Playa Grande Golf Course, fourth hole

nature-made and required few earthworks. This is the 13th, a brawny 249-yard par three that plays downwind over a boiling cove on the far side of the water. It is poised to take its place among the most thrilling one-shotters in the world. The green here, because of the demands of the shot, is sizable, but overall Nicklaus's targets have begun to shrink. At Punta Espada, the average green is under 5,000 square feet and subtly undulating.

Las Iguanas, Cap Cana's second Nicklaus course, will break ground in late 2006 and will feature five oceanside holes, while the third venue will skirt the base of a 200-foot curtain bluff and bring cavernous sinkholes into play. There is also room at the far-flung complex for two or three additional courses to be laid out by other designers.

Golf is just one piece of the puzzle at this landmark Dominican development, which at 47 square miles is comparable in size to Walt Disney World in Orlando. In addition to 5.3 miles of oceanfront and dazzling beaches along Lujillo Bay, Cap Cana will boast one of the largest man-made marinas in the Caribbean

(over 1,000 slips), upscale hotels, permanent and part-time residences, health spas, tennis facilities, a polo and equestrian club, luxury shops, trendy bars, a European-style casino, a 5,000-seat open-air ampitheater—the whole enchilada. The project's final build-out will be completed by 2015.

One of Cap Cana's first hotels will be the **Golden Bear Lodge,** which marks Nicklaus's first foray into the hospitality business. (Having conquered the world of golf as a player and designer, the hospitality industry may be Jack's final frontier.) Jack's wife, Barbara, will decorate the Spanish colonial–style lodge. Each two- and three-bedroom unit will have its own private swimming pool and veranda. The Lodge is scheduled to open in 2007.

ONE TO WATCH

Located on the island's east coast 20 miles from Punta Cana International Airport, **Westin Roco Ki Beach & Golf Resort** is yet another promising new development in the Dominican Republic. The 315-room resort, slated to open in late 2006, aims to honor the island's ancient Taina culture. (Major chains are getting better at this sort of thing as they steer clear of generic getaways.) The resort's Nick Faldo–designed course skirts a palm-lined beach and plays through dunes, meadows, and a forest of mangroves before reaching a dramatic finale at holes 17 and 18, which are etched across a massive bluff high above the sea.

There are very few secrets in the world of golf anymore, very few places where the path to a special course has not been beaten. Yet a truly great course remains relatively undiscovered on the north coast of the Dominican Republic an hour's drive east of Puerto Plata, a major tourist center. This is **Playa Grande Golf Course,** reputedly the last project Robert Trent Jones actively worked on. Completed in 1997 after a protracted series of fits and starts, this 7,046-yard stunner has 11 holes perched on bluffs and headlands 100 feet or more above the turquoise-blue sea, qualifying it as the "Pebble Beach of the Caribbean."

The majestic layout, named for a mile-long stretch of sandy beach set far below the clifftop 13th hole, bears all of Jones's trademarks: runway tees, wide fairways, cloverleaf bunkers, and giant rolling greens, most of them left open in front to accept bump-and-run approach shots, a good option given the ever-present wind. From the tips, better players can choose to bite off as much of the gaping ocean coves as they dare, notably on holes 3, 4, 7, 12, 14, and 18. The forward tees offer much less perilous routes. Unlike many championship-class courses, Playa Grande was not designed solely for professionals and low handicappers. Targets are wide. Bail-out areas are generous.

There are many, many first-rate holes at Playa Grande, which like Pebble Beach has an elongated figure-eight routing, although the holes here change direction more frequently. The 17th, a 220-yard par three, occupies its own promontory and calls for a solid shot into a stiff onshore breeze. The target, a two-tiered, 40-yard-deep green, is projected on an arm of rock high above the ironshore and thrashing sea. It is a place of unsurpassed beauty. The 18th is a memorable finale, a sharply angled, do-or-die par five

bent around a wave-tossed cove that ranks among the most heroic holes Jones ever built. These two holes account for one of the most exhilarating finishes in the sport.

Wedged between a jungled mountain ridge and the sea, this reclusive beauty offers something more than a worthy test in an intoxicating tropical setting. Playa Grande is, to quote the caddies, "*mas bonito lugare*"—the most beautiful place. It has a wild grandeur all its own, the lush hills flattening into a plain that ends abruptly at the sea-blackened cliffs. In an age of manufactured venues, there is very little evidence of earthmoving or artifice.

Playa Grande is my favorite Trent Jones course in the world. I rank it ahead of Spyglass Hill, Mauna Kea, and Valderrama. The golf course, which generally plays firm and fast, is currently in the hands of the central bank, which is seeking a buyer to take over the existing course and perhaps build a second venue.

MEGA-RESORT ON THE HORIZON

Shortly after a Canadian firm announced in 2004 that it will build the world's largest resort off the coast of Grand Bahama (see above), a French resort mogul unveiled plans for **Atlantica,** a multi-billion-dollar development on the Dominican Republic's northwest coast to be modeled after St. Tropez, the jewel of the French Riviera.

Described as a multi-use, residential/resort community that will become the Caribbean's "leading yachting destination and a golf capital," Atlantica would add 25,000 beds to the nation's hotel room inventory. The development, to be built on 12 natural islands and peninsulas in Luperon Bay, calls for seven villages with some 3,000 homes and 20 hotels, including luxury boutique properties as well as high-end international brands. In addition, two golf courses are planned, with room for a third. The Arnold Palmer–designed **Ocean Course** is laid out on cliffs high above the Atlantic. The **Canyon Course,** by Jim Fazio, will have four holes stretched along the coast with the remainder set within the lush, tropical canyons of Luperon's Colina. The first course is slated to open in late 2006.

Jamaica

It is said that Jamaica, birthplace of reggae, has a little bit of everything to be found in the Caribbean. Its beauty is seductive: tall mountain ridges sweeping down to lush valleys, rivers, waterfalls, long sandy beaches. Here's the place to sample local cuisine like jerk chicken and pepperpot soup in roadside cafés, to tune your ear to the lilting patois, to learn that Bob Marley's songs are national anthems.

Most of the island's golf courses are found east and west of Montego Bay on the island's north coast, the main resort area. Happily, a new coast road has made traveling in and around "Mo-Bay," as it is known, much easier. The profile of Jamaica's time-honored resorts, including Tryall and Half Moon Bay, were raised significantly in 2000 with the opening of a new Ritz-Carlton, the first major chain affiliate built in the region since 1974, and its stellar new golf course, the White Witch.

Somewhat surprisingly, the Ritz-Carlton Hotel Company, long synonymous with luxury lodging and first-class service, had been slow to dip its toe into the golf pool, an even bigger surprise given the financial and sporting profile of its typical guest. The debut of the **Ritz-Carlton Golf & Spa Resort, Rose Hall,** a lavish 428-room property located 15 minutes east of the international airport in Montego Bay, brought a new level of luxury to Jamaica. The AAA Five Diamond property, set on 4,000 acres, also signaled a tremendous vote of confidence by Ritz-Carlton in Jamaica's ability to revalidate its stature as one of the most appealing islands in the Caribbean, an appeal that had slipped in the 1990s.

It was the dream of John W. Rollins, a self-made billionaire and philanthropist from Delaware, to transform a portion of the historic Rose Hall Plantation and adjoining lands, which he bought in 1960,

Ritz-Carlton Golf & Spa Resort, White Witch course, 17th hole

into a self-contained resort community that would attract sophisticated travelers and fertilize the local economy. Robert von Hagge, who had a longstanding handshake agreement with Rollins to design the project's golf course, rolled up his sleeves when the time finally came to build. "I have seen golf course property like this in an accessible and fine market location only three or four times in my life," says von Hagge, who has designed more than 250 courses. "The mountainous terrain offered opportunities for amazing diversity."

Von Hagge and design partner Rick Baril had all they could handle on the exceedingly rugged site. Located five minutes by complimentary shuttle from the hotel, the **White Witch** course is named for Annie Palmer, a plantation mistress who is reputed to have murdered three husbands and many slave lovers in the early 1800s. She herself was killed in 1831. Locals say her ghost still roams the Rose Hall Great House at night. (Daytime tours are available.) The layout itself is an engineering marvel blasted from granite and marl, the holes bellied into valleys or etched across the tops of ridges and spurs nearly 1,000 feet above sea level.

"Designing [resort] golf courses is show biz," von Hagge says. "We're in the business of entertainment, creating places of fun and enjoyment." Visually striking, 16 of the 18 holes on this 6,719-yard, par-71 layout serve up panoramic views of the Caribbean Sea. An upcountry tropical gambol and theatrical tour de force rolled into one, the target-style White Witch emphasizes tactics, course management—and the need to play a second round in order to divine a few of its secrets. Several of the holes are quirky, one-of-a-kind creations that are faithful to the terrain despite their conspicuous landforms, i.e., high-peaked mounds beside the fairways. These holes might not pass muster in the states. But here, bounded by fruit-bearing trees and jungle-covered mountains, the sea flooding the horizon and tradewinds sweeping the fairways, the White Witch beguiles, especially in the company of cheerful "golf concierges" (half of them women) who impart local knowledge, cite yardage, read putts, clean clubs, and generally make the round enjoyable.

The first tee, set below the clubhouse veranda and aimed to the sea, sets the stage for the game. Tee shots on this spectacular par five drop nearly 200 feet into the saddle of a deep-cut valley staked out by large inkblot bunkers. A drive can hang in the air 10 seconds or more before falling to earth. On the way home, the par-three 17th, its tilted, kidney-shaped green set against the sky and ringed by five bunkers, is perhaps the best one-shotter in Jamaica.

There is ample playability from the middle and forward tees on the Witch, as landing areas are generous and green entries are mostly open, but the layout's wickedly contoured putting surfaces are the great equalizer. Still, with green-throated parrots and other exotic birds flitting from tree to tree and the sea air heavy with the scent of flowers, the White Witch is not the kind of track where players groan about missed opportunities. It is, quite simply, a one-of-a-kind wonder that has helped to re-establish Jamaica as a premier golf destination.

The open-air veranda of the clubhouse, with its top-of-the-world ocean views, is a great place to relax after the round. There's also a Nike Golf School and first-rate practice range at the facility.

LODGING & DINING

The **Ritz-Carlton Rose Hall** aims to please. More than 23,000 Jamaicans were interviewed for 850 jobs at the hotel. Staff members, hospitality experts all, are quick with a smile. The physical plant—white stucco buildings with peach-colored roofs—stands in stark contrast to the typical urban Ritz-Carlton. Sweeping lawns, lovely gardens, and swaying palms set back from the sea create a sense of languor. Moreover, the hotel's interior design pays homage to Jamaica's historic plantation homes, the traditional British Colonial décor offset by the bold, vibrant colors of the Caribbean.

Among the five restaurants at the resort is Jasmines, which features "Jamasian" cuisine, an imaginative blend of local foodstuffs and Oriental spices. To give guests a true taste of Jamaica, the hotel in 2002 opened the Reggae Jerk Center, where island chefs prepare authentic jerk-spiced chicken and pork dishes. These dishes are served informally on West Beach to the accompaniment of live reggae music.

SPA & OFF-COURSE ATTRACTIONS

Fresh allspice. Wild yam. Sweet star apple. These are some of the ingredients used in the resort's spa treatments. The sugarcane body scrub, an exfoliating therapy, is one of the more popular treatments, while the peppermint-scented steam room is a great place to relax after the round.

The adventurous can sign up for a half-hour rafting trip on the Martha Brae River 30 minutes from the resort. After dark, the younger set can check out the nightclubs along the oceanfront "Hip-Strip" in Montego Bay.

If there's one drawback to the resort, it's the beach, which is man-made and small. A larger beach more typical of the island is available at the Rose Hall Beach Club 10 minutes east of the property.

Seagrape Terrace at Half Moon Resort

Next door to the Ritz-Carlton is **Rose Hall Resort & Country Club,** a former Wyndham property now under the LXR Luxury Resorts flag. Prior to the ownership change, von Hagge and Baril were tapped to completely revamp its dramatic but quirky golf course. Reopened in 2001 after a $4.3-million overhaul, with several new holes superimposed on the old site, the course is called **Cinnamon Hill,** after the late Johnny Cash's vacation home located off the 14th hole. A shotmaker's track stretching to 6,637 yards (par 71), Cinnamon Hill has an excellent blend of seaside and interior holes.

The opening stretch takes players past the Rose Hall Plantation house and the walled graveyard of Elizabeth Barrett Browning's family, but then the course plays nip and tuck with the sea at Nos. 7 and 8 before rambling alongside the foundations of an old sugar mill and aqueduct. The back nine climbs into the verdant foothills of the mountains, the holes sketched across heaving land framed by huge spreading trees, with a few forced carries over vegetation-choked chasms. The signature hole is the par-four 15th, which hops a ravine and drops 75 feet to a waterfall-backed green made famous in the James Bond movie, *Live and Let Die*. The par-five 18th, a brilliant risk-reward hole that dares players to carry a chasm with their second shots, is set below plantation ruins. Cinnamon Hill will always be overshadowed by the White Witch, but it is an excellent test with more change of pace than any other course in Jamaica.

After the round, players can cool off in the 488-room resort's Sugar Mills Falls, a $7-million water complex. The water park features a 280-foot-long, 30-foot elevation thrill slide; three terraced pools; a "lazy river" for tubing, rafting, and swimming; and a swim-up bar extending into the main pool.

In the wake of a major refurbishment completed in 2005, members of the British royal family and many other long-time guests might be hard-pressed to recognize the vintage Robert Trent Jones course at **Half Moon Resort,** a venerable retreat on the outskirts of Montego Bay. The widening of the coastal road that divides the property necessitated the shifting of corridors at several holes, but the course overall was long overdue for a trimming of its dreadlocks. And while long-time Trent Jones protégé Roger Rulewich believes "the course is like a beautiful lady who only needed a touch of makeup to recapture her youth," he actually treated the 1961 design to a much-needed facelift.

After ripping out invasive casuarina pines to better highlight the layout's stately palms, Rule-wich widened fairways, reshaped and repositioned bunkers, divided the long runway-style tees into separate pods, expanded and resurfaced the greens, and installed a new drainage system. As before, the first four holes play downwind, but the middle section of the round plays into the teeth of a stiff Caribbean breeze. A sea-level layout designed for walkers, the course, Jamaica's longest, remains a test for the best from the tips at 7,199 yards. Caddies are available; their local knowledge adds immeasureably to the enjoyment of the game.

In addition to the remedial work, Rulewich also refashioned the resort's practice facility (it's home to a David Leadbetter Golf Academy) and built an 18-hole putting course on the hotel grounds. It's the perfect place to hone your stroke following afternoon tea. The colonial-style pastel clubhouse is one of the prettiest in the islands, while the resort's well-appointed cottages are spaced along a beautiful crescent-moon beach.

A major rehabilitation prior to the Johnnie Walker World Championship in the 1980s transformed the hilly layout at **The Tryall Club** from a good course to a great one, and a second round of renovations completed in late 2003, notably a new irrigation system, have improved the course even more. The links, located 15 miles west of Montego Bay, starts off along the half-mile-long beachfront before climbing into lush mountain foothills, the fairways and greens framed by coconut groves and an abundance of fruit trees. A highlight is the massive, slow-turning water wheel in view at the seventh tee. It was used to crush sugarcane on the 2,200-acre estate in the 1700s. From the blue tees, the ball must be driven unflinchingly through the arch of the waterwheel's stone viaduct to find the sloping fairway. Players must negotiate forced carries over creek beds and gullies on the rugged upcountry holes, a daunting task from the tips at 6,772 yards, but the white tees at 6,221 yards offer a fun, satisfying experience, even when the tradewinds blow. Tryall's caddies, by the way, will always hand you the right club and will always have the same reply if you question their selection: "Hit the ball, mon."

A word about the best time of day to play at Tryall. Unlike most tropical environments, mornings are muggy on Jamaica's north coast. Afternoon, however, brings drier air and cooler breezes. Morning is the time to linger over a breakfast of sliced tropical fruits, coconut pancakes served with Jamaican rum syrup, and a bottomless cup of Blue Mountain coffee, and later take a dip in the spring-fed pool or snorkel among the coral reefs offshore.

Puerto Rico

Puerto Rico has been attracting vacationing golfers for decades to a storied line-up of courses, notably the designs of Robert Trent Jones at Dorado Beach. But this Latin-flavored corner of the Caribbean, praised for its beauty by Columbus in 1493 and today a U.S. Commonwealth, now has updated many of its mainstays as well as adding several exciting new projects. The list of off-course attractions here is long and diverse. Puerto Rico boasts the only rain forest (El Yunque) in the National Park System. There's also the bustling, salsa-flavored capital of San Juan, with its giant casinos and glitzy hotels, and its counterpart, Old San Juan, where pirates once scrambled across the mossy ramparts of El Morro, an imposing fortress high above the Atlantic. The island's golf courses are somewhat less impregnable. Except when the tradewinds blow.

Carved from a 1,000-acre coconut and grapefruit plantation an hour's drive west of San Juan, **Dorado Beach** showcases two exceptional layouts by Robert Trent Jones, both of which feature sloping pedestal greens and lots of sand and water. In 2005, major renovations were completed by the Raymond Floyd Group on the venerable **East Course,** Dorado's flagship track, a jungle-encased masterpiece famous for its heroic par-five fourth hole (formerly the 13th), a Z-shaped double dogleg bent around a pair of ponds that plays to a seaside green. The par-four 18th, which sweeps to the left, plays to a green set below the oceanside clubhouse. (The nines were switched so that the round would conclude here). Always swept by sea breezes, the East's 18th is a grand finale on the consensus number-one course in Puerto Rico, a course good enough to host 10 Champions Tour events and two World Cups.

Floyd also reworked the **West Course,** a slightly shorter layout with several holes bent in hairpin turns around a lagoon. As on the East, all tees on the West were stripped and leveled, all greens were regraded, and all fairway and greenside bunkers were redone. The course, which boasts a brilliant quartet of par threes, reopened in 2003. It lacks the seaside charge of the East but is a fine test in its own right.

In the spring of 2006, Dorado Beach Hotel Corporation, owners of the property, terminated its management agreement with Hyatt Hotels, which had operated the landmark resort for 48 years. At press time, the hotel founded by Laurance Rockefeller in the late 1950s was scheduled to be closed. The golf courses, however, were expected to remain open.

Dorado's sister property, formerly the Hyatt Regency Cerromar Beach Resort, is now a timeshare operation known as Hyatt Hacienda del Mar. Its golf component, the **Plantation Club,** offers its own pair of vintage (1970) Robert Trent Jones layouts. Routed on drier, more open land, they were always a rung or two below the original Dorado Beach designs. But in the wake of a creative teardown, these virtually new courses are well worth a visit.

Beach club at Palmas del Mar

Above: Palmas del Mar, Flamboyan Course, 13th hole
Opposite: Westin Rio Mar Beach Resort & Golf Club, River Course, seventh hole

Ray Floyd and his design staff built six new holes and completely redid three others on the back nine of the former South Course, now called the **Sugarcane Course.** Lakes, rivers, and waterfalls accent these much improved holes, while the front nine retains most of the pre-existing holes but also features a new par three. From the back tees at 7,119 yards, the revamped layout is a strong, stern test of golf marked by deep bunkers and sharply contoured greens.

Cerromar's former North Course, renamed the **Pineapple Course,** also has been completely redone, its revised routing accommodating both new and reconfigured holes. By design, the Pineapple Course is more of a sporty, resort-style layout, with softer bunkering and somewhat flatter greens than the Sugarcane Course, though the finishing holes have plenty of muscle from the tips, which stretch to 7,030 yards. One hole retained from the original layout is the par-three 12th (formerly the seventh), which plays from a new elevated tee to a large green backdropped by the sea. It is one of the prettiest par threes in Puerto Rico.

The Plantation Club's revised courses are anchored by an impressive 50,000-square-foot clubhouse, its sweeping balconies wrapped around the first and second floors.

Fronting three-and-a-half miles of sandy beach, the refurbished **Palmas del Mar Country Club** on Puerto Rico's southeast coast, located 45 minutes from San Juan, offers two of the more interesting courses on the island. The **Flamboyan Course,** a solid 7,117-yard layout by Rees Jones opened in 1998, is a multi-theme design woven through wetlands,

meadows, and coconut palms, with several holes bordering the Caribbean Sea. Having updated several of A.W. Tillinghast's classic courses, Jones took a page from the old master's book, building what he called "Tillinghast ramps, or grassy avenues, in front of the greens so golfers can bounce it in or fly it in," depending on wind velocity and direction. The layout's signature hole is the 12th, a sturdy par three that calls for a solid shot into the prevailing wind, with the shimmering sea and the island of Vieques backdropping the elevated green. Jones also reworked the resort's 6,675-yard, par-71 **Palm Course,** originally designed by Gary Player, creating three new holes and revamping several others.

In addition to the two layouts, which are served by a 20,000-square-foot clubhouse, Palmas de Mar, a 2,700-acre resort and residential community, offers several restaurants, swimming pools, an equestrian center, a beach club, 200-slip deep-water marina, nature preserves, and one of the largest tennis facilities in the Caribbean. Accommodations are available in one-, two-, and three-bedroom rental villas with sea or garden views.

The **Westin Rio Mar Beach Resort & Golf Club,** opened in 1997, is a 600-room extravaganza on the island's northeast coast. If location is everything, this sprawling resort occupies one of the best: Encircling the property are El Yunque Rain Forest, the Atlantic, and the Mameyes River, which divides the resort beach from Luquillo Beach, a beautiful strand shaded by tall palms. The seven-story Caribbean manor house–style hotel, with its pitched terra-cotta tile roofs and three-story atrium overlooking a grotto pool and gardens, has sweeping ocean vistas from its public areas and dining spots. Spacious guest rooms have private terraces or balconies angled to the mountains or the sea. In addition to 12 dining and entertainment venues at the resort, there's a full-service casino, beachfront pools, international boutiques, large tennis complex, fitness center and spa, and an extensive array of water sports. The resort is heavily patronized by corporate groups, but the conference center and group check-in area is separate from the resort's public areas.

Rio Mar's pair of golf courses hail from different eras. The **Ocean Course,** a solid 6,782-yard layout opened in 1975 as a private club, was designed by George and Tom Fazio. The course is known for its par-three fourth hole, where hundreds of iguanas, some up to five feet in length, loiter around the pond that fronts the green. However, the best par three is the breezy, 238-yard 16th, which skirts the sea from start to finish.

Westin Rio Mar, Ocean Course, 16th hole

The **River Course,** debuted in 1997 and one of Greg Norman's first design efforts, is a 6,931-yard test with seven holes routed alongside the Mameyes River. Fairways are hemmed in by marshes and wetlands throughout, but forced carries from the forward tees are rare. Not only are the ocean and mountain backdrops outstanding, the region's lush, exotic vegetation has been carefully preserved. The course hosted the 2004 World Amateur Team Championship.

Also situated in Rio Grande near the Westin property is **Coco Beach Golf & Country Club,** a 36-hole complex designed by Tom Kite and Bruce Besse. Set on a lovely stretch of coastal property with inland views of El Yunque rain forest, Coco Beach has four distinct nines—Lakes, Ocean, Palms, Mountain—that offer six different 18-hole configurations. The golf complex, opened in 2005, is anchored by **Paradisus Puerto Rico,** a luxury all-inclusive property (the island's first).

ONE TO WATCH
Located a short distance from Rio Mar, **Bahia Beach Plantation** is a beautiful public course, carved out of a beachfront coconut grove, featuring a scenic three-hole stretch along the sea on the back nine. At press time, Bahia Beach was slated for a major makeover by Robert Trent Jones, Jr. In addition to upscale real estate offerings, the property was planning to build a 142-room St. Regis resort hotel on site.

A newcomer worth noting is located on the south coast of the island a few miles from the historic downtown area of Ponce, Puerto Rico's second-largest city. This is the **Hilton Ponce Golf & Casino Resort** and its 27-hole **Costa Caribe Golf & Country Club.** Opened in 2003, two of the layout's nines trace the shore of the palm-fringed sea, while the dramatic par-three 12th hole, set on a peninsula, is home to Puerto Rico's first island green. A posh 32,000-square-foot clubhouse overlooks Ponce's Central Mountains and the ocean. The hotel, beautifully landscaped with lush gardens, borders the south coast's striking black-sand beaches. The Hilton, located 90 minutes from San Juan, also boasts one of the largest casinos on the island.

Also located on the south coast is **El Legado Golf Resort,** a Chi Chi Rodriguez–designed layout set on a former thoroughbred horse farm near the town of Guayama. Opened in 2004, this challenging course, a stout 7,217 yards from the tips, offers ocean and mountain views. A system of interior lagoons puts water in play on 15 holes. Interestingly, there is no 13th hole at El Legado ("The Legacy"). According to Rodriguez, "We're going to be just like an elevator—no unlucky 13th on my golf course. You'll skip from the 12th hole to the 14th and finish on the 19th hole." Future plans call for 313 golf villas on site as well as a luxury hotel and spa.

St. Kitts & Nevis

St. Kitts, the larger of this two-island nation, welcomed in 2003 the **St. Kitts Marriott Resort & The Royal Beach Casino,** a 641-room property located on Frigate Bay 10 minutes from the capital city of Basseterre. The beachfront hotel, the island's first international-class resort property, is designed around a Mediterranean-themed main building and 15 three-story Garden Houses, each beautifully landscaped. Facilities include a swimming area with a natural reef, six specialty restaurants, a nightclub/disco, a health club and spa, and a Kids Club. Among the area attractions and landmarks are Brimstone Hill, a restored 38-acre fortress and a UNESCO World Heritage Site; and the St. Kitts Scenic Railway, its 10-car, 280-seat train carrying passengers along 30 miles of narrow-gauge track built in 1912 to transport sugarcane.

There's also **Royal St. Kitts Golf Club,** an entirely new course superimposed by Canadian Tom McBroom on the site of a previous design. The 6,859-yard, par-71 layout, which straddles a sandy peninsula on the island's narrow bottleneck, has three holes set along the wave-tossed Atlantic Ocean and two holes flanked by the limpid Caribbean Sea. Broad fairways and large greens effectively widen the margins of error, a nice plus for wayward hitters when the tradewinds blow. Water hazards, 80 well-placed bunkers, and clusters of palm trees enhance the challenge at Royal St. Kitts. The five seaside holes are outstanding, but McBroom has crafted an excellent test of golf with fine mountain views that holds everyone's attention from start to finish. The course, which debuted in 2004, is surfaced in paspalum, the only grass that would (or could) grow on site.

ONES TO WATCH

No fewer than three courses are planned for the dramatic hillsides and beautiful seashore of a destination that for decades bided its time as one of the sleepy backwaters of the West Indies. Like Jamaica, Barbados, and other Caribbean islands with a British heritage, St. Kitts has begun to target affluent international golfers who travel frequently and spend roughly 35 percent more per trip than the average visitor.

Slated to open in 2006 in the Sandy Point area on the island's northwest coast is **La Vallee,** a links-style nine-holer that will offer fine views of the Caribbean Sea, neighboring St. Eustatius, and 3,792-foot Mount Liamuiga, a dormant volcano. Future plans call for an additional nine holes, villas, a marina, and a sports complex.

California-based Auberge Resorts plans to build a $295-million luxury resort complex on a peninsula in the Sand Bank Bay area of St. Kitts. (The development was previously known as Whispering Head, but was unnamed at press time.) The project will feature a 250-room, five-star property and a Rees Jones–designed golf course to be followed by retail shops, a beach club, and up to 750 villas. The resort,

Four Seasons Resort Nevis, 11th hole

Infinity-edge pool at Four Seasons Resort Nevis

scheduled to open in 2008, is located on the island's southeastern tip within sight of Nevis.

Wales's Ian Woosnam, the 1991 Masters champion, has gotten into the golf design game. He is signed to build a course at **Kittitian Heights Resort** at Belmont Estate in northwest St. Kitts about 12 miles from Basseterre. The $140-million development, expected to be completed in 2011, will feature a boutique hotel built as a series of cottages, a spa and wellness center, a recording studio, and an artist's village.

Separated from its sister island by a two-mile-wide channel, the tiny island of Nevis (*knee*-vis) is home to **Four Seasons Resort Nevis,** a 196-room property on Pinney's Beach consistently rated one of the Caribbean's premier resorts. Fully recovered from the wrath of Hurricane Lenny—the property reopened in 2000 following a complete refurbishment—the resort's accommodations are found in 12 low-rise, West Indian plantation–style cottages trimmed in gingerbread and shaded by palms, their modest exteriors concealing sumptuous guest rooms (mahogany furniture in the bedrooms, marble everything in the bathrooms) as well as screened verandas. Estate homes and multi-bedroom villas perched on the green slopes of Mount Nevis, a dormant volcano rising 3,232 feet from the center of the tiny isle, are also available. Guests can lounge beside the pair of lagoon-like, infinity-edge pools and be handed chilled, eucalyptus-scented towels (or spritzed with

Evian water); soak in one of the spa's large outdoor hot tubs built to resemble the ruins of a sugar mill; or a join a naturalist-led "eco ramble" up the verdant slopes of Mount Nevis.

Or you can tee it up on the resort's golf course, a spectacular Robert Trent Jones, Jr. design that commences at sea level, climbs over 450 feet into jungle-covered foothills, and returns home to the sandy shore. Along the way, players can see and hear vervet monkeys chattering in the treetops—and admire every shade of green in the palette.

As for exquisite ocean views on this 6,766-yard, par-71 layout, mount the back tee of the par-five 15th, a gargantuan 663-yard hole where the ball must carry 240 yards from the tips across a verdant gorge to reach the fairway. Best of all for serious golfers, the Four Seasons Resort layout is generally underplayed. Because most guests visit the resort to relax or engage in water sports, tee times are at a premium for only an hour or so in the morning. Which means this luxurious slice of golf paradise is wide open most of the day, even in high season.

ONE TO WATCH

At press time, an as-yet-unnamed golf course by Canadian designer Doug Carrick was slated to be built adjacent to the Four Seasons Resort Nevis. Tentatively scheduled to open in 2008, the layout will climb the foothills of Mount Nevis, its fairways framed by mature coconut groves.

Other Islands

ANGUILLA

Anguilla, a British Crown Colony settled in 1650, is renowned for its quiet sophistication and exquisite, powdery beaches. The eel-shaped island, only 16 miles long and three miles across at its widest point, has to date supported only a very modest nine-hole layout. Enter the tandem of Flag Luxury Properties and St. Regis Hotels & Resorts, which hopes to define the deluxe golf experience in the islands in fall 2006 with the opening of the Greg Norman–designed **Temenos Golf Club.**

For an island with a reputation as flat, the layout boasts a surprising 87-foot elevation change, the holes crisscrossing a central ridge above Rendezvous Bay on a site where a derelict hotel had to be torn down and a biologically dead saltwater pond needed to be restored. There are 28 acres of water on the course, mostly in the form of saltwater lagoons that come into play at 13 holes. Like all of Norman's work, Temenos is championship-class from the tips at 7,144 yards, but it is first and foremost a resort course. It announces its intentions at the very first tee, where players are greeted by a stunning view across the sea to the mountainous coast of St. Martin seven miles

to the south. Thatched palm, a rare midget species, and other native vegetation salvaged from the former Sonesta hotel site was used to landscape the course.

The development, set beside a mile-long stretch of pearl-white beach, will have at its center **Temenos Anguilla—a St. Regis Resort,** an ultra-luxe, 120-room property slated to debut in 2008. The decentralized, low-rise hotel, none of its buildings taller than two stories, promises to "exceed five-star standards and expectations by offering a style of luxury development that doesn't exist anywhere in the Caribbean," according to the principals.

Temenos will one day have company on Anguilla. At press time, Jack Nicklaus had signed a contract to design a course at the eastern tip of the island at **Savannah Bay.**

BRITISH VIRGIN ISLANDS
ONE TO WATCH

At press time, Jack Nicklaus had committed to build a golf course at **Trellis Bay Estate,** a budding resort and residential community on the island of Tortola. The course will be the first in the BVI, a lovely chain of islands known as a sailor's paradise.

Swimming pool at Raffles Resort Canouan Island

Trump International Golf Club, 11th hole

ST. LUCIA

In St. Lucia, one of the Caribbean's most strikingly beautiful islands, Greg Norman broke ground in 2005 at **Le Paradis, Praslin Bay,** a new resort nestled in a pocket of scalloped coastline on the east side of the island. The 554-acre site, located along 2 ½ miles of reefs, keyhole bays, and peninsulas, fronts the Atlantic near the fishing village of Dennery and the Fregate Island Nature Reserve. Praslin Bay is 20 minutes from the international airport in Castries, St. Lucia's capital.

According to Norman, "This site is absolutely breathtaking, and we have strategically positioned golf holes on sheer cliffs that sit hundreds of feet above the ocean." The layout climbs to 600 feet before descending to four stunning coastal holes wrapped around Galet Bay.

In addition to the golf course, a 323-room, four-star branded hotel, a world-class spa with beachside treatment cabanas, and 100 deluxe residential units are slated to open at Praslin Bay in 2007. Phase 2 will feature a 40-room, five-star boutique hotel and a marina village encompassing waterways and moorings for up to 70-foot yachts.

ONE TO WATCH

At press time, discussions were under way for the construction of a Jack Nicklaus Signature course to be built at **Point Hardy**, on the island's northern tip. The $100-million project will include a high-end lodging entity and up to 50 single-family homes on a 360-acre site that features two-way views of the Caribbean Sea and the Atlantic Ocean.

ST. VINCENT & THE GRENADINES

This strand of 32 islands and cays at the southern end of the Windward Islands between St. Lucia and Grenada claims the region's first top-drawer golf course on the tiny isle of Canouan (prononced *can*-no-wan). The boot-shaped island, ringed by coral reefs, wide shallows, and ribbons of powdery white sand is only three square miles, population 1,100. Located 15 minutes by plane from St. Vincent, the serene little island is the setting for **Raffles Resort Canouan Island,** a $200-million ultra-luxe property designed with tropical flair by a pair of Italian architects.

Reopened in 2004 after closing its doors for a $40 million renovation, the resort, the first in the hemisphere to be managed by Raffles, the Asian luxury chain, features 156 one- and two-story villas, all with private terraces or patios overlooking the sea. Accommodations feature custom-made Italian linens, Indian fabrics, Mexican furnishings, and original works of art depicting objects found on Canouan. The resort offers a variety of exquisite beaches, plus water sports, private yacht moorings, a signature Raffles spa (Amrita), one of the Caribbean's largest fresh-water pools, four restaurants, two bars that offer 88 different types of martinis, and an elegant casino that commands the top of a cliff and overlooks the sea.

The resort's unfinished course was turned into a Jim Fazio–designed layout known as **Trump International Golf Club** (Donald Trump has a real estate interest within the development). Several holes on the newly created back nine climb a sloping hillside to nearly 800 feet above sea level, offering spectacular views of the Grenadines, including Mustique, Bequia, and the Tobago Cays. What the course lacks in distance—only 6,483 yards—it more than makes up for in steep drops, narrow fairways, and unforgiving rough.

The layout's photogenic back nine disappears into a lush jungle as it ascends to high ground, bringing players face-to-face with cascading waterfalls and vertigo-inducing ridges. The signature hole on this improbably remote and lovely course is the par-three 14th, which plays from tees slotted into rock at the top of a mountain. The green beckons from a natural bowl more than 100 feet below.

According to Fazio, "The front nine offers a great experience for players of all abilities. The back nine is more challenging—the wind on the top of the hills is formidable, as are the elevation changes and the roughs and wooded areas. It's also quite a bit cooler on these holes." After a series of fits and starts, the golf course, one of the most ravishing in a part of the world dominated by beautiful layouts, opened in 2004.

TRINIDAD & TOBAGO

Tobago, the sleepy island where Robinson Crusoe was shipwrecked, got a shot in the arm in 2001 with the debut of **Hilton Tobago,** a British Colonial–style hotel located on the south end of the island a short drive from the airport. Each of the spacious rooms and suites at this 200-room property overlook the ocean. A mile-long beach, large free-form pool, and easy access to world-class snorkeling and scuba diving sites are among the amenities at this kid-friendly resort. Guests have access to **Tobago Plantations,** a budding real estate development built around a 7,009-yard, links-style layout set on a former sugar-

Seaside pool at Hilton Tobago

cane plantation. What the course lacks in elevation change, it more than compensates with well-placed hazards (notably lagoons and creeks), a steady ocean breeze, and beautiful indigenous vegetation accented by native plantings. The feature hole is the third, a 416-yard par four that plays through "Naked Indian" trees to the far end of a peninsula, with fine views of Scarborough, Tobago's capital, in view from the seaside green. The resort's nine-hole Sugar Mill Course, a gentle 2,800-yard layout (par 35), is a perfect venue for carefree play. There's also a Stephen Ames Golf Academy with a variety of instructional packages available.

Europe

Europe is a big place with 44 distinct countries, a continent that has unified and prospered in the post–World War II era. Scotland, the cradle of the game, is the European nation most closely associated with golf, but it has not produced many new course designs, perhaps reasoning that 475 layouts give or take a few is enough. Ireland, on the other hand, has surged forward with dozens of new developments since the mid-1990s and has significantly raised its profile as a golf destination.

Four Seasons Resort Provence at Terre Blanche, France

Leading the way on the continent is Portugal's Algarve, which has added to its already impressive list of courses with several excellent newcomers. Despite the shortness of the season, Scandinavia, notably Sweden and Finland, will soon debut several excellent new facilities. Among the former Soviet Bloc nations, the Czech Republic has made the biggest inroads, adding to its already impressive courses in the old spa towns west of Prague. Bulgaria has two fascinating projects in the works that have the potential to rank among the best in Europe. Other nations that have worked hard to expand their appeal as golf destinations are Austria and Cyprus.

Ireland

It wasn't so very long ago that Ireland was one of Europe's untidy stepchildren, a rural place with a checkered past, quaint but rundown, its lace curtains, plastic leprechauns, and faux Blarney Stones nearly overshadowing its wonderful pubs. By the mid-1990s, however, Ireland was enjoying a renaissance. Even once-grimy Dublin was attracting international hipsters.

Then there's golf in Ireland. Scotland is the acknowledged birthplace of golf, but Ireland rocked the game out of the cradle, bathed it in mother's milk (a euphemism for creamy stout), and set it loose upon the seaside dunes and verdant meadows. It has thrived and prospered ever since. This quote from the late golf scribe Henry Longhurst, written in the 1960s, sums it up best. "Some of the Irish links, I was about to write, stand comparison with the greatest courses in the world. They don't. They *are* the greatest courses in the world, not only in layout but in scenery and 'atmosphere' and that indefinable something which makes you relive again and again the day you played there."

Today, Ireland now outstrips Scotland in the total number of golfers it welcomes from abroad each year. Some 450,000 rounds are expected in Ireland in the Ryder Cup year of 2006.

But numbers tell only half the story. The Irish people are among the wittiest and most welcoming on earth. The landscapes for golf, from towering sand-hills hard by the Atlantic to serene parkland marked by specimen trees and lazy rivers, are amazingly varied. As first-timers quickly discover, the color green is its own palette in Eire.

The entire nation has experienced a tremendous boom in new course openings, but the most interesting developments have taken place in the austere but captivating Northwest; and south of Dublin in counties Kildare and Wicklow.

Ballyliffin Golf Club, Glashedy Links, 15th hole

THE NORTHWEST

Sadly, there are precious few discoveries to be made in Ireland anymore. It could be said that Ireland has become a victim of its own success. Sky-high green fees, hard-to-get tee times, busloads of Yanks, five-hour rounds—jaded caddies—all have come to Emerald Isle.

But there is one place left that is to grail seekers what Alaska is to wilderness lovers: the Last Frontier. This is the wild northwest corner of Ireland, counties Donegal, Sligo, and Mayo. Here are found new as well as reworked and vintage links routed among heaving, bearded dunes in view of treeless hills, blue loughs, and the white-capped North Atlantic. This is the Ireland you've heard about from old-timers, a briny, thinly populated place where sheep clog the roads and peat fires warm the pubs, where *craicks* (conversations) elicit soft, musical Gaelic and where the rural hospitality is genuine. Golf in the Northwest invites discovery; it remains an adventure.

Financially, the roaring Celtic Tiger of the '90s is now a meowing pussycat throughout most of Eire, but the Northwest, thanks to a pair of canny Irish architects and a few resourceful clubs, has forged ahead and can now lay claim—sorry St. Andrews—to the greatest collection of links courses on earth. And since it is still largely undiscovered, it's a place where the golf is half the price and twice as much fun as the better-known Irish venues.

The best way to commence a counterclockwise tour of this elemental region is to begin in County Donegal and make your first stop at **Ballyliffin Golf Club,** Ireland's most northerly club. Ballyliffin presents two completely different venues. The **Old Course**, built in 1948, is a rumpled rug of a links where maybe a few teaspoons of sand were displaced to make way for tees and greens. After visiting in 1993, Nick Faldo called it "the most natural golf links I have ever played."

Rosapenna, Sandy Hills Links, 10th hole

There are no flat lies. You'd get seasick if you drove this quirky links in a cart, so pronounced are its ripples and wrinkles. But then, the sea and mountain views are spectacular.

Ballyliffin's second course is the **Glashedy,** named for the muffin-top of rock that rises from Pollan Bay. Designed by Pat Ruddy and Tom Craddock in 1995, this newer links is a much sterner test parted through a lunar landscape of taller dunes, its peat-revetted bunkers fiendishly positioned to snare offline shots. The par-three seventh and 14th holes both drop nearly 100 feet to their targets. Atop the world on these tees, you can almost see Santa and his workshop on the horizon. From the tips at 7,217 yards (par 70), the Glashedy is a beast. The finish, marked by wicked doglegs threaded through corridors of shouldering dunes, is unusually strong. There are courses with more charm, but few with more bite than the Glashedy.

After repairing to the modern clubhouse to recover from the round or rounds (tackling the Old Course and Glashedy in one day is an experience unto itself), make the half-hour drive to Malin Head at the very tip of the Inishowen Peninsula. Here, from a cliff at the northern extremity of the Ireland, can be seen the North Atlantic shipping lanes as well as white rocks spelling EIRE that once guided World War II aviators. Be sure to take a few deep breaths of what is reputed to be the freshest and purest air on earth.

Loop around to Donegal's next splayed peninsula and head north to **Rosapenna Hotel & Golf Links,** a full-service resort that extends a very warm welcome to guests. There is history here. A century ago, the unhurried Northwest was the preferred retreat of British aristocrats. Rosapenna was built in 1891 as a top-shelf getaway by the fourth Earl of Leitrim, who brought in Old Tom Morris of St. Andrews to build a golf course. In the ensuing decades, Harry Vardon and James Braid also came and left their design mark. The current hotel course, called the **Old Tom Morris Links,** is a near-perfect holidaymaker's track with beautifully sited greens. By all means have a go at its ledged fairways and punchbowl greens, and savor the wonderful stretch of holes set in a low valley that runs beside the sea. But don't expend all your energy upon it. Save it for Ireland's best new course of the millennium.

Rosapenna's **Sandy Hills Links,** unveiled in 2003, is a brawling, witchy, in-your-face links, its tossing fairways woven through massive dunes blanketed in spongy, thigh-high marram grass. The golf course is the creation of Pat Ruddy, Ireland's answer to Pete Dye. Ruddy, a Sligo man and as iconoclastic as they come, found his ideal canvas here: tumbling dunes that bottleneck impressively, magnificent views of

haystack-shaped peaks to the south, equally fine views of combers pounding the vast deserted beach far below the fairways. Rarely is the scenery a match for the challenge on a top-notch course. It is at Sandy Hills.

Like Dye, Ruddy is aghast at the advances in modern equipment, specifically the ever-lively ball. He uses doglegs, carries over valleys, and both sunken and domed greens to create shot values and press his advantage in the battle of wits between designer and player. Brilliantly routed, each hole at Sandy Hills is tucked in its own compartment of dunes. Bogey shooters who recognize their place and who manage to keep the ball in play can survive an outing from the white tees, but this steroidal links will pillage an overconfident ace from the tips at 7,155 yards. Accuracy, placement, and sensible course management count for everything. A good short game, too, assuming your putt means something. Go for too much, fail to pull off a gamble, and you're finished. If you're the type who pounds driver off every tee no matter what, they'll take you away in a donkey-cart when you're done.

Golf at Rosapenna is a work in progress. At press time, Ruddy had completed a series of new holes that will eventually replace the back nine on the Old Tom Morris Links. These new holes form a seamless connection with the Morris-designed valley holes, the heart of the layout. The new 18-hole configuration will be known as the **Morris Ruddy Links.** Stretching to 7,100 yards from the championship markers, the revamped course is a testing combination of traditional and modern links holes that bridge a century of golf design. Remaining holes from the original links designed by Vardon and Braid will be crafted into a stand-alone Academy Course. No resort anywhere can boast of such a pedigree.

LODGING

Assuming you're staying at **Rosapenna Hotel,** far and away the best lodging choice in these parts, look for owner Frank Casey, but don't blink—you'll miss him. Son of the resort's former head waiter, Casey learned the hospitality trade as a barefoot caddie and later as a barman. The place runs like a Swiss watch because he's always there, a dervish attending to every detail, and always turned out in a tux at night to greet his guests for dinner.

Meals are served in a pleasing window-walled room overlooking the bays of Sheephaven and Mulroy, and the food is as good as the bar is lively. An indoor pool, whirlpool, and steam room are recent additions. Two lovely beaches are close by, as is the local fishing village of Downings, its sandy shore, caves, and rock pools much appreciated by children.

One of the genuine highlights of a journey to the Northwest is **Portsalon Golf Club,** located a short drive east of Rosapenna on an adjacent peninsula. The club, founded in 1891, occupies a stunning location on the shores of Lough Swilly. It piddled along as an innocuous little links for generations, but the ubiquitous Ruddy was brought in to build 11 new holes, revise the others, and knit the work together in 2000–01. The result is a premier member's course that is pure joy to play. Ruddy's new holes, stitched among virgin dunes set back from the golden beaches of Ballymastocker Bay, are magnificent, their slippery crowned putting surfaces—including a pair of giant double greens—hard to hit and harder to hold. The opening sequence, which crosses an inlet of the sea and skirts a long, tawny strand, is dazzling. The sixth, emblematic of the new Portsalon, is a killer par four with a tiny ribbon of fairway parted through a valley in the dunes that curves gently left to a platform green embraced by swales and hollows. When the sun hits the high hurdle of rock-studded hills to the east, the links positively glows.

Ruddy was wise enough to leave well enough alone on the interior portion of the layout. A case in point is the par-four 14th, Matterhorn, which plays from a high, wooded rocky alcove to a narrow, tumbling fairway with two distinct shelves. Portsalon (pronounced Port-SAL-on) is a sleeper with an elegant beauty all its own. One caveat: measurements here and here only are in meters.

Heading south from these splendid peninsulas, one reaches Donegal Town, a pleasant little city with a main square called the Diamond. It's a good place to shop for heathery tweeds at Magee. On the outskirts of town alongside an estuary is Donegal Castle, a foursquare edifice circa 1505 that is worth a visit. A few miles south of town on the Murvagh Peninsula is **Donegal Golf Club,** a burly Eddie Hackett design stretching to 7,280 yards (par 73). Completed in 1976, it was for years the longest course in Europe. The views of white-capped Donegal Bay and the Blue Stack Mountains are "hauntingly beautiful," as the late British golf scribe Peter Dobereiner described them.

In the 1990s, Ruddy was brought in to revamp a few greens and re-orient a few fairways, notably the stretch from 12 through 14. He also made lethal use of a stream that cuts through the links. Coupled with its prodigious length, Donegal, or Murvagh as it is often called, presents a formidable test, for this is a course

Portsalon Golf Club, second hole

writ large that calls for big hitting. On a windy day, it gives Sandy Hills a run for its money as the toughest links in the Northwest. Wear your newly-purchased woolies.

ONE TO WATCH

Not far from Rosapenna and sharing the same wild Donegal scenery is **St. Patrick's Golf Links**, a virtually unknown 36-hole complex that should rank among the best golf facilities in Ireland by the end of the decade.

A bit of history. **Magheramagorgan,** the first of the two courses, was designed by Eddie Hackett in 1982. However, construction did not begin for 11 years and was not fully completed until 1996—the last piece of sod was laid six weeks before Hackett's death. The second links, **Tra Mor** (Gaelic for "big strand"), was designed in 1993 by Joanne O'Haire, a former Royal County Down assistant pro who worked with Hackett on the main course. It is said to be the only course in Ireland designed by a woman.

In late 2005, the Relton Development group, a fixture in the hotel, bar, and restaurant business in the greater Dublin area, contracted Jack Nicklaus to redesign the existing 36 holes of seaside golf. At press time, reconstruction of the courses was slated to begin in early 2006. According to Tim Kenny, executive vice president of Nicklaus Design, "The land and the dunes comprising St. Patrick's is what Ireland golf is supposed to be—raw, natural, wild, windy, with bunkers carved and created by Mother Nature. It is absolutely an incredible site." Both courses, backed by mountains, are threaded through bearded dunes near a mile-long beach fronting Sheephaven Bay.

Upon completion, St. Patrick's Golf Links will consist of a five-star luxury hotel as well as a spa and complete leisure facilities. A future phase will include up to 200 luxury apartments, houses, and retail outlets.

Heading south along the N-15, a pleasant thoroughfare threaded through the Dartry Mountains in County Leitrim, a land feature looms into view that looks totally out of place among the thatched-roof homes and rolling green hills. In fact, the massive limestone mesa known as Ben Bulben could double for Table Mountain in Cape Town, South Africa. This is the elephant-legged monolith that inspired W.B. Yeats, the revered Irish poet who put into words what everyone feels about a region he dubbed "the land of heart's desire." Golfers and pilgrims alike should pause to pay their respects to the great poet in the tree-shaded Drumcliffe churchyard, and to read the sobering words inscribed on his gravestone:

Enniscrone Golf Club, 13th hole

Cast a cold eye
On life, on death.
Horseman, pass by!

A short distance away on a neck of land jutting into the sea is **County Sligo Golf Club,** a.k.a. **Rosses Point.** The club was founded in 1894, but the current links, designed by H.S. Colt, dates to 1927. Portmarnock, Ballybunion, and Northern Ireland's two Royals, County Down and Portrush, are generally regarded as Ireland's top four tracks. While off the beaten path, lesser-known Rosses Point is their equal.

The first two holes on this venerable links play straight uphill, the better to give players a top-of-the-world view of Ben Bulben, the Ox Mountains to the south, the shining sea in Drumcliffe Bay and, looking back, the white-washed homes in Sligo Town. It is one of the most stunning panoramas in the sport. The course provides sublime links golf, subtle and cunning, where shot-makers will prosper—if they can avoid the narrow stream, called here a "drain," that flanks or crosses the fairways.

A long-time site of the West of Ireland Championship and many other competitions, Rosses Point has

enough land to build new holes on sandy duneland and may consider abandoning the opening holes on the hill, which are wonderful but are quite out of character with the rest of the course. The verdict is still out on whether or not tampering with an H.S. Colt masterpiece is a good idea.

Departing Sligo and heading west on N-59, what little civilization exists in these parts tends to disappear in the rear view mirror. The pilgrim's next destination is **Enniscrone Golf Club,** yet another Northwest club that, after a long, hard look in the mirror, decided to undergo a facelift. The original course, which dates to 1918 and was extended to 18 holes by Eddie Hackett in the mid-1970s, was known as a solid test with a dull start. Enter Donald Steel, the English designer, who in 2001 built six stunning new holes among skyscraper dunes, their sheer alpine faces rising 80 feet above the fairways. The U-shaped corridors for these new holes are nothing short of majestic, while elevated tees serve up inspiring views of Killala Bay and distant mountains. Four of the new holes are par fives, each brawny and awesome, but the highest praise must go to the new 15th, called

Carne Golf Links, 17th hole

LODGING & DINING

Several good seafood restaurants line the quayside along the harbor near the County Sligo club, notably the Waterfront. For tippling, Yeats Tavern, north of town, is a favorite of locals and visitors alike, though Hardagan's, on Old Market Street, is a dark but inviting public house with an old marble bar. This is where the poets go.

There are several fine hotels in Sligo (**the Radisson SAS,** for one) as well as a number of historic guest houses. The best of these is **Coopershill,** a grand 18th-century Georgian manor located 20 minutes south of town. But the most convenient place to stay is the **Yeats Country Inn** directly across the street from the club. To wake up in the morning, see the flags flapping in front of the black-and-white Tudor clubhouse and know that a round awaits on this tantalizing links, well...that is something Yeats, though a non-golfer, would undoubtedly describe poetically.

The Strand, a 421-yarder that curves along the shore and leads to a three-tiered green defended in front by a grassy knob. In a stiff wind, it's one of the most fearsome par fours in Ireland.

With its revamped links, this friendly, welcoming club stands shoulder-to-shoulder with its neighbors and qualifies as a destination course that belongs on any Northwest itinerary. If you happen to catch a chill on the links, have the barman make you a hot Irish whiskey: boiling water, a shot of Paddy's, a lump of brown sugar, with a slice of lemon and a clove or two floated on top. What a reviver!

ONE TO WATCH

Six-time major champion Nick Faldo, who has turned his competitiveness as a player into a passion for golf design, describes **Bartragh Island** in County Mayo, which he purchased in 2003, as "the most magical and most extraordinary property I have ever seen." Located in Killala Bay not far from where the River Moy, a salmon fishery, empties into the sea, the 365-acre island is dominated by massive, heaving sand dunes. Faldo and his design team have produced a preliminary out-and-back routing in the shape of an elongated figure eight that takes full advantage of the towering sand hills. "Our aim is to roll back the years and handcraft the golf course: It could be Royal County Down, Ballybunion, Royal St. George's, and Royal Dornoch all rolled into one—and on an island, no less," he wrote in *Links Magazine* in 2004. "We will not be 'building' a golf course so much as 'discovering' it." The only structures on Bartragh Island are a stone wall and a 200-year-old manor house which Faldo says will be "a challenge and a pleasure to restore." The only detail to be worked out, once the project receives the necessary environmental and planning consent, is transportation: The island's closest point to the mainland is 600 yards.

Every journey relies upon a colossal detour to preserve the memory of the trip. In Ireland's Northwest, that journey is a Marco Polo–like expedition to the far west of the Republic, across miles of a vast, desolate blanket bog to the Mullet, a talon-shaped peninsula thrust far into the North Atlantic. The County Mayo seaside town of Belmullet has a quaint cheerfulness—this is still Ireland, after all—but you can feel a detachment from civilization here. Despite its remoteness, the town decided to build a golf course in the early 1990s to spur tourism. The man brought in to work the ancient commonage beside Blacksod Bay was Eddie Hackett, then in his late 70s. (He died in 1996, three years after the course opened.)

Hackett, a Dubliner who worked as a pro at Royal Dublin and later Portmarnock, set about the task of finding golf holes in the wild with the vigor of a man half his age, producing along the way the finest work of his career. (He also pocketed a little more than 10,000 Irish pounds plus train fare for his troubles. It wasn't about the money for Eddie.)

Of course, Hackett was the first to admit that **Carne Golf Links,** as the links is called, is great because the site is beyond belief. Huge dunes in turmoil, like colliding freight trains, merge here. There is a scale and grandeur here seen only at Ballybunion and a few other places. There are only 18 formal bunkers: The tumultuous land is defense enough.

The green sites, natural plateaus or amphitheaters, are brilliant. So is the routing. The front nine climbs the dunes, swings past agricultural land, then doubles back to the shaggy pyramidal hills. The back nine can be forgiven the short, kooky, hairpin-shaped par fours at 11 and 12. Hackett tended to err on the side of an eccentric hole rather than move dunes to create textbook golf. However, the payoff at Carne is sublime. Holes 15 and 17, each a majestic par four set on rising land, are among the finest natural two-shotters in all of golfdom. The verdict is still out on the par-five 18th.

A deep valley that could hide a herd of brontosauri stands between player and green following the drive. "A conundrum," Hackett called it, deigning not to fill it.

Even for experienced travelers who have seen a few courses in their time, Carne ranks as one of the great adventures in links golf, offering four-and-a-half hours of astonishment. The Mullet is a place apart, Ireland's Patagonia. For those who have made the journey, Carne, a cult classic, is and always will be the most remote great course beyond the ken of Middle Earth. As a bonus, American designer Jim Engh, who adores Carne, had at press time begun to build an additional nine holes, presumably to keep the pilgrims coming.

LODGING

Located in tiny Ballycastle in County Mayo is the **Stella Maris Hotel,** a former coast guard headquarters and later a convent that is today a charming hotel with a scenic observatory overlooking Downpatrick Head. The hotel is run by former PGA of America official Terry McSweeney and his Irish wife, Frances. The reason to stay here, in addition to the fact that the staff lays a great table for supper, is that Stella Maris, "Star of the Sea," is an ideally situated base for those who wish to play Enniscrone and Carne.

DAY TRIP

Five miles west of Ballycastle on the road leading to Carne are the Ceide Fields, an extensive Neolithic landscape of world importance that has changed perceptions of Stone Age farmers. Preserved under a 5,000-year-old blanket bog lies a farming countryside of stone-walled fields, the oldest enclosed landscape in Europe. These fields were already deserted and bog-ridden before the pyramids were built in Egypt! The interpretive center has exhibitions, an audio-visual show, and tearooms. Guided tours enable you to walk on the bog or even probe for a buried Neolithic wall.

PUBS

The pubs of Ireland need no introduction. Pubs are where the life of Ireland originates and where its lore is born. In toto, there are more than 11,000 pubs in the country. The ones in the Northwest tend to be smaller, friendlier, and homier than those in the nation's more populous regions. Seek out your own. Ask around. Make discoveries. The clubhouses at the aforementioned courses all have bars. They're warm and welcoming, but they're not pubs. Pubs, ruled by the witty asides, genial quips, and occasional song of regular patrons, are another reality altogether. God bless, as they say, and raise a toast if you happen to find one where the traditional music stirs your blood.

DUBLIN

Perhaps you've been to Ireland, if only in your dreams. After all, what golfer's education is complete until the Emerald Isle has been experienced to the fullest one way or another? You've spread out the map and traced your finger along the coastline, where the great links reside. You played them. Or maybe they played you. It's not that the weather was bad. It's just that there was a great deal of it. You've been blitz-krieged at Ballybunion, whiplashed at Waterville, pelted at Portmarnock.

Great as they are, there is an alternative to the brawling links of Ireland, a kinder, gentler place to pursue the game. Very quietly, a number of first-class parkland spreads have sprung up south and west of Dublin since 2000, joining several established venues. Oh, there's enough rain to keep everything green, mind you, but County Kildare, horse country, and County Wicklow, the "Garden of Ireland," are two of the sunniest places in Eire. The Dublin area's refined inland layouts offer pleasant respite from the salty chill of the coast. And when the round is done, you're convenient to one of the most vibrant and interesting cities in Europe, home of James Joyce and Guinness and U2.

Starting in County Kildare, there is The Kildare Hotel & Country Club, located in the tiny village of Straffan west of Dublin and now known universally as **The K Club,** a high-toned resort that continues to set the pace for Irish golf in the 21st century. The golf world will converge on this sleepy corner of Kildare in 2006, when the Ryder Cup Matches, the first to be held in Ireland, arrive at The K Club. The expansive resort is the brainchild of Michael Smurfit, a successful businessman who completely revived the domain and recast it along the lines of an exclusive American country club (though open to the public). After restoring the grand Georgian estate on site, Smurfit brought Arnold Palmer and his design team to Kildare.

The club's original layout, now called the **Palmer Course**, is a magnificent parkland creation that traces the River Liffey and winds around Straffan House, which dates to 550 A.D. and is today one of Ireland's most luxurious hotels. Home of the Smurfit European Open, the course, which suffered from poor drainage initially, has been tweaked and reworked dozens of times since its debut in 1991. The 7,337-yard layout reflects the go-for-broke personality of its

The K Club, Palmer Course, seventh hole

Formal grounds at The K Club's Straffan House

designer, with several watery risk-reward scenarios sprinkled throughout. In fact, players must contend with man-made lakes and the ever-present river at more than half the holes. The double-dogleg, par-five seventh is a case in point. A big drive tempts bold players to cross the River Liffey and reach the green in two, but the more prudent approach is to steer clear of the river on the second shot. The payoff shot is fraught with danger, as the green crowns an island between two arms of the Liffey and is framed by bunkers and huge specimen trees.

The well-groomed layout, its peak season green fee of 265 euros (at press time) the highest in the land, was joined in 2003 by a second Palmer design routed on a flat, treeless pasture on the opposite side of the River Liffey. Known as the **Smurfit Course,** the gently undulating 7,313-yard layout, marked by rolling man-made berms and large cloverleaf bunkers, has water in play at nearly every hole, including an island green at the par-five 18th. There's even a Hollywood-like stage set of faux rock walls and water cascades at the signature par-five seventh hole, a million-euro,

606-yard extravaganza reportedly inspired by the quarry holes on the Green Monkey course at Sandy Lane in Barbados. Randomly landscaped with gorse, bracken, and other native vegetation, this breezy inland links lacks the enchanting beauty of the original, but it does present a dramatic (and watery) test for the best.

In addition to a full-service clubhouse and two elegant dining rooms, notably the Byerley Turk restaurant (French haute cuisine with an Irish twist), seasonal golf packages are available at The K Club, Ireland's top-rated resort hotel. The opulent guest rooms are individually appointed with fine antiques, while the public rooms are highlighted by paintings in the Jack B. Yeats collection, the famous poet's brother.

Tucked into a storybook setting—a walled 1,100-acre estate on the outskirts of Maynooth that served as the ancestral home of the Earls of Kildare—the **Mark O'Meara Course** at **Carton House Golf Club,** debuted in 2002, is a 7,006-yard gem that makes

splendid use of the historic demesne's rolling hills and specimen oak, cedar, and copper beech trees. Holes 13, 14 and 15—a pair of par threes wrapped around a heroic par five—cross the lazy loops of the River Rye, a tributary of the Liffey. This parkland course supreme is plenty tough from the tips, but O'Meara intended it to give pleasure from the regular tees. The course exists in perfect harmony with its serene setting and is one of the prettiest inland courses in Ireland. It's also a putter's delight: The velvety bentgrass greens are exceptional. Beyond the hills and trees, Tyrconnell Tower, a hilltop "folly," looms into view during the round, as does the palatial 18th-century Carton House.

The facility's **Colin Montgomerie Course,** opened in 2003, is altogether different from the O'Meara layout. Although bordered in places by the estate's beautiful trees, the course is relatively flat, nearly treeless, and quite barren in places, its well-contoured fairways parted through tall, shimmering fescues in the open countryside. Deep, recessed pot bunkers, each well-positioned, were designed to gobble

offline shots. The large greens, notable for their broad slopes and interesting contours, were planted with an advanced strain of bentgrass. They are even finer and faster than the O'Meara's. At full stretch—7,301 yards—Monty's links-style creation, which offers a fine mix of long and short holes, is championship stuff, a fact not lost on the European Tour, which tapped the Montgomerie Course to host the 2005 Irish Open. Montgomerie admitted that while his creation can't technically be called a links course, "it plays like a links and has all the characteristics of a links." Especially on a breezy day, when the bunkers become genuine hazards.

At press time, Carton House had under construction a 160-room luxury hotel that carefully integrates the existing mansion. Fifteen bedrooms will be located within the stately Carton House itself, while the main hotel will feature a full-service spa, a leisure center, and a fine dining restaurant that will offer views of the formal gardens. The hotel is scheduled to open in 2006.

Carton House Golf Club, Colin Montgomerie Course, 18th hole

Set on the magnificent Palmerston Estate in Johnstown an hour's drive southwest of Dublin, **PGA National Ireland** is yet another significant new golf development within County Kildare. Debuted in 2005, the club joins a prestigious PGA family that includes Gleneagles in Scotland (site of the 2014 Ryder Cup Matches) and The Belfry in England.

Using Augusta National as his model, designer Christy O'Connor, Jr., working from an earlier routing devised by Jack Nicklaus and the late Payne Stewart, fashioned a brawny but gorgeous 7,419-yard layout that rambles along the outskirts of a once-famous stud farm. (Thoroughbreds still canter to and from the estate's stables.) O'Connor clearly built a course to challenge experts from the tips, but this refined parkland spread presents a fair test from the forward tees. Many of the holes are framed by specimen hardwoods, transplanted laurel trees, and an abundance of flowers, though the signature features of PGA National are sand and water. Water comes into play at nearly every hole. Bunkers are deployed in echelon—whole constellations of them guard key landing areas and green sites. The only gimmicks on the course, if they can be called that, are the sham-

rock-shaped bunkers on the first and 18th holes.

Until a five-star hotel is built on the estate, visiting players can stay at the **CityWest Hotel,** a popular conference destination located near PGA National Ireland.

Moving to County Wicklow, an hour's drive south of Dublin, we start with **Druids Glen Golf Club,** site of Murphy's Irish Open from 1996–99. It's a brilliantly conceived layout by Pat Ruddy and Tom Craddock, a crafty test that rewards shot-makers who can maneuver the ball to sloping fairways and well-defended greens. Built by Hugo Flinn, an engineer who made a fortune in large-scale civil engineering projects in Africa, the layout is marked by subtle earthworks, formal topiaries, gurgling waterfalls, and unusual suspension bridges. The entries to several of these bridges are planted in herbs that, trodden underfoot by passing golfers, release their aroma.

The first seven holes at Druids Glen, each self-contained, occupy rolling, wooded land; the middle stretch descends into a quiet, mystical glen. There are no easy holes at the Glen, but there's one, the 13th, that is decidedly world-class. A long granite ledge

PGA National Ireland, 16th hole

was sheared away to make room for the elevated tee and fairway at this spectacular 471-yard par four, where the tee shot must find a fairway angled sharply to the right and bisected by a stream. The second shot is daunting—a long carry over a pond to a narrow green set among spreading oaks and chestnuts, with water left and grassy swales right.

Druids Glen is anchored by Woodstock House, a restored 1770 manor house. Each of its rooms is dedicated to a famous personage in Irish history, while the view of the Irish Sea from the roof is sublime. A genuine landmark, it is one of the coziest clubhouses in all of Ireland.

Typically, it wasn't enough for Ruddy to construct a course that was named the European Golf Course of the Year in 2000. The peripatetic designer returned to build **Druids Heath,** which opened to immediate acclaim in 2003. A multi-theme spread routed among billowing hills, with fantastic views of the Irish Sea and distant mountains from its fairways, the layout rambles around old farm ponds and descends into the mini-canyons of spent rock quarries. On a clear day, the hills of Wales can be seen 200 miles to the east. At full stretch, Druids Heath, an artful blend of links,

parkland, and heathland design styles, presents one of Ireland's strongest tests of golf. The golf club, by the way, is located in a mouthful of a town—Newtown-mountkennedy.

The course is located beside the **Druids Glen Marriott Hotel & Country Club,** a pleasant 148-room property nestled between the Wicklow Mountains and the Irish Sea that opened in 2002. Despite the Marriott name, this is a very individual property built with stone and wood harvested on site during the construction of Druids Heath. Light-filled and airy, its lines clean and modern, the hotel offers golf packages that include full Irish breakfast.

Situated on an exquisite estate that dates to the 16th century and is now owned by the Slazenger family, **Powerscourt Golf Club** is a 36-hole golf resort that has quietly taken shape in Enniskerry. The club's 7,051-yard **East Course,** laid out by Peter McEvoy in 1996, has a good mix of parkland and links-style holes, their fairways serving up fine views of the Wicklow Mountains. Deep bunkers and small, multi-tiered greens provide plenty of challenge, but take heart: All the par threes play downhill.

Druids Glen Golf Club, 17th hole

Far grander is Powerscourt's **West Course,** a majestic 7,029-yard design by Scotsman David McLay Kidd. The course, routed on much hillier ground than the original layout, has shallower bunkers and larger greens. With its towering pines and 80-foot elevation change, the fledgling layout, opened in 2003, could pass for a rugged track in the Scottish Highlands. "Given the broad nature of the landscape, I aimed for broad, soft movement of the terrain," said Kidd, "with most of the greens open to a running approach shot." The scenery is very fine: Sugar Loaf Mountain and the Irish Sea can be spied from the topmost holes of the West Course.

After the round, be sure to tour the estate's 45 acres of walled and tiered English, Italian, and Japanese formal gardens, a sublime blend of flowers, statuary, terraces, lakes, and a very tall waterfall. These are the prettiest gardens in Ireland and among the loveliest in Europe. The gift shop sells seeds of nearly all the flower species cultivated at the estate.

At press time, Ritz-Carlton had announced plans for a 203-room resort at Powerscourt to include four restaurants and lounges, a 30,000-square-foot spa,

and extensive meeting facilities. A late 2006 opening was forecast for the Ritz-Carlton Powerscourt, the luxury chain's first hotel in Ireland.

SIDETRIP: THE EUROPEAN CLUB
On a primeval piece of ground hard by Brittas Bay an hour's drive south of Druids Glen is **The European Club,** the inspired creation and perpetual work-in-progress of journalist-turned-designer Pat Ruddy, whose immodestly titled tour de force features *20* brilliant holes set in bearded dunes high above the Irish Sea.

Opened in 1993 but revised by Ruddy many times over the years, this brawling course, with two 10-hole loops on offer, is a clever counter-puncher that rewards good shots but punishes thoughtless or inept efforts. The sleeper-lined bunkers are deep, the rough off the fairways is impenetrable, and some of the greens, notably the 127-yard-long putting surface at the 12th, are designed, declares Ruddy, "to see the great three-putt restored to the game." By turns the most exhilarating and exasperating links in Ireland, this is a genuine original cherished by purists. The

The European Club, 17th hole

heart of the round—holes seven through 12—features six very challenging (and lengthy) par fours interspersed by hole 7a, a cute little par three tucked in the sand hills.

Marked by a small, boxy concrete clubhouse, The European Club is truly a place unto itself. It is run with studied informality by Ruddy and his grown children. Despite the owner's incessant tinkering, the links has grown in stature every year since its opening.

A DUBLIN PRIMER

What was once referred to disparagingly as "dear, dirty Dublin" has been transformed by the "Celtic Tiger" economy and a younger generation (half the population is under 30) into a lively, upbeat city. Grafton Street, a bustling pedestrian thoroughfare with St. Stephen's Green at one end and Trinity College (1592) at the other, is a prime shopping and people-watching zone. For many, no trip to Dublin is complete without a visit to the Guinness Storehouse at St. James Gate. The story of the famous stout begins over 250 years ago and ends in Gravity (a bar

in the sky) with a complimentary pint and a panoramic view of the city. Temple Bar, Dublin's cultural and nightlife quarter, is a pulsing enclave of pubs, cafés, shops, and art galleries. Bookish types can trace the Irish literary tradition at the Dublin Writers Museum, which occupies a grand 18th-century mansion and celebrates the works of Joyce, Shaw, Wilde, Yeats, Beckett, Swift, and other Irish writers. The pubs, needless to say, are everywhere.

LODGING

In addition to the aforementioned resort hotels, visitors can also stay in Dublin and make day trips to the golf courses south and west of town. Among the city's finest hotels is the **Four Seasons Hotel Dublin,** a newcomer situated in the residential and embassy district of Ballsbridge. The 258-room, Georgian-style property is set within the Royal Dublin Society's 42-acre show grounds. Chauffeur-driven or self-drive transportation as well as tee times can be arranged by the concierge. The hotel's location on the south side of Dublin makes it that much closer to the great new parkland courses in Kildare and Wicklow.

Portugal/Algarve

Situated at the far western edge of the Iberian peninsula, a world apart from the rest of continental Europe, Portugal is a small country the size of Maine that had superpower status during the Age of Discovery. Then as now, the sea is the horizon from every Portuguese summit.

In the north of the country are found mountains and vineyards, while vast cereal plains stretch southeast from Lisbon. These plains end abruptly at a ridge of *serras* (mountains) that block the flow of cold air to the south. Beyond lies the Algarve, an ancient kingdom with a strong Moorish influence. It

was to the Algarve that many Britons emigrated in the 1950s for sun and relaxation. A decade later, golf courses began to spring up. In fact, it was Sir Henry Cotton, the legendary British champion, who put the Algarve on the golf map in 1966 with his seminal design at Penina, reclaimed from a rice paddy and the region's first proper grass course.

The Algarve's courses are set back from a sawtooth terrace of canary-yellow and burnt-orange cliffs in the *barrocal*, or foothills of the mountains. Cork oaks cover the dry, folded land. So do umbrella pines, their coarsely-barked trunks opening to rounded bon-

San Lorenzo, sixth hole

nets of greenery. Closer to the Atlantic are olive and almond, fig and carob trees. Citrus groves and cactus plants are also present, for the weather in the Algarve is invariably dry and sunny in autumn and spring, the region's prime golf seasons.

Golf development along the coast between Lagos and Faro, gateway to the Algarve, has been strong of late. In fact, the region more than doubled its inventory of courses in the 1990s, with several fine new tracks opened shortly before and after the millennium. In addition, a number of vintage designs have been significantly revised to keep pace. The Algarve,

with some 30 courses, boasts one of the highest ratios of golf holes per square kilometer in the world. Yet despite recent expansion, the region, formerly a beach destination popular only in summer, feels more carefree than crowded.

Vilamoura is a burgeoning 90-hole complex that ranks among the largest in Europe. Its **Old Course** was one of the first (and finest) courses built in the Algarve, and has been treated to an extensive renovation. Laid out on elevated ground that rises and falls through a forest of umbrella pines, the make-

Vilamoura, Old Course, ninth hole

over retains Englishman Frank Pennink's original 1969 design, which captures the feeling of a British heathland spread, though golfers are never far from the maritime influence here. Wiggle your feet into the coarse Atlantic sand in the bunkers, and little cockleshells rise up around your shoelaces.

The newest of the five courses at Vilamoura is the **Victoria Clube de Golfe.** Laid out by Palmer Course Design, it attracted immediate notice as one of Europe's finest new venues. Chosen to host the 2005 WGC-World Cup, the 7,174-yard spread was built on virtually flat terrain covering 220 acres. The other courses at Vilamoura have rolling hills and umbrella pines to define them, but Vicki Martz, Palmer's on-site architect, moved 750,000 cubic yards of dirt and built 20 acres of lakes to add pizzazz.

Large-scale landforms designed to mimic the surrounding hillsides are covered in native grasses and shrubs, with carob, olive, and almond trees along with well-placed bunkers framing the fairways. So pleased was the resort's management by the creation, they named the course for the designer, though Martz claims the resort owner's granddaughter is also named Victoria.

The **Millennium** course, debuted in 2000, also significantly boosted Vilamoura's stature. Designed by Englishman Martin Hawtree, a third-generation architect who cobbled together a pre-existing nine to nine new holes of his own design, the course, set on rolling terrain dotted with umbrella pines, is an attractive, enjoyable design.

Vilamoura has several lodging partners, including a trio of four-star properties in the Dom Pedro Hotels group. The most scintillating accommodations, however, can be found at the **Vilamoura Marinotel,** a luxurious 383-room hotel ideally located near the resort's golf courses and offering fine views of the marina and beach.

Generally ranked among the top 10 courses in continental Europe and one of Portugal's very best layouts, **San Lorenzo,** designed by Joe Lee in 1988, was treated to a makeover in the 1990s. The masterly layout, the most visually striking in the Algarve, sits beside the Ria Formosa Nature Reserve, a tidal estuary that serves as a staging area for migratory birds. Not only are the holes along the estuary unforgettable, but the panoramic views of the ocean, forest, dunes, and mountains are sublime. Golf-wise, the well-groomed layout artfully blends the demanding and the dramatic. Higher handicappers who play it safe will enjoy the course, but better players will be tantalized by the risk-reward scenarios. The button-hook-shaped par-four 18th, with water to the left of the narrow fairway and a tiny peninsula green projected into the estuary, is a controversial but somehow fitting finale to the round.

The golf course is attached to **Le Meridien Dona Filipa,** a well-situated, 154-room hotel on the Vale do Lobo estate with a heated outdoor pool and two fine restaurants, the Dom Duarte (formal dining) and the Primavera (a la carte Italian). San Lorenzo is a short courtesy bus ride from the hotel.

Vale do Lobo, Royal Course, 16th hole

The marquee course at the venerable **Le Meridien Penina Golf Resort** is one of the longest, flattest, and most challenging in the Algarve. Fashioned by Sir Henry Cotton from a field of sodden, brackish rice paddies, the brawny par-73 layout, framed by towering fir and eucalyptus trees, is a test for the best from the tips. A 10-time host of the Portuguese Open, most recently in 2006, the layout, crisscrossed by waterways and pockmarked with numerous bunkers, looks better than ever in the wake of a facelift. The resort also has two sporty nine-holers for casual play.

The resort, built in the 1960s by an English family with rice producing and port wine interests in the north of Portugal, still retains a traditional Brit-ish flavor. In addition to a good variety of spacious accommodations, most with balconies overlooking the golf courses, the resort maintains its own clubhouse at the beach, a five-minute shuttle bus ride from the hotel. There are five restaurants at the hotel, but most golfers usually make a detour to Sir Henry Cotton's Club, a classic 19th-hole bar.

The original layout by Henry Cotton at **Vale do Lobo** ("Valley of the Wolf") has since been expanded into the Royal and Ocean courses. If there's an American look and feel to the **Royal Course,** it's because Rocky Roquemore, who worked with the late Joe Lee on several Algarve projects,

Quinta do Logo, 17th hole

upgraded Cotton's core 18 in the late 1990s. The layout is celebrated for one of the most thrilling and photographed holes in all of Europe. This is the par-three 16th hole (formerly the seventh on the Yellow course), a daunting one-shotter propped on honey-colored bluffs more than 100 feet above the beach far below to the left. From the back tees at 224 yards, the tee shot must carry a gap-toothed pair of indentations in the sandstone cliffs and hold a green fronted by a yawning bunker.

Vale do Lobo's shorter **Ocean Course,** cobbled together from the former Green and Orange nines, winds through umbrella pines and offers a firm, fair test. In 2003, redevelopment work on the Ocean's first and ninth holes created two entirely new holes, each longer and more difficult than their predecessors.

One of the Algarve's landmark developments, **Quinta do Lago** ("Farmhouse on the Lagoon") offers 36 holes. The **South Course,** created from what was

while a little shorter than the South, offers an imaginative and well-varied test sprinkled with great par fives that require both power and accuracy to play them well. With two exceptions (at holes 10 and 13), all the par fours on the North are doglegs that demand precise tee shots.

The **Hotel Quinta do Lago,** one of the most luxurious resorts in the Algarve, is spread across a rolling, wooded 2,000-acre estate flanked by a golden-sand beach and the Ria Formosa tidal inlet. The resort is built around four lakes, one of which is used for "non-polluting" sports such as sailing and windsurfing. If horseback riding is your pleasure, be sure to pack some boots along with your golf shoes—the resort has some of the finest riding trails in southern Europe. The hotel itself offers 141 rooms, each with private terrace. The two restaurants are superb. Ca d'Oro serves fine Venetian cuisine in an elegant room, while Briso do Mar features Portuguese specialties.

TOP NEWCOMERS

Located at the western end of the Algarve, **Boavista Resort** is perched on a headland high above the Atlantic, with views to Praia de Luz on one side and the Bay of Lagos on the other. There are also fine panoramas of the distant Monchique mountains and, from the seventh hole, the headland at Sagres, the southernmost point in continental Europe. Designed by Englishman Howard Swan, the layout, opened in 2001, traces the natural contour of the hillsides and incorporates in the strategy of the holes a system of interconnected lakes. The collection of par threes is unusually strong, while the greens are quite large and very undulating.

Located inland from Portimao and Penina in the foothills of the Monchique mountains, **Morgado do Reguengo,** a rolling course that debuted in 2003, is laid out on a former private estate marked with small, undulating valleys and dotted with lakes. The par-73 course doubles as a prized waterfowl habitat. The front nine traces a now-dry riverbed; the back nine meanders along gently undulating slopes above it. Wind, as is usual on the Algarve, plays a key role in the challenge of the holes, according to architect Russell Talley of European Golf Design. So do the deep, well-placed bunkers. A second 18-hole course is already underway.

Located roughly midway between Lagos and Faro in the center of the Algarve, the original 1995 design at **Salgados,** by Portuguese architect Pedro de Vasconcelos, was later restyled by American Robert Muir Graves. The course is not overly long, yet nearly every hole brings a water hazard into play. Placement, not raw distance, is the order of the day, as an accu-

known as the B and C nines, was laid out by the American designer William Mitchell in 1973. This time-honored test, a seven-time site of the Portuguese Open, has water in play on several holes and fine views of the sea from its elevated tees.

Quinta do Lago's **North Course,** formerly known as Ria Formosa, combines the subtle artistry of a Mitchell-designed nine with a newer compilation of holes laid out by Rocky Roquemore. The seemingly disparate designs are an asset: the North Course,

Briso do Mar restaurant at Hotel Quinta do Lago

rate drive will set up an approach to the well-guarded but relatively flat greens.

The first of two courses opened in 2002 east of Faro, the Rocky Roquemore–designed **Quinta da Ria** layout occupies gently rolling land between Tavira and the foothills of the Serra do Caldeirao. Because of its location at the eastern boundary of the Ria Formosa Nature Reserve, hundreds of trees— olive, carob, oak, and almond—were transplanted during course construction. Also, five lakes were built for irrigation and come into play frequently on the back nine. In addition to mountain and sea views, citrus groves and vineyards surround the course.

Located near Quinta da Ria is **Quinta de Cima,** another Rocky Roquemore creation, which shares comparable scenery and also debuted in 2002. The inspired routing features a good mix of holes that bend left and right. The smooth bentgrass greens are well-defended by sand or water or both, particularly at the finish. The layout, a little shorter but no less challenging than Quinta da Ria, is characterized by a series of lakes connected by a stream with dams, with flowing water crossing a number of holes.

Situated at the now-blossoming eastern end of the Algarve near Tavira, **Castro Marim** was unveiled in

2000. In addition to beautiful views over the Atlantic Ocean, the River Guadiana, and a nearby nature reserve, the so-called "Atlantic Course" at Castro Marim makes good use of the rolling terrain and the many ornamental lakes that sprinkle the site. Prevailing onshore winds dictate strategy at the layout's more exposed holes.

ONE TO WATCH

Located in the eastern Algarve near the Spanish border, **Monte Rei Golf & Country Club** is a 36-hole project that represents Jack Nicklaus's first design foray into Portugal. Routed among rolling hills and valleys, the first of the two courses was slated to open in 2006, with the second to follow shortly afterwards. The development, which will feature low-density housing, is set on 1,000 acres near Tavira. When completed, the layouts will offer panoramic views of the sea; both are backdropped by the dramatic Serra do Caldeirao mountains. To lend the courses maturity, indigenous shrubs and flowers have been transplanted alongside the fairways. This vegetation complements the thousands of trees that have already been planted throughout the site.

Horseback riding at Quinta do Lago

DAY TRIP/PORTIMAO

Sardines, those tiny members of the herring family, rarely are sold fresh at fish markets. Even more than tuna, sardines are closely associated with a tin can, and a key-opened one at that. But in the Algarve, *Sardina picchardus* grows to a length of 10 inches and makes for one of the most appetizing seafood lunches in southern Europe.

The sardines make their way from boat to plate via a hardy breed of fishermen who in the middle of the night motor their heavy trawlers into the chilly Atlantic, where they surround large shoals of the fish with purse seine nets (a style of fishing adapted from the Carthaginians) and return to port in mid-morning with their catch.

Portimao, one of the Algarve's busiest seaside towns, is a good place to observe the return of the fleet. Owners of sidewalk cafes stop by to place their orders and carry their purchases a few hundred yards to their establishments. There the fish are cleaned and sprinkled with rock salt. Shortly after noon, patrons begin to arrive at a string of alfresco charcoal grills situated along the estuary near the town's old iron bridge. Men in plastic aprons guide passersby to tightly packed café tables, where the table d'hote is a heaping plate of grilled sardines. For a pittance, diners receive a dozen large sardines cooked, as the food reviewers say, to "moist perfection." Needless to say, Portimao's fresh-grilled sardines are miles beyond the canned variety in taste.

After lunch, there is ample opportunity to tilt back your head, close your eyes, and feel the warmth of the Algarvian sun, which shines often. Even with their molded plastic chairs and unsteady little tables, Portimao's cafes are a fine place to observe the passing scene of a town reputedly founded by Hannibal before he got involved in difficult alpine crossings.

DAY TRIP/SAGRES

For anyone with a sense of history and an appreciation of geography, a drive to Sagres and Cabo de Sao Vicente in the western Algarve is a must. As the road nears the most southwesterly point in Europe, the land turns stony and desolate. Goat tracks crisscross the moors atop the cliffs. Fishermen inch down the lichen-covered rocks to secure a foothold in the cliffs. At the very tip of the wind-blasted promontory, huge rollers thunder into the rocks, the water churned to a milky froth. It was here that Henry the Navigator assembled the finest seamen and navigators of his day to launch the Age of Discovery in the 15th century, here where the Old World ends and the new begins, here where—unless you knew better—the world really looks rather flat.

Czech Republic

Sweeping political changes in the early 1990s caused the Iron Curtain to crumble and disintegrate as Communism fell. Of course, several nations in central Europe had a tradition of playing golf that predates World War I—the first Hungarian golf club was formed in 1889 in what is now Slovakia. With nations of the former Eastern Bloc trying to get their arms around democracy, plans are afoot to renovate old courses and build new ones. At present, the Czech Republic is setting the pace. (Bulgaria, based on a pair of Gary Player designs set to open in 2007–08 and a Jack Nicklaus project on the drawing board, also bears watching.)

The geographic center of Europe and the only country in which golf was still played during the Communist era, the Czech Republic, half of what was formerly known as Czechoslovakia, has a long tradition of top quality golf. The country's first golf courses were established 70 miles west of Prague in the spa towns of Karlovy Vary (1904) and Marianske Lazne (1905). With the fall of the Iron Curtain, the resorts and courses of the West Bohemia area, tucked among rolling, wooded hills, are returning to the elite status they once enjoyed. Spring, when the fruit trees lining the roads are in bloom, is the best time to visit this sleeper destination.

Formerly known by its Austrian name of Karlsbad, **Karlovy Vary's** original nine-holer was established in 1904 in an exceedingly lovely valley. The current 18-hole course was built in 1932, but was later refined by shareholders that included the stately Grandhotel Pupp-Moskva (founded in the early 1700s and one of Europe's oldest surviving hotels). The layout, with distant mountains backdropping its rolling fairways, is one of the prettiest in central Europe. A luxurious clubhouse built in 1997, its terrace overlooking the 18th hole, is a perfect complement to the layout.

Marianske Lazne, known as Marienbad in Germany, was established as a spa in 1808 and was patronized by such notables as Richard Wagner and King Edward VII of England. The golf course, the nation's oldest 18-hole layout, is a compact parkland spread set at 600 meters above sea level. Like Karlovy Vary, the course, anchored by a beautifully restored

Golfpark Plzen, 11th hole

Belle Epoque–style clubhouse, is a charmer from another time.

Located in the far west of the Czech Republic near the German border, **Frantiskovy Lazne,** opened in 2002, is set near the West Bohemia region's famous spa towns and historic places of interest. A solid test carved through the rolling countryside, the layout features undulating fairways framed by hardwoods and pines, with well-contoured greens.

Situated near the village of Darova in the picturesque Berounka river valley, **Darovansky Dvur Golf Resort** is a full-service resort (including a luxury hotel and a heated covered pool) that offers a plethora of activities, including mountain biking, canoeing, and river rafting. In addition to a challenging, full-length 18-hole course, there's a sporty nine-hole course.

Gary Player, who prides himself on designing courses in some of the far corners of the globe, recently laid out the par-70 spread at **Cihelny,** which is located in a lovely valley on the river Tepla not far from Karlovy Vary and on the way to Marianske Lazne. Boasting one of the largest practice centers in Eastern Europe, Cihelny, in addition to the full-sized 18, also offers a pitch-and-putt layout.

Set among birch and alder groves, **Golfpark Plzen** is an attractive resort course located near the famous town of Pilsen, which has produced world-famous Pilsner Urquell beer since the Middle Ages. The par-71 golf course, designed by Christoph Stadler, is embraced by the Klabava river and the placid Ejpovice lake. The resort is conveniently located off the highway an hour's drive from Prague.

Located 30 miles southwest of the city is **Golf Resort Karlstejn,** a superb layout by Canadian designers Les Furber and Jim Eremko that is spread across 250 hilly acres at the edge of the tree-covered valley of Berounka. Opened in 1995, the course is a favorite of Czech executives. Heaving fairways and elevated tees serve up fine views of the white towers and red-slate roofs of the 14th-century Karlstejn Castle built by Charles IV. Site of the Czech Open on several occasions, the challenge at hand on this championship-class course is riveting: Clever doglegs hinged on huge fairway bunkers skirt rivers and ponds and lead to tricky greens.

Moving to the southeast of Prague, a noteworthy newcomer is **Golf Resort Konopiste,** unveiled in 2002 and boasting 27 holes, with a fourth nine on the way. The layout rambles through rolling, wooded hills, with hazards discreetly deployed. The resort's refurbished Manor House doubles as an excellent hotel and conference center.

Grandhotel Pupp-Moskva in Karlovy Vary

Scandinavia

Think of Scandinavia as a midsummer night's fairy-tale of Vikings and trolls, of saunas and smorgasbords, of lakes, canals, and fjords, and a golf season that, while short, is enjoyed to the fullest by natives and visitors alike. Often overlooked in the pantheon of Europe's top golf destinations, Scandinavia, peaceful, safe, and pristine, offers majestic open spaces and increasingly is finding room for new courses. This is especially true in Sweden and Finland.

Now that Annika Sorenstam has achieved iconic status as one of the game's greatest players, her home country has loomed into focus as a destination.

With nearly 500,000 players for nearly 300 18-hole courses, Sweden, where the game is an egalitarian affair, is one of Europe's leading golf nations. In fact, the only country in Europe with more golfers is the United Kingdom. The quality of the golf is catching up, especially with four new projects scheduled to open in 2006–08.

Situated on a beautiful, sand-based site, a 27-hole layout by Nicklaus Design is taking shape in the town of Habo overlooking Lake Vattern, Sweden's second-largest lake. Known as **Branninge Golf & Country Club,** the course, slated to open in 2007–08, winds

Kytaja Golf, seventh hole

through dense pine forest and open fields, with meandering creeks in play. Branninge, which traces its origins to the 18th century, has an old farmhouse that will be converted into a hotel and restaurant.

Located in the major seaport of Gothenburg, a pleasant city of wide avenues and verdant parks on Sweden's west coast, is **Hills Golf Club**, scheduled to open in 2006. The course will measure over 7,700 yards from the back tees, making it one of the longest courses close to sea level in all of Europe. Designed by Arthur Hills,

the club has dramatic elevation changes and may develop into Sweden's most rigorous test of golf.

Hills also is designing **Sand Golf Club** in Jonkoping, located not far from the Nicklaus course at Branninge. The course, which is being carved out of rolling, wooded terrain, is slated to open in 2006, with European and PGA Tour performer Fredrik Jacobson acting as player-consultant.

The PGA of Sweden National Golf Resort, near Malmo and a 30-minute drive via bridge and tunnel from Copenhagen Airport in Denmark, will be one of the epicenters of Swedish golf when it debuts in

Oulu Golf Club, fourth hole

2007–08. Designed by American architect Kyle Phillips, a former Robert Trent Jones, Jr. design associate who has made a name for himself in Europe, the first phase of this ambitious development will feature two full-sized 18-hole layouts intended for championship play, plus a complete practice center and a nine-hole par-three course.

The growth over the past two decades or so has been dramatic in Finland. Despite the relatively short season (May to September), Finland has over 100 courses to offer, most of them built since 1980. More than 20 layouts can be found within an hour's drive of Helsinki, a beautiful seaside city renowned for its cultural offerings. Players who spray the ball may wish to invest in a ball-retriever before heading to Finland. The nation counts nearly 188,000 lakes greater than two acres in size!

Located on the outskirts of Helsinki an hour's drive from St. Petersburg (the Russian one), **Kytaja Golf** is Finland's top newcomer. The sprawling 11,000-acre complex, built by a Finnish timber-and-mining baron, features two premier courses by Canadian designer Tom McBroom, with a third venue expected to open in 2006–7. Kytaja's **South East** course, debuted in 2003, is a beautifully sculpted parkland-style layout dotted with deep bunkers. The facility's **North West** course, unveiled in 2004, is a

rugged yet refined layout cut through firs and pines high above the shores of a pristine lake that borders the back nine of the South East course.

Way up in the north of Finland, a few courses offer round-the-clock golf during the endless days of the midnight sun from June to August. Among the newcomers are a pair of layouts by Ron Fream, the globetrotting American designer. A mere 60 miles from the Arctic Circle is **Oulu Golf Club,** which dates to 1992 and is well-known for its Midnight Golf competitions. Laid out in a forest among hilly moors and small ponds near the Saginjoki River, Oulu debuted a third nine by Fream in 2004 and at press time was adding a fourth nine to accommodate rising play. (The club typically registers more than 50,000 rounds per year).

Not far from Oulu is **Paltamo Golf,** which made an informal debut in 1992. Fream completed the final five holes on the course, considered one of the most beautiful in Finland, in 2000. Several of the holes trace the shoreline of Lake Oulujarvi, with trees, cliffs, and ponds in play throughout. Visiting players will find a warm welcome at the nearby **Katinkulta Resort & Spa,** which has a fine 18-hole course of its own and is classed among the finest resorts in Scandinavia.

Austria

Hailed by the International Association of Golf Tour Operators as the "Undiscovered Golf Destination of the Year" in 2004, Austria, known mainly for Mozart, mountains, and *The Sound of Music*, offers nearly 140 courses stretching from the skyscraping Alps in the west to the sophisticated capital of Vienna in the east.

Austria, it should be noted, is no Palm Springs or Pinehurst as a golf destination. Many of its courses are modest nine-holers, though the clubhouse amenities and practice facilities are generally excellent, as are the numerous four- and five-star hotels in close proximity to the venues. And, in addition to the majestic alpine panoramas, the people of Austria offer a warm and friendly welcome, a take-things-as-they-come attitude known as *Gemütlichkeit*.

The most outstanding newcomer in Austria is **Golf Eichenheim,** an epic and memorable test conjured by American designer Kyle Phillips in a picturesque region outside the postcard Tyrolean town of Kitzbühel. Steep rocky slopes and thick deciduous forests characterize the 6,750-yard, par-71 layout, which opened in 2001 and already is considered to be Austria's finest course. Sharp doglegs, huge bunkers, and thick rough place a premium on accuracy. Fearlessness comes in handy, too. More than one hole, for example, calls for a tee shot over a 200-foot-deep precipice. But it is the aesthetic diversions that set this brilliant layout apart. Backdropping several fairways is the awesome Wilder Kaiser ("Wild King") mountain range, its lofty spires, deep gorges, and sheer granite cliffs providing a spellbinding backdrop for the game. At press time, the club had an upscale hotel under construction on site.

Golf Eichenheim, third hole

Golf Eichenheim, 13th hole

France

With two coastlines, towering mountains, winding rivers, famous vineyards, the City of Lights, and a Gallic populace that has perfected the art of living, France has everything a visitor could want in a European vacation. That includes scores of underappreciated golf courses, many of them built in the 1980s and '90s. At present, there are roughly 500 golf courses scattered around the country, but the region that strikes the most resonance with travelers is the south of France, notably the magical region of Provence, a sun-drenched land set back from the Mediterranean.

Renowned for its flavorsome cuisine, delicate rosé wines, and exquisite landscapes, the south of France is also known for its sunlight, from soft and gauzy to hard and brittle. Van Gogh lived and painted in the city of Arles, while Paul Cezanne settled in Aix-en-Provence to drink in the climate, the culture, the light. In 1961, Picasso moved to Mougins, a storybook village tucked in the hills above Cannes, where he lived until his death in 1973. Mougins and other tiny settlements set inland from the sea are bathed in luminous light, a fact not lost on visiting players who find their way to the well-known courses stretched along the glamorous French Riviera between Nice in the east and St. Tropez in the west, with Cannes in the middle. Royal Mougins, La Grande Bastide, Cannes-Mougins, Saint Donat, Esterel Latitudes, Opio-Valbonne—these are among the stellar layouts in the south of France. However, given the preciousness of real estate along the coast and in the hills above the sea, there is scant room left for golf, which is why enterprising developers have pushed deep into the interior regions of Provence to turn up new sites for the game.

In a secluded domain near the village of Fayence an hour's drive from Nice and even closer to the Cote d'Azur's fabled playgrounds is **Four Seasons Resort Provence at Terre Blanche,** the luxury chain's first resort in Europe. Built by SAP co-founder Dietmar Hopp, Europe's answer to Bill Gates, the low-rise complex, opened in 2004, looks from its wooded perch to limestone-specked hills, huddled medieval villages, and distant peaks in the Alpes-Maritimes.

Hopp, an avid golfer, brought in Englishman Dave Thomas, a former tour pro with over 100 designs to his credit, to build two courses. **Le Chateau,** championship-caliber at 7,235 yards, is a straightforward parkland test bellied into a valley, its pitfalls and perils—rock-lined creeks, man-made lakes, grass-faced bunkers—in plain view. The most distinctive hole is the par-five sixth, both for its crook-shaped fairway indented by water and the austere 19th-century cha-

teau that sits high above the green. (The edifice once belonged to Sean Connery.)

The second course, **Le Riou,** occupies the domain's upper valley, its shorter, narrower holes carved from oak- and pine-clad hills. What it lacks in length, the 6,567-yard course more than repays with steep drops, sharply-angled doglegs, and liberally-contoured greens. Le Chateau is sober and stern; Le Riou is sportier and more scenic. Both courses are extremely well-groomed. At their center is an elegant clubhouse, its terrace restaurant overlooking Le Riou's water-

Four Seasons Resort Provence at Terre Blanche, Le Chateau, 10th hole

guarded 18th hole. Luxurious locker rooms and a boutique-style golf shop are complemented by an excellent practice facility and golf academy. Golf is played year-round in Fayence, but spring, when the air is rich with the scents of rosemary, thyme, and wild lavender, is the time to go.

The resort's 115 suites, housed in one- and two-story hillside villas, are connected by meandering walkways landscaped with bougainvillea and other flowering shrubs. The ochre-colored, barrel-roofed villas are plain on the outside, but interiors offer a sleek, sophisticated interpretation of Provence, with natural wood and stone finishes accented by rattan chairs, loose-weave rugs, terra-cotta headboards, and vibrant artwork. French doors open onto a private terrace. This is a relaxing, tranquil retreat with a full-service spa and infinity-edge pool. The resort's main restaurant, Faventia, serves eclectic Mediterranean cuisine turned out by Phillippe Jourdin, who earned his stripes at Tour d'Argent in Paris.

Cyprus

Situated off the southern coast of Turkey, Cyprus, the third largest island in the Mediterranean, lies at the crossroads of ancient civilizations. After decades of British rule, Cyprus won its independence in 1960 for the first time in 3,500 years. Turkey occupied the northern third of Cyprus in 1974 but the southern two-thirds, inhabited mainly by Greek Cypriots, is the only part of the rugged island to receive international recognition and is where golf has taken root.

The island's first grass course, **Tsada Golf Club,** debuted in 1994 and is located on the western tip of the island near Paphos, a small, charming harbor town located near the Tombs of the Kings, an early necropolis marked by Doric columns and dating to the fourth century B.C. The golf course, laid out by Donald Steel on the grounds of a 12th-century monastery at 1,650 feet above sea level, is swept by cool breezes and framed by citrus groves, vineyards, and trees. Holes move gently uphill and downhill, with the undulating terrain and well-placed bunkers heightening the challenge.

Laid out in a lovely valley dotted with colorful rock formations and staked out by specimen trees and beds of flowers, **Secret Valley Golf Club** was the island's second course, welcoming players in 1996. Situated on the opposite side of Paphos convenient to Limassol, the island's wine-making center, Secret Valley offers a pleasant, scenic test. The course is not long, and the front nine is padded with four relatively easy holes, but the longer, tougher back nine, marked by several water hazards, presents a formidable challenge.

The top newcomer is **Aphrodite Hills,** unveiled in 2002 as the first integrated golf, leisure, and real

Massage pavilion at InterContinental Aphrodite Hills Resort

Aphrodite Hills, fifth hole

estate development to open in Cyprus. Located on the outskirts of Paphos near "Petra tou Romiou," the legendary birthplace of Aphrodite, the Goddess of Love, the golf course, designed by Cabell Robinson, is a magnificent championship-caliber track with five sets of tees per hole. The fairways, carved from thick groves of carob and olive trees, occupy two high plateaus divided by a plunging ravine. All but a handful of holes at Aphrodite Hills command superb views of the Mediterranean from a prospect nearly a thousand feet above the sea. Fairways are generously wide, though cloverleaf-shaped bunkers defend the prime landing areas. The large, sloping greens are well-defended by sand.

Ranked among the region's most thrilling one-shotters is the seventh, its tee box a narrow platform cut from the side of a deep, trenchlike ravine. The tee shot is played across the chasm to an undulating green tucked in a grove of olive trees more than 100 feet below the tee. An easy pitch for Zeus; difficult for mere mortals. Needless to say, golf carts are mandatory given the ruggedness of the terrain at Aphrodite Hills.

The golf course is attached to the **InterContinental Aphrodite Hills Resort,** a 290-room hotel opened in 2004. The resort offers the Retreat, an authentic Greco-Roman thermae, its series of rooms of varying temperature combined with cooling showers; indoor and outdoor pools; and four restaurants, including Mesogios, which features fine Mediterranean cuisine served on an open-air terrace overlooking the course and sea.

A five-minute drive from the resort is "Petra tou Romiou," also known as Aphrodite's Rock. According to legend, Aphrodite, the patron goddess of Cyprus and the mythological personification of love and beauty, is said to have risen naked and perfect from the sea foam. There were other pre-Hellenic fertility deities on Cyprus, but Aphrodite reigned supreme.

Rest of the World

With roughly half the world's golfers located outside the U.S., up-and-coming destinations beyond the shores of America offer the greatest potential for growth. In fact, golf is just beginning to flex its global muscles as more and more nations embrace the ancient game.

Curiously, much of the game's expansion is being realized in places not ordinarily associated with the game. A British heritage explains in part the growth of golf in Australia, New Zealand, and South Africa. But how to explain the golf bug catching in places as disparate as China and Dubai? It boils down to the game's intrinsic appeal as well as its status as a sport that attracts upscale visitors. So long as land is available, enterprising developers worldwide will continue to build golf courses to satisfy what they believe is a pent-up demand for the game.

Terravista Golf Club, Brazil

Dubai

One of seven sheikhdoms within the United Arab Emirates and by far its most glamorous, Dubai is *sui generis*, a booming destination born of hubris and vision and money. Located on the western shore of the Persian Gulf, Dubai, a former pearl-diving center and smuggler's haven, has in a very short period of time asserted itself as the business goliath of the Middle East as well as a major tourism player.

Dubai's push for visitors came out of necessity. With oil, the mainspring of its economy, running low, the crown prince and sultans of Dubai concluded that the best way to prepare for the day some three decades hence when the oil runs dry was to exploit the city-state's salubrious climate and reinvent itself as a financial center, duty-free shopping mecca, and luxury travel destination rolled into one. Heavily westernized, with hundreds of technology companies among its tenants, the traditional Arab culture is nearly absent in Dubai, where more than 80 percent of the population of about one million are expatriates hailing from more than 160 nations.

Despite the strife in the Middle East, Dubai is the fastest-growing tourist destination on earth, according to the World Tourism Organization. It's not from doing much to attract travelers on a budget. Nearly all of Dubai's major developments are either ultra-luxe or over the top. Dubai's standout hotel is the spinnaker-shaped, 1,053-foot Burj Al Arab, which bills itself as "the world's most luxurious hotel" and, with rates starting at just under $1,000 per night, is also one of the most expensive.

Golf, of course, is a part of the boundless enthusiasm for all things new and fun in Dubai. The model for Dubai's top venues is the upscale American country club. From golf carts outfitted with automated GPS yardage devices and roving beverage carts to clubhouses with fine dining rooms and golf shops stocked with designer apparel, Dubai has taken ultra-luxe to another level.

Fall, winter, and spring are the best (and perhaps only) seasons to visit Dubai for golf—summer temperatures often exceed 115 degrees.

Emirates Golf Club and its Bedouin village-style clubhouse

The Montgomerie, Dubai, ninth hole

The Majlis Course at **Emirates Golf Club,** opened in 1988, was the first grass golf course in the Middle East. Laid out by American designer Karl Litten on rolling desert terrain, the beautifully landscaped, 7,101-yard course, long-time host of the European Tour's Dubai Desert Classic, swings around huge waste bunkers. Majlis was followed by a second Litten-designed venue, the **Wadi Course,** in 1996. Its signature feature is a landscaped river that flows through the layout. At press time, the Wadi Course was undergoing a redesign by Nick Faldo. Both courses are served by a spectacular clubhouse designed to resemble a tented Bedouin village.

First opened in 1993, **Dubai Creek Golf and Yacht Club,** a traditional parkland-style test known for mature date and coconut palms lining its fairways, underwent a major transformation in 2004. European PGA Tour star Thomas Bjorn, a Dane who is based in Dubai, was brought in to completely redesign the front nine to boost its challenge and add strategic interest. Dubai Creek's back nine has remained virtually unchanged, though at press time

plans had been hatched for a new par-five signature 18th hole to be built along the peninsula. Dubai Creek's clubhouse, designed to resemble the sails of a traditional Arab dhow (lateen-rigged boat), is a local landmark. The course is the centerpiece of a resort that includes a Park Hyatt hotel and spa, a 121-berth marina, yacht club, and other leisure facilities.

The Montgomerie, Dubai, designed by Scottish pro Colin Montgomerie and the late Desmond Muirhead, is an exquisite test of golf that significantly boosted Dubai's appeal as a golf destination when it opened in 2002. The well-groomed layout, marked by undulating fairways, has the look of a Scottish links course, except for the 14 lakes. The notorious par-three 13th plays to a 58,000-square-foot green that is reputedly the world's largest and is designed in the shape of the United Arab Emirates, though most golfers will be too busy trying to avoid three- or four-putting to notice. A grand clubhouse, unveiled in 2005, features 21 luxuriously appointed guest rooms with butler service.

The only way to really beat the desert heat is to play at night, and **Nad Al Sheba,** a floodlit, links-

The distinctive clubhouse at Dubai Creek Golf and Yacht Club

style layout provides the opportunity. The back nine is built inside the oval of the Nad Al Sheba Race Course, home to the Dubai World Cup, the world's richest horse race, with the front nine routed along the track's home stretch. Night or day, this 6,503-yard, par-71 layout offers a pleasant test.

Opened in 2004, **Arabian Ranches Golf Club,** designed by Ian Baker-Finch in association with Nicklaus Design, eschews water hazards and instead embraces the desert, which serves as an enormous, everpresent bunker. According to Baker-Finch, the 1991 British Open champion and a golf analyst for ABC Sports, "Our design concept for this course was to build a true desert-style course similar to those found in Palm Springs and Scottsdale." The site, he added, is "rich with gently rolling sand dunes that allowed us to literally melt the golf holes into the existing terrain." The lush tees, fairways, and greens, framed by the barren desert, create a dramatic contrast on a target-style links that stretches to 7,698 yards and is rated by many as the toughest course in town. A second course is expected to open at a later date.

Another newcomer, opened in 2005, is **Al Badia Golf Resort,** located within Dubai Festival City, the waterfront "city-within-a-city." The Robert Trent Jones, Jr.–designed layout stretches along the eastern bank of Dubai Creek, an inlet of the Gulf and one of the world's oldest seaports. Centerpiece of an enormous mixed-use development—the golf course is but one of 15 distinct zones within Dubai Festival City—Al Badia ("Land of the Bedouins") is an oasis-like layout marked by 11 lakes as well as several gently flowing streams that feed into Dubai Creek. In addition, sculpted fairways are pinched by waste areas that Jones calls "rivers of sand." Late afternoon, when long shadows created by the design features are cast across the links, is the best time to appreciate Jones's artistry.

An eco-sensitive creation, Al Badia utilizes salt-tolerant paspalum grass, which can be irrigated with brackish or tertiary water. An iconic blue glass, golden-roofed clubhouse overlooking the ninth and 18th holes is slated to open in 2006.

In addition to the golf complex, Dubai Festival City's first phase includes a marina, a waterfront

Thoroughbred racing at Nad Al Sheba Race Course

promenade and canal with water taxi transport, over 400 retail outlets from around the world, more than 100 international restaurants, a 600-room resort hotel, and a Mediterranean-style residential community.

ONES TO WATCH

Nakheel, one of Dubai's top property development companies, has formed a golf division and hired Greg Norman to build four courses at **Jumeirah Golf Estates,** a gated residential community on The Palm Jumeirah, a huge man-made island being built in the Gulf. These environmentally-themed courses, inspired by the elements of Earth, Fire, Air, and Water, have been branded as "Eco-Signature" courses. Along with dramatic elevation changes, a first for Dubai, the Earth course will accent indigenous flora, including olive, date, and fig trees. The Earth and Fire courses are scheduled to open in 2006–07, with the Air and Water courses to follow.

Nakheel Golf is also building **The Lost City,** a development that will accurately recreate several old lost cities from various parts of the ancient world. The Lost City's Norman-designed golf course, dubbed **The Inspiration,** will be based on a recreation of Norman's favorite holes from around the world, to include six each from the Americas, Europe, and Australia.

A 50-million-square-foot mixed-use metropolis that purports to be the world's first integrated purpose-built sports city, **Dubai Sports City** will be situated within the confines of a $5 billion entertainment complex called Dubailand. Slated to open in 2007, Dubailand, twice the size of Disney World, will feature aquatic- and dinosaur-themed amusement parks, a space-age hotel, and the world's largest shopping center. The centerpiece of Dubai Sports City will be **The Dunes,** an Ernie Els–designed course in Victory Heights, a gated residential community. Says Els, "Unlike, say, the nearby Emirates Golf Club, which is very manicured with lots of water hazards, The Dunes is going to have a more natural look and feel about it."

South Africa

Blemished for years by the stain of apartheid, South Africa recast its destiny in 1990 following the release of long-jailed leader Nelson Mandela. In its post-liberation era, South Africa has blossomed into a prime destination for visitors, many of whom are drawn to Africa's top game parks. Much like Australia, South Africa is absolutely mad for sports, from rugby and cricket to soccer and golf.

In addition to the more than 400 courses sprinkled across the tip of the continent, several new projects by the game's top designers are currently taking shape across the land. All the ingredients for world-class resort golf are found here: temperate weather, dramatic landscapes, excellent hotels, superb cuisine with wines to match, and the bonus element of neighboring game parks where one or more of the "Big Five"—elephant, rhino, lion, leopard, and buffalo—can be viewed.

Like most nations where the British asserted themselves, South Africa has a strong golf heritage. It's a little known fact, but the South African Open is older than the U.S. Open. But it's the new courses on the drawing board that will soon elevate this forward-looking nation into an elite group of the world's most desirable destinations.

South Africa's most promising new developments can be found along the Garden Route, a resplendent coastal plateau bounded by the Indian Ocean on one side and mountain ranges on the other. The Route is perhaps misnamed. There are gardens, yes, but here sheer cliffs plunge into the roiling sea, golden beaches stretch away from charming coastal villages, amber-colored rivers flow from fertile valleys, and rugged peaks in the Outeniqua Mountains rise behind the serrated coast. Located four hours east of Cape Town, the Eastern Cape, as it is known, also embraces South Africa's largest remaining indigenous forest. The town of George, which occupies a coastal plateau at the foot of the mountains and is the nation's sixth-oldest city, is the unofficial gateway to the Garden Route and its many new golf projects.

Outdoor terrace at Fancourt Hotel

Fancourt Hotel and Country Club Estate, Links, 14th hole

The finest resort in the area—and the nation—is the **Fancourt Hotel and Country Club Estate.** Located on the outskirts of George, the resort's beginnings date to 1847, when Henry Fancourt White established a worker's base at the foot of the Outeniqua Mountains for the construction of the Montagu Pass. The original manor house has been declared a national monument, but many more buildings have been added over the years. Today, Fancourt is a full-service resort with 72 holes of golf, a health spa, swimming pools, squash courts, lawn bowling, luxurious accommodations, and superb restaurants.

Gary Player was the man entrusted with the design of Fancourt's courses. The **Montagu,** debuted in 1989, is a parkland-style spread that originally set the standard for golf course conditioning in South Africa. The course, marked by large, oval bunkers and very slippery greens, is a scenic delight that takes in mountains, lakes, and wildlife. Not content to rest

on its laurels, the resort brought in Scottish designer David McLay Kidd to burnish and lengthen the Montagu. The tastefully revamped course opened in 2005.

Similar in design to the Montagu, Fancourt's **Outeniqua** course, completed in 1997, lacks some of the Montagu's inherent drama but does offer plenty of challenge. The setting is magnificent—blocky mountain peaks, which range in color from blue to amber depending on the light, backdrop holes beautified by flower beds and ponds. A meandering creek on the back nine can prove ruinous to a good score.

The resort's third course, the **Links,** is the one that put Fancourt and South Africa squarely on the international golf map. The Links was the site of the storied 2003 Presidents Cup, where the United States and an International team battled to a tie. The course is probably the greatest something-from-nothing layout Player has ever built. On a former

airfield, Player and his design team moved 700,000 cubic meters of earth and clay to transform the dead-flat land into a facsimile sand dune environment typical of Ireland. Opened in 2000, this windswept 7,234-yard, par-73 behemoth resembles Ballybunion on steroids. Everything is outsized, from the mounds and swales to the monstrous topsy-turvy greens. Currently ranked 59th on *Golf Digest's* list of the "100 Best Courses Outside the United States," the Links at Fancourt is generally grouped among the top three in Africa.

Player later returned to round out Fancourt's golf facilities with **Bramble Hill,** a "pay and play" public facility. (The other three courses are open to members and resort guests only). A parkland-style course with links features, Bramble Hill incorporates a little bit of the other three courses in its design, though it is not as long or as daunting from the tips as the core courses.

ONES TO WATCH

Located five miles outside George, **Oubaai at Herold's Bay** is a budding golf estate overlooking the Indian Ocean and the Gwaing River Valley that is home to the first Ernie Els signature golf course in South Africa. Slated to open in 2006, the Kuwaiti-funded development will feature a championship-caliber golf course that will stretch across a broad peninsula high above the sea. The golf course, designed to minimize environmental impact, will have forest, sea, river, and mountain views. A luxury hotel, golf academy, retail village, restaurants, residential units, and hiking and biking trails are also in the works.

Le Grand George Golf Resort, adjacent to Oubaai, occupies a pristine peninsula between the Indian Ocean and the Gwaing River. Bordered by a densely vegetated valley and the Outeniqua Mountains to the north, the resort's Greg Norman–

One of Sun City's many pools

designed golf course is scheduled to open in 2006–07. The goal, says Norman, is "to preserve a natural, stand-alone rural atmosphere that will deliver a unique golfing experience."

The Jack Nicklaus–designed **St. Francis Links** at the new St. Francis Bay development on the Eastern Cape near Port Elizabeth has the potential to develop into a world-class facility. The seaside estate, backed by a $300 million investment, will feature a 60-room luxury boutique hotel, 120 golf chalets, and 400 homes. A 2007–08 debut is anticipated.

In the northern part of the country is Johannesburg, South Africa's largest city, which was born out of a gold rush in the late 19th century. Two hours to the northwest, another type of gold was struck in the bushveld by Sol Kerzner, who in the late 1970s first imagined and then built **Sun City,** a sprawling resort and casino complex set in a natural ampitheater ringed by the Pilansberg Mountains. A spectacular man-made oasis, Sun City is a fantasy world of lush gardens, gurgling streams, and cascading waterfalls. More than 1,300 guest rooms are found in four different hotels, including the Palace of the Lost City, a sublime 322-room palace fabled to be the royal residence of an ancient king. With its hanging gardens, simulated ocean waves, spectacular 80-foot-high rotunda, and African-themed objets d'art, it's a Cecil B. DeMille epic come to life.

In addition to the Lost City, casino gambling, and several al fresco entertainment areas, there's the **Gary Player Country Club** at Sun City, annual host of the Nedbank Golf Challenge, one of the world's richest pro events. Routed within the crater of an

Gary Player Country Club at Sun City

The Palace of the Lost City

extinct volcano, this long, demanding course opened in 1981. Player returned in 1992 to create the **Lost City Golf Course,** a desert-style layout cut through the bushveld, its gently rolling fairways framed by baobob trees, assorted cacti, and large waste bunkers. In addition to the normal hazards found on a golf course, the infamous 13th hole at Lost City introduces a hazard of another kind. Inhabiting the pond located between the tee and the Africa-shaped green at this par three are nearly 40 crocodiles. Needless to say, golfers are strongly discouraged from retrieving their wayward tee shots from the croc pool. A full-fledged safari can be organized in nearby Pilansberg National Park, a 137,000-acre preserve where rhino, lion, and elephant are plentiful.

ONE TO WATCH

Located 90 minutes north of Johannesburg and an hour's drive from Sun City and Pretoria, **Waterberg,** featuring a first-ever design collaboration between Jack Nicklaus and Ernie Els, combines golf and a major game preserve. The 6,900-acre estate, bordering on one of South Africa's four UNESCO Biosphere Reserves, is centered around a layout that meanders through a lovely valley in the bushveld. Two main rivers and numerous streams crisscross the property. The safari-style golf course, which Nicklaus said could stretch to 8,000 yards given the mile-high altitude, is scheduled to open in 2007.

In addition to residential lots plus golf and bush lodges, Waterberg, a $250-million development, will feature a luxury hotel, conference facilities, and a wellness center. A world-class game reserve on site will offer a predator sanctuary and feature most of the region's major species. In addition, an equestrian center will offer guided horseback safaris. Guided game drives and overnight safaris in tented camps will also be available.

China

Behind what used to be known as the "Bamboo Curtain," golf, along with the Chinese economy, is positively booming in the 21st century. Chairman Mao may have denounced golf as a bourgeois game of millionaires, but his time has come and gone.

The modern history of golf in China, excluding the British colonial presence in Hong Kong, dates only to 1984, when the Chung Shan Hot Springs Golf Club, an Arnold Palmer design, opened in the province of Guangdong not far from Macao, a Portuguese colony on the South China Sea. Since then, nearly 200 golf courses have mushroomed across the mainland, making China one of golf's fast-growing and most promising frontiers.

The world of professional golf has embraced China as a prime venue for its events. In 2005, the prestigious Johnnie Walker Classic was one of five European Tour championships held in China. As many as 11 pro tournaments were tentatively scheduled in the country in 2006. After years of closure during a downturn in the Asian economy, Jack Nicklaus re-opened a design office in Hong Kong in 2003 to oversee his burgeoning projects in the region. At press time, he had 12 courses open for play in China, with another seven in development, including three

in Beijing. Robert Trent Jones, Jr., who has worked extensively in Asia, has designed more than a dozen courses in China since the 1990s.

It's hard to imagine that China only opened its doors to international travelers in the late 1970s, for today the country is the fourth most-visited in the world (behind France, Spain, and the U.S.) and brims with fine hotels.

The largest golf club in China—and on the planet—is **Mission Hills Golf Club.** A sprawling 23,000-acre complex in the Pearl River Delta near the city of Shenzhen an hour's drive north of Hong Kong, Mission Hills boasts no fewer than 10 18-hole courses plus a David Leadbetter Golf Academy, surpassing the eight courses of Pinehurst Resort and Country Club in North Carolina.

The brainchild of Dr. David Chu, the club's chairman and founder, Mission Hills was made possible by Deng Xiaoping's market-oriented reforms, one of which was the designation of Shenzhen as China's first special economic zone in 1980. Since then, what had been a sleepy fishing village near Hong Kong has grown to a city of 10 million. Golf-wise, the region's salubrious climate has been compared to that of

Mission Hills Golf Club, World Cup Course

Jacksonville, Florida, only the Shenzhen area has mountains and denser vegetation.

Just as the Great Wall of China was built one stone at a time, the club got its start in 1994, when Jack Nicklaus designed the first course. A solid test stretching to 7,323 yards, the layout hosted the World Cup of Golf in 1995, an event captured by Americans Fred Couples and Davis Love III. It is now known as the **World Cup Course.**

Following the success of the first course, the Scottsdale, Arizona-based firm of Schmidt-Curley Golf Design was brought in to work with a stellar cast of internationally famous golfers on the next eight courses. There's never been another golf construction project to match it. To complete the task, a labor force of 2,000 worked round-the-clock shifts on the rugged, wooded site, utilizing 700 dump trucks and 250 excavators to move more than 25 million cubic yards of earth. Workers uprooted and transplanted 500,000 trees, laid more than 20 miles of cart paths, and built 36 stone bridges.

The first four of those courses were crafted with Nick Faldo, Ernie Els, Vijay Singh, and Jumbo Ozaki. The final four solicited the design insights of Jose Maria Olazabal, David Duval, David Leadbetter, and Annika Sorenstam. Surprisingly, no two are alike. They run the gamut from the **Olazabal Course,** a daunting 7,356-yard brute staked out by 155 menacing bunkers; to the **Annika Course,** Sorenstam's first stab at golf design and the only course at Mission Hills that measures less than 7,000 yards from the tips. Not surprisingly, this shorter, tighter shot-maker's layout demands precision and accuracy.

Arguably the strongest test of golf at Mission Hills is found on its 10th and final venue, the **Norman Course,** a.k.a. the Tournament Course. Opened in 2004, this 7,214-yard dragon of a layout has already been acclaimed as one of the most difficult and challenging in Asia. The front nine, marked by back-to-back par fives at Nos. 7 and 8, meanders through a succession of small valleys; the back nine, which builds to a very strong finish, is spread across a single large valley walled in by steep slopes. Dense forest and flash-faced bunkers gobble stray shots on nearly every hole.

In essence a gated residential community—a Chinese version of the American model, with British names (Rosedale, Knightsbridge, Mayfair) for its neighborhoods—the club welcomes visitors to a luxurious 315-room hotel. Anchored by a pair of enormous, palatial clubhouses, Mission Hills also has a full-service spa, Asia's largest tennis facility, and a fabulous array of restaurants, from Cantonese to Japanese. Demonstrating a flair for democracy, the

Mission Hills Golf Club, Norman Course

club charges the same price for each course. (At press time, green fee rates ranged from $137.50 weekdays to $206.25 weekends.)

Mission Hills bustles with 4,500 employees, more than half of them caddies. The club has a fleet of 2,000 power carts. One fine day in May of 2004, 2,366 golfers teed it up at Mission Hills, another world record.

More than one commentator has noted that Mission Hills may be the golf equivalent of the Great

Wall of China, the greatest building enterprise ever
undertaken by man. But there's one important difference. The Great Wall was built to repel invaders.
Mission Hills was designed to attract visitors. Judging by the fact that nearly 400,000 players made their
way to Mission Hills in 2004, Dr. Chu, who reportedly spent $400 million to fashion the club from
rural farmland, has realized his dream of creating a
world-class golf destination.

Australia

Melbourne, Australia's second-largest city after Sydney, is a cosmopolitan city and gateway to a geological oddity known as the Sand Belt. Southeast of the city center near the shores of Port Phillip Bay, this 25-square-mile area is characterized by sandy, undulating terrain, native gum and tea trees, and fine-bladed grasses. It is, in short, the perfect medium in which to create naturalistic, links-style golf courses, a fact readily apparent to Alister MacKenzie, who arrived by passenger steamer in 1926 and departed several months later with a handful of masterpieces (notably the West Course at Royal Melbourne) to his credit. There are eight world-class layouts in the Sand Belt. It is, for many, the densest concentration of superlative courses on earth. And while none touch the ocean, they are influenced by sea breezes.

Great as they are, the Sand Belt courses are getting some serious competition from a new generation of courses sketched across the Mornington Peninsula located 90 minutes south of Melbourne. Flanked by Port Phillip Bay and projected into the Bass Strait, this boot-shaped peninsula is home to charming bayside villages, the region's best beaches, and numerous vineyards that produce some of Australia's finest wines. In "The Cups" region along the western coast of the peninsula, heaving dunes, sandy ridges, and rippled ground created by eons of wind and wave action provide a perfect canvas for authentic links golf. The Sand Belt courses are elegant and time-honored, but for a taste of Aussie-style links golf, the Mornington Peninsula, home to the finest collection of coastal layouts in the southern hemisphere, is Scotland and Ireland with better weather. October through April is the best time to visit, though golf is played year-round Down Under.

The Golf Club St. Andrews Beach, Gunnamatta course, 14th hole

The new shining star of the Mornington Peninsula is **The Golf Club St. Andrews Beach,** which will be ranked among the top 36-hole facilities in the world when its second course debuts in 2007. A tall statement? Not when the architect and the land are brought into closer view.

Tom Doak, fresh off his triumph at Pacific Dunes in Oregon and deciding perhaps to emulate Alister MacKenzie, his golf design idol, took on a number of commissions in Australia and New Zealand shortly after the millennium. These plum jobs included Barnbougle Dunes in Tasmania and Cape Kidnappers in New Zealand (see below). Doak took a special liking to the St. Andrews Beach development, and for good reason. The undulating land, a series of large bowls set below sandy ridges, was ideally suited to the creation of genuine links-style courses. According to Doak, "Great golf courses are unquestionably a product of great terrain, and the land at St. Andrews Bay is as good as it gets." The land's built-in defenses, including natural blowouts, deep swales, and tabletop plateaus, were expertly harnessed by Doak in his plotting of two 18-hole layouts as well as a composite course that will utilize nine holes from each design to host championships.

Situated within earshot of the thundering surf at Gunnamatta Beach, the club's first venue opened in 2004. Called the **Gunnamatta** course, this 6,660-yard, par-70 creation is, says Doak, "the easiest golf course I've ever built." One of the few architects working today who has the discipline to leave well enough alone, Doak and his crew displaced fewer than 20,000 cubic yards of material, a pittance. The result is a naturalistic, lay-of-the-land links framed in places by rolling grasslands and ancient Moo-

The Golf Club St. Andrews Beach, Gunnamatta course, fourth hole

nah trees, the strategy of each hole dictated by the strength and direction of the wind.

Free of unnecessary adornments, the Gunnamatta blends into the landscape and flows through billowing hills, its elevated tees serving up magnificent panoramas of the coastal terrain. The greens, well-varied in size and contour, from pulpits to punchbowls, tie in seamlessly with their surrounds. There are only two par fives at Gunnamatta, but the overall range and variety of holes, especially among the shorter par fours, is outstanding.

According to Doak, "In my studies of great courses, short par fours seem to separate the cream from the crop. Courses like Cypress Point, St. Andrews, and Royal Melbourne have several great ones." So does Gunnamatta, notably holes 2, 8, and 9. At each, the lack of distance is more than compensated for by cunning defenses, including bunkers with sharp earthen lips rimmed with native grasses built in the classic Sand Belt style.

Scheduled to open in 2007, the **Fingal** course at St. Andrews Beach, according to its peripatetic designer, bears a brotherly resemblance to the Gunnamatta course, with a similar style of bunkering and well-contoured greens. However, the undulations of the ground are slightly choppier, increasing the frequency of uneven stances for second shots, and there are more trees on the margins of the fairways and near the greens. The finish of the 6,750-yard Fingal course, a pair of long, strong holes in the expansive valley below the clubhouse, will be used as the home stretch on the composite layout. At 7,055 yards against a par of 71, the composite course at St. Andrews Beach is destined to become a world-class test of golf.

In time, the facilities at St. Andrews Beach will include a five-star eco-resort with a small deluxe hotel, multi-bedroom golf lodges, casual and fine dining restaurants, a lounge bar, conference facilities, a pool and health spa, a full leisure center with tennis and squash courts, and a croquet pitch.

The Dunes, set among towering sand hills that rival Ireland's tallest dunes, is a splendid, treeless links, laid out by little-known Australian designer Tony Cashmore. A strong test from the tips at 7,009 yards, the layout's sloping fairways meander through tufted knolls and long, matted ridges dotted with wind-twisted vegetation. Greens on this elemental test are large and firm, the surfaces typically sheltered in natural ampitheaters or set on raised promontories

The National Golf Club, Old Course, seventh hole

Moonah Links, third hole

and exposed to brisk breezes that sweep in from the Bass Strait.

The strengths of the course are its naturalness and variety: Players are required to hit blind shots over aiming stones and must find fairways that dogleg sharply left and right through the shouldering dunes. Opened in 1997, The Dunes, with its quirks, is a course that demands to be played more one once. Though 10,000 miles from its ancestral home, this links is as plaid and tartan as anything in Scotland.

Something a little more forgiving? **The Cups,** an executive-style course, has fast greens and cavernous bunkers like The Dunes, but the distances—and challenge—are significantly reduced.

Located in beautiful Cape Schanck next door to The Dunes, **The National Golf Club,** a 54-hole facility that is American in style but Aussie at heart, put

the Mornington Peninsula on the golf map when its first layout, now called the **Old Course,** debuted in 1988. Designed by Robert Trent Jones, Jr. and set a few hundred yards inland from the sea, the course occupies rugged, heavily wooded terrain. The style is old-fashioned: Most of the tees are perched on hilltops, with drives played into valleys and approach shots aimed to sharply elevated greens. The greens are often multi-tiered and heavily contoured. Despite its inland setting, the ocean views from the topmost tees are breathtaking.

The National's next two courses, both links-style layouts for walkers only, both opened in 2000. Australian Peter Thomson, a five-time British Open champion, used his intimate knowledge of the great links courses in the U.K. to fashion the **Ocean Course.** Wide fairways defended by large, tufted-edge bunkers lead to greens that utilize the site's natural features, the surfaces ranging from perched to sunken. Rarely are they flat. While not as long as some courses in the vicinity, this well-conceived, windswept track calls for all the shots.

The National's finest layout overall is the **Moonah Course,** a Greg Norman design. A minimalist, lay-of-the-land creation, the Moonah, named for the famous gnarly trees that define the landscape, has narrow fairways but a virtual absence of rough. The bunkering is extensive and dramatic, but Norman encourages players to employ bump-and-run shots to chase the ball onto the greens. It's yet another Mornington Peninsula course that closely resembles the links of Scotland.

Next door to The National is the self-proclaimed "Home of Australian Golf," **Moonah Links,** with two first-rate venues. The stadium-style **Open Course,** laid out by Peter Thomson with design partners Michael Wolveridge and Ross Perrett in 2002, is the first-ever course specifically built to host a national championship. Exceptional viewing points for spectators are located throughout the prodigious 7,418-yard layout, which hosted the Australian Open in 2003 and 2005. Intended by Thomson and his team to present a mighty and ferocious test to the game's best players, the layout nevertheless has great flexibility. Staggered tees, for example, enable it to be played at varying lengths, though even from the forward tees there isn't a single pushover among the 18.

In addition to the fine natural contours that bless every course on the Mornington Peninsula, from long sandy ridges to broad open basins, the Open Course is swept by winds that blow from every direction. These winds dictate the strategy at every hole and bring the fairway bunkers, which are *in* the fairways, not alongside them, into play. The layout's trans-valley par threes are daunting and classic, but the hole everyone remembers is the 18th, a beastly par five with a minefield of 11 bunkers sprinkled from tee to green to snare careless efforts. This is a course to humble the giants or confirm their greatness.

The **Legends Course,** the facility's second venue, is a shorter, friendlier track laid out by Perrett. The course, a loop of 18 holes with non-returning nines, follows a series of valleys through a variety of landscapes ranging from ancient Moonah woodlands to open, treeless linksland. The landing areas on the Legends are generous, and the putting surfaces are gently contoured, but the bunkering is bold and, in classic Sand Belt fashion, a little wild and scruffy in appearance. Challenge-wise, the Legends is not a match for the Open Course, but neither is it a pushover.

The largest golf tourism development in recent Victorian history, Moonah Links offers a full-service clubhouse with restaurants, bars, conference facilities, and a large viewing deck. The club is also the headquarters of the Australian Golf Union, including the Australian Institute of Sport Golf Academy, Australian Golf Museum, and Golfing Hall of Fame.

If you've traveled from afar and wish to extend your stay on a gorgeous peninsula within striking distance of Melbourne, there are dozens of established courses that were built at a more carefree time when a pleasant outing, not a championship test, was the goal. These kindler, gentler courses include **Portsea, Sorrento, Flinders, Eagle Ridge,** and **Cape Schanck.**

SIDETRIP: TASMANIA

Tucked away on the remote northeast coast of Tasmania, Australia's island state, is **Barnbougle Dunes Golf Links,** a course that proves beyond the shadow of a doubt that a great track can thrive anywhere, even behind God's back. Like a lot of the world's great out-of-the-way links, there's a story behind the development of this one-of-a-kind course.

Greg Ramsay, a 23-year-old Tasmanian who had spent a year caddying at St. Andrews in Scotland, returned home having developed a passion for links golf. On the outskirts of the laid-back beach town of Bridport, population 1,500, he came upon a coastal farm with a two-mile stretch of towering sand hills rising to 60 feet. At first the farmer who owned the land wouldn't give Ramsay the time of day, but the young man's persistence paid off. The farmer agreed to lease the land for the development of a golf course. Ramsay then dashed off an e-mail to Tom Doak, a man like himself who had caddied at St. Andrews and whose work he'd read about in books and periodicals.

Ramsay's choice was wise, for Doak, along with Aussie co-designer Mike Clayton, a former European Tour player, were the perfect interpreters for the tumbling terrain. Nestling holes into valleys below bearded dunes, they conjured a masterful 6,755-yard layout bounded on three sides by the ocean, a tidal estuary, and tea tree wetlands. Barely out of diapers, it was voted the No. 1 public-access course in Australia shortly after it opened in 2004. The following year, it placed 49th on *Golf Magazine's* list of the Top 100 Courses in the World, a remarkable achievement for a remote newcomer.

As at Pacific Dunes in Oregon, Doak, a true minimalist who handles prime sites with plenty of T.L.C., displaced very little material to make way for Barnbougle Dunes. The front nine, looped to the west, has

Barnbougle Dunes Golf Links, seventh hole

among its feature holes the 120-yard seventh hole, "Little Devil," a hole that has already become an icon for golf in Tasmania.

The back nine offers an incongruous array of memorable holes splayed out among wrinkled dunes. A central fairway bunker at the par-four 15th gives players a choice of *four* lines of attack, while the grand 442-yard 17th, which bends along the mouth of the Great Forester River, is simply one of the great two-shotters Down Under. Doak did not impose his will on the land but rather created a fascinating test where players can plot their own routes and devise their own strategy based on their skill level. On any given day, the wind dictates a few decisions, too. Surfaced from tee to green in fescue grasses, the links plays fast and firm.

After the round, golfers can relax in a welcoming clubhouse perched on a dune between the ninth and 18th greens. On a sunny Tasmanian day, the prevailing condition on the island's north coast, the outside deck, overlooking Barnbougle Beach and the sparkling waters of the Bass Strait, is a great place to savor the superb seafood preparations turned out by the kitchen. The Tasmanian wines are just as exotic as a links that appears airlifted from County Kerry and has created a new destination an hour's flight from Melbourne. Sixteen sea-view cottages tucked in the dunes out of sight from the course are the perfect place to stay. For collectors of unique links experiences, Barnbougle Dunes is worth the journey.

New Zealand

An unspoiled kingdom on the other side of the world, a land brilliantly showcased by *The Lord of the Rings* film trilogy, New Zealand lies adrift in the South Pacific 1,500 miles east of Australia. A magical place best described by Rudyard Kipling as "last, loneliest, loveliest, exquisite, apart," this dual island nation's reputation as one of the most beautiful places on earth is fully deserved.

There are a number of courses that can be built into an extended golf itinerary, including Titirangi, New Zealand's only Alister MacKenzie–designed course; and Muriwari, which overlooks the Tasman Sea and a black sand beach. But the most notable developments of late are a pair of courses built by an American billionaire who believes New Zealand's North Island, where he and his family have lived on and off since the late 1970s, closely resembles the Monterey Peninsula of 75 years ago.

The two newcomers, Kauri Cliffs and Cape Kidnappers, are worth crossing an ocean as broad as the Pacific to play. In addition to the fantastic seaside landscapes and world-class challenges found at both, visitors can look forward to exceptional food and cuisine, a superlative array of off-course attractions, and the genuine friendliness of the "kiwis," as New Zealanders call themselves.

Underwritten by hedge fund tycoon Julian Robertson, who was hailed as "the Wizard of Wall Street" in his heyday, **Kauri Cliffs Golf Club** occupies a remote 4,000-acre ranch and farm perched above Matauri Bay 150 miles north of Auckland. Robertson had originally planned to buy the farm as an investment, but when he descended in a helicopter to one of the property's three beaches, he "saw" the site for a golf course, a course that would tightrope 200-foot-high bluffs and overlook the Bay of Islands National Park. Think Big Sur and Pebble Beach with a Polynesian lilt.

Partnering with David Harman, an experienced designer who had worked with Arnold Palmer and Jack Nicklaus before founding his own firm, a routing plan was devised with six holes placed on sheer cliffs that drop to the sea. Fifteen of the 18 holes offer views of the ocean, and the three that don't, each bellied into a canyon, are outstanding in their own right. Given the ever-present wind, which blows from all directions, Harman built wide fairways and open-entry greens that welcome run-up shots. An aesthetic marvel with shot values to match, Kauri

Kauri Cliffs Golf Club, seventh hole

Lodge at Kauri Cliffs

in the coast to a perched green, takes in magnificent views of the Cavalli Islands, while the top-of-the-world 14th plays downhill to an infinity-edge green framed by Cape Brett and Waiaui Bay. Yet even holes that are not draped along the rocky bluffs are memorable. Several fairways trace the natural contours of inland promontories or skirt streams, wetlands, and groves of totara trees.

With its smooth ryegrass fairways and slick bentgrass greens, Kauri Cliffs is the best-maintained course in New Zealand. Its exceptional condition is helped by the fact that play is very light. Tee times, which rarely are necessary, are spaced *30 minutes* apart. Once you make the four-hour drive from Auckland (or a short helicopter flight), this rugged but walker-friendly course, 7,119 yards at full stretch, is yours. The golf complex also includes an exceptional practice facility backdropped by the Bay of Islands.

Robertson didn't stop with the golf course. Working with architects from the U.S. and New Zealand, the financier and his wife, Josie, built the **Lodge at Kauri Cliffs,** a splendid colonial-style property with 11 spacious cottages nestled in a thicket of trees near the main lodge. Overlooking the golf course and the ocean, this exquisite lodge, a member of the prestigious Relais & Chateaux group, is the epitome of refinement. The airy main lodge, in particular, reflects the Robertsons' simple yet refined tastes, its

Cliffs was lauded as the international course of the year when it opened in 2000.

According to Michael Campbell, New Zealand's top golfer and the club's ambassador, the fourth hole, its green backdropped by the majestic, rocky coast, "is one of the great par fives in golf." The layout's one-shotters, meanwhile, are simply jaw-dropping. The par-three seventh, which plays over an indentation

Stylish interior, the Lodge at Kauri Cliffs

The pool at the Lodge at Kauri Cliffs

wrap-around porches inspired by a sheep rancher's homestead. The restaurant's Pacific Rim–influenced cuisine, featuring local produce and seafood as well as prime New Zealand lamb and beef with local wines to match, is exceptional.

Had it only world-class golf and a beautiful lodge to offer, Kauri Cliffs would be worth the journey. But there's more. Mountain biking, sea kayaking, fishing (inshore and deep-sea), scuba diving, sailing, and other activities, including nocturnal possum hunting, are available. So is a full-service spa and gym. The resort boasts three private beaches, one of them a rare pink sand beach located near the sixth green where a barbecue is held each week in summer. A pleasant two-hour hike from the lodge leads to a magnificent waterfall. Guided nature tours and four-wheel drive farm tours are also available, though ancient sequoia-like kauri trees up to 900 years old can be viewed 10 minutes from the lodge.

Once Julian Robertson got the golf development bug under his skin at Kauri Cliffs, he couldn't stop. His second project, **Cape Kidnappers Golf Course,** ladled out on fingers of land nearly 500 feet above Hawke's Bay on the east coast of the North Island, is a vertigo-inducing tour de force creased by ravines and patrolled by gannets. Indeed, this unique links-in-the-sky belongs more to heaven than to the earth. Perhaps this is the place Abel Tasman, a Dutch navigator who sighted New Zealand in 1642, was thinking of when he wrote, "It is a land uplifted high."

Several holes on this stellar creation are pressed to the edge of serrated cliffs, the deep "saving" bunkers placed by designer Tom Doak to snare balls headed

for oblivion. The visceral rush provided by Cape Kidnappers is off the charts, as is the epic scale of the 5,000-acre property the designer was handed by Robertson for his first overseas project. The land, says Doak, "tilts toward the sea on a broad plane, with

Cavalli Islands offshore of Kauri Cliffs

deep valleys dividing it into a series of ridges jutting out toward the edge of the cliffs." The soil is volcanic, not sandy, and lacks the subtle undulations of a true links, yet Doak believes "the Cape," with its firm turf and steady winds, offers seaside golf at its finest. This Down Under delight is a masterpiece of minimalist design, but with maximum views.

A layout that effectively redefines the parameters of headlands golf, Cape Kidnappers, its sloping fin-

Cape Kidnappers Golf Course, 15th hole

gers linked by a dozen bridges, is the ultimate thinking man's course. Doak uses clever angles, crossing gullies, and seemingly misplaced fairway bunkers to create resistance to scoring. Given the scale of this exalted, nearly treeless plateau, depth perception is difficult. The course may at first appear to favor power, but like all of Doak's courses, the Cape rewards placement off the tee and finesse around the greens. There are more than a few death-or-glory scenarios here, but only highly skilled players should be tempted by them. And only world-class players should tee it up from the back tees at 7,137 yards (par 71).

Never one to shy from controversy, Doak ends the round with a quirky par four that calls for a semi-blind approach to a punchbowl green. A "counter-intuitive" finishing hole, he calls it, meaning that the best way to attack the hole is not to aim for the pin.

Located six hours by car southeast of Auckland or an hour's flight to Napier (Hawke's Bay) airport, Cape Kidnappers reinforces the belief that connoisseurs will travel far and wide to savor a special experience on a golf course that, despite its relative infancy, was ranked 27th on *Golf Magazine*'s list of the Top 100 Courses in the World in 2005. Lunch, refreshments, and golf merchandise are available in

Cape Kidnappers Golf Course, 16th hole

a wool-shed–inspired clubhouse constructed from recycled timbers and corrugated iron. Here's the place to relax on a leather couch, warm yourself by an open fire, and take in sweeping views of one of the most spectacular courses in the world.

The name for the peninsula occupied by the course and still roamed by sheep dates to 1769, when local Maori tribesman attempted to "rescue" Captain Cook's Tahitian translator from the *Endeavour* by kidnapping him. The course, which has no members and at press time commanded a $280 (U.S.) green fee, is located on the doorstep of the Hawke's Bay wine country, a warm, sunny region recognized for its award-winning wines. (The Craggy Range sauvignon blanc is exceptional, as are many of the reds.) Until lodging is built on site, charming inns can be found nearby in and around the colorful art deco town of Napier.

ONE TO WATCH

Located three hours south of Auckland in the Lake Taupo district, **The Kinloch Club,** a Jack Nicklaus-designed facility nestled in a sheltered bay on the shores of New Zealand's largest lake, is expected to open in 2006–07. Conceived as a resort and golf community, Kinloch will offer world-class fly-fishing for brown and rainbow trout in the alpine streams that feed Lake Taupo. The recreation-minded club will also offer kayaking, sailing, boating, horseback riding, water skiing on the lake, snow skiing on Mt. Ruapehu, and wilderness trekking. Kinloch is also located an hour's drive from Rotorua, the cultural center of the native Maori population and an area of intense geothermal activity. Bubbling mud pools, spouting geysers, and colorful silica terraces abound, as do active fumeroles.

The 630-acre parcel on which the golf course is designed offers a good mixture of rolling terrain, with holes framed by hills that slope to Lake Taupo. A limited number of villas and residential estates will complement the refined parkland-style spread. The Lodge, still in the planning stages at press time, will feature deluxe accommodations, fine and casual dining, a cocktail bar and lounge, a full-service spa, tennis, swimming pools, and a billiards/game room.

Other Hot Spots

BRAZIL

With a landmass roughly comparable in size to the continental U.S., Brazil, the world's fifth most populous country, counted more than 100 18-hole courses as of 2005, with many more in the works.

Known for its fabulous beaches, the state of Bahia, located north of Rio de Janeiro on Brazil's east coast, showcases several notable courses designed by Dan Blankenship, a Pete Dye disciple. Chief among them is **Terravista Golf Club,** a spectacular layout in Transcoso that debuted in 2004. The front nine of this sturdy 7,212-yard course is tunneled into a rain forest, but the back nine brings players to the brink of chalky white cliffs 130 feet above the sea, with four holes, including the dazzling par-three 14th, calling for carries over indentations in the coast. Blanken-

ship also built the **Ocean Course at Comandatuba,** a gorgeous spread located on an island off the Bahia coast. Opened in 2000, the holes on this 6,928-yard spread are routed between the sea and a mangrove swamp, its fairways framed by coconut palms and huge waste bunkers.

Even Donald Trump has fallen for Brazil's charms. In the hills of Itatiba some 50 miles outside São Paulo, the financial capital of South America, Trump has joined forces with Ricardo Bellino, a young Brazilian entrepreneur, to build a luxury residential development around a Jack Nicklaus–designed course. **Villa Trump International Golf Club** is slated to open in late 2006.

Serrated cliffs at Terravista Golf Club

Club at Nine Bridges, fourth hole

SOUTH KOREA

Located 60 miles off the southern tip of South Korea, Jeju Island, a tiny volcanic nub in the Sea of Japan an hour's flight from Seoul, is a popular honeymoon capital. Many of the newlyweds who arrive en masse are now packing their golf clubs. Ever since 20-year-old Se Ri Pak captured the 1998 U.S. Women's Open, Korea has gone ga-ga over golf. Because more than 70 percent of the South Korean mainland is mountainous, flat land is given over to agriculture and housing, not golf. Which means Jeju Island, a resort paradise that Koreans equate with Hawaii (it's roughly the size of Maui), is where most new golf projects are taking shape. Thanks in part to its designation in 2002 as a "free international city development center," tax incentives for business development on the island have led to a wave of new golf projects. (Its new status is ironic, for Jeju was once a place of political exile.) At press time, Jeju Island had 15 courses open for play, with *40 more* expected to be completed by 2010.

While the island has the potential to become the Hilton Head of Southeast Asia, the topography here is far cry from the Lowcountry. For example, the **Club at Nine Bridges,** built at a cost of $125 million by Korean tycoon Jay Lee, scion of the family that founded Samsung, is carved from the verdant green flanks of Mount Halla at 3,500 feet above sea level. Opened in 2001, Nine Bridges, designed by Americans Ron Fream and David Dale, offers an Asian version of the Scottish Highlands, moving from pine forests to ancient lava fields to ravines filled with bracken and fern. Host to an LPGA Tour event, Nine Bridges was the first course in Korea to offer a bent-grass playing surface from tee to green.

Among the bright newcomers on the horizon is a Greg Norman–designed course to be built for Hanwha Land, a major Korean developer. Like Nine Bridges, it will be terraced up the volcanic slopes of Mount Halla, at 6,398 feet Korea's tallest peak. The course, slated to open in 2007, has remnants of stone walls from the Chosun Dynasty as well as distant ocean views.

Antalya Golf Club, Pasha course, fourth hole

TURKEY

A fast-developing holiday destination on Turkey's southern coast, Antalya's Belek area, a.k.a. the "Turkish Riviera," offers six fine courses, all of them built since the late 1980s. While not quite in competition with Spain's Costa del Sol, the region, known for its mild, sunny winters, continues to grow as Turkey becomes more westernized. In pine and eucalyptus woodlands backdropped by the snow-capped Toros Mountains and fronted by beaches along the Mediterranean Sea, European designers have laid out a handful of excellent courses. Five-star beachfront hotels are associated with the clubs.

Belek's most ambitious new golf facility is the 36-hole **Antalya Golf Club.** The **Pasha** course, opened in 2002, is framed by eucalyptus trees, with lakes forcing risk-reward decisions at many holes. The **Sultan** course, debuted in 2003, occupies a much larger parcel and makes a strong appeal to the better player. **National Golf Club,** generally rated the nation's top layout, could pass for a course in coastal South Carolina, its winding fairways carved from pines and other native trees. Water comes into play early and often on this first-class spread. **Gloria Golf Resort,** attached to Turkey's premier resort hotel and located

Minarets in Antalya's skyline

at the foot of the mountains, added a third nine in 2002 and at press time was planning to unveil another 18-hole layout by French designer Michael Gayon in late 2005.

Tat International, set between the mountains and the sea, offers 27 holes and is hillier than the region's other courses. **Nobilis Golf Resort,** built on the site of a Roman settlement (the colonnaded clubhouse boasts a statue of Julius Caesar swinging a golf club atop a triumphal arch!), skirts the Belek Acisu River. The newest facility is the 27-hole, Nick Faldo–designed course opened at the **Cornelia Golf Resort** in late 2005.

An hour's drive from Belek's golf scene is Perge, a Greco-Roman city with some of the best-preserved stadiums of antiquity. The Lycian city of Myra, with its famous church dedicated to St. Nicholas, is located near Antalya, a walled port city 25 miles west of Belek that boasts a picturesque harbor, a renovated beach, and lively bars.

Directory

United States

NORTHEAST

PLYMOUTH, MASSACHUSETTS

Atlantic Country Club
Plymouth, MA
www.atlanticcountryclub.com

Crosswinds Golf Club
Plymouth, MA
www.golfcrosswinds.com

Pinehills Golf Club
Plymouth, MA
www.pinehillsgolf.com

Waverly Oaks Golf Club
Plymouth, MA
www.waverlyoaksgolfclub.com

BOSTON

Granite Links Golf Club at Quarry Hills
Quincy, MA
www.granitelinksgolfclub.com

Red Tail Golf Club
Devens, MA
www.redtailgolf.net

UPSTATE NEW YORK

Turning Stone Resort & Casino
Verona, NY
www.turningstone.com

MID-ATLANTIC

ATLANTIC CITY, NEW JERSEY

Architects Golf Club
Lopatcong, NJ
www.thearchitectsclub.com

Atlantic City Country Club
Northfield, NJ
(609) 641-7575

Blue Heron Pines Golf Club
Cologne, NJ
www.blueheronpines.com

Harbor Pines Golf Club
Egg Harbor Township, NJ
www.harborpines.com

McCullough's Emerald Golf Links
Egg Harbor Township, NJ
www.mcculloughsgolf.com

Sand Barrens Golf Club
Swainton, NJ
www.sandbarrensgolf.com

Sea Oaks Golf Club
Little Egg Harbor, NJ
www.seaoaksgolf.com

Seaview Marriott Resort & Spa
Galloway, NJ
www.seaviewmarriott.com

Shore Gate Golf Club
Ocean View, NJ
www.shoregategolfclub.com

Twisted Dune Golf Club
Egg Harbor Township, NJ
www.twisteddune.com

Vineyard Golf at Renault Winery
Egg Harbor City, NJ
www.renaultwinery.com

PHILADELPHIA

Glen Mills Golf Course
Glen Mills, PA
www.glenmillsgolf.com

Jeffersonville Golf Club
Jeffersonville, PA
www.westnorritontwp.org/golf.htm

Makefield Highlands Golf Club
Yardley, PA
www.makefieldhighlands.com

RiverWinds Golf Club
West Deptford, NJ
www.riverwindsgolf.com

Scotland Run Golf Club
Williamstown, NJ
www.scotlandrun.com

Tattersall Golf Club
West Chester, PA
www.tattersallgolfclub.com

BALTIMORE

Beechtree Golf Club
Aberdeen, MD
www.beechtreegolf.com

Bulle Rock
Havre de Grace, MD
www.bullerockgolf.com

Mountain Branch Golf Course
Joppa, MD
www.mountainbranch.com

Patriots Glen Golf Course
Elkton, MD
www.patriotsglen.com

FREDERICK, MARYLAND

Clustered Spires Golf Course
Frederick, MD
(301) 624-1295

Hollow Creek Golf Club
Middletown, MD
www.hollowcreekgolfclub.com

Maryland National Golf Club
Middletown, MD
www.marylandnational.com

Musket Ridge Golf Club
Myersville, MD
www.musketridge.com

P.B. Dye Golf Club
Ijamsville, MD
www.pbdyegolf.com

Whiskey Creek Golf Club
Ijamsville, MD
www.whiskeycreekgolf.com

Worthington Manor Golf Club
Urbana, MD
www.worthingtonmanor.com

SOUTH

TENNESSEE'S BEAR TRACE

Bear Trace at Chickasaw
Henderson, TN
www.beartrace.com/chickasaw

Bear Trace at Cumberland Mountain
Crossville, TN
www.beartrace.com/cumberland

Bear Trace at Harrison Bay
Harrison, TN
www.beartrace.com/harrison

Bear Trace at Ross Creek Landing
Clifton, TN
www.beartrace.com/rosscreek

Bear Trace at Tims Ford
Winchester, TN
www.beartrace.com/timsford

GEORGIA'S LAKE COUNTRY

Golf Club at Cuscowilla
Eatonton, GA
www.cuscowilla.com

Harbor Club
Greensboro, GA
www.harborclub.com

Reynolds Plantation
Plantation, Great Waters, National,
Oconee, Reynolds Landing courses
Greensboro, GA
www.reynoldsplantation.com

ORLANDO

ChampionsGate Golf Resort
ChampionsGate, FL
www.championsgategolf.com

Eagle Creek Golf Club
Orlando, FL
www.eaglecreekgolf.info

Legacy Club at Alaqua Lakes
Longwood, FL
www.legacyclubgolf.com

Marriott Grande Pines Golf Club
Orlando, FL
www.grandepinesgolfclub.com

Mystic Dunes Golf Club
Celebration, FL
www.mysticdunesgolf.com

Orange County National
Winter Garden, FL
www.ocngolf.com

Reunion Resort & Club
Reunion, FL
www.reunionresort.com

Ritz-Carlton Orlando, Grande Lakes
Orlando, FL
www.ritzcarlton.com/resorts/orlando_
grande_lakes

Shingle Creek Golf Club
Orlando, FL
www.shinglecreekgolf.com

Victoria Hills Golf Club
DeLand, FL
www.joetowns.com/victoriapark/golf.asp

MIDWEST

SHEBOYGAN COUNTY, WISCONSIN

The American Club
Blackwolf Run (River and Meadow
Valleys courses), Whistling Straits
(Straits and Irish courses)
Kohler, WI
www.destinationkohler.com

The Bull at Pinehurst Farms
Sheboygan Falls, WI
www.golfthebull.com

MINNESOTA'S FAR NORTH

Fortune Bay Resort Casino
Wilderness Golf Course
Tower, MN
www.fortunebay.com

Giants Ridge Golf and Ski Resort
Biwabik, MN
www.giantsridge.com

Superior National Golf Course
Lutsen, MN
www.superiornational.com

ROCKIES

SUMMIT COUNTY, COLORADO

Breckenridge Golf Club
Breckenridge, CO
www.breckenridgegolfclub.com

Keystone Resort
Keystone, CO
www.keystoneresort.com

The Raven Golf Club at Three Peaks
Silverthorne, CO
www.intrawestgolf.com

VAIL VALLEY, COLORADO

Eagle Ranch Golf Course
Eagle, CO
www.eagleranch.com

Lodge & Spa at Cordillera
Edwards, CO
www.cordillera.rockresorts.com

Red Sky Golf Club
Avon, CO
www.redskygolfclub.com

SOUTHWEST

LAS VEGAS

Aliante Golf Club
North Las Vegas, NV
www.aliantegolf.com

The Badlands
Las Vegas, NV
www.badlandsgc.com

Bali Hai Golf Club
Las Vegas, NV
www.waltersgolf.com

Bear's Best
Las Vegas, NV
www.bearsbest.com

Boulder Creek Golf Club
Boulder City, NV
www.bouldercreekgc.com

Cascata
Boulder City, NV
www.caesars.com/Cascata

DragonRidge Country Club
Henderson, NV
www.dragonridgegolf.com

Lake Las Vegas Resort
Reflection Bay Golf Club,
The Falls Golf Club
Henderson, NV
www.lakelasvegas.com

Las Vegas Paiute Golf Resort
Las Vegas, NV
www.lvpaiutegolf.com

Red Rock Country Club
Las Vegas, NV
www.redrockcountryclub.com

Revere Golf Club
Henderson, NV
www.reveregolf.com

Rio Secco Golf Club
Henderson, NV
www.riosecco.net

Royal Links Golf Club
Las Vegas, NV
www.waltersgolf.com

Shadow Creek
Las Vegas, NV
www.shadowcreek.com

Silverstone Golf Club
Las Vegas, NV
www.silverstonegolfclub.com

TPC at the Canyons
Las Vegas, NV
www.tpc.com/daily/the_canyons

Tuscany Golf Club
Henderson, NV
www.tuscanygolfclub.com

Wildhorse Golf Club
Henderson, NV
www.golfwildhorse.com

Wynn Las Vegas
Las Vegas, NV
www.wynnlasvegas.com

HOUSTON

Augusta Pines
Spring, TX
www.augustapinesgolf.com

BlackHorse Golf Club
Cypress, TX
www.blackhorsegolfclub.com

Cypresswood Golf Club
Spring, TX
www.cypresswood.com

Magnolia Creek Golf Links
League City, TX
www.magnoliacreekgolf.com

Meadowbrook Farms Golf Club
Katy, TX
www.meadowbrookfarms.com

Memorial Park Golf Course
Houston, TX
www.houstontx.gov/municipalgolf/
memorial

Redstone Golf Club
Humble, TX
www.redstonegolfclub.com

Tour 18 Houston
Humble, TX
www.tour18golf.com

The Woodlands Resort and
Conference Center
The Woodlands, TX
www.woodlandsresort.com

WEST

BANDON, OREGON

Bandon Dunes Resort
Bandon, OR
www.bandondunesgolf.com

LOS ANGELES

Angeles National Golf Club
Sunland, CA
www.angelesnational.com

Lost Canyons Golf Club
Simi Valley, CA
www.lostcanyons.com

Moorpark Country Club
Moorpark, CA
www.moorparkcountryclub.com

Ojai Valley Inn & Spa
Ojai, CA
www.ojairesort.com

Robinson Ranch Golf Club
Santa Clarita, CA
www.robinsonranchgolf.com

Rustic Canyon Golf Course
Moorpark, CA
www.rusticcanyongolfcourse.com

Tierra Rejada Golf Club
Moorpark, CA
www.tierrarejada.com

Trump National Golf Club, Los Angeles
Rancho Palos Verdes, CA
www.trumpgolf.com/trumplosangeles

SAN DIEGO NORTH

Barona Creek Golf Club
Lakeside, CA
www.barona.com

Four Seasons Resort Aviara
Carlsbad, CA
www.fourseasons.com/aviara

The Grand Golf Club
San Diego, CA
www.thegrandgolfclub.com

La Costa Resort and Spa
Carlsbad, CA
www.lacosta.com

Maderas Golf Club
Poway, CA
www.maderasgolf.com

Torrey Pines Golf Course
La Jolla, CA
www.torreypinesgolfcourse.com

International

CANADA

NIAGARA FALLS

Grand Niagara Resort
Niagara Falls, ON
www.grandniagararesort.com

Hunters Pointe Golf Course
Welland, ON
www.hunterspointe.ca

Legends on the Niagara
Niagara Falls, ON
www.niagaraparksgolf.com/legends

Niagara-on-the-Lake Golf Club
Niagara-on-the-Lake, ON
www.notlgolf.com

Royal Niagara Golf Club
Niagara-on-the-Lake, ON
www.royalniagara.com

Thundering Waters Golf Club
Niagara Falls, ON
www.thunderingwaters.com

Whirlpool Golf Course
Niagara Falls, ON
www.niagaraparksgolf.com/whirlpool

TORONTO

Angus Glen Golf Club
Markham, ON
www.angusglen.com

Copper Creek Golf Club
Kleinburg, ON
www.coppercreek.ca

Eagles Nest Golf Club
Maple, ON
www.eaglesnestgolf.com

Osprey Valley Resorts
Caledon, ON
www.ospreyvalley.com

Royal Woodbine Golf Club
Toronto, ON
www.royalwoodbine.com

Wooden Sticks
Uxbridge, ON
www.woodensticks.com

MUSKOKA

Bigwin Island Golf Club
Lake of Bays, ON
www.bigwinisland.com

Deerhurst Resort
Huntsville, ON
www.deerhurstresort.com

Grandview Golf Club
Huntsville, ON
www.clublink.ca

Lake Joseph Club
Port Carling, ON
www.clublink.ca

Rocky Crest Golf Club
Mactier, ON
www.clublink.ca

Taboo Resort
Gravenhurst, ON
www.tabooresort.com

The Rock
Minett, ON
www.therockgolf.com

PRINCE EDWARD ISLAND

Andersons Creek Golf Club
Stanley Bridge, PE
www.andersonscreek.com

Belfast Highland Greens
Belfast, PE
www.peisland.com/belfast

Belvedere Golf & Country Club
Charlottetown, PE
www.belvederegolf.com

Brudenell River Resort
Cardigan, PE
www.roddhotelsandresorts.com

Eagles Glenn Resort
Cavendish, PE
www.eaglesglenn.com

Eagles View Golf Course
Murray River, PE
www.eaglesviewgolf.com

Fox Meadow Golf & Country Club
Stratford, PE
www.foxmeadow.pe.ca

Glasgow Hills Resort & Golf Club
Hunter River, PE
www.glasgowhills.com

Green Gables Golf Course
Cavendish, PE
www.greengablesgolf.com

Links at Crowbush Cove
Morell, PE
www.roddhotelsandresorts.com

Mill River Resort
O'Leary, PE
www.roddhotelsandresorts.com

Rollo Bay Greens
Rollo Bay, PE
www.rollobaygreens.com

MEXICO

LOS CABOS

Cabo del Sol
Cabo San Lucas, Mex.
www.cabodelsol.com from U.S.

Cabo Real Golf Course
Cabo San Lucas, Mex.
www.caboreal.com

One&Only Palmilla
San Jose del Cabo, Mex.
www.palmillaresort.com from U.S.

Raven Golf Club
Cabo San Lucas, Mex.
(888) 328-8501 from U.S.

PUERTO VALLARTA

Four Seasons Resort Punta Mita
Bahia de Banderas, Mex.
www.fourseasonshotel.com/puntamita

Los Flamingos Golf Club
Nuevo Vallarta, Mex.
(329) 296-5006

Mayan Palace
Nuevo Vallarta, Mex.
www.mayanpalace.com/nuevo

Paradise Village Resort
El Tigre Golf Course
Nuevo Vallarta, Mex.
www.paradisevillage.com

Vista Vallarta Golf Club
Puerto Vallarta, Mex.
www.vistavallartagolf.com

CANCUN/RIVIERA MAYA

Club de Golf Cancun
Cancun, Mex.
www.cancungolfclub.com

Cozumel Country Club
Cozumel, Mex.
www.cozumelcountryclub.com

Golf Club at Moon Palace
Cancun, Mex.
www.palaceresorts.com/Golf/
MoonGolf/MoonGolf_index.asp

Golf Club at Playacar
Playa del Carmen, Mex.
www.palaceresorts.com/Golf/
PlayaGolf/Golf_Intro.asp

Iberostar Paraiso Maya
Riviera Maya, Mex.
www.iberostar.com

Mayakoba
El Camaleon Golf Course
Riviera Maya, Mex.
www.mayakoba.com

CARIBBEAN

BAHAMAS

Four Seasons Resort Great Exuma at
Emerald Bay
Great Exuma, Bahamas
www.fourseasons.com/greatexuma

One&Only Ocean Club
Paradise Island, Bahamas
www.oneandonlyresorts.com

Our Lucaya Beach & Golf Resort
Grand Bahama Island, Bahamas
www.ourlucaya.com

Royal Oasis Golf Resort & Casino
Grand Bahama Island, Bahamas
www.cpgrandbahama.crowneplaza.com

BARBADOS

Barbados Golf Club
Christchurch, Barbados
www.barbadosgolfclub.com

Royal Westmoreland
St. James, Barbados
www.royal-westmoreland.com

Sandy Lane
St. James, Barbados
www.sandylane.com

DOMINICAN REPUBLIC

Cap Cana
Santo Domingo, Dom. Rep.
www.capcana.com

Casa de Campo
La Romana, Dom. Rep.
www.casadecampo.com

Guavaberry Golf & Country Club
Juan Dolio, Dom. Rep.
www.guavaberrygolf.com

Los Marlins Golf Resort
Juan Dolio, Dom. Rep.
(809) 526-3315

Playa Grande Golf Course
Playa Dorada, Dom. Rep.
www.wyndham.com/hotels/POPPD/
golf/grande/main.wnt

Punta Cana Resort and Club
Santo Domingo, Dom. Rep.
www.puntacana.com

JAMAICA

Half Moon Resort
Montego Bay, Jamaica
www.halfmoon.com

Ritz-Carlton Golf & Spa Resort,
Rose Hall
St. James, Jamaica
www.ritzcarlton.com/resorts/
rose_hall_jamaica

Rose Hall Resort
St. James, Jamaica
www.rosehallresort.com

Tryall Club
Montego Bay, Jamaica
www.tryallclub.com

PUERTO RICO

Coco Beach Golf & Country Club
Rio Grande, P.R.
www.cocobeachgolf.com

Dorado Beach Country Club
Dorado, P.R.

El Legado Golf Resort
Guayama, P.R.
www.ellegadogolfresort.com

Hyatt Hacienda Del Mar
Plantation Club
Dorado, P.R.

Hilton Ponce Golf & Casino Resort
Ponce, P.R.
www.hilton.com

Palmas del Mar Country Club
Humacao, P.R.
www.palmascountryclub.com

Westin Rio Mar Beach Resort
Rio Grande, P.R.
www.westinriomar.com

ST. KITTS & NEVIS

Four Seasons Resort Nevis
Charlestown, Nevis
www.fourseasons.com/nevis

Royal St. Kitts Golf Club
Bassaterre, St. Kitts
www.royalstkittsgolfclub.com

ST. VINCENT & THE GRENADINES

Raffles Resort Canouan Island
Trump International Golf Club
Canouan Island, St. Vincent &
The Grenadines
www.rafflescanouan.com

TRINIDAD & TOBAGO

Tobago Plantations Beach & Golf Resort
Lowlands, Tobago
www.tobagoplantations.com

EUROPE

IRELAND

Ballyliffin Golf Club
Ballyliffin, Co. Donegal, Ire.
www.ballyliffingolfclub.com

Carne Golf Links
Carne, Co. Mayo, Ire.
www.carnegolflinks.com

Carton House Golf Club
Maynooth, Co. Kildare, Ire.
www.carton.ie

County Sligo Golf Club
Rosses Point, Co. Sligo, Ire.
www.countysligogolfclub.ie

Donegal Golf Club
Murvagh, Co. Donegal, Ire.
www.donegalgolfclub.ie

Druids Glen Golf Resort
Newtownmountkennedy, Co.
Wicklow, Ire.
www.druidsglen.ie

Enniscrone Golf Club
Enniscrone, Co. Sligo, Ire.
www.enniscronegolf.com

The European Club
Brittas Bay, Co. Wicklow, Ire.
www.theeuropeanclub.com

The K Club
Straffan, Co. Kildare, Ire.
www.kclub.ie

PGA National Ireland
Johnstown, Co. Kildare, Ire.
www.palmerstownhouse.com

Portsalon Golf Club
Letterkenny, Co. Donegal, Ire.
Powerscourt Golf Club
Enniskerry, Co. Wicklow, Ire.
www.powerscourt.ie

Rosapenna Hotel & Golf Links
Downings, Co. Donegal, Ire.
www.rosapenna.ie

PORTUGAL/ALGARVE

Boavista Resort
Lagos, Port.
www.boavistaresort.com

Castro Marim Golfe and Country Club
Castro Marim, Port.
www.castromarimgolfe.com

Le Meridien Penina Golf Resort
Portimao, Port.

Morgado do Reguengo
Portimao, Port.

Quinta da Ria
Vila Nova de Cacela, Port.
www.quintadaria.com

Quinta de Cima
Vila Nova de Cacelta, Port.

Quinta do Lago
Almancil, Port.
www.quintadolago.com

Salgados Golf
Albufeira, Port.
www.nexus-pt.com/salgados

San Lorenzo Golf Club
Almancil, Port.

Vale do Lobo
Almancil, Port.
www.valedolobo.com

Vilamoura Golf
Vilamoura, Port.
www.vilamouragolf.com

CZECH REPUBLIC

Cihelny Golf Course
Karlovy Vary, Czech.

Darovansky Dvur Golf Resort
Darova, Czech.
www.darovanskydvur.cz/en

Frantiskovy Lazne
Hazlov, Czech.

Golf Park Plzen
Pilsen, Czech.
www.golfparkpl.cz/en

Golf Resort Karlstejn
Belec, Czech.
www.karlstejn-golf.cz

Golf Resort Konopiste
Tvorsovice, Czech.
www.gcko.cz/en

Karlovy Vary
Karlovy Vary, Czech.
www.golfresort.cz

Marianske Lazne
Royal Golf Club
Marianske Lazne, Czech.
www.golfml.cz

SCANDINAVIA

Hills Golf Club
Gothenburg, Sweden

Katinkulta Resort & Spa
Vuokatti, Finland

Kytaja Golf
Kytaja, Finland

Oulu Golf Club
Oulu, Finland

Paltamo Golf
Paltamo, Finland

Sand Golf Club
Jonkoping, Sweden

FRANCE

Four Seasons Resort Provence at
Terre Blanche
Tourrettes, France
www.fourseasons.com/provence

AUSTRIA

Golf Eichenheim
Kitzbühel, Austria

CYPRUS

Aphrodite Hills Resort
Paphos, Cyprus
www.aphroditehills.com

Secret Valley Golf Club
Kouklia, Cyprus
www.cyprusgolf.com/sv_about_us.htm

Tsada Golf Club
Tsada, Cyprus
www.cyprusgolf.com/tsada.htm

Rest of the World

DUBAI

Al Badia Golf Resort
Dubai, U.A.E.
www.albadiagolfresort.com

Arabian Ranches Golf Club
Dubai, U.A.E.
www.arabianranchesgolfdubai.com

Dubai Creek Golf & Yacht Club
Dubai, U.A.E.
www.dubaigolf.com

Emirates Golf Club
Dubai, U.A.E.
www.dubaigolf.com

The Montgomerie, Dubai
Dubai, U.A.E.
www.themontgomerie.com

Nad Al Sheba Club
Dubai, U.A.E.
www.dubaigolf.com

SOUTH AFRICA

Fancourt Hotel and Country Club
Estate George, S.A.
www.fancourt.co.za

Sun City Resort
Sun City, S.A.
www.suninternational.com

CHINA

Mission Hills Golf Club
Shenzen, China
www.missionhillsgroup.com

AUSTRALIA

Barnbougle Dunes Golf Links
Bridport, Australia
www.barnbougledunes.com

The Dunes Golf Links
Rye, Australia
www.thedunes.com.au

Golf Club at St. Andrews Beach
St. Andrews Beach, Australia
www.standrewsbeach.com

Moonah Links
Fingal, Australia
www.moonahlinks.com.au

The National Golf Club
Cape Schanck, Australia

NEW ZEALAND

Cape Kidnappers Golf Course
Hawke's Bay, N.Z.
www.capekidnappers.com

Kauri Cliffs Golf Club
Matauri Bay, N.Z.
www.kauricliffs.com

BRAZIL

Ocean Course at Commandatuba
Commandatuba, Brazil

Terravista Golf Course
Porto Seguro, Brazil
www.terravistagolf.com.br

TURKEY

Antalya Golf Club
Belek, Turkey
www.antalyagolfclub.com.tr

Cornelia Golf Resort
Belek, Turkey

Gloria Golf Resort
Belek, Turkey
www.gloria.com.tr

National Golf Club
Belek, Turkey
www.nationalturkey.com

Nobilis Golf Resort
Belek, Turkey
www.meditalya.com/nobilisgolf.html

Tat International
Belek, Turkey

SOUTH KOREA

Club at Nine Bridges
Jeju Island, S. Korea

Index

Photo Credits

Editor: David Barrett

Designer: Robert McKee

Production Manager: Anet Sirna-Bruder

Picture Research: Cristian Peña, Laurie Platt Winfrey, Carousel Research, Inc.

Library of Congress Cataloging-in-Publication Data

McCallen, Brian.
   Golf's best new destinations / Brian McCallen.
      p. cm.
   ISBN 10: 0-8109-5745-0 (hardcover)
   ISBN 13: 978-0-8109-5745-9
   1. Golf courses—Guidebooks. 2. Golf courses– –Directories. 3. Golf courses—Design and construction. 4. Golf resorts—Guidebooks. 5. Golf resorts—Directories. I. Title.

   GV975.M338 2006
   796.352'068—dc22

                                   2006013207

Text copyright © 2006 Brian McCallen

Published in 2006 by Abrams, an imprint of Harry N. Abrams, Inc.

Printed and bound in China
10 9 8 7 6 5 4 3 2 1

HNA
harry n. abrams, inc.
a subsidiary of La Martinière Groupe
115 West 18th Street
New York, NY 10011
www.hnabooks.com